Rural Houses of
the North of Ireland

To Estyn Evans

Rural Houses of
the North of Ireland

ALAN GAILEY

Keeper, Department of Buildings
Ulster Folk and Transport Museum

JOHN DONALD PUBLISHERS LTD
EDINBURGH

ISBN 0 85976 098 7

The publishers acknowledge the financial assistance
of the Scottish Arts Council in the publication of this
volume.

Exclusive distribution in the United States of America
and Canada by Humanities Press Inc., Atlantic
Highlands, NJ 07716, USA.

Phototypesetting by H.M. Repros, Glasgow.
Printed in Great Britain by Bell & Bain, Ltd., Glasgow.

PREFACE

STUDY of traditional rural houses in Ireland has generated a specialist bibliography of a couple of hundred titles, published almost exclusively as articles in academic, and in local historical or archaeological, periodicals. It may seem a basis for criticism that no substantial book has yet been published in this field, but some extenuating circumstances exist, and these are outlined in Chapter 1. Ireland, too, is a fairly small place; even so, this book deals only with the northern third of the island, that is with rather more than the political unit of Northern Ireland, or even than the historical Province of Ulster. Sadly, it must be said that although there was a fine start to the study of vernacular architecture throughout Ireland, the next stage, of detailed local field and documentary study, has been commenced only in the north. Hopefully, conclusions reached in this book about house types, roof forms and timbering systems, building materials, and later (mainly nineteenth- and early twentieth-century) adaptations and elaborations of traditional houses responding to social changes in the same period, will provide a point of departure for future development of vernacular architecture studies in the rest of Ireland.

A second aim is to provide a readily accessible synthesis of work on northern Irish rural housing in particular, and to some extent also of rural housing in Ireland in general. Recently there have been indications that scholars in other countries are taking note of the existence of important evidence in Ireland when speculation is being advanced about the origins of many traditional architectural features, and when attempts are made to account for their distributions in the British Isles,[1] and more widely in western Europe.[2] So it seems timely to contribute to a series of regional monographs, setting the northern Irish evidence beside that already published on rural Scotland,[3] and on Brittany.[4]

If this book alerts more people in Ireland, and perhaps elsewhere also, to the richness of formally undocumented cultural material in the countryside, perhaps they will become more aware of their environment and its history, and some indeed may be inspired to take up the study for themselves. The prime requirement for anyone to become involved in vernacular architecture study is interest. The necessary skills: of measuring and drawing up buildings, photographing them, and analysing the consequent corpus of data; of viewing this material against what is already known, and marrying the field evidence with what can be culled from documentary sources; and finally, of fitting into all of this the oral testimony of those who live in vernacular houses — and the relevance of such oral history should never be underestimated; all of these skills can be acquired along the way. Starting only with the necessary interest, the rewards are immediate. Long before the formal results of field and historical study begin to materialise, the invariable openness and kindliness of ordinary people living in ordinary (and sometimes extraordinary) houses provides an unforgettable, heart-warming experience.

In the last twenty years I have never encountered obstructiveness in the course of my field investigations. Occasional and readily understandable wariness as to what I was about has always disappeared as quickly as the proverbial snow off a ditch once I explained my interests, and once those interests were seen as genuine, doors immediately opened wide. Local interest, but more importantly involvement, in local history runs very deep in rural Ireland. It is perhaps all the more remarkable that this hospitality has survived during the recent years of social strife and disorder in Northern Ireland. I could not have written this book in the absence of the ready acceptance and friendliness I have met with throughout the north of Ireland, and it would be invidious to the rest to single out those in any house I have visited over the years. I thank them all.

Professor Estyn Evans opened my eyes to the interest of traditional rural houses in his lectures in human geography which I attended almost thirty years ago at Queen's University, Belfast. The topic was only a tiny element in the course he was teaching, but I soon found

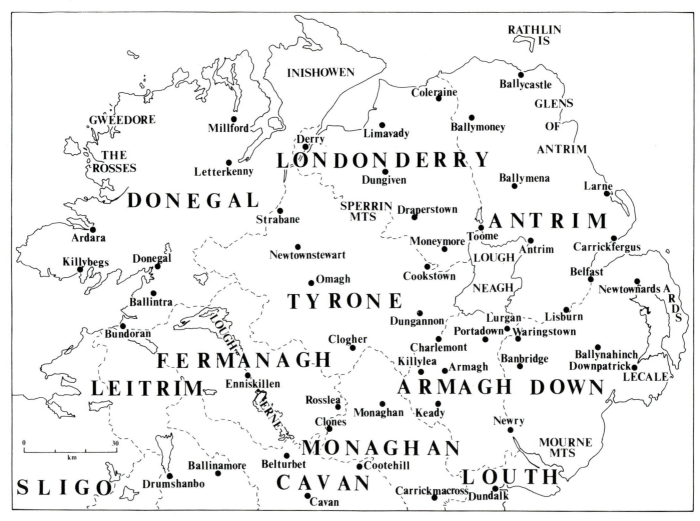

myself privately recording old houses in the west of Ireland, in districts which I had known from my boyhood there. This interest remained largely a leisure activity, although I was able to make use of it in studying rural settlement changes in the south-west Highlands of Scotland in the late 1950s. Leisure interest became part of my professional commitment when I joined the staff of the new Ulster Folk Museum in 1960, and in a sense I then rejoined Professor Evans, who was one of the museum's founding trustees; he in only now, as I write this preface, relinquising his trusteeship. I count myself fortunate indeed that I sat in his lectures and have for so long enjoyed and benefited from his advice, interest in the work of the museum, and stimulation of exposure to his ever critical mind. Readers will recognise, therefore, the honour he does me, and the pleasure I derive, in his agreement that I may dedicate this book to him.

Here also I pay tribute to my family, especially to my wife, who during holidays in various parts of the north of Ireland during the 1960s, with great forbearance and often much amusement endured my inability to distinguish between work and leisure in the matter of examining interesting buildings. They have, too, in recent years, given me much peace at home when writing has been attempted.

The importance of the field evidence will be apparent to any reader. Coupled with the problems of the nature of the documentary record explained in Chapter 1, my decision not to include a list of sources used will I hope be understood. Such a list, of course, can be compiled from the references as can a bibliography of northern Irish vernacular architecture studies. It would be superfluous, however, to burden this book with a specialist bibliography when most of the titles therein are not easily accessible, and when the bibliography itself already exists elsewhere.[5]

Alongside contemporary photography as part of the field work on surviving buildings, there must be set study of photographs taken in earlier periods. Northern parts of Ireland are well served in this respect, and I am indebted to the Trustees and Director of the Ulster Museum, Belfast for permission to use some photographs taken about the turn of the centruy by the late R. J. Welch, whose collection is in their care; and to the Trustees and Director of my own museum for similar facility in respect of photographs from the W. A. Green collection, which is slightly later (Green, in fact, learnt his photography from Welch). Thanks are also accorded to the Ulster-American Folk Park near Omagh, county Tyrone for providing illustrations of the Mellon and Hughes houses which appear in Chapter 11.

Text references to the illustrations occur mainly where the dominant point each illustrates is dealt with. Many, however, cover a variety of points. Insertion of text references in all cases would have made for disjointed reading; readers should be aware that the photographs throughout the book should be scanned in relation to many subjects discussed in Chapters 4 to 10 especially.

I owe a large debt to many friends and colleagues with whom over the years I have discussed matters raised in this book; in particular, in Ireland, Caoimhín Ó Danachair and Desmond McCourt; in Scotland, Sandy Fenton and Bruce Walker; in England, Ronald Brunskill and Nat Alcock; in Wales, Peter Smith; in America, Henry Glassie. My membership of Northern Ireland's Historic Buildings Council since 1976 has brought me into fruitful contact with other Council members, and with Colin Hatrick and Dick Oram of the Historic Monuments and Buildings Branch of the Department of the Environment for Northern Ireland, and Hugh Dixon of the Northern Ireland Archaeological Survey. Nick Brannon of the Archaeological Survey has kindly provided preliminary information on his excavations at Tildarg, Camphill and Dungiven. I thank them all, and

hope that my specialist interest in vernacular buildings has been of some value to them.

Staffs in three institutions have been helpful as I have searched for documentation bearing on traditional housing: the Library, Queen's University, Belfast; the Public Record Office of Northern Ireland; and the Muniments Room, the Library, Trinity College, Dublin. I am grateful to the Deputy Keeper of the PRONI, and the Keeper of Manuscripts, TCD, for permission to work from, refer to, and occasionally to quote directly from original documents in their care.

Last, but by no means least, I am indebted to the Trustees, Director and colleagues at the Ulster Folk and Transport Museum. The Trustees and Director have actively supported my field and archival work on vernacular buildings over many years and I hope that they will feel justified in having done so when they read this book, and recognise it as one outcome (there are others, of course) of that support. Many colleagues have provided practical assistance in all aspects of the work and in preparation of the typescript and illustrations. In warmly thanking them all I know they will not take it amiss if I single out one for special mention. Philip Robinson has, since he joined me in the autumn of 1974, provided a critical sounding-board for tuning my ideas, and he read through this book in draft form, making helpful suggestions. Nevertheless, shortcomings in the finished product are mine alone. It is my earnest hope that further endeavour, in the north and indeed throughout Ireland, will sooner rather than later supersede my work, prompting further writing in this field.

Alan Gailey

CONTENTS

ONE

Vernacular Housing and the Built Environment

The Built Environment

AWARENESS of the quality of the total stock of buildings and their relationships to one another, the 'built environment' in which we live and work, has long been regarded as essential to the training of professional architects. General realisation of the need to protect the quality of our built environment, and of the need to maintain a balance between old and new, is however a fairly recent phenomenon. The National Trusts in the United Kingdom and An Taisce in the Republic of Ireland do much to preserve important buildings of the past and thereby, and in other ways, to educate the population at large about architectural history; if the emphasis has been on the grand houses of the upper classes, some homes of humbler people have been preserved, notably by the National Trust for Scotland. Legislation on the preservation of buildings of architectural and historic significance has long been in force in Great Britain, but its advent in Ireland, restricted to the north, was only in 1972. The importance of this legislation is that it applies to all classes of buildings, not just to the masterpieces of the professional designers of the past. At least in theory, a reasonable sample from the totality of the historic built environment may now be preserved, though no sensible preservationist wishes to see entire architectural environments stultified in the process. There must be accommodation between retaining something of the flavour of the past and the demands of rapidly changing modern society.

The built environment encompasses the entire stock of buildings of all kinds, however grouped together or scattered widely in rural areas. This book considers only the traditional or vernacular houses of the northern Irish countryside. Passing reference is made to buildings in the towns and smaller agglomerations and to larger, formally designed rural houses, but the primary concern is with rural houses of traditional type. Only brief consideration is given to other structures, the range of out-buildings associated with farmhouses in particular.

Houses come in all shapes and sizes, or so it seems at first glance. Yet until recently there was some pattern to the range of possible sizes and designs encountered in the countryside. By selecting broad categories of houses, thatched, slated, one-storeyed, two-storeyed, and so on, order comes out of the seemingly endless variety. A more consistent way of regarding northern Irish rural houses, or indeed any portion or all of the built environment, is to consider the sources of design inspiration involved. The work of the trained, professional designer, the architect, is readily appreciated. He designs in the abstract in response to the demands, means, and ideas of his client, and also having regard to the restrictions and inhibitions placed upon him by the wider society, in modern times for example through planning controls and building regulations. Thus circumscribed, the architect yet expresses his own ideas, aesthetic and otherwise, and except where modern designs are replicated as in urban housing schemes, each design is unique, sometimes an artistic expression.

Most observers sensitive to variations in their surrounding built environments recognise a different category of buildings, constructed to accord with locally accepted tradition. On enquiry, it is discovered that the builder was the designer, and sometimes both were also the owner. Conformity with local tradition produced familiarity for all, perhaps a sense of social ease; yet close examination reveals that no two traditional thatched houses, for example, were identical — an extra few inches in length here, a slightly varied position of a window there, no attempt at symmetrical handling of facade elements on one house, addition of a dummy chimney next door to try to veer in that direction. Design variation for the individual was possible, but within culturally defined and generally accepted limits.

To consider only these two categories is to ignore

Fig. 1. Dunbar House, Magheradunbar Td., Co. Fermanagh. Nicely proportioned formal Georgian house. UFTM L 986.8

Fig. 2. Greenfield, Magherally Td., Co. Down. Simple formally laid-out rural house. UFTM L 975.3

Fig. 3.   Tullyverry Td., Co. Londonderry. Degenerate-formal farmhouse with four ground-floor rooms opening off a central front 'hall'. UFTM L 899.19A

Fig. 4.   Corrarod Td., Co. Cavan. Degenerate-formal Georgian farmhouse. Note chimney stacks and facade piercing not quite symmetrically placed. UFTM L 1378.20 +

many buildings worthy of attention. If it is easy to recognise the clear categories of formal or academic Architecture, and vernacular buildings, reality is a continuum of buildings between those representing the extremes of the formal and the vernacular (Figs. 1-8).[1] For example, in the late eighteenth and early nineteenth centuries, as local builders constructed the designs produced by the professionals, giving the masterpieces of so-called Georgian architecture (Fig. 1), they became familiar with the various architectural elements involved. These professional ideas were spread even more widely, sometimes, through the use of pattern books. But the builders did not always appreciate the design relationships between the elements (Figs. 3, 4), and in the course of time the original design concepts became debased or degenerate as local builders tried to reproduce professional designs.

In a similar way, builders of traditional houses (Figs. 8, 10) took over individual elements from professional designs and tried to apply them to their vernacular buildings (Figs. 6, 7). This urge to copy standards from higher up the social scale is a recurrent theme in study of vernacular houses; most widespread was the adoption of Georgian-style windows. In a different context, one sees it too in the massive gate pillars at entrances to farmyards, so characteristic in many parts of Ulster, inspired by the grand estate entrances created by landlords.

Somewhere in the centre of this continuum are houses whose design ancestry is uncertain (Fig. 5); they are too degenerate to be referred to as formal architecture, too elaborated or deviant internally and externally to be regarded as vernacular. However, few rural houses in Ulster cannot be assigned to one end or other of this building continuum. Also, an individual house may be moved along the continuum as time passes and it is enlarged or otherwise 'modernised'. But it is interesting that a good formal house is difficult to hide under the later accretions, and a truly vernacular layout is more likely to have been demolished than to have been altered out of recognition. If a 'grey area' between formal and vernacular exists, the truly indeterminate middle of the continuum is restricted in extent.

Design influences moved in both directions along the building continuum. Even casual observers of rural housing in Ulster will recognise Georgian windows, or various styles of Victorian panelled doors replacing older forms in many houses. A more subtle response to ideas coming from the formal into the vernacular sphere was the 'drive' towards symmetry in handling facade elements (Figs. 6, 7). So often, however, symmetry was never quite achieved, because the implications of internal layout of kitchen and other spaces, and of hearth

Fig. 5.   Tullyah Td., Co. Armagh. Simple farmhouse with byre under left-end bedroom. Kitchen chimney second from left.

positions, could not be fully accommodated. The idea that design concepts should come in this direction, from formal towards vernacular, will surprise few readers. It is expected that the 'lettered' will have influenced the 'untutored' in this way.

More surprising to many people is the fact that design ideas moved in the opposite direction. Examples may be more difficult to find, but they exist. The internal layout of many late eighteenth- and nineteenth-century estate gate-lodges, for example, clearly owed its inspiration to a vernacular tradition, whether witnessed in Ireland or in Britain, that allowed the construction of lodges two rooms wide with central door and chimney, internally having a screen wall between the entrance and the fireplace, the whole under a hipped roof. This symmetry was achieved by only minor adjustment of the entrance position of a vernacular form, that with the hearth-lobby entry layout discussed in Chapter 8. Comparable small landlord-inspired houses were also built, apparently based on northern Ireland's other vernacular layout, with the entrance at the opposite end of the kitchen from the hearth (Fig. 9).

A more interesting example of the professional world borrowing design ideas from vernacular experience occurred at the beginning of the twentieth century. Legislation had been passed encouraging construction of rural labourers' cottages in Ireland. A design competition was organised in Dublin, the winning cottage designs to be available on application to local authorities in all rural districts throughout Ireland. Some designs submitted were certainly inspired by vernacular models, and many of these small dwellings are still seen in the countryside. For example, the Cooley peninsula in north-east county Louth is truly 'littered' with old rural district council cottages, many now modernised, having an internal layout with a screen wall between entrance and principal hearth. This layout was common elsewhere in Louth, but was apparently unknown in the Cooley peninsula before the building of these cottages. Similarly 'alien' vernacular forms were introduced at this period into parts of Ulster, for example in the Ards peninsula of east county Down,

Fig. 6.   'Bloomvale', Bleary Td., Co. Down. Formalised facade hides a vernacular hearth-lobby interior, apparent externally from entrance/kitchen chimney relationship. UFTM L 969.15

Fig. 7.   Cappagh Td., Co. Down. Attempted formality not achieved. Enlarged vernacular farmhouse of hearth-lobby type. Note entrance/kitchen chimney relationship UFTM L 965-16

Fig. 8.   Derryall Td., Co. Armagh. Vernacular hearth-lobby farmhouse. Note entrance/kitchen chimney relationship. UFTM L 1002.17

Fig. 9.   Dunminning, Co. Antrim. Landlord-influenced hipped-roof dwelling of gate-lodge type. UFTM L 974.3

and in the borderlands of south Tyrone and north Fermanagh.

Comparable interaction between formal and informal, high and low culture — there are many designations for the extremes[2] — exist in other segments of cultural experience and achievement. Consider the distinction between 'classical' and 'folk' music — yet recall the inspiration a classical composer like Béla Bartok drew from folk tradition in Hungary and Rumania. Consider likewise the distinction between the great 'classic' literatures and what has come to be known as 'oral literature' — perhaps a contradiction in terms, but a useful enough label for the whole range of traditional narrative. At least two of Shakespeare's plays, *Cymbeline* and *The Merchant of Venice*, make vital use of themes and structures common in international tale-types that were spread widely throughout the Old World. No scholar has argued that the oral forms always derive from the literary creations. Shakespeare was only a more recent exponent of a very old tradition of literary inspiration drawn from oral culture. Homer had done the same thing long before. Movement in the opposite direction, of course, also took place. Aesop's fables, or some of them, literary creations, found their way into Irish oral tradition perhaps through the medium of National School reading books in the nineteenth century. There need be no surprise, then, that there were significant two-way movements of ideas along the building continuum, and these are still reflected in many houses surviving in rural Ulster.

Returning to the categories of formal and vernacular architecture, it requires little reflection to realise that they belong to broader areas of cultural experience distinguished from each other by the principal means of transmitting ideas. Formal architecture for long has been developed and passed on through the medium of penmanship, if not writing in the narrower sense. It is the prerogative of a formally educated group in society, and the further back its predecessors are traced in history, the more privileged they were. They belonged within a literate, educated 'Great Tradition', as the creators and propagators of great music and literature similarly belonged. Vernacular architecture on the other hand stems from a 'little tradition' within which ideas have been transmitted mainly informally and orally, where the possibilities for individual innovation have been closely circumscribed by the attitudes of the community at large, transmitted over the generations.[3]

The Nature of Irish Vernacular Building

Given the two-way interaction along the continuum between vernacular and formal architecture, a useful enough definition of vernacular architecture study follows. It is concerned certainly with the vernacular end of the continuum, but it must also deal with the 'grey area' in the middle, accounting for buildings inspired by influences flowing in both directions.

It is in the nature of traditional culture that it expresses itself strongly in regional variants, and nowhere more so than in the sphere of buildings. Popular house forms change only slowly both through time and across space, and their study is usually dominated by attention to form, or type, contrasting with the emphasis on style or decoration so characteristic of histories of formal architecture. Study of vernacular architecture does not belong within the fine arts, as architecture does; rather its practice has close affinities with disciplines like ethnology and archaeology.

Those who built traditional houses did so according to norms that were widely known and accepted. Builders, designers and clients, to use the formal descriptions, shared in a common cultural experience. It was enough for someone to decide he needed a house of three rooms — he knew what that meant and so did the builder-designer. Also, because vernacular buildings were ubiquitous in times before it became economic to transport materials over considerable distances, local materials imposed their own uniformities upon local building. The traditional building was the outcome of an ecological situation in which the cultural expectations of its occupants, the potentialities of their surrounding physical environment, and economic forces were dominating factors. All of these changed through time. However, so long as the general cultural setting leads people to demand houses of traditional *type*, even when economic considerations may mean it is more sensible to import materials foreign to the area rather than use the stone or clay and straw seemingly so conveniently to hand, then still there is vernacular architecture. Earlier examples of traditional houses were always built of local materials, while those constructed after the mid-nineteenth century increasingly used imported slates, tiles, concrete, timber and other materials. But in northern Ireland, it was usually well into the twentieth century before traditional house types or forms were abandoned for others whose inspiration stemmed from modern industrial society.

A significant portion of this book deals, then, with the traditional *types* of house found in northern Ireland; with the internal relationships between the elements

Fig. 10.   Brackenagh Td., Co. Down. Mourne Mountains vernacular farmhouse. Each unit a single room front-to-rear, axially placed chimneys, absence of gable windows. UFTM L 1217.3

comprising them, enshrined in plan forms and visibly expressed in their elevations; with their regional variations and distributions; with explanation of their historical development; and briefly, with speculation on their possible origins.

All vernacular houses in Ireland share some fundamental characteristics. Generally they are a single room deep between the front and rear walls. End walls are seldom pierced by doors, and rarely by windows except for small upper-floor attic lights, often placed to one or both sides of a chimney stack carried on the roof ridge. This placing of chimneys on the ridge line, reflecting axially located hearths internally, is a further regularity (Figs. 6—12).

In earlier historical periods most vernacular houses had a ground floor only, and they were usually covered with thatch, with certain outstanding local exceptions such as the use of local 'Tullycavey' slate in the Ards peninsula of east county Down since at least the seventeenth century. Remarkable surveys of the Londonderry family's estates in north and east Down in 1848 and of the Trinity College estates in northern Ireland a few years earlier, clearly illustrate the dominance of this traditional form; between 94% and 99% of rural houses on these estates

were of one storey. This experience was repeated in most parts of rural Ireland, as revealed by the figures of the 1841 census. Two- to four-room houses accounted for 40.1% of all the dwellings in rural Ireland and one-room houses for a further 37.0%. If a tiny minority of these houses of 1841 were two rooms up and two down in form, the remainder were all single-storeyed. Small wonder, then, that the pioneering studies of Irish vernacular architecture concentrated on the single-storey thatched dwelling.

Whenever in northern Ireland larger multi-storeyed vernacular houses are encountered, they almost invariably conform, on their ground floors, to the patterns represented by the smaller dwellings. Many were created by simple enlargement of the older houses, bedrooms being added above. Others were built to this enlarged pattern from the outset, but their design ancestry based on enlarged vernacular single-storeyed houses is unmistakable.

A further feature of vernacular houses in Ireland, as they have survived until recent times, is the fact that the walls surrounding each room extend up to the roof structure (Fig. 12). Since the walls are always of mass materials, stone or earth, they are also load-bearing,

Fig. 11.   Tyanee House, Tyanee Td., Co. Londonderry. Two-storey vernacular farmhouse, axially placed chimneys, only gable window lights roof-space. UFTM L 1263.2

Fig. 12.   Milltown, Moyheeland Td., Co. Londonderry. Rear view of ruinous vernacular farmhouse of 1791, showing division of interior into units separated by load-bearing walls rising to roof ridge (cf. Fig. 202). UFTM L 1252.11

support the weight of the roof, and absorb its thrust. So each 'room' may be considered a structural *unit*. A slight qualification is necessary to the statement that the vernacular house is always one room wide. This is true when one thinks in terms of these structural units. Double-pile houses having load-bearing walls between front and rear walls and parallel to them are not vernacular houses when found in Ireland. However, in many cases units, especially those at the ends of houses, were divided by non-load-bearing walls to provide front and rear apartments. Gables and internal transverse partition walls almost always rise to the roof ridge in surviving vernacular houses. A roof supported between the ends solely on timber trusses, and at the ends also in the case of hipped roofs, is unknown in surviving vernacular houses in northern Ireland constituted with two or more units.

These structural units provide an interesting case of the intrusion of the vernacular into the realm of formal architecture. In Britain larger formal houses, and many vernacular ones also, have their roofs carried on timber borne on walls carried to wall-head height only. Their counterparts in Ireland, especially those of the Georgian period, had internal walls carried to ridge level to bear the weight of the roof.[4] Builders of these houses must have been familiar with vernacular building practices, their tradition reinforced by scarcity of load-bearing timber in Ireland generally after the middle of the eighteenth century. Indeed, vernacular practice itself may date back only to that time, and there is some evidence for non-load-bearing partition walls of mass construction at vernacular level, more particularly in southern parts of Ireland.[5]

Structural units as defined here formed the conceptual 'building blocks' in the design of traditional houses. A unit had a fairly standardised size, variation reflecting poverty or affluence rather than tradition. One unit provided the principal living space and often also fulfilled all other domestic functions. Other units were added to provide separate sleeping areas, formal parlours, and as the tradition of combined accommodation for humans and their cattle died away, to provide separately entered housing for the latter under the one roof. Extension of the dwelling was in length to start with, the idea of upward enlargement coming later, though once it began to spread, multi-storeyed houses were built as such from new.

Study of Vernacular Housing in Ireland

Study of Irish vernacular houses started at the end of last century. In the 1890s, incorporated into comprehensive ethnographic and physical anthropological studies of communities in western Galway and Mayo, brief accounts of housing were published.[6] For present purposes they have little more than curiosity value. There was no continuity with later work which commenced in the 1930s with visits by two scholars, one German and one Swedish, again mainly to western districts. A generation had passed, one in which fundamental changes had occurred in academic attitudes to the study of culture. European countries had nurtured study of one's own people and their life styles, and modern European ethnological studies including those in vernacular architecture had been born.

Ludwig Mülhausen gathered data in counties Kerry, Galway and Donegal, and in spite of a strong linguistic emphasis, like that of the Swedish scholar Åke Campbell, his work provided a model for the future.[7] Campbell's work,[8] mainly in Kerry and Galway, was to be more influential. He proposed classification of Irish houses on the basis of chimney position — *gable-chimney* and *central-chimney* houses. This became the foundation upon which later study was to develop until at least the mid 1960s, albeit with the distinction recast in terms of hearth rather than chimney position, a small shift in emphasis, but fundamentally moving attention to plan types.

Campbell had been brought to Ireland in the 1930s by those behind the nascent Irish Folklore Commission, to lay a basis for study in material culture. His viewpoint was that of his day, concentrating on matters of typological classification and a search for origins in classic linear evolutionary fashion. The Commission appointed Caoimhín Ó Danachair as its specialist in material culture. He built ably on Campbell's foundation[9] at a time when Estyn Evans was working from Belfast and studying Ulster conditions especially but not exclusively.

Wartime circumstances in the first half of the 1940s slowed progress, but did not halt it. Ó Danachair published his first regional study, of north county Kerry housing, where the problems posed by the gable hearth/central hearth distinction were already implicit. He later made this problem plain in an important paper on hearth and chimney development, a study based on archival data and fieldwork, the former gathered by a postal enquiry system which he organised with great efficiency during the 1940s.[10]

Estyn Evans taught geography at Queen's University, Belfast, and before 1939 had co-operated in setting scientific archaeology in Ulster on its feet. Wartime conditions put an end to excavation work, and Evans turned to analysis of materials on traditional culture he had gathered all over Ireland, building from an important pair of papers published in 1939 dealing with north-west Donegal.[11] His book *Irish Heritage*, published in 1942,[12] was very influential, inspiring students and public alike, the first developing a tradition of research later carried on in an institution whose creation in 1958 was eased by the receptiveness of the latter — that institution was the Ulster Folk Museum.

Campbell, Ó Danachair and Evans were the founders of vernacular architectural research in Ireland. Although it has developed since their beginnings and been influenced by the course comparable studies have taken in other countries, yet the debt still owed to their pioneering efforts is immeasurable. Unfortunately, events since 1945 in the two parts of Ireland have taken very different courses, leading to a situation where a book such as the present one may be attempted dealing with northern Irish vernacular houses, but a counterpart dealing with houses elsewhere in the island is still not possible. Detailed local fieldwork remains to be carried out throughout much of Ireland.

The Irish Folklore Commission in Dublin was a research and archival institution until its first Director, James Delargy, retired in 1973. Only then, when it became a teaching department in University College, could Ó Danachair significantly influence students, and amongst those who have carried out research in material culture studies, one has recently worked in vernacular architecture.[13] Fruitful contact was however made during the 1960s between Ó Danachair and F.H.A. Aalen, a geographer teaching in Trinity College, Dublin.[14]

By contrast, Evans encouraged a number of his students between the 1940s and the 1960s to undertake research into traditional culture, concentrating especially on housing. This work was a spin-off from a school of settlement study which he fostered. Desmond McCourt's seminal research was on Irish openfield organisation and its associated settlement form, but he also studied house types[15] and roof timbering systems[16] in Ulster. Ronald Buchanan investigated the evolution of settlement and socio-economic organisation in the barony of Lecale, county Down, a veritable laboratory for examining the impact of English influences on the native culture; he also studied house types and thatching techniques.[17] Alan Gailey first studied geography under Evans in Belfast, but his post-graduate work on vernacular housing started in western Scotland. He returned to Ulster in 1960 to take up an early professional post in the Ulster Folk Museum, later starting systematic field recording and archival work on Ulster vernacular housing[18] with one of the last of Evans's students in geography, Philip Robinson, who joined the museum staff in 1974.[19] During all of this time, Evans himself kept up a steady flow of published

analytical ideas, and reporting of fundamental details of housing which he had gathered during his career.[20] His second book, *Irish Folk Ways* in 1957,[21] was the last of the pioneering studies, still based on the classification of houses depending on hearth position, and written just before important work began to be published, especially by McCourt, on such topics as roof timbering systems, and before the distributions of so many elements of traditional housing became apparent. It was the last great study cast in general terms, for also soon afterwards descriptions of individual buildings began to play a more significant role in Irish vernacular architectural writing.

A fundamentally different approach to vernacular architecture has been evident in Ireland from that which developed in Britain. Following the great works of Innocent[22] and Addy,[23] British studies concentrated on analysis of individual buildings, and Fox and Raglan's classic study of Monmouthshire houses[24] really initiated detailed regional interpretation of house forms and structural systems and details. In more recent times the work of the Royal Commissions on Historic Monuments,[25] coupled with the studies by students of the Manchester School of Architecture first inspired by the late Professor Cordingley and then ably led by Ronald Brunskill, have both extended the base, and elaborated regional analysis and an overall synthetic approach.[26] This work has been closely linked with study of local history in many areas, and has been prosecuted by people, professional and lay, from many disciplines and backgrounds. Historians, architects, archaeologists, some trained in human geography and many simply interested committed people, often without formal training, have all been involved.

Studies of Irish housing, as we have already seen, built on origins created by European ethnologists, while of the local pioneers, Ó Danachair was trained first as an archaeologist and took further training in European ethnology, while Evans, coming from the renowned school of anthropo-geography at Aberystwyth to teach geography at university level in Belfast, was influential in establishing teaching there of both archaeology and anthropology. Human-geographical and archaeological interests and attitudes have been and remain evident in Irish research in vernacular architecture. Relatively speaking, much more is known about overall distributional aspects of Irish housing than is known of vernacular housing in Britain — by contrast, published studies of individual structures were few and far between before the 1960s,[27] since when they have developed especially in northern areas, and detailed publication of many structural details, particularly of roofing techniques, dates from the same time.

It is at present difficult to foresee expansion or intensification of study of Ireland's vernacular architecture in years to come. Teaching emphasis in the Department of Irish Folklore at University College, Dublin is on oral tradition; to judge from published literature, the folk-life department of the National Museum of Ireland in Dublin is not active in this field. Teaching departments of architecture in Ireland are uninterested — Ireland shows no signs of developing a counterpart to the energetic recording carried out from the School of Architecture in Manchester University since the 1950s, and more recently from the Duncan of Jordanstone College of Art in Dundee. Statutorily based recording of monuments in Ireland has not extended work sufficiently into the vernacular field as has happened in Britain. Activity in local history in Ireland, which has blossomed recently, has not moved in this direction either. Systematic, concentrated field study of vernacular architecture has been confined to northern Ireland, developing since the 1960s.

Survey work carried out beforehand, by the pioneers and by Evans's students, provided a base upon which the Ulster Folk Museum, established at the end of 1958 as a national institution — since 1967 known as the Ulster Folk and Transport Museum — could begin development of an open-air museum or folk-park section. Legislation[28] instituting the museum insisted upon a research role which implies development of archival resources. Systematic data collection dealing with aspects of popular culture in northern areas commenced in the winter of 1960-61. Field experience soon revealed the necessity to broaden the concept of the vernacular house to include all dwellings of traditional design, whether of one or two storeys, whether constructed using local materials or not. As the museum grew and staff were recruited, a small Department of Buildings emerged in the early 1970s, which now carries out recording both of individual rural and urban vernacular buildings, and of their architectural and cultural contexts.

Also in the late 1960s, in anticipation of enactment of historic buildings legislation in the early 1970s, recording of potentially statutorily listable buildings started. An Historic Monuments and Buildings Branch of the Department of the Environment for Northern Ireland came into being following the 1972 reorganisation of local government. Listing started in 1973, including representative coverage of vernacular buildings, and a major photographic archive underpinning this statutory work now exists within the Branch. Most regrettably, due to serious understaffing within the Branch, access to this archive cannot realistically be made generally available.

Much earlier, in the early 1930s, Estyn Evans became involved in the work of the Northern Ireland Ancient Monuments Advisory Committee (later Council) which was charged with oversight of historic monuments. In 1950 an Ancient Monuments Branch of the Northern Ireland Ministry of Finance was set up, advised by the Council, its professional staff taking responsibility for monument conservation and starting systematic field survey of archaeological sites and historic architecture. In 1972 this work became the Historic Monuments element of the new, combined Department of the Environment for Northern Ireland Branch, together with Historic Buildings, the Branch being advised by its two Councils, one for Monuments and one for Buildings. One archaeological inventory volume covering county Down was published in 1966,[29] which included some attention to vernacular buildings, drawing on Ronald Buchanan's work based in Lecale which he extended elsewhere in the county to contribute to the volume. Interestingly, some houses were included in this volume either on historic or general architectural grounds, the vernacular significance of which was not then recognised. Work towards completion of the second inventory volume, dealing with county Armagh, is well advanced, while preparatory work for a volume dealing with Fermanagh has long been in hand, and fieldwork on the county Antrim survey is in progress.

All of this officially sponsored activity in Northern Ireland testifies to the primacy of field investigations and recording of surviving buildings. Only the Ulster Folk and Transport Museum with its slightly wider brief extends systematic recording work beyond the limits of the six counties of Northern Ireland. Field study is essential when dealing with buildings which, as virtually always throughout Ireland, are not dealt with individually in written records. Here lies a reason for the different emphasis in vernacular architecture studies in Ireland compared with Britain. Ireland lacks the documentary resources comparable to those which Professor Barley used so tellingly in *The English Farmhouse and Cottage*.[30] All of the pioneers of our study in Ireland, Mülhausen, Campbell and Ó Danachair in south-western and westen, and Evans and Mülhausen in north-western parts of Ireland, based their work firmly on field investigations. Some, especially Mülhausen, also considered what linguistics could contribute from study of traditional terminologies associated with buildings, and this approach has been used occasionally since.[31] The possible value of the linguistic element will be seen within this book also. However, it cannot be too strongly emphasised that the essential requirement for study of vernacular buildings anywhere, but especially throughout Ireland, is detailed fieldwork. New data survive to be recorded everywhere, even in Northern Ireland where a more systematic approach to survey work already exists than seems yet to be contemplated elsewhere in the island.

Henry Glassie's *Passing the Time*, published in 1982, deals with the whole spectrum of popular culture, including vernacular architecture, in a small district in west Fermanagh lying south of Belnaleck and north of the Arney River. Firmly based on field evidence, his book brings new approaches to the study of Irish housing. His intention is to explore the social processes responsible for design changes in the development of the local vernacular architecture, and he applies a structuralist theoretical analysis to this end. 'Always in process, unstoppably changing, houses record the local will, the cultural history of the . . . people.'[32] Glassie's approach is more sociological and cultural-anthropological than has hitherto been applied to the study of vernacular architecture in the British Isles, yet his effective setting of his analysis in an historical dimension gives his conclusions a depth often missing from anthropological and folkloristic academic endeavour. He essays an understanding of how the people who built and lived in vernacular houses viewed their own dwellings, what were the motivations for change, what values they placed on comfort, convenience, sociability and privacy, and he is less concerned to examine the historical development of the construction of the house and its structural details. His conclusions for the very small area he studied are theoretically interesting, and importantly valid for that area, but it is his methodology which will be important for work in vernacular architecture elsewhere in Ireland.

Other sources of valuable information exist of course. A substitute of a kind for actual examination of buildings, externally and even internally, is old photographs. Mention need only be made of the two major collections in Northern Ireland, that of R.J. Welch dating to the turn of the century,[33] and of W.A. Green surviving from about World War I, together with the all-Ireland collection of W. Lawrence held in the National Library in Dublin. Other pictorial sources are valuable but increasingly scarce the further back in time we seek material. Works by Irish artists are sometimes useful, especially for the late eighteenth and nineteenth centuries. The linen industry illustrations of William Hincks of 1783 are amongst the earliest illustrations we have of housing and of many other aspects of life and activity in east Ulster.[34] There are also occasional illustrations in collections of estate papers, for example decorating estate maps, or included as illustrations in estate surveys. Some of the nineteenth-century tourists who wrote accounts of their experiences included illustrations in their books; however, these are seldom detailed enough for accurate structural descriptions to be based on them. Tourists visiting Ireland, including the north, usually did so for one of two reasons. What were then recognised as the scenic parts of Ireland are scattered around the coasts, and in western areas these coincided with regions of great poverty, a condition that had grown to gross proportions by the mid-nineteenth century. Here was the other reason why the visitor came — to see at first hand what the growing agitation regarding the circumstances of life for the poor in Ireland was really about. Obviously the tourists provide neither regional nor social coverage of all the realities of life in rural Ireland, from the time of Arthur Young in the 1770s, who consciously sought places where he knew or thought there were landlords interested in 'improvement', to the post-Famine accounts of the consequences of starvation and the related flight of people from the land.

In the nineteenth century there are fortunately some consistently useful general sources for our purposes. Data collected from the 1841 and later censuses on the quality of housing, provided they are correctly interpreted, are revealing. Evidence gathered by the Commissioners who reported on the circumstances of the labouring poor all over Ireland in the mid-1830s[35] can, in northern areas, be set against fuller accounts of parochial conditions in the same decade preserved in the Ordnance Survey memoirs.[36] Half a generation earlier, W. Shaw Mason had set out to emulate the Statistical Account of Scotland; he failed, but left three volumes of valuable parochial surveys which give a sample of conditions all over Ireland about 1812.[37]

The earliest countrywide survey, clearly modelled on the county surveys of agriculture in Britain, was initiated by the Royal Dublin Society just after 1800 in its series of county statistical surveys. Depending on the interests and thoroughness of their authors, these volumes can be most useful, containing generalised descriptions of housing for both man and beast together with information on domestic, agricultural and economic matters.[38]

In northern parts of Ireland two archival collections contain quantities of relevant documentation. In other contexts the Ulster Folk and Transport Museum has been referred to. One of its functions has been to accumulate relevant documentation, including data gathered by means of systematic questionnaire surveys of various themes within traditional and popular culture. It is fortunate that its resources are strongest and most thorough in those districts of east and mid Ulster where the analogous resources of the Department of Irish

Folklore at University College, Dublin (formerly the archive gathered by the Irish Folklore Commission) are least representative.

Potentially the most important archive source for north Irish buildings of all kinds is the Public Record Office of Northern Ireland. Here local and national governmental documentation is housed together with family and estate records. Regrettably, sources bearing on vernacular buildings in this repository are few and far between. That this is so casts no reflection on the comprehensiveness and quality of the work done in the Public Record Office in recent decades. Rather, it testifies to the lowly position that housing of the mass of the population held in the estimation of landlords and legislators until after disaster struck rural Ireland in the 1840s in the potato famine. As a general rule this seems proven by the few exceptional documentary morsels that do exist. Records dealing with the nature and extent of British settlement in northern Ireland from 1610 onwards are on deposit, some in the Public Record Office of Northern Ireland, some dealing with county Londonderry in the records of the London Livery Companies, some in other archives, and some have been published.[39] In the 1660s there is a detailed survey of leases for the Brownlow properties about and including Lurgan which throw valuable light on materials used in vernacular building.[40] A series of Quaker domestic inventories survives for a community in north county Armagh between 1715 and 1740,[41] while for about 1700 there is a useful if brief survey of the Manor of Castledillon in the same county, containing information on building materials.[42] Later estate surveys usually dealt more with tenure and agriculture, less often with buildings, but notable exceptions are for the Gosford estates,[43] and Drumbanagher in Armagh,[44] in the early nineteenth century. The 1848 survey of the Londonderry family's estates in north Down and those for the Trinity College estates in Down, Armagh, Fermanagh and Donegal also in the 1840s[45] provide the most amazing detail, which can be related to the near contemporary census data of 1841.

The general poverty of documentation generates a major problem for study of vernacular architecture in Ireland, especially in the light of the usually undecorated nature of the buildings themselves. Dating buildings anywhere in Ireland is difficult, often impossible. Absence of decorative features such as mouldings and chamfer stops denies the possibility of building up typological sequences to provide at least relative chronologies in a built environment where timber-framed structures were

either not known or have not survived. Many owners believe, however, that they hold documents dealing with their houses; invariably these prove to relate to the property on which the buildings stand. Before the end of the nineteenth century most people in rural Ireland were tenants, and in circumstances where the landlords did not usually provide housing for their tenantry it is understandable that documentation, especially leases and deeds, deals with land and not buildings, certainly not buildings of vernacular character.

Later chapters show how difficult it is to date northern Irish traditional buildings. A very slow pace of design change at vernacular level coupled with considerable time lags from place to place in changes in building materials, such as changing brick sizes, makes it almost impossible to draw up workable chronologies. A few buildings carry date-stones in original positions, but some also have date-stones re-used from other buildings on the same site or elsewhere.[46] Even in the one facet of dating where there has been recent remarkable progress, the dendrochronologist must be wary of sampling timbers re-used from an earlier building.

It is through the application of dendrochronology to the problem of dating vernacular buildings that startling results have become available in recent years. Dendrochronology is based upon the measurement and analysis of annual growth rings in timber. The techique originated in North America, using timber samples from the long-lived giant sequoias. Master reference tree-ring growth curves are constructed against which samples either from timber buildings or recovered from archaological excavations can be matched and therefore dated. The principle involved has been applied to native oak in Ireland by Michael Baillie of Queen's University, Belfast with a remarkable degree of success. With a master reference curve extending back into prehistoric times, developed as part of an integrated programme to refine scientific dating procedures generally, it is now possible to date samples of oak from Irish buildings. If some bark or the curved surface between bark and sapwood survives, a felling date for the timber accurate to one year can be provided; if only some sapwood survives, a date subject to a small statistical variation can be given; if no sapwood remains, a generalised statement about dating probabilities may be possible. Resulting from Baillie's work, accurate dates for the possible year of building are now to hand of a number of seventeenth- and early eighteenth-century houses, where before 1970 only educated guesses were possible.[47]

TWO

Early and Medieval Houses

ANY account of Irish rural housing traditions commences with a discontinuous chain of evidence for early periods. Field study of vernacular houses is illuminated by reference to documentary sources dating from the seventeenth century onwards, the two allowing a reasonably connected account of regional housing variations and their development. There is good evidence also for the culturally important period in northern areas about 1600 A.D., when older domestic conditions were under pressure from ideas introduced by British settlers. For all earlier periods the evidence is patchy. Medieval rural houses in Ireland are hardly known. Only a mere handful of neolithic habitations have been discovered, and evidence for the bronze age is as sketchy. By contrast, there is a relative wealth of both archaeological and documentary evidence for housing from about 400 A.D. until about the end of the twelfth century. Later chapters refer back to the earlier evidence as occasion demands, for example when discussing certain building materials or the evolution of plan form. This short chapter briefly surveys the earlier archaeological and documentary evidence in its own right. Readers will recognize that where the evidence is sparse, especially for the neolithic and medieval periods, generalisation based on available evidence from anywhere in Ireland is all that can be attempted. A northern Irish viewpoint is usually impossible. On the other hand data relating to native housing traditions in the late sixteenth and early seventeenth centuries presented in this chapter are of northern provenance, and derive mainly from the unique documentation generated by the Plantation of Ulster. It was a scheme of planned colonial settlement inspired from Britain which was closely monitored. A series of surveyors' reports charted the progress of the scheme. Together with other contemporary material, they provide a comprehensive account of native and imported building traditions in Ulster during the first quarter of the seventeenth century.

In contrast to the wealth of neolithic funerary sites in Ireland, representing well-defined regional cultures, there are few excavated neolithic houses to provide possible origins from which later domestic architecture may descend. Rectangular and curvilinear houses are known from the earlier part of the neolithic. Two circular post-built houses 5 m. in diameter stood on Slieve Breagh in county Meath, and rectangular houses (Fig. 13) occurred at Site A on Knockadoon, Lough Gur, county Limerick, at Ballyglass in north Mayo, and at Ballynagilly in east Tyrone.[1] The Knockadoon house measured 14 m. by 4.5 m. externally, had low wall footings of stone built around a framework of upright posts, and there were four rows of internal posts presumably supporting a roof structure. The door was in one of the long walls at the south-west corner, and the hearth was centrally located. At Ballyglass there was a house 13 m. by 6 m. with an entrance in the north gable. Walls were framed with posts sunk deeply in the ground in wall trenches. The wall posts presumably supported the roof, and further posts separated an entrance end, possibly with a porch, from the main living area where the hearth lay on the long axis of the building. At the end away from the entrance was another small room. The Ballyglass house was intentionally demolished to make way for construction of a tomb, so little evidence remained of constructional techniques used for the walls. The Ballynagilly house, however, provided evidence of quite sophisticated carpentry work, with walls of radially split oak planks. Also rectangular, 6 m. by 6.5 m., material from the wall foundation trenches provided radio-carbon dating of about 3300–3200 BC. The longer sides ended in substantial posts, and two other post holes within the house may have marked the positions of roof supports.[2]

Other neolithic evidence for houses in Ireland is meagre. Possibly forty-seven circular enclosures on the Mullaghfarna promontory in the Carrowkeel area of county Sligo were habitations of diameters within the range 6 m. to 13 m. Also from the Passage Grave culture, a large number of stake holes at the Townleyhall II site on the north side of the river Boyne may indicate habitation, but of what kind excavation did not

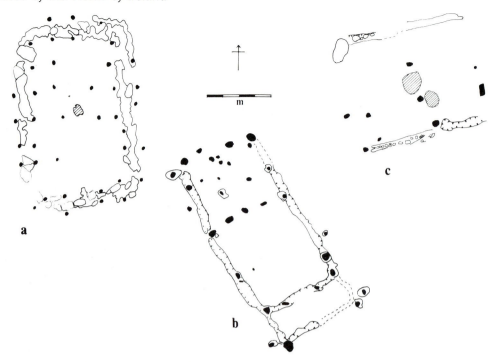

Fig. 13.   Excavated plans of Irish neolithic rectangular houses.
a: Knockadoon, Co. Limerick (after Ó Ríórdáin);
b: Ballyglass, Co. Mayo (after Ó Nualláin);
c: Ballynagilly, Co. Tyrone (after ApSimon).
Post and stake holes, black; hearths shaded.

determine. Given the occurrence of late neolithic (Sandhills culture) sites in Ulster, as at Dundrum, it is possible that the rectangular post-built house at Ronaldsway in the Isle of Man (of the Sandhills culture) is an example of a house type that also occurred in the north of Ireland. A site at Whitepark Bay on the north Antrim coast, where there were twenty circular huts about 6 m. in diameter, may demonstrate continuity with mesolithic domestic circumstances. Finally, at Knockadoon, Site A gave evidence also of a rectangular house about 6 m. wide. The south wall was marked by two rows of post holes, the line of the north wall only by a wall-trench. Sites C and D produced remains, however, of circular or curved-wall houses; at Site C they were about 5 m. across, had post-built walls set either in wall trenches or in individual post holes, and the hearths were central.[3]

Bronze age evidence for dwellings is even scantier than the neotholic material. In chronological order it is as follows. At Monknewtown, in county Meath, a wooden house, trapezium-shaped with a central hearth, was found in a hollowed-out area; there may have been rectangular houses up to 20 m. long also occupied by Beaker peoples at Newgrange in the Boyne valley. After

2000 B.C. Food Vessel people built two rectangular structures on Coney Island in Lough Neagh. One had sod walls possibly with a hearth close to one wall; it measured 2.75 m. × 6.1 m. The other smaller house had wall posts. No Urnfield people's houses are known, but at Knockadoon, Lough Gur, county Limerick, two structures in which bronze casting was carried on were excavated. A hut at Site D measured about 5 m. by about 3 m., while the other at Site F was rectangular, 8.25 m. × 6.3 m; both had the lower portions of their walls built of stone, the upper parts of perishable materials, perhaps of sods. In the final part of the bronze age, wicker or wattle-and-daub structures were found in the lower levels of Ballinderry No. 2 crannog, under an early Christian level. Nine small circular ones, 1 m. to 2.17 m. in diameter, are too small to have been habitations, but a larger area nearby, covered by parallel beams with mortices to take upright stakes, possibly represents some kind of house, interpretation of which is difficult.[4]

Houses at Cush in county Limerick span the period from the later bronze age to the early iron age.[5] Like the neolithic and bronze age evidence cited above, this site provided traces of circular and rectangular forms, and walls consisted of both stonework and of wattling. Given

Fig. 14. Kilmalkedar church, Dingle peninsula, Co. Kerry. Note gable finials, antae and projecting eaves course. UFTM L 1452.10

the small number of examples of early houses of which adequate details are known, it is unwise to suggest whether round or rectangular forms predominated at any period until early Christian times. At the start of the early Christian period the usual dwelling was a round wicker or post-and-wattle structure, without substantial roof supports, often with a stone slab-lined hearth and the house surrounded by a shallow drainage gully.[6] Literary sources confirm this view. It is of interest that early Christian church buildings seem also to have made use either of wattling or of hewn timberwork.[7] Unlike the round houses, however, the earliest churches invariably were rectangular with plank-built or boarded walls and shingled roofs. Similar buildings are represented by eighth-century bronze shrines and by house-shaped terminals on some tenth-century high crosses, like the Cross of Muiredach and the West Cross at Monasterboice in county Louth, the cross at Durrow in county Offaly and the Cross of the Scriptures at Clonmacnois in the same county. Perhaps some contemporary domestic buildings belonging to privileged ranks in society were similarly constructed.

Full-scale skeuomorphs of wooden construction survive in some early churches and oratories, of which the best known may be Kilmalkedar in the Dingle

peninsula, county Kerry (Fig. 14). Here the antae, gable finials, and projecting eaves courses combine to represent a timbering system, of wall posts, wall plates and principal rafters, or possibly cruck-like features with wall plates. However, by the seventh century, Tírechán specified a rectangular earthen church of turf 'because there was no wood nearby', a fairly clear indication that building in sod or turf would also have been acceptable domestically at that time.

Fuller information is available about domestic conditions between the fifth and twelfth centuries A.D., even if its interpretation is difficult.[8] More than 160 houses are known from about 120 excavated sites, mostly raths or ring-forts, but some from contemporary cashels and crannogs. Searching analysis of the excavation reports shows that between about the fifth and eighth centuries circular buildings predominated, whereas by the eleventh and twelfth centuries the principal house shape was rectangular. The earlier houses were mainly of light timbering and wattlework, the later of heavier timber framing, often coupled with stone foundation courses for the walls. At a number of sites where there was a succession of houses of different shapes, for example at Dunsilly and Ballymacash in county Antrim and at Nendrum and Rathmullan in

Fig. 15.   Simplified detail drawing of The Temple of Jerusalem, from The Book of Kells, f. 202v.

county Down, the change in each case was from round to rectangular. Sites with round houses only, like Big Glebe in county Londonderry, and Dressogagh in county Armagh, fall within the earlier centuries mentioned, and those with rectangular buildings only, like Ballynarry and Duneight, both in Down, seem to belong to the end of the period. The change was largely complete by about 1000 A.D. Small rectangular post-and-wattle houses used by the Vikings in Dublin probably did not inspire the change, which was accompanied by a shift in building techniques with greater emphasis afterwards on joinery work, stone walling and clay, possibly used both as bonding and plastering. Given that the earlier round houses used constructional procedures similar to those employed in the Viking houses of Dublin, had the Viking houses provided inspiration for the change in house form, it is unlikely that constructional methods would also have changed. Possibly the desire to construct the canonically correct rectangular early churches to acceptable standards of workmanship not only developed carpentry traditions, but also in time spread the idea of rectangular buildings into the domestic sphere, this change coming perhaps at about the same time as earlier timber churches were being replaced by stone ones.

Documentary sources for domestic buildings in Ireland over the same period are relatively plentiful, but their interpretation is difficult because of a number of problems.[9] Many were written in older forms of Irish, and original meanings of words have been lost. Also, because they were writing documents for contemporaries who understood the nature of the buildings described, the writers often abbreviated their accounts, omitting fundamental details. For example, the eighth-century law

tract, *Críth Gablach*, quotes the sizes of houses suited to different social grades, but only by listing a single dimension in each case.[10] It is difficult to know if this represents the length or breadth of a rectangular building, or the diameter of a circular one. The laws, too, depict an ideal view of society, one possibly already archaic when they were committed first to writing, given the oral transmission of culture that preceded them. Jurists' concepts of what was fit and proper probably only remotely reflected regional and other variations of reality, and may have over-represented the norms of a 'metropolitan' area in the east of Ireland. Nevertheless, at some point they were based on actual buildings and to that extent must contain valuable insights. Similarly, with care in interpretation, the other documentary sources, the secular sagas and poetry and the *vitae* of the saints, also contain valuable clues.

Few references in the early documentation relate to ground plan. Perhaps a single plan type was ubiquitous and so it was unnecessary to detail it. The earliest written sources relate to the eighth century, and possibly rectangular buildings were already involved. No sources seem to imply circular buildings, whereas some do refer to the four sides of a building.[11] Sizes, as already noted, are described by a single measurement. It is probable this is the length, particularly when a church is measured as 60 ft. (18.3 m.) in Tírechán's *Life of Patrick*, for we know that churches were always rectangular.[12]

Most descriptions of wall construction relate to use of wood or wattle. Undoubtedly this reflects a northern, eastern and midland emphasis; the archaeological record already discussed, showing a greater diversity of walling materials, draws from more extensive areas of Ireland.[13] Perhaps here the archaeological and written records combine to demonstrate regional variation, at least in the latter part of the early Christian period. If wattlework is predominantly noted in the sources, some indicate a more massive type of construction. Adamnán's *Life of Columba* tells of use of both oak and pine in house building, and jointed planking is attested for churches if not for houses.

Few sources suggest a single entrance to the house, whereas *Críth Gablach* describes the house of the *ócaire*, the lowest grade of freeman, as having opposed entrances, and the story of the voyage of *Mael Dúin*, dating to about 1100, indicates the same arrangement with a more substantial door in the windward side.[14] Opposed entrances have been discovered archaeologically, but in medieval rather than in early Christian or dark age contexts.

Hearths within domestic buildings are occasionally noted, for example in both the early laws and in

Adamnán's *Life of Columba*, but only three sources specify a central location, all referring to socially exceptional structures like Queen Maeve's palace at Cruachan. Various kinds of internal divisions and arrangements are suggested; they are difficult to interpret, but some may provide descriptions of antecedents for the bed-outshot tradition reported in vernacular housing in north-west Ireland in the nineteenth and twentieth centuries.[15] Other details referred to are windows and some kind of external balcony.

Roofs are mentioned in a number of contexts. *Crith Gablach* describes the house of the *ócaire* as:

> Wattle to the lintel, a pair of rafters between every two sections of wattle from the lintel to the *cleithe* [ridge][16]

— surely a description of some kind of principal-rafter or comparable roof-framing system. Thatch is often specified as the roof covering. The laws cite fines to be paid for interference with one's neighbour's thatch, presumably at the eaves. This hints at the height of the walls and extent of overhanging eaves.[17] Wooden shingles are also mentioned, at least on Maeve's palace.

Hilary Murray has conveniently summarised much of the documentation by suggesting what the houses of an *ócaire*, the lowest grade of freeman, and an *aire túise*, a farmer of noble grade, would have looked like.[18] In the early laws, the *ócaire* was rather less prosperous than average. His house was roofed with thatch on pairs of rafters rising from wattled walls. It was unpartitioned internally, probably rectangular, and measured perhaps about 5.8 m. long by 3.9 m. wide. Opposed entrances were probably closed by a wooden door on the windward side, and a wattle door on the lee side. No evidence is available to tell if the roof was hipped or gabled; both forms are found in contemporary representations. The *aire túise* had a larger but otherwise rather similar house, perhaps about 8.8 m. × 5.9 m. Some form of internal divisions provided specially defined sleeping spaces, and these had corner posts supporting curtain rails, probably to facilitate privacy as occasion demanded.

The sources also describe exceptional buildings like Maeve's palace, which are hardly representative in design, even if they shared in the constructional techniques characteristic of more lowly habitations. What the sources do not reveal is the nature of the housing of the poorest element in society, those people without rights and share in control of property, with which the laws were primarily concerned. This same element is apparently not represented in the archaeological record either.[19] Yet it is amongst the poorest in society that we

might expect to discover persistence of older building traditions, of materials and design, superseded as time went on amongst their social superiors. Such certainly was true in later historical times.

Documentary representations of buildings also exist. Well known are the plans of the 'banqueting hall' at Tara, interpretation of which has been disputed.[20] The plans really relate more to concepts of social precedence amongst those who might be present in the building and tell little about its construction and design. More pertinent is the drawing of the Temple of Jerusalem in the Book of Kells (Fig. 15). It is rectangular, with a framed door in the

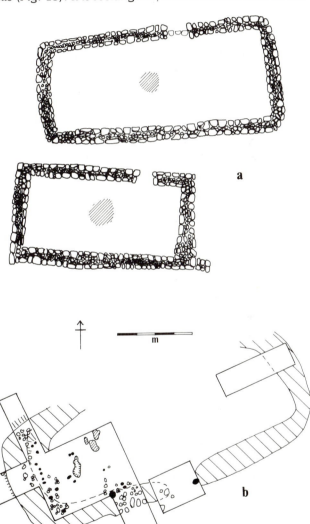

Fig. 16.   Excavated plans of Irish medieval houses.
a: Caherguillamore, Co. Limerick (after Ó Ríordain and Hunt);
b: Tildarg, Co. Antrim (based on unpublished data kindly provided by the excavator, N.F. Brannon, Northern Ireland Archaeological Survey).
Stake and post holes, black; hearths, shaded.

middle of at least one side wall. Decorative bands at top and bottom of the wall suggest wall plate and ground sill respectively, so presumably it was timber-framed. The steeply pitched roof is hipped at the ends, with only a short ridge where pairs of rafters cross to end in animal-decorated finials. Some kind of tiles or shingles cover the roof. Illustrating the Temple, this representation is perhaps of an oratory rather than a dwelling; the probable relationship between these two classes of structure has already been noted. At the very least it suggests the level of skill and range of techniques and structural ideas known to contemporary builders.

Information on medieval houses, or indeed buildings of any kind below upper-class level, is extremely difficult to come by.[21] There has still been excavation of only two peasant dwelling sites, at Caherguillamore in county Limerick more than forty years ago, and near Tildarg in county Antrim in 1982 (Fig. 16).[22] At Caherguillamore the remains of two houses with clay-bonded stone foundation courses to the walls were discovered. Both were rectangular, the larger having two rooms and measuring 13.1 m. × 6.1 m. externally, the other being of a single room 9.85 m. × 5.55 m. The smaller house had straighter walls and squarer corners than the larger one, but was less well built. Each had a single entrance in one of the long walls, with a hearth placed off-centre on the long axis of the building, set between the entrance and one end of the smaller house, and between the entrance and an internal partition in the larger. Inside the latter the wall surfaces were plastered on a framing of wattling, which in the small inner room covered a blocked-up second external door, in the corner of the house on the side opposite the main entrance. External

wall surfaces of this house seem also to have been rendered. Excavation finds attributed occupation to the period from the fourteenth to the sixteenth centuries. The Tildarg house has only been partially excavated but seems broadly similar to the Caherguillamore ones and is datable perhaps to the sixteenth century.

Some other medieval buildings, probably not houses, have also been uncovered by excavation. They are important in that they suggest variations in plan and materials that may have been represented amongst medieval dwellings too. Foundations of a thirteenth-century trapezium-shaped stone-walled building were uncovered in the excavation of the Ballynarry rath, county Down.[23] It was described by the excavator as a house, but the absence of hearth, its dimensions of 3.65 m. × 4.25 m. internally, and its 1.2 m.-wide door opening, all suggest it may have fulfilled some purpose other than that of a dwelling. It had stone walls with well-built faces and perhaps also clay bonding, and a single post hole against the inner face of one wall may indicate some kind of timbering of the upper parts of the walls as well as the roof. Also in county Down and attributed to a thirteenth-century secondary occupation phase, Ballyfounder rath contained a small rectangular structure some 3.65 m. × 2.15 m., represented only by post holes: it was timber-framed.[24] Another small, 3.65 m.-square building was discovered in the north rath at Glenkeen, county Derry, and it may be medieval. The structure was defined by a charcoal spread, with settings of flat stones at the corners which probably formed pads for the bases of timber posts.[25]

To complete the archaeological record, mention may be made of rectangular peasant houses excavated in a

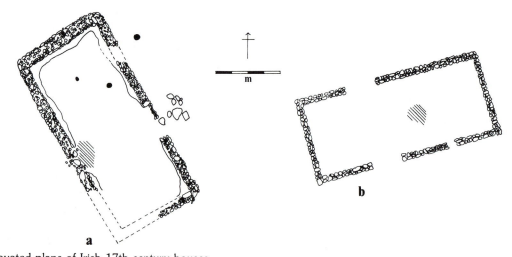

Fig. 17.   Excavated plans of Irish 17th-century houses.
a: 'Thady's Fort', Shannon Airport, Co. Clare (after Rynne);
b: Liathmore-Mochoemóg, Co. Tipperary (after Leask and Macalister). Post holes black; hearths shaded.

rath at Shannon Airport in county Clare,[26] and at Liathmore-Mochoemóg in Tipperary, both dating to the seventeenth century (Fig. 17).[27] The 'Thady's Fort' house at Shannon Airport was 13.4 m. × 6.2 m., with stone walls surviving to about 0.6 m., but even when fallen stone recovered from the excavation is allowed for, they were probably originally no more than 0.8 m. high. External and internal faces consisted of dressed stones, the largest in the bottom courses with smaller irregular stones in the wall cores. They were 0.75 m. thick, and loose earth amongst the stones was interpreted by the excavator as the remains of original sod upper courses above the stonework. An entrance off-centre in one of the long walls was matched by the position of some kind of chimney structure against the opposite wall, to judge from the evidence of the hearth position. The inner surfaces of the house walls were plastered with a yellowish mortar. No evidence survived to suggest how the house was roofed. Suggested dating is in the first half of the seventeenth century, and it is most interesting that the surrounding rath seems to have been contemporary with the house.

The larger house at Liathmore-Mochoemóg is equally interesting; measuring 12.2 m. × 5.6 m., with 0.5 m.-thick walls of small field stone surivng to a maximum height of 0.4 m., it had opposite doors set off-centre in the long walls. The hearth was on the long axis in the larger portion of the interior, set slightly to the opposite side of the centre of the house from the 'cross passage' between the doors. The same site provided another rectangular structure, obviously an outbuilding of some kind on account of the absence of a hearth and its small dimensions of about 4.9 m. × 2 m. internally.

The present extreme poverty of the medieval record for rural Ireland, by comparison with the apparent richness of the archaeological and documentary sources from early Christian times until the Anglo-Norman invasion, throws into high relief the value of the last of the evidence on north Irish housing before 1600 A.D. The northern part of Ireland had been a constant source of trouble to English administration during the second half of the sixteenth century, and the flight of the Earls of Tyrconnell and Tyrone marked the final collapse of effective native resistance to English domination. Confiscation of the northern counties, apart from Antrim and Down which had already seen substantial British — mainly Scottish — settlement, and Monaghan, paved the way for a planned settlement by British people: the Plantation of Ulster, under James VI and I. Suddenly, then, Ulster provides plentiful documentation, both of circumstances before this plantation and of the progress of the domestic details of the settlement itself. A considerable corpus of individual references to native north Irish housing conditions is included in this record, and it must be realistic to extrapolate backward in time from this material reaching towards the housing traditions of earlier periods already discussed in this chapter. It immediately becomes clear from the sources that there were two contemporary traditions of domestic structures co-existing in northern areas of Ireland.[28]

Impermanent dwellings, some rectangular but most mainly oval or circular in shape, are widely attested. They were post-and-wattle dwellings, the walls of which were not of mass construction and therefore may not directly have supported their roofs. They were thatched, chimney-less, and were associated with transhumant, extensive use of territory for grazing cattle. Misunderstood by contemporary English and other observers, who regarded their inhabitants as nomads without permanent dwellings, these flimsy habitations known as 'creats' are usually described in derogatory terms.

In county Fermanagh in 1607 Sir John Davies described the dwellings of the people as '. . . so wild and transitory as there is not one fixed village in all this country . . .',[29] and in the next year Sir Arthur Chichester advised that the native population of Ulster should '. . . be drawn from their course of running up and down the country with their cattle . . .'[30] A source referring to Augher in east county.Tyrone told that the impermanent huts built by such people could be put up within an hour.[31] David Wolf, S.J. in 1574 referred to these huts as tents,[32] while some contemporary military maps include representations of shelters for the soldiery (Fig. 18) which were similar.[33] Illustrations of such huts also occur in maps of Newry, Carrickfergus (Fig. 19) and Armagh,[34] those at Carrickfergus being hemispherical without suggestion of eaves or walls in any way separate from roofs. Armagh about 1600 was in ruins, and a map of the period shows wattled, curved-walled houses with dome-like thatched roofs (Fig. 20),[35] an interpretation echoed in a reference to '. . . a few small wattle cottages . . .' in the ruined city.[36] There can be no doubt that these flimsy huts continued the early Christian traditions of circular wattled houses. They must surely have had counterparts somewhere in the entire social range of habitations, during the centuries after the transition from round to rectangular house already discussed as being completed by 1000 A.D., and before the Plantation of Ulster.

The building of such impermanent houses was not entirely restricted to the Irish in late sixteenth- and early seventeenth-century Ulster. Scottish craftsmen who came to north-east Down in 1606 with Sir Hugh Montgomery

Fig. 18.   Detail of soldiers' encampments, from drawing of capture of Inisloughan Fort, Co. Antrim, 1602, in Hayes-McCoy, *Ulster and Other Irish Maps, c.1600* (Dublin, 1964), Plate VI.

. . . soon made cottages and booths for themselves because sods and saplins . . . with rushes for thatch and bushes for wattle were at hand . . .[37]

but these they occupied only until they had built stone-and-lime houses. A plantation grantee in county Armagh in 1622 erected a comparable temporary house. Similarly basic structures, presumably for short-term initial occupation by British settlers, were reported in Tyrone, Fermanagh and Cavan.[38]

Existence of these transient dwellings has long been known to Irish historians. Less obvious was the existence of another vernacular type, which can be called the Irish 'coupled' house, a couple being a transverse structural frame supporting the roof. The full significance of this tradition has only recently become apparent, following exhaustive study of all the contemporary source materials.[39]

Irish coupled houses are mentioned in several surveys of the progress of the Plantation of Ulster in the early seventeenth century. Many settlers were bound by the conditions of the plantation to build 'English' houses in timber and cagework or in stone, but a considerable number put up houses described in the surveys as 'Irish'. In county Donegal in 1622 some places had numbers of houses referred to as being built of timber; 'of birch timber, thatched' in Rosguill, for example.[40] It is unlikely that these birchwood structures were the same as the timber cagework houses 'after the English fashion' built elsewhere. It is remarkable that in Donegal only *these* timber houses were regarded as Irish: in Ballyshannon there were '. . . about 30 Irish houses and two stone houses . . .'[41] In 1613 in county Cavan timber and wattle are noted as having been made ready for an Irish house,[42] and in Fermanagh Sir Henry Foliat had 'caused a great Irish house to be framed',[43] while another settler had put up 'an Irish house strongly timbered and very large'.[44] Again in county Donegal Walter McLaghlin McSwine erected three Irish houses, one of which had a 'double chimney of stone'.[45] Of more particular concern, however, are references to Irish houses from counties Donegal, Tyrone, Fermanagh and Cavan, showing them to have been coupled. For example, Sir Oliver Lambert in Cavan had 'some couples and other timber upon the land for an Irish house'.[46]

Fig. 19. Late 16th-century creats at Carrickfergus, Co. Antrim. Detail from 'The Platt of Knockfergus', British Museum, reproduced in Camblin, *The Town in Ulster* (Belfast, 1951), frontispiece.

Fig. 20. Wattle-walled Irish houses, c.1600, city of Armagh. Detail from Hayes-McCoy, *Ulster and Other Irish Maps c.1600* (Dublin, 1964), Plate III.

The especial value of the series of plantation surveys is that they permit comparison of successive descriptions of the same buildings by different observers. From these it is obvious that 'timber house', 'Irish house', 'Irish coupled' house, or simply 'coupled' house were one and the same thing. There is no doubt that to the plantation surveyors there was a consistent Irish tradition of timbered houses whose roofs were supported on couples. It is unclear, however, if these couples were simply truss blades supported on the tops of the side walls of the houses, or if, as in contemporary Lowland Scotland,[47] couples really meant crucks. Crucks are load-bearing timbers supporting the roof of a building, springing from ground level, or from a position within the side walls somewhat above the ground. The documentation clearly shows that Irish coupled houses did not have stone walls, and there is little secure evidence for a tradition of mass walls of earth or mud in northern parts of Ireland before the end

of the sixteenth century. Also, northern Irish vernacular housing is characterised by an absence of wall plates; the lower ends of truss blades always rest in or on the heads of mass walls. So it seems unlikely that there was a system of timbering of walls heavy enough to have carried couples, such as anything like the contemporary lowland English half-timbered box framing. For all these reasons an identification of Irish couples with crucks is quite possible.

If the change from the tradition of post-and-wattle walling recognisable in Irish housing from prehistoric to early medieval times occurred in the medieval period, to mass walls of stone, earth or sod, such as typify vernacular houses in the seventeenth and eighteenth centuries, certainly this change had not been completely achieved in northern areas by 1600. Survival of the older frame tradition is clearly documented. Some houses combined the two traditions,[48] but it is impossible to say to

C

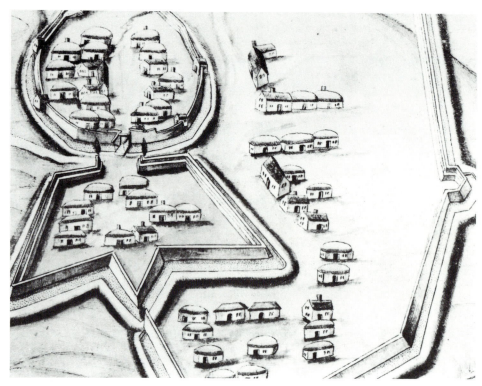

Fig. 21.   Irish houses inside and outside the fort, Mount Norris, Co. Armagh, *c.1600. Detail from Hayes-McCoy, Ulster and Other Irish Maps c.1600* (Dublin, 1964), Plate II.

what extent use of mass walling had spread into Ulster. Walls combining frame and mass constructional techniques would be expected in sod or earth houses where the problems of supporting the weight and thrust of a roof are considerable. The same combination might, however, also be found in a transitional phase where the older framing tradition was being superseded, perhaps because of lack of popular confidence in the potentialities of the newer mass-walling building technique.

Unquestionably the best illustrative evidence for pre-plantation house types in Ulster comes from military maps of about 1600 by Richard Barthelet, official cartographer to the Mountjoy campaign against the Earl of Tyrone.[49] Most of the native houses he shows were single-storey, thatched structures, mainly rectangular in plan, usually with a more or less centrally located door, and apparently having hipped roofs (Fig. 21). More of the houses inside the military forts had chimneys than those outside, and the few gabled roofs were found only within the forts. The only evidence Barthelet provided for roof structure comes from representation of several partly demolished houses.[50] Couples are shown in association with low walls of mass construction (Fig. 22). The intention of these drawings presumably was to show

where sizeable timbers could be taken from Irish houses for military purposes. It is remarkable that the couples are shown slightly curved. The very low walls might accord with the archaeologically attested use of low stone walls with timbering or wattling above with timber-supported roofs and therefore provide further confirmation that, about 1600, 'couples' were in fact crucks. The drawings suggest that by 1600 the mass walls, whether low or not, were either clay, earth, or earth-and-wattle walls plastered and whitened on the exterior.

Further illustrations of native houses in county Londonderry are available in the Phillips maps drawn by Thomas Raven of the settlements of the London Companies (Fig. 23).[51] All were shown with hipped roofs, and less than half had chimneys, of which only three are shown at the gable position, the chimney and so the hearth being located somewhere near the centre of the house. Windows are shown, but usually small ones pushed high under thatch eaves. There is broad agreement between the two map sources in the manner in which they represent native houses, and they probably reflect a widespread housing tradition in northern parts of Ireland.

Documentary and cartographic sources descriptive of

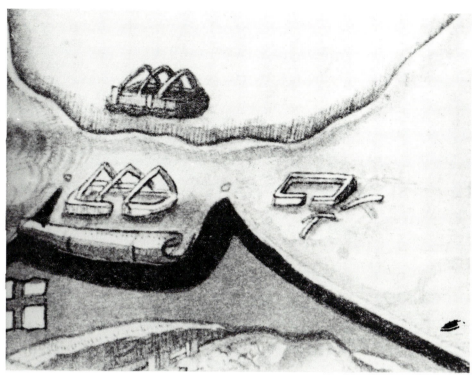

Fig. 22. Dismantled Irish houses of *c.*1600 showing low mass walls and curved roof-truss blades. Detail from a view of an attack on a crannog, perhaps in Co. Tyrone, in Hayes-McCoy, *Ulster and Other Irish Maps c.1600* (Dublin, 1964), Plate V.

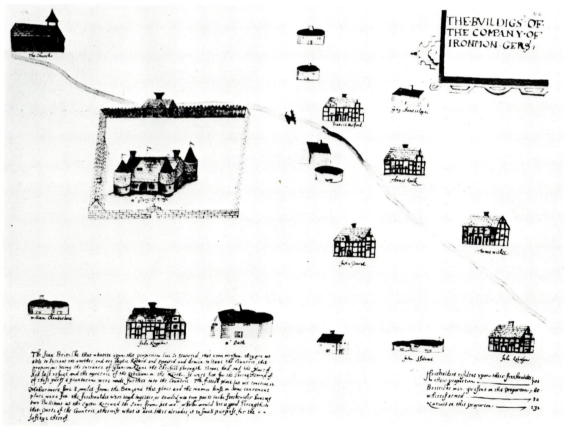

Fig. 23. Early 17th-century housing at Agivey, Co. Londonderry. From 'A Plat of the Ironmongers' Buildings' by Thomas Raven, included in Sir Thomas Phillips's survey of the Londonderry plantation in 1622, reproduced in Chart, *Londonderry and the London Companies, 1609-1629* (Belfast, 1928), Plate 21.

early seventeenth-century pre-plantation Ulster houses thus show clearly the existence of a house type co-existing with the impermanent circular wattled huts which so attracted the attention of contemporary observers. These more substantial houses were rectangular in plan, perhaps with rounded ends outside, normally without chimneys, but where they did have them, their position consistently indicates a more or less centrally located hearth. Walls were thick, of earth and post construction with perhaps a wattle skin, and the use of plastered wattling on the inner surface of one of the Caherguillamore houses should be remembered here. Roofs were carried on couples, probably crucks springing from the ground or from a position in the walls close to ground level.

THREE

Construction and Size

House Building

AS outlined in Chapter 1, design and construction of vernacular housing took place within a 'little tradition' dominated by non-formal methods of passing information and ideas between generations. Cultural prescription generated uniformities in aspirations based upon comparable uniformities of experience, and kept the level and pace of innovation to a minimum over long periods. Community loyalties and norms predominated over long periods, and dominated individual initiative. These circumstances acted against development of individual specialism, because almost everyone had first-hand experience of vernacular houses since they lived in them. Specialist designers were unnecessary; because many men in rural areas at one time or other had helped someone else build a dwelling, an outhouse, or merely a field boundary, essential techniques were widely known. Men who lived in thatched houses usually grew their own thatch material, and cut the necessary osiers (scollops) or twisted the straw or bog-fir ropes to keep it in place, and if they were putting on a new roof, they had the necessary spades to cut the scraws (sods) for underthatch. When the passage of time demanded that deterioration in a vegetable roof, due to rotting, be made good, usually a man went up on his own roof to put things right, provided he still counted himself 'souple' enough. At most, he sent for a neighbour. Specialist thatchers were few outside the towns until recently; there are now only a couple of thatchers left throughout east Ulster. Dissemination of other building skills was as widespread throughout rural parts of northern Ireland as thatching, except fine masonry work for which there was little demand within the 'little tradition'. Specialist tradesmen were not employed in house building in part of west county Donegal until the end of the nineteenth century[1] when application of centralised schemes to aid house improvement in the west brought about greater standardisation of construction techniques as well as introducing non-local materials like slate to replace thatch; in these circumstances building specialists inevitably came to the fore.

Only by arguing thus can one explain the poverty of documentary references to building specialists outside the towns. Reference to them even within the towns is scanty enough, sometimes rather oblique, as in a listing of the costs per day for various building trades in Garvagh, county Londonderry, in the late 1830s.[2] Prices for carpenters, slaters, masons and bricklayers, plasterers, stonecutters, cabinet-makers and labourers are listed, but there is no mention of how many of each were involved. At the beginning of the seventeenth century building craftsmen appear in the documentation of British settlement in Ulster, especially carpenters and masons. However, they too were largely employed in building the new towns of the plantation scheme.[3]

There is indeed little record of any kind of the building of vernacular houses at any period. Some of the early seventeenth-century accounts by British administrators of circumstances in northern parts of Ireland tell how rapidly houses could be put up, but they usually refer to the 'creats' or booley houses associated with the seasonal use of pastures at some distance from the permanent houses. An account of Augher, in county Tyrone, tells that they could be completely built within about one hour.[4]

Emphasis on a communal approach to building is illuminated in a description of the building of a house in Lecale in south-east county Down in the second half of the eighteenth century:

> When they want to build new houses the method they took was as follows. They first provided timber and cut sods of a certain size and set them on their edges to dry. Also cut 'scraws' and made straw ropes sufficient, they gave notice that the house was to be built. The Clachan was gathered with their 'Slide Cart', the timber being bound with a foot under each end reaching the ground to bear up the *Copple*. Then they laid on the first course of sods by proper hands when two men followed with 'Batstaves' beating the wall and dressing or trimming it and so continued building . . . the side wall was about six feet high and gable in the centre four more and the ribs, wattles & scraws was laid on on one end of the house and thatcher set to cover it in, while the

other end was building. A man also was set to, and was to warp a rung-like gate with straw ropes and daub it over with Cow droppings mixed with water for a door which was hung to the frame with a plait rope of straw. The roof being thus covered then was roped diamond like the better ones in net-work if time would allow. A chimney was set on in the centre wrought as the door from which the Crook hung as the fire was always in the middle of the house round which they seated themselves to partake of the feast prepared for the occasion.[5]

Certainly this description relates to construction of the housing of poor people, but various elements and constructional details in it were known in houses lived in by better-off farmers, and the communal appoach to building was possibly fairly widespread in rural areas, both earlier and later. About 1840 it was said that the building of new houses, 'though troublesome to them', was not an expensive operation for tenants on Lord George Hill's Gweedore estate in west Donegal:

> As the custom on such occasions is, for the person who has the work to be done, to hire a fiddler, upon which *engagement* all the neighbours joyously assemble, and carry, in an incredibly short time, the straw and timber upon their back to the new site: men, women and children alternatively dancing and working while daylight lasts, at the termination of which they adjourn to some dwelling where they finish the night, often prolonging the dance to dawn of day, and with little other *entertainment* but that which a fiddler or two affords.[6]

Later oral evidence gathered this century shows that in parts of county Donegal stones for house building were gathered co-operatively, and that in Townavilly the team of workers who helped a neighbour build his house on a church holiday was known as a 'gathering'.[7] John M. Synge, in his *Aran Islands*, gives a graphic account of a similar approach to thatching in the early 1900s.[8]

Breakdown in the older communal pattern of life in rural areas in the second half of the nineteenth century meant that young men setting up a household on their own account often carried out all the work themselves. I recall being told of such a man near Newtownbutler in south Fermanagh who used his own horse and cart to draw all the stones required for his house from the quarry opened some years previously to provide material for the building of Monaghan's Roman Catholic cathedral, which places his labour sometime about the 1880s. His son went on proudly to relate that his father had built the house virtually unaided; on examination it proved to fit exactly within contemporary vernacular norms.

Relatively little folklore associated with housebuilding has been recorded. Older beliefs about selection of a suitable site for a dwelling, to ensure that it was not on a fairy pathway or suchlike are known, and the burying of

tokens like coins for good luck within the fabric of the house is shared with many other parts of Europe. For example, in Clonallan parish in south county Down, before building a house or outhouse it was customary to place two large stones in the positions where the corners of a gable would be. On top of these stones lamps were placed and lighted. If they were not interfered with after a few nights, it was considered safe enough to proceed with building on the site, but otherwise the site was not considered lucky.[9] Of two practices, however, much more is on record. A widespread practice all over Ireland was to bury a horse's skull under some part of the house, usually at the threshold, or under a hearth stone or some other part of the kitchen floor. It has been suggested that some kind of foundation sacrifice was implied at the inception of this custom.[10] A more practical reason accrues from the rigidly enclosed, largish empty space represented by a horse's skull. Once buried under the floor, the skull becomes a hollow space which acts as a sort of 'sounding box'. At many of the places where the practice has been reported, it has been said that the dwellings involved were ceilidhing houses, where singing and dancing were common. Two houses I visited during the 1960s to see horse skulls, one near Crumlin in county Antrim, the other in mid Down at Drumaghlis (Fig. 24), were similar in that the skulls were placed under the position where it had been decided a piano should stand. In the Drumaghlis case, indeed, portions of half a dozen skulls were found.[11] Placing a horse skull in the floor underneath where a piano stood, to improve the tone, is also reported from Knocknamuckley south of Lurgan in county Armagh.[12] Horse skulls under the floors of late nineteenth-century community halls are also on record.

A building custom persisting today is more restricted geographically in east and central Ulster together with the extreme north of county Louth.[13] When a house is being constructed, upon reaching the highest point the builders raise a flag or piece of cloth (Fig. 25), which traditionally stayed in place until they were rewarded either with suitable refreshment or with 'roof money'. In recent years the custom has been largely confined to houses built for private clients; public housing schemes have not usually been involved. Its incidence is generally urban and suburban. There is some indication that until the 1960s at least, the practice was spreading westward from a core area in Down, Antrim and east Armagh (Fig. 26). These facts imply that the custom is historically of fairly recent introduction, perhaps in the nineteenth century, and that its spread has been associated both with growing urbanisation of the northern Irish population, and with the consequent development of a substantial specialist building industry. Obviously, owner-builders did not

Fig. 24. Horse skulls under floor in a farmhouse, Drumaghlis Td., Co. Down. UFTM L 424.1

Fig. 25. Flag raised on chimney of modern bungalow under construction, Donaghmore, Co. Tyrone. UFTM L 530.16

Fig. 26.   Distribution of the custom of raising a flag during house building.

reward themselves with 'roof money', and in the absence of knowledge of any other motivation for the custom, like some kind of celebration, and in view of the general absence of the custom from rural areas, it is unlikely that it formerly was widespread in Ulster.

Building Costs

Little information is available as to the cost of rural house-building in the seventeenth century. Documents in London companies' archives give remarkably detailed information on the erection of some houses in the Plantation of Ulster in county Londonderry, including costs of materials and labour but invariably the buildings concerned were in towns. Understandably, when tenants and cottiers were also builders, accurate assessments of costs would have been difficult if not impossible to provide, apart from the fact that landlords by and large for whom the surviving documentation was created, normally left their tenantry to construct their own dwellings. This arrangement commonly persisted until the end of the nineteenth century. The few exceptions were landlords sufficiently interested in 'improvement' in their estates, like, for example, Mr. Irving. In the 1830s he owned ten of the thirteen townlands in the parish of Glynn in south-east county Antrim,[14] and provided those of his tenants who would enlarge their houses by addition of a second storey with lime, slates, and timber for flooring and roofing, and slates and lime to others who would build or improve one-storey houses. He also

provided free lime for white-washing. Even here, however, no assessment is given of costs involved in this improvement work; possibly Mr. Irving was not very concerned about costs.

Arthur Young's assessments of house-building costs in the 1770s are subject to the reservation that they are notional, 'guestimates' probably, difficult to judge because of the lack of dimensions for some houses or cabins he quoted:

> Co. Donegal. 'Expense of building a mud cabbin £3; of stone and slate £40.'
> Co. Fermanagh. 'Building a sod cabbin, £2. Ditto of stone and thatch £15.'
> Co. Cavan. 'Building a mud cabbin, £4. Ditto of stone and lime, 37 feet [11.28 m.] by 15 [4.57 m.], £17.'[15]

One must query the reality of the Donegal cost of a cabin of stone and slate, for there is no evidence that any such were ever built. Probably the figure was invented by a landlord with whom Young stayed who wanted only to impress on him how uneconomic it would be to improve the domestic circumstances of his tenantry.

A covenant in a 1792 lease from the Earl of Erne to John Willson of property in Tiriville, county Fermanagh stipulated that a dwelling was to be constructed of stone or brick and lime mortar within six years, to a value of not less than £10.[16]

Authors of the county statistical surveys of the early 1800s gave more consistent but still meagre data on peasant house building costs. M'Parlan wrote that the average cost of cabins in Donegal was £5 to £10,[17] and he quoted comparable figures for neighbouring parts of north Connacht.[18] Coote in the Cavan survey reported that improved houses built by Lord Farnham for tenants on his property in the barony of Loughtee 'consisting of every necessary apartment, and two stories high', cost £60 'which is quite too much'.[19] However, Coote gave greater detail of 'The expense of building a comfortable cottage' in county Armagh:

Mud-working and plastering	£3 - 8 - 3
Roofing	1 -14 - 1½
Thatching and Straw	2 - 5 - 6
Door, and leaded windows	0 -11 - 4½
	£7 -19 - 3

He added that some cottages were put together for £3 to £5 using inferior materials.[20] Comparable housing in Tyrone was cheaper. A house '24 × 14 feet [7.32 m. × 3.66 m.] in the clear, side wall 6 [1.83 m,] feet, 2 gables' was itemised by McEvoy as follows:

Stone, and clay mortar	£1	-10	- 0	
Three couples, or principals	0	-15	- 0	
Three dozen ribs	0	-15	- 0	
Two wheel-car loads of wattles	0	- 5	- 5	
One brace-tree or beam, to support a chimney	0	- 8	- 0	

The above articles are procured from the improvements [i.e. plantings].

Two door-cases of bog oak	0	- 4	- 4	
Two doors of foreign stuff	0	- 8	- 8	
Two windows, cases and glazing with lead-light	0	- 6	- 6	
Thatch. I set down at	1	- 0	- 0	
Labour of roofing, thatching, etc.	0	-15	- 0	
	£6	- 7	-11	

'A cabin of the above description, is reckoned in the country a respectable and comfortable mansion for a cottager.'[21] McEvoy's figures are based on an experience where obviously a landlord was insisting on use of timber cut from his own plantings for roofing; surviving buildings of the period are often roofed with bog wood. Obviously, again as with Arthur Young's earlier figures, estimates are involved, especially in the two final items, for a tenant provided his own labour as well as design expertise, and produced his own thatch inevitably in growing grain crops for rent and subsistence. Similar estimates are involved in Sampson's set of figures for the 'Expense of building a Mud Cottage' in county Londonderry:

To 3 bays of mud-work, ready for roofing	£3 - 8 - 3				
To straw, laid in to the workmen, for mixing with the mud	0 - 3 - 4	3 -11 - 7			
To 2 couples of birch	7 - 7				
To 27 ribs at 6½d	14 - 2				
To wattling, brought home	4 - 4				
To binding couples	5 - 5				
To other work	2 - 2	1 -13 - 8			
To 1 door and case of deal	8 - 8				
To 2 lead windows, 18 inches by 12	4 - 8	0 -13 - 4			
To straw for thatching drawing straw, 100 sheaves at 2d	16 - 8				
To scollops, for ditto, at 8d 3 hundred	2 - 0				
To thatcher, 6 days, at 1s.7½d	9 - 9				
Labourer, at 1s.1d	6 - 6				
Scraws and divets	10 -10	2 - 5 - 9			
	[22] Total	£8 - 4 - 4			

The Armagh and Londonderry figures are roughly comparable, for example both as to overall cost, and when one abstracts and totals the elements relating to roofing alone. It is more difficult to compare the Tyrone figures with those for the other two counties. If '3 bays of mud-work' implies a three-room house, as seems probable in the Londonderry house, and this is maybe supported by the presence of two couples, or collar or tie-beam trusses, and if the Armagh house was comparable, then a cost per room works out at about £2.14s. Dimensions quoted for the Tyrone house, however, seem to imply a two-room dwelling, giving a cost per room of about £3.4s. On the other hand, this house has three trusses, an interpretation that agrees with the number of ribs quoted, giving a frame consisting of a ridge purlin and four purlins on each side of the roof, allowing of course that the house has stone gables. Obviously, it is impossible to reconcile these sets of figures directly with one another. Too many questions of design, size, labour input and other matters are involved for which no information is given. The principal value they have lies in their listing of elements, to be discussed in later chapters.

Later nineteenth-century evidence on house building costs usually refers to the houses of the poor or to improved dwellings advocated by landlords, or, late in the century, by official agencies such as led to the construction of the 'labourers' cottages' from the late 1890s onwards in the various rural district council areas (see Chapter 9). A suitable example is provided in the evidence gathered by the Devon commission of the 1840s which enquired into the law and practice regarding occupation of land throughout Ireland. Just as the Ordnance Survey memoir for the parish of Glynn quoted earlier showed that landlord improvement of dwellings was in progress in south-east Antrim in the 1830s, no less than 106 dwellings and 231 barns, stables and byres had been built on the estate of Charles M'Garel at Magheramourne in the same district, the tenant supplying skill and labour, the landlord making timber, slates, ridges, tiles, and lime available to him. On a farm paying less than £20 per annum, a dwelling of two rooms, each 12 ft. by 16 ft. [3.68 m. × 4.88 m.], lofted at one end, cost the landlord £18.8s., and the tenant's contribution was estimated at half that sum. Suitable outhouses, a barn 16 ft. [4.88 m.] square and a byre 14 ft. by 16 ft. [4.27 m. × 4.88 m.], probably under the one roof, cost £14, and although the witness did not say so, this sum probably represented only the landlord's outlay. A larger farm paying an annual rent of up to £30 had a two-roomed house lofted throughout, each room 15 ft. by 18 ft. [4.57 m. by 5.47 m.], at an outlay of £26, and a barn/byre at £16.10s.[23] Scraps of evidence from the mid-1830s in Down and Monaghan suggest how exceptional these south-east Antrim buildings were. Houses in Lecale in south-east Down cost £12 when constructed of good materials and consisting of two rooms; a one-room cabin cost £5.[24] Also in 1835 it was reported that in Aghabog parish, county Monaghan, thatched, roughcast houses, with clay walls 0.60 m. thick, of a 'superior description' cost about £10 to build and they were fairly permanent buildings, but the 'usual class of cabin', which seldom survived longer than fifteen to twenty years, could be put up for not more than £3.[25]

The evidence on house building costs in south-east Down above was provided by Jonathan Binns, the poor inquiry commissioner. His personal account of his travels as a commissioner also provides figures of £5 to £6 for providing a cabin in upper Iveagh barony in county Down, and £4 to £5 in northern parts of county Monaghan.[26] Formal evidence presented to the poor inquiry suggests figures of £4 to £5 in the extreme north of county Louth for one- and two-room cabins; £4 for some two-room cabins built about 1830 in the Loughtee baronies of county Cavan; the same amount for similar cabins in Tirkennedy barony in Fermanagh and for one-room examples in Monaghan barony where, however, two-room cabins cost £8; and as much as £12 for cottages in Lecale in south-east Down where good materials were used.[27] The scale of the change wrought by the trauma of the Great Famine period is well illustrated by a cost of £198.5s.11d. for a cottage built under the Landed Property improvement Act, 10 Vic. Cap. 32 Labourers' Dwellings in 1876 on the Blessingbourne estate in county Tyrone.[28] Pre-famine improved cottages were also provided by enlightened landlords. On the Earl of Erne's Lisnaskea property, five cottages went ahead in Carrickawick townland in the mountains about 1839 at a cost of £68 each.[29] However, they were sophisticated houses for their period, with cut stone dressings, sills and lintels, and slate roofs. Houses like this were far from typical at that time, and built outside vernacular farmhouse norms about which formal documentation simply does not exist.

Dimensions

Already three ways of referring to the size of a house have been mentioned. There is the obvious enumeration of measured dimensions. In the eighth century the law tract *Críth Gablach* used this approach, but cited a single dimension for the ideal house of each of the social grades with which the tract deals. It is probable that length was

intended[30] but breadth has also been advocated.[31] Dimensions of excavated houses from the neolithic period onwards have been given in Chapter 2; it suffices here to refer back to the seventeenth-century houses at Thady's fort in county Clare, 13.4 m. by 6.2 m., at Liathmore-Mochoemóg, 12.2 m. by 5.6 m., and to the medieval houses at Caherguillamore, 13.1 m. by 6.1 m., and 9.85 m. by 5.55 m. Sizes of native houses are not commonly noted in the early seventeenth-century documentation in the north of Ireland; they are usually described as coupled, framed, or simply as 'Irish'. Details of some planters' stone-walled houses are recorded, revealing a preponderance of front-to-rear dimensions in the range 5.48 m. to 7.62 m., with lengths commonly 6.00 m. to 7.32 m., 10.00 m. to 12.80 m., 14.60 m. to 15.24 m., and 18.00 m. to 18.30 m. Given that the larger buildings are probably castles and other dwellings of a socially superior group of undertakers and servitors, a common tenant's smaller house averaging perhaps 12.20 m. by 6.10 m. has been suggested, which would have contained two rooms[32] with internal dimensions 5.20 m. by 4.90 m., assuming they were of equal size.

Later in the seventeenth century a lease of 1675 for lands at Killymaddy in county Tyrone specifies that a house of lime and stone 15.24 m. long and 5.28 m. wide was to be constructed by the lessee within seven years.[33] In rural areas on the Lurgan-based Brownlow estate in north county Armagh about the same time a common length was 9.14 m., breadth 4.88 m., with wall heads at between 2.44 m. and 3.05 m. high. These dimensions probably imply two-room dwellings, possibly with lofts given the height of the walls, although the Brownlow leases only specify lofts in houses in the town of Lurgan. One of these Brownlow estate houses, in Kilnargett, was described as 'English' — it was to be 12.19 m. long, with wall heads 3.66 m. high, and a planked or shingled roof.[34]

A generation later the survey of the manor of Castledillon in north county Armagh by Thomas Ashe in about 1700 provided overall dimensions of three houses. In Dromadmore 'a good convenient countrey house made of stone and clay' was 15.24 m. long and 4.88 m. wide, 'a good mud wall house' in Mullabane was 18.29 m. long, and 'a good sod wall house' in Turkarry and Drumsolagh was 12.19 m. long and 3.96 m. wide.[35] Also in 1700 a lease of two townlands in county Tyrone specifies a house 15.24 m. long and 3.56 m. high 'of good oak timber with two upright gavels the walls of stone and lime'.[36]

Later in the eighteenth century, at Eskreagh in Tyrone, Thomas Knox in 1778 was to see that a house of stone or brick, 13.67 m. long by 5.18 m. wide, was built; a very similar house was to be built at Sandholes in the same county four years later, with walls 2.74 m. high; and in 1778 in Derrylard, county Armagh a house 9.14 m. long and 4.88 m. wide was stipulated in a lease, while construction of an almost identical dwelling is included in a covenant in a county Tyrone lease of 1806.[37]

The dimensions of the Tyrone house quoted by McEvoy in 1802 (above) as 7.32 m. by 3.66 m. 'in the clear', which presumably means internal measurements, stand almost alone in the nineteenth century until some data are available from the Ordnance Survey memoirs and from evidence given before the inquiry into the condition of the poor in 1835. Houses of the poorer classes of farmers in Dunboe parish, county Londonderry, in 1835 were 9.75 m. by 4.88 m. internally, divided into two rooms.[38] Half a generation earlier in 1814, similar measurements were reported for the parish of Dungiven in the same county, where larger three- and four-room farmhouses were also noted.[39] Dwellings occupied by cottiers and the poor were generally smaller than farmhouses, although a comfortably accommodated cottier in the east may be better housed than a farmer in the west or in a mountainous district. Sizes varied from 6.41 m. to 6.71 m. by about 4.88 m. for a two-room cottage in the north-west parish of Seapatrick,[40] to a single-room cabin 2.90 m. by 2.50 m. in the Ballinamallard district of county Fermanagh seen by Jonathan Binns.[41] Evidence representative of all nine Ulster counties from the poor inquiry of 1835 shows that one- and two-room cabins were usual, with lengths of from 4.9 m. to 9.1 m. and widths in the range of 3.0 m. to 4.6 m; wall heads were usually at 1.8 m. to 2.1 m., with a few as high as 2.45 m. It is pointless quoting from the variety of sizes reported within this range. However, analysis of all the contemporary evidence on the housing of the poor before the Great Famine of 1845–9 shows that the little one-room dwellings were often scaled-down versions of the principal living space, the kitchen, of the more commodious farmhouses. They were part of the vernacular tradition, constructed in traditional ways, using local materials, sometimes retaining archaic architectural features like wattle doors.[42]

Experience of surviving vernacular farmhouses and published details of others suggest that their sizes fell within fairly well-defined limits, illustrating all of the possiblitities mentioned in the earlier documentation cited above. These limits may have been dictated by the possibilities of available building materials, particularly of timber suitable for roofing.[43] Before the mid-eighteenth-century disappearance of native forest timber fit for building purposes, longer lengths capable of forming the

bigger roof trusses required to span internal widths up to 6.4 m. or more were available. A characteristic of some earlier houses of the seventeenth and early eighteenth centuries is their large roofs consequent on the size of such trusses. Then also, as thereafter when shorter timbers made a restricted internal width essential, room widths of about 4.9 m. were also common. Late in the eighteenth century and especially until about 1850, as settlement was pushed into poorer localities often higher in the hills, and as good timber became increasingly difficult to acquire either because vernacular house builders could not afford to buy imported timber, or because suitable growing timber no longer existed in the countryside, fossil timber from peat bogs came into increasing use for house building. It was often recovered in shortish lengths, and internal house widths were sometimes reduced to 4 m. or less. I recall being shown some years ago a stone-walled house of this period on the southern flank of Slieve Gullion in south county Armagh only minimally more than 3 m. wide inside.

Kitchens tended to be square, or slightly longer than wide, but not invariably so. Other rooms, certainly by the nineteenth century, were often wider than long, except in the linen-weaving districts like north-west Down and north and mid Armagh where the weaving 'sheds' or 'shops', integral parts of the weavers' houses, could be as long as 6m. It was in the fine adjustment of dimensions to cater for individual needs that the vernacular builder/designers most readily exercised variation within their tradition, without interfering with the basic concepts of vernacular layout, of axially placed hearths having well-defined relationships with entrances, and maintaining the uniformity of single-pile structures. Once the dimensions were laid down, even the spacings of windows could vary only within close limits, since there were norms as to the sizes and numbers of windows regarded as suitable for lighting the various internal spaces. So, a three-room house might be as short as about 9 m. or as long as 15 m., but the front-to-rear external measurement was more closely confined within the range 5.5 m. to 6.4 m. In these circumstances, it is understandable that other methods of referring to house size would be used.

Bays

Some documentary sources, and to a degree colloquial speech in rural areas even yet, refer to houses being of so many 'bays'. In the most general terms a bay may be defined as the length-wise space in a building between adjacent transverse roof supports, whether roof trusses, gables or internal walls rising to roof-ridge level. Obviously since to refer to a house as of a certain number of bays is to denote its length, the bay carries the implication of a known, fairly standard span from front to rear. Early usage of the term applied to distances between roof trusses, and in vernacular architectural writing this meaning is common. However, because roof carpentry traditions vary considerably from place to place, bay sizes show much variation — larger heavier trusses are normally more widely spaced than those with members of light scantling. If, as suggested in the previous chapter, the native Irish house of about 1600 A.D. was cruck-framed, it was probably conceived as consisting of a small number of bays separated by a few cruck trusses of heavy timbers relatively widely spaced from one another. Commonly, cruck trusses also provided a frame within which an otherwise flimsy internal partition could be provided, to separate internal space into rooms. Perhaps the same interpretation still applied to the usage enshrined in a ninety-nine-year lease of 1701 relating to a tenement in Ballymenoch, county Antrim. It included a covenant to build a house of

> five bayes with stone clay and oack timber, five foot high on the syd wall . . . [the] same to be perfyted with thatch.

The lessee was to furnish wood for the alteration of partition walls where needed, perhaps suggesting perpetuation of the older provision of such walls within and supported by roof trusses above.[44]

Later changes in walling to use of load-bearing mass materials and in the nature of roofing as suitable large timbers became difficult to find, together brought about a shift in colloquial use of the word to mean a 'room', or more strictly a 'structural unit' as defined in Chapter 1. It is this colloquial usage that must be applied to the mud cottage in county Londonderry costed by Sampson in 1802. It consisted of '3 bays of mud-work, ready for roofing', that is earth walling. Having only two couples, or collar-beam rafter trusses, we can recognise that the end walls supported the roof. It is difficult to know, however, if in 1802 a bay still referred narrowly to the spacing of roof trusses, in which case the house might only have two rooms possibly separated by a light partition. The list of costing is equivocal here, for the wattling mentioned may have been for roofing, or it may also have included materials for partitions and even a chimney canopy. Alternatively, the later meaning of bay may apply, and the house had three rooms. The fact that it cost more than the Tyrone house of dimensions 7.23 m. by 3.66 m. may be significant. In an 1826 county Armagh deed of transfer of property, '3 bays of houses'

and one acre of land were being exchanged for a larger acreage and similar housing,[45] and probably rooms were here intended by 'bays'. Certainly the modern colloquial usage was already established by 1835 when thatched mud-wall one-storey cottages in Loughgall parish, county Armagh were described as being 'divided into 2 or 3 bays or rooms'.[46] Other citations explicitly making the identification of bay with room occur in the poor inquiry evidence of the mid-1830s for counties Armagh and Monaghan.[47] Usage in this book restricts 'bay' to mean the spacing between adjacent roof trusses, or between a truss and a gable or internal cross wall; 'unit' or structural unit to the space enclosed by adjacent load-bearing cross walls including gables; and 'room' to a space that may be identical to a unit, or may be a sub-division within one, the context making clear which is involved. It may incidentally be noted that an architectural usage of 'bay' provides another variation. From the seventeenth century at least, many bays and/or units were lighted by a single piercing in the facade of the building. Identification of the bay with facade piercing, however, is later applied indiscriminately to buildings more extensively provided with windows and doors, and the word ceases to have any direct relationship to the roof structure or internal divison of the building. This is noticeable in descriptions of formal Georgian and later houses with rooms each lighted by two or even more windows in the facade. A three-unit house can be described as having a five-bay facade but its roof timbering may include no trusses (it is supported on purlins only); two, four, or some other number of trusses giving a variety of possibilities for the number of bays; or the roof may consist solely of a common-rafter system to which the idea of bays is foreign.[48]

Window and Hearth Taxes

This problem of the relationship between windows and the number of rooms internally is one reason why returns of window tax levied in Ireland are of little value in assessing house sizes. Equally important is the fact that only a minority of houses, apparently, were subject to this tax. In 1810, 51,318 dwellings are enumerated for the whole of Ireland as being involved.[49] No window tax was paid on 'houses of the commonest kind', some of which although of substantial proportions had few windows, or even none. The window-tax figure should be compared with the hearth-tax total for Ireland of 700,292 houses subject to it in 1791,[50] and population numbers grew rapidly between 1791 and 1810. Even though the hearth-tax figures were underestimated,[51] they are rather more useful. Hearth tax was introduced in Ireland in 1662, using as a precedent the recent similar tax levied in England. If by the mid-seventeenth century fixed hearths were common in English housing, the same was not true in Ireland; this problem was early recognised for in 1665, when fines were imposed for the concealment of hearths, it was decided that houses without fixed hearths should be counted as having two. What was meant by a hearth is implicit in the original wording of 1662 to the effect that 2/-per annum 'be paid out of all chimneys, stoves and hearths'. English-introduced stone or brick chimneys, or even clay-plastered wattled canopies, are already evident in the early seventeenth-century plantation documentation, but were slow to take hold generally. The Brownlow Lease Book dealing with property in north county Armagh from 1667 onwards makes clear that such chimneys were still a novelty to the extent that the landlord had to write their provision into his leases.[52] At the beginning of the nineteenth century, Dubourdieu, writing of county Down, suggested that many farmhouses had only a kitchen fire because the other hearths had been closed off to avoid payment of an augmented rate of hearth tax, or at least to reduce it:

> Had parliament at that period made every house with two fireplaces pay for one, at the usual rate, little loss would have accrued to the revenue, as very few would in that case have built up the second; but the additional two and eight-pence-halfpenny, on one side, paid for two hearths, and the temptation of not paying anything by having but one, has operated both against the revenue and the comfort of the people, who for so trifling a consideration have deprived themselves of the satisfaction of a second fire, and consequently no longer possess the advantage of ventilation, which from an open chimney they formerly obtained in their bedrooms . . .[53]

Obviously therefore, apart from the problems of definition of a hearth, there was not necessarily a direct relationship between the number of hearths and the number of rooms in a house. Furthermore, later in the century Down was the best provided-for county in housing, and this regional advantage probably prevailed at earlier periods.

Hearth-tax figures for 1791[54] in fact suggest that there was regional variation in housing standards. Assuming that regional variation in the degree of underestimation of the figures was not so severe as to invalidate the exercise, percentages of the total houses in each county can be worked out for houses having one hearth, two hearths, and exempted pauper houses. The pauper houses may broadly be considered to have included one-room and some two-room dwellings: one-hearth houses would have accommodated most farmers, probably having two or three rooms; and almost certainly two-hearth houses

had three or more rooms, being the homes of more prosperous farmers and perhaps also professional people like clergy and teachers resident in the country. However, it is impossible in these figures to make any distinction between rural and urban proportions.

TABLE 1. PERCENTAGE OF TOTAL HOUSES. HEARTH TAX 1791

County	1 Hearth	2 Hearths	Exempted Pauper Houses
Antrim	73.7	6.4	12.3
Armagh	82.1	3.4	10.3
Cavan	76.8	3.1	15.2
Donegal	61.6	4.9	28.8
Down	81.2	5.2	7.8
Fermanagh	72.7	3.4	19.9
Londonderry	61.7	4.7	25.9
Monaghan	77.6	2.8	15.7
Tyrone	73.4	4.6	17.0

This table includes neither houses with more than two hearths, which predominantly would have been those of the landed class and in towns, nor exempted new houses; consequently the percentages for any county do not total 100.

In the 1840s Dublin and Wexford shared with Down in being the most favoured counties in the matter of housing. Since no allowance can be made for the city of Dublin, a comparison may only be made with Wexford, which had 70.6% of houses with one hearth, 6.3% with two, and 16.4% exempted pauper houses. So not only Down, but Antrim, Armagh and even Cavan and Monaghan had lower proportions of pauper houses than Wexford had at the end of the eighteenth century. Obviously Down, Antrim and Armagh, eastern counties, were better off for housing than western ones like Donegal, Londonderry and Fermanagh. Most impressive is the predominance everywhere of one-hearth houses, the majority of which must have been two- or three-room farmhouses.

Rooms

Enumeration of house sizes by number of rooms, implicit in these hearth-money data, is difficult to interpret, as is the same implication in the meaning that the word 'bay' had taken on by the first half of the nineteenth century. It becomes a reality in the 1841 and later official censuses of Ireland. In 1841 houses were divided into four categories, and enumerations were published by parishes and larger administrative areas. Class 4 houses had a single room; class 3 houses had two to four rooms; class

2 houses had five to nine rooms and included the larger farmhouses and also town houses; and class 1 houses were all those with ten or more rooms and were either lived in by the landed class or were urban. Fortunately also, the data distinguish between urban and rural totals.

The unrefined definitions of the census categories pose problems of interpretation. Class 2 houses included minor examples of formal architecture in rural areas, as well as enlarged and elaborated vernacular ones. Class 3 houses consisted mostly of thatched single-storey farmhouses and larger cottier houses, until late in the nineteenth century when some of the more elaborate labourers' houses might have been included. The later nineteenth-century phenomenon of more extensive specialisation of space use in the house usually meant physical separation of internal areas from one another, without significant increase in space. So a class 3 house in 1841 might be larger than a class 2 house at the end of the century. However, in 1841 in parts of east Ulster, class 3 included a few four-room two-storey farmhouses. Class 4 houses encompassed both the tiny cottier houses (Figs. 27, 28, 29), cabins and hovels found throughout the north of Ireland in 1841 as well as the larger unpartitioned dwellings that provided combined accommodation for people and cattle, especially in western areas. Furthermore, one does not know into which category former byre-dwellings were put, having a sleeping area separated from the living quarters only by large pieces of furniture such as the dresser. Non-structural partitions or 'walls' of this kind were unlikely in the far west. A list of the belongings of the entire parish of Tullaghobegley in north-west Donegal in 1837 includes not a single large item of furniture that could have fulfilled this purpose,[55] and in 1841 almost 63% of all the houses in that parish were included in class 4. Such may not have been true elsewhere, however.

The figures in Table 2, showing the percentage of county totals of rural houses in the different categories in which we are interested in 1841 and 1851, demonstrate

dramatic changes during the decade which included the Great Famine, and that these changes varied regionally. Eastern counties like Down, Armagh and Monaghan, with percentages of class 4 houses in 1841 less than 30, were obviously better-off than Donegal with almost 44 and Fermanagh and Londonderry close to or over 35. In terms of two- to four-room houses (class 3), the spread of percentages is more restricted, all falling between 41 and 51. By 1851, however, the position had altered. Down was joined by Antrim and Londonderry in having the lowest percentage of single-room dwellings, and the spread of values in class 3 housing had both increased its level and widened. By 1851, too, no fewer than five counties had more than a third of their rural houses with between five and nine rooms, whereas only Down had had more than 30% in this category ten years earlier; much of this change is attributable to internal subdivision rather than to fundamental enlargement of houses. Upsurge in the demand for greater specialisation in the use of space in the rural house really commenced in the decade 1841–51.

Generalised county figures conceal enormous local differences in the revolution in rural housing during the 1840s. Data for the extreme counties of Donegal in the west and Down in the east, calculated to show the percentage changes, 1841–51, in the numbers of houses in classes 3 and 4, illustrate this clearly, for selected baronies, and for individual parishes within them. It should be noted that Down had the lowest percentage of rural one-room houses in all Ireland in 1841; Donegal, however, was far from being worst off, the west Connacht counties having even higher percentages than Donegal's 43.8%.

The Donegal decline of almost 80% in one-room houses, 1841–51, compared well with the figure for Down; the big contrast was in what happened to the two- to four-room houses, which increased their numbers from 19,992 in 1841 to 27,462 in 1851 in Donegal, while those in Down dropped in number by 719 to 23,729 in 1851. Conditions in the north-west Donegal barony of Kilmacrenan, and in Banagh in the south-west, showed that experience even in the far west varied. Class 4 houses in Kilmacrenan actually declined at a rate below the county average, but below that in Banagh in the south-west; but the extreme north-western and south-western parishes show even greater extremes. Tullaghobegley was in a parlous state, with a much lower rate of disappearance of one-room houses than the county average, unlike Glencolumbkille where the rate was actually slightly higher; but also, the class 3 houses were increasing their numbers at a slower rate than in Glencolumbkille. Raphoe barony in east Donegal is in a

TABLE 2. PERCENTAGE OF TOTAL RURAL HOUSES. CENSUS 1841 AND 1851

County	Class 4		Class 3		Class 2	
	1841	1851	1841	1851	1841	1851
Antrim	30.0	3.9	44.6	57.0	23.9	36.4
Armagh	29.6	9.8	49.5	57.3	19.9	30.9
Cavan	34.9	12.1	47.8	58.6	16.6	27.8
Donegal	43.8	10.8	42.0	66.3	13.5	21.3
Down	22.5	4.0	44.3	49.4	31.7	43.7
Fermanagh	36.4	11.4	42.2	52.1	20.8	34.9
Londonderry	34.7	5.2	41.1	57.2	23.2	35.5
Monaghan	28.0	7.6	50.7	58.3	20.5	32.8
Tyrone	33.6	6.3	45.3	58.1	20.4	33.8

Fig. 27. Derelict one-room house, Meenagarragh Td., Co. Tyrone, before removal to UFTM. UFTM L 322.15

Fig. 28. Occupied one-room house, Ballycronan More Td., Co. Antrim. UFTM L 1098.10

Fig. 29.   Fisherman's one-room house, early 20th-century, Co. Donegal. UFTM WAG 1196

kinder physical environment than that of west Donegal, and Leck is one of the best parishes in it. Leck's apparently poor performance in the disappearance of single-room houses must be seen against the fact that it started from a percentage of such houses that was amongst the lowest in the county in 1841, apart from in the extreme south near Ballyshannon.

The contrast Down provides with Donegal is enormous, but so are the variations within it. The Ards peninsula displays characteristics comparable with parts of Donegal, largely accounted for by circumstances in the south of the peninsula, such as in St. Andrew's parish,

with its enormous decline in one-room houses, and its great growth in class 3 houses. Mourne (barony and parish) shows a high rate of decline also in class 4 houses, but little change in the matter of larger houses. In the north-west of the county, however, Moira is typical of its barony, a prosperous district with increasing drift from the land in the middle of the nineteenth century, especially as the linen industry mechanised. There were typically large declines in the numbers of single-room houses, but there was also significant decline in the numbers of larger houses in rural areas.

Detailed examination of the 1841 parish figures for

TABLE 3.   % CHANGES IN CLASS 3 AND CLASS 4 HOUSING, 1841-1851. COUNTIES DOWN AND DONEGAL, AND SELECTED BARONIES AND PARISHES THEREIN

County	Barony/Parish	Class 3	Class 4	County	Barony/Parish	Class 3	Class 4
Donegal		+37.36	−78.09	Down		− 2.94	−83.68
	Kilmacrenan/	+45.78	−74.73		Ards/	+21.47	−89.00
	Tullaghobegley	+67.08	−48.51		St. Andrews	+44.80	−91.33
	Banagh/	+49.98	−82.44		Mourne	− 3.93	−81.72
	Glencolumbkille	+84.00	−78.23				
	Raphoe/	+42.66	−80.63		Iveagh Lr./	−14.51	−75.22
	Leck	+28.57	−23.59		Moira	−10.32	−73.39

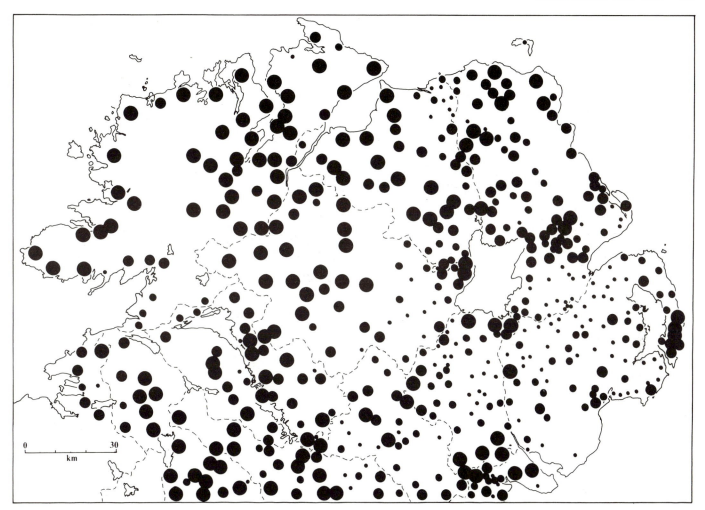

Fig. 30. Parish percentages of one-room houses, 1841. The four circle sizes represent, in ascending size order, quartiles with the following percentages limits: 0-22.1; 22.2-31.9; 32.0-40.2; 40.3-100. Based on census data.

single-room houses (Fig. 30) shows that they were least prevalent throughout almost all of county Down except the south end of the Ards peninsula in the east, south Antrim, the area in the vicinity of Coleraine, Armagh except for the mountainous south and the boggy lands bordering the south shore of Lough Neagh, east Tyrone and the extreme south of county Londonderry about Moneymore, across Monaghan and into south Fermanagh and mid Cavan, and lastly into north Fermanagh and neighbouring parts of south Donegal. Parishes with percentages of these little houses in excess of 40 were in most of Donegal, mid and west Tyrone, most of mountainous parts of Londonderry, a scatter throughout county Antrim apart from the south, the south half of the Ards peninsula, south Armagh, and the hilly parts of Monaghan and Fermanagh. In 1841 half of all the parishes had at least a third of their houses consisting of a single room.[56]

Historians dispute the rate at which Irish population increased after 1841. Probably the rate of increase was in decline before the Great Famine of 1845-9, but absolute numbers continued to rise. Growth was almost certainly greatest amongst the poorest levels of society, so the 1841 figures are not the greatest that ever existed for single-room houses. Thus the rapid decline to the levels recorded in 1851 is all the more remarkable testimony to the ravages of the potato famine period amongst the poorest people. That decline persisted throughout the remainder of the nineteenth century. In 1901 Cavan had the greatest percentage of its houses in class 4 of any Ulster county, at 1.5%, and the numbers everywhere were insignificant. So it is easy to understand why now, and in recent decades, it has been unusual to discover survivors of this socially very important category of mid-nineteenth-century housing in the north of Ireland. Its disappearance, however, although testimony to a

D

revolution in living standards, and therefore important in social historical terms, is less significant for the study of vernacular architecture; as already noted, most of these tiny dwellings represented an integral part of the vernacular tradition, and almost certainly the rise of the one-room house to numerical significance was a product of the unique demographic history of Ireland between 1750 and 1845. One-room houses were present much earlier, for example in the early seventeenth century. These earlier examples were largely in the tradition of combined byre-dwellings, not necessarily tiny buildings, forerunners of those survivals in west Donegal especially which make interpretation of the census class 4 house statistics problematic in some districts.

Storeys

By way of tailpiece to this discussion of house size, it should be remembered that another crude method of generalising about a house's accommodation is to refer to the number of storeys it contains. Early references to Irish housing, as we have seen in Chapter 2, imply one-storey houses, and such larger dwellings as are mentioned or noted on military maps of the early seventeenth century were mostly in towns or fortified settlements, obviously the houses of a minority, socially superior group. Rural houses are invariably shown with a single storey. Even where 'English' houses were being constructed, as in the plantation towns of county Londonderry before 1641, they are shown as at their largest when dormer windows rise into their roofs to light an attic floor. In the late 1660s similar houses may have been built in some places, to judge from the Brownlow Lease Book already discussed when dealing with house dimensions. Houses described in the manor of Castledillon in county Armagh about 1700 are predominantly of a single storey, although the tenant (as distinct from his under-tenants) on Turkarry had a large castle of brick 'except the low storey', but a building denominated a mansion on Dromoher was not necessarily large, for the 'mansion' on Mullinasillagh may have had wattle walls.[57] At the same period on the lands of the Archbishopric of Armagh there were at least three multi-storey houses, but all seemingly occupied by wealthy people, and their houses did not conform to vernacular norms. In county Armagh, in Ballebrolle townland, the lessee Jonat Powell, noted as a 'Gent', had constructed but not completed a 'good Stone House 2 Stories high and Garretts'; in Mucklagh also in Armagh there was 'a very Pritty House well tymber'd and regularly built. It is two Story high. There are good Chambers and Garretts above Staires a hansome Parlor, a common Hall a kitchen sellars . . .'; and in Tulledowe, county Tyrone,

'a very good Brick House' had 'Preety Appartments both above and below Stairs', including 'a common Hall a kitchen Sellar . . .'[58]

Two-storey houses were only beginning to spread in 1816 in rural parts of county Antrim, where a traveller in northern Ireland described conditions generally: 'When the circumstances of the farmer enable him, and the size of his farm justifies him in doing it, he usually erects a dwelling-house two stories high . . .'[59] The evidence of the Ordnance Survey memoirs two generaitons later shows that some two-storey farmhouses were present in most of the parishes across south county Antrim, in a few in south county Londonderry and the eastern half of Down, and in a few isolated parishes elsewhere. The same source mentions two-storey cottages in only three parishes, one each in mid and east Antrim, and one in Lecale barony in south-east Down. Two-storey dwellings were only beginning to spread in rural areas in the 1830s, perhaps from an innovative area in south Antrim as this evidence seems to suggest. Uneven coverage in the Ordnance Survey memoirs may conceal similarly innovative parishes in north Down also. However, the memoirs make it clear that everywhere the numbers of these larger dwellings were still small. In the 1840s Maurice Collis, an estate surveyor and valuator from Dublin, carried out surveys of the Londonderry family's estate in the vicinity of Newtownards and Comber in north Down (dated 1848), and of Trinity College's estates in the north of Ireland (dated 1845, but enumerated 1843). The latter included a few townlands in mid Lecale, south-east Down; a few townlands immediately to the south of Charlemont in north-west Armagh; a large estate stretching from Killylea to south of Keady and Darkley in west Armagh; another extensive estate in south-east Fermanagh including the town of Rosslea; a few townlands in south Donegal lying about Bundoran, and Ballymacward to the north of the Erne estuary; a large estate lying south of Donegal town which included the villages of Laghy and Ballintra; and an estate in Kilmacrenan in north Donegal lying about Millford village. Collis's surveys included great detail about housing, summarised by townlands; from his data Table 4 (as well as others later in this book) has been compiled,[60] to provide estate summaries for rural housing only, from which a comparative view across the north of Ireland emerges. There was a remarkably consistent dominance of the one-storey house across all of these estates. Two-storey houses attained about 5% of rural dwellings only in north Down, west Armagh, and in the Ballintra estate in south Donegal, all areas which in 1841 had low proportions of their total rural housing stocks consisting of one-room dwellings.

TABLE 4. PERCENTAGES OF TOTAL RURAL HOUSES
BY NUMBER OF STOREYS IN 1840s

Estate	1 Storey	2 Storeys	3 Storeys	Total Rural Houses
North Down	95.5	4.3	0.2	1863
Lecale, Down	98.3	1.7	0	118
Charlemont, Armagh	98.9	1.1	0	378
Killylea-Keady, Armagh	93.6	6.0	0.4	2122
Rosslea, Fermanagh	98.1	1.8	0.1	828
Bundoran, Donegal	96.3	2.4	1.3	294
Ballintra, Donegal	94.0	5.5	0.5	1530
Kilmacrenan, Donegal	98.1	1.8	0.1	1336

There is a small number of two-storey thatched farmhouses, widely scattered across the north of Ireland, some of which can be dated to the later seventeenth and early eighteenth centuries, some obviously of English architectural inspiration (see Chapter 8); but they did not serve as exemplars for any widespread development of multi-storey rural dwellings. Nor did the formally designed Georgian farmhouses and their derivatives, built in many areas in small numbers after about 1780, generate an appreciable move to enlargement of vernacular farmhouses until well into the following century. It was not until after 1850 that two-storey, usually slated farmhouses became numerous. This happened at first by upward enlargement of earlier smaller houses, but these enlargements themselves rapidly became exemplars for new larger houses, yet still constructed within vernacular parameters so far as their ground-floor plans were concerned.

FOUR

Wall Materials

Wattle

USE of wattle as a walling material is clearly attested in early and medieval houses in Ireland, and about 1600 it was widely used in both the normal native house and in the seasonally occupied creat. Drapers' Company records of their building operations about Moneymore c. 1615 tell of the gathering of '10 lods of wattells' to 'cyver cabbynnes with'. The mode of completion of these dwellings is suggested in an account that was paid for 'making a grett cabbyne and cyeringe it with sodde'.[1] Wattling then, and well into the eighteenth century, consisted of weaving pliable lengths of wood (osier, briar

and various kinds of twigs) horizontally or vertically through stouter framing timbers. It was then usually plastered with clay or mud to seal the interstices, but as suggested above, wattling may have served as a frame to support a covering of sod. While there are few references to wattled exterior walling in northern Ireland, about 1700 on the Armagh manor of Castledillon, an undertenant still lived in 'a small wattled walled house' in Turkarry and Drumsollagh, and there was mud-plastered wattling as already noted in the tenant house in Mullinasallagh.[2] Five years later concern about depredations upon surviving woods and forests in Ireland generally was sufficient for the Irish parliament to forbid

Fig. 31. Remains of interior partition wattling of ruined house near Smithborough, Co. Monaghan. From a transparency. UFTM L 1661.7

Fig. 32. Straw ropes laced around timbers as a core for clay-plastered partition wall, Waringstown village, Co. Down. From a transparency. UFTM L 1661.8

people to use 'in wattling the walls of houses or cabbins, or out-buildings, any kind of gadd or gadds, wyth or wyths, of oak, ash, birch, hazel or other tree whatsoever . . .'[3] Thereafter wattling was used more sparingly in house construction, perhaps more in response to the rapid depletion of forest resources for reasons other than house-building, than in direct response to the Act of 1705. Wattling survived throughout the eighteenth and nineteenth centuries for construction of internal partition walls and for fabrication of elements like doors and chimney canopies, which could be set in place once mass walls had been constructed. Houses in county Monaghan were reported in 1946, built in the nineteenth century if not before, in which wattling was used.[4] And Professor Estyn Evans has illustrated the wattled upper triangular portion of an internal partition wall in a house at Drummany, county Cavan, which he saw in 1945.[5] I saw survivals of wattling twice during the 1960s in ruined houses — between Monaghan and Smithborough a two-room stone-walled house had a wattled partition wall which seemed not to have risen above wall-head level into the triangular roof space (Fig. 31), and in Formil townland, south of Derrylin in county Fermanagh, a disused door opening giving access through the upper

part of a partition wall into a loft area had been blocked off with clay-plastered wattling. All of these instances relate to wattling as described above. A variant form, of twisted straw or hay ropes laced around and between stout timbers, the whole plastered with clay, is also fairly widely attested elsewhere in Ireland. Only once, in a partition wall in a house with cruck trusses in Waringstown village in county Down, have I seen this technique (Fig. 32), but it may have been more widespread in northern areas, for it was reported in the 1940s in a house described by an informant in county Cavan.[6]

Structural Timber

The native house of *c.* 1600 A.D. described in Chapter 2, with its walls of non-load bearing materials, has been interpreted as probably having been framed with crucks. Descriptions of these houses as having walls of posts and wattle therfore ignore the fact that either the posts were carried to roof-ridge level, or that the principal roof-bearing timbers were jointed in some manner to the wall posts, without the interposing of a horizontal wall-plate.

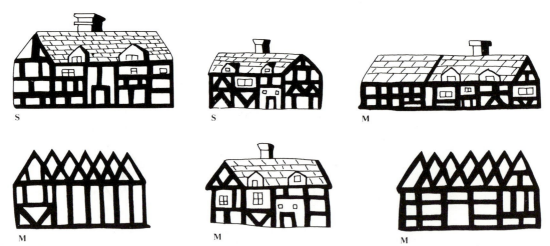

Fig. 33.   Early 17th-century timber-framed house in Co. Londonderry, after Thomas Raven's originals in the Phillips survey, reproduced in Chart, *Londonderry and the London Companies, 1609-1629* (Belfast, 1928). S: Salterstown; M: Moneymore.

Because cruck trusses support the roof, they will be discussed later with roof timbering. It must be significant that survivals of cruck systems have been found, but survivals of any other timber-framing system have never been reported in the field. Change to extensive use of mass materials in house wall construction took place during the seventeenth century; because so few houses of this period survive for study and because the documentation of house building, apart from Plantation records, is so imperfect, it is impossible to chart in detail the progress of the change from use of wattling to mass materials.

Houses built by British settlers in Ulster in the early decades of the seventeenth century were of two kinds: those with stone walls, and those of timber box-framing. The latter are well authenticated, even illustrated in the maps drawn by Thomas Raven (Fig. 33) of the London companies' estates in county Londonderry.[7] Some fifty box-framed houses appear on these maps. None is shown with cruck framing. The box frames have both diagonal braces and horizontal ties. However, a description of a house on the Ironmongers' property is of half-timbering with spaces between the structural timbers about the same width as that of the timbers themselves, the spaces nogged with riven oak, then plastered over.[8] So there was some variety of carpentry tradition. Most of the timber-framed houses were built in the new planter towns, but a few were built in rural areas also. Some survived the incendiarism of the 1641 rebellion by the native Irish, the last few disappearing in the nineteenth century. Most British settlers who rebuilt after the rebellion invariably put up houses with mass walls. However, there are occasional references to later houses with structural timberwork in the walls, like one in 1675 at

Killymaddy in Tyrone, 15.24 m. long by 3.49 m. wide.[9] An 'English house' to be constructed about the same time at Carne, near Buncrana in north Donegal, may have been another.[10] In an account of north Armagh in 1682 we learn that 'The great plenty of oak wood . . . makes our houses much better than those of other parts where that assistance is wanting.'[11] In the early nineteenth century some timber-framed houses remained in Ballyscullion parish in east Londonderry,[12] and in the nearby Antrim parish of Duneane one had been erected as late as about 1770,[13] but in Lissan parish on the Londonderry/Tyrone boundary an oak-framed house in Killybaskey townland had been rebuilt in stone, perhaps in the late seventeenth or early eighteenth century.[14]

In one special context structural wall timbers were used in Ireland, although to judge from the evidence, not widely in northern areas. Sod (turf) is not inherently a load-bearing material, and so timber supports were occasionally placed within the walls to provide rigidity and a stable base for support of the roof. The same was also done in some cases of clay or mud walling. In an unspecified locality in county Antrim 'posts were stuck in the ground, one at each corner of the size of house required. The clay was softened with water to a thick plaster, and then put up in spadefuls and flattened down and left to dry in the sun.'[15]

Undoubtedly the principal reason why traditions of structural wall timbers disappeared from northern Irish vernacular house building was the reluctance of landlords, mainly of British descent, to permit use of woodland resources except for exportable or saleable products: charcoal for iron making, staves for barrels for the provision trade, and so on. Then because by the mid-eighteenth century the woods had disappeared due to

Fig. 34. Sod house near Toome Bridge, Co. Antrim, early 20th-century. UFTM WAG 269

Fig. 35. Sod house, Magilligan, Co. Londonderry, *c*.1900. UM WO7/48/1

exploitation for these purposes, even the potential for wall timbering had also gone, and so traditions of stone and earth walling became fixed.

Turf or Sod

The grassy, root-matted surface of the ground, cut into blocks of suitable size, may represent a poor building material with little inherent stability, yet it has the merit of being everywhere readily available. Tenants evicted from their houses in some places were able to go to the property of a landowner not ill-disposed towards them and there construct, within a day, a house to live in.[16] Poor inquiry evidence of the 1830s shows that sod was then used as a building material in many parts of Ulster, except in the most favourable eastern counties of Antrim, Down and Armagh. By contrast, the contemporary evidence of the Ordnance Survey memoirs shows that the dwellings of the better-off classes of rural society, the farmers, weavers and other cottiers, that is those with some tenurial status, seldom had sod walls.

Sod was not just a building material of the poor. Rather, it seems that the poor in the early nineteenth century fell back on a known traditional material, use of which had been superseded at higher social levels. Thatched sod-wall houses of the Newtown Saville estate in east Tyrone about 1800[17] were matched by sod-wall houses occupied by under-tenants on various properties in the manor of Castledillon in mid Armagh a century earlier,[18] although they were noted as either 'small' or 'ordinary'. Even though its use was not highly regarded by those who reported on the building work of the early phases of British settlement in the Plantation period, sod was used in a number of places for the protective 'bawn' walls within which the undertakers and some servitors were expected to erect their new houses. Professor Evans places evidence such as this in a wide context, temporally and geographically, seeing a common tradition of sod construction in areas about the Irish Sea stretching back to prehistoric times and forward to survivals in the present century.[19] There are widespread recordings of use of sod in vernacular housing. Packing courses are commonly found on wall heads to seal the space between the top of the stone- or clay-work and the underside of the roof, and in the Duncrun cottier house from north Londonderry, of perhaps late eighteenth-century origin, now at the Ulster Folk and Transport Museum, the upper portion of the inner face of the hearth gable is faced with sods, seemingly to serve as a 'holding' material into which the wattle ends of the chimney canopy were stuck.[20] Most ubiquitous of all, of course, is the almost invariable use of a layer of sods or 'scraws' as underthatch, even on roofs on which roped thatch is normal where the sods are not needed to anchor thatching pins (scollops) in place.

Visual records of three sod or turf houses survive. A small cabin was photographed near Toome Bridge in county Antrim (Fig. 34) about the World War I period. It graphically portrays the inherent instability of sod walling, with its end propped up by timbers. This hints that some means of supporting the weight of the roof independently of the walls was needed when sod was used. A more expert building technique may have been used as in the much larger house photographed at Magilligan in north Londonderry (Fig. 35), but even in this case some settlement of the walls would have been inevitable.

Hard black peat used presumably like bricks has been reported by Professor Evans in a house in Mullyard townland in south Fermanagh which he recorded in 1945. They were used to form walls separating small bedrooms in one end of the house, laid in six-inch layers separated by wooden laths which would have imparted some stability, the whole whitewashed all over.[21] In 1940 he recorded and photographed a house excavated from solid peat, its roof supported on posts placed in lines along the inner and outer wall faces, and in two rows along the interior (Figs. 36,37). This unique house had door and window openings cut into the front wall, the upper triangular part of its gables built up of layers of sods, a thatched roof and a chimney of bricks and basalt blocks. It stood in an area of reclaimed bog in Leck townland, near Ballymoney in north Antrim.[22] The manner in which it conforms to so many vernacular-house design and constructional details reinforces the view already put, that sod and turf houses were not always merely impoverished makeshifts, but were constructed within traditional patterns.

Stone

Stone is the most commonly encountered wall material in surviving vernacular houses, although it is difficult to recognise as such because external rendering has normally been applied. The transition from wattle and timber to mass materials in the seventeenth century has been mentioned. Almost all of the few seventeenth-century houses that survive, mainly from after 1650, have stone walls. Houses built by planters in county Londonderry about 1620 were regarded as of superior quality when constructed in stone.[23]

Fig. 36. House excavated from peat, Leck Td., Co. Antrim, from a photograph in the possession of Professor E.E. Evans. UFTM L 2.5

Fig. 37. House excavated from peat; plan, section and perspective view, not to scale (after E.E Evans).

TABLE 5. PERCENTAGES OF TOTAL RURAL HOUSES
BY WALL MATERIALS IN 1840s

Estate	Mud	Mud/Stone	Stone	Brick	Total Rural Houses
North Down	0.6	0.2	99.1	0.1	1863
Lecale, Down	—	—	100.0	—	118
Charlemont, Armagh	97.4	—	2.1	0.5	378
Killylea-Keady, Armagh	40.3	0.8	58.7	0.2	2122
Rosslea, Fermanagh	2.2	14.5	83.3	—	828
Bundoran, Donegal	7.5	—	92.5	—	294
Ballintra, Donegal	1.2	0.1	98.7	—	1530
Kilmacrenan, Donegal	0.4	0.4	99.2	—	1336

Fig. 38.   Basalt field-stone walling, Feumore Td., Co. Antrim. UFTM L 1147.15

Collis's estate surveys summarised in Table 5[24] illustrate the overall predominance of stone building. The only other building material used to a significant extent in the 1840s on the estates he surveyed was mud (earth), which in north-west Armagh in the Charlemont area was used to build most houses, as it was throughout most of north Armagh, for example in the low-lying boggy lands south of Lough Neagh colonised mainly in the eighteenth century. Nevertheless it is noticeable in the latter area that the more substantial older farmhouses, carefully sited on the drier flanks of drumlins protruding through the areas of bog, had stone walls.

Of course the potentialities provided by local solid and drift geology strongly influenced the pattern of local building. On the Londonderry family's north Down estate, no fewer than 1847 of the rural dwellings were built with stone and lime walls; only twelve had mud or earth walls, and there was a single brick house. All the houses on this estate in the towns of Newtownards and Comber had stone walls.[25] Good building stone is readily available in north Down, mainly a slaty Silurian greywacke, but the New Red Sandstone of Scrabo Hill was an important resource. Carboniferous sandstones and limestones were widely quarried in south-east Tyrone, and Fermanagh. It was said in 1739 that their availability encouraged many 'even of the small farmers to build neat little stone cabbins'.[26] A generation later Arthur Young reported that cabins in Clonleigh parish in county Donegal could be built for £5, of stone which was plentiful, with clay mortar instead of lime.[27] In many parts of Ulster field stones, cleared in the course of agricultural work, were used in house building (Fig. 38). They were often used without any surface dressing, although sometimes a fairly even face was prepared for the surface of the wall. The best stones, of sufficient size, worked to rectangular shapes for a good fit, were reserved for the interlocking 'quoins' at corners. Sometimes even though quarry stone was to hand, the only use made of it was for quoins (Fig. 44), window sills and door and window dressings,[28] field stone collected by the farmer/builder himself constituting the remainder of the wall material. An interesting technique of building a very dry wall is reported from Connor in mid Antrim. Old houses in the district had walls two-and-a-half to three feet thick, constructed as two mortared facings leaving an inner space about nine inches wide filled with loose stones of up to about three inches diameter laid in without any mortar whatever.[29]

Field stones were used mainly in random rubble building, a technique used in most seventeenth-century stone houses that survive. Coursed rubble building is seen earliest in better houses, and by the eighteenth century was common at all social levels except in the houses of the landless poor and usually also in the byre-dwellings and their derivatives in west Donegal where large, unworked granite boulders imparted a distinctive coarse texture to the surfaces of house walls (Fig. 39). By contrast, in the Newry and Mourne granites of south Down and neighbouring parts of Armagh, worked stone in coursed building was commoner (Fig. 42), but here there was a long-standing tradition of quarry-work. Surviving houses throughout Antrim and east Londonderry have walls built of basalt, used both as random rubble when the boulders are usually field stones (Fig. 42), and in coursed rubble work when the stones

Fig. 39.   Granite boulder walls, with glacial erratics as quoins, dry-stone work, *c.*1880s, Gweedore, Co. Donegal. UFTM L 440-16

Fig. 40.   Cabin, largely of dry-stone walling, *c.*1900, Glencolumbkille, Co. Donegal. UM WO4/13/12

Fig. 41.   Dry-stone walling using rounded boulders and flat, platy stone as packing, early 20th century, probably north Co. Donegal. UFTM WAG 3330

Fig. 42.   Random quarried basalt walling, Ballymakeown Td., Co. Armagh. UFTM L 1287.10

Fig. 43.   Coursed quarried granite walling, Carcullion Td., Co. Down. UFTM L 1287.5

Fig. 44.   Random silurian greywacke walling with granite quoins, Imdel Td., Co. Down. UFTM L 966.13

Fig. 45.   Packing around roughly dressed field stones, Ballykeel Artifinny Td., Co. Down. UFTM L 932.21

were either quarried, or mason-dressed or split field stones.

Bonding with lime mortar goes back at least to the seventeenth century, and lime for this purpose is referred to in the plantation documentation, but this in general implies socially superior usage. The common earlier bonding in domestic buildings was with clay mortar, use of which is also attested in an early church at Raholp in county Down.[30] Its use persisted into the nineteenth century, especially in the housing of the poor, for poor inquiry evidence of the 1830s shows that it was widespread in county Down except the north of the county, south Armagh, a restricted part of west Armagh

and south-east Tyrone, and the relatively low-lying areas of north and north-west Londonderry and east Donegal. Unmortared, dry-stone walling was also used, especially in earlier periods. A traveller in 1835 near the town of Donegal came across houses 'built of unshapen stones, loosely placed together, without mortar or even clay to stop up the crevices, and thus but ill calculated to keep out the weather'.[31] Dry-stone walling was common in the far west (Figs. 39, 40), and perhaps more widely, for houses are occasionally discovered elsewhere with clay or lime mortar pointing of the surfaces only, almost certainly not applied in the original construction. Clay mortar persisted in use until the end of the eighteenth century in such places, for example near Downpatrick, because of the costs of transporting lime from the source areas, especially from the kilns where Cretaceous chalk was burned in county Antrim.[32] Nineteenth-century improvements in transport greatly altered the situation, and by the 1830s only the houses of the poor persisted with the poorer clay bonding in their stone walls, although there was a significant proportion of houses in the south-east part of Fermanagh in the 1840s with walls of mud/stone (Table 5). This evidence may be interpreted as either stone walls with clay mortar, or as houses with some walls of stone, others of earth, like one I saw in the Newtownbutler area some years ago with external front and rear walls and gables of stone, and internal partition walls of solid earth (mud). In contrast, leases of the 1660s on the Brownlow estate in north Armagh specified lime and stone house walls in Lurgan and in the surrounding country, but in some cases, in the town especially, this was only for a wall-foot two or three feet high; the leases do not tell whether the superstructure was to be of earth walling or some form of timber framing, although an 'English' house in Kilnargett may have been entirely of stone and lime. Likewise houses in Toberhewnie and Ballynamoney, and the gable end of a house in Balliblagh in 1671 were to be of lime and stone.[33] In reporting that many Tyrone farmhouses in 1802 were built of lime and stone, John M'Evoy in his statistical survey went on to state that in his opinion 'far too many are built with clay-mortar as a cement. In the angles of houses, jaumbs of doors, &c. lime-mortar is commonly used, in order to strengthen the walls; but, notwithstanding, the walls frequently bulge outwards, wherever clay mortar is concerned',[34] presumably due to outward thrust transmitted to the wall-heads by the roof timbering.

In the minority of houses with coursed rubble work there is decorative treatment, but usually only on the facade. 'Galleting' consists of pressing small stones, usually dark in colour to contrast with the lime mortar,

Fig. 46.   Packing around roughly dressed sandstone, 1772 datestone, coursed dressed sandstone in later upper storey, Lurganville Td., Co. Down. UFTM L 1362.17

Fig. 47.   Facade galleting, Bleary Td., Co. Down. UFTM L 969.18 (cf. Fig. 6)

Fig. 48.   Facade galleting (1791 datestone), later rendering fallen away, Moyheeland Td., Co. Londonderry. UFTM L 1252.13 (cf. Fig. 12)

into the bonding between the stones. There is a notable example in the walls of a fine thatched house in Bleary townland south of Lurgan (Fig. 47), and I have seen another example dating to 1791, in a now ruinous, slated farmhouse in east county Londonderry (Fig. 48). The latter in Moyheeland townland is interesting, because the facade originally treated in this decorative manner was later rendered. Galleting as decorative treatment, however, should not be confused with the packing of spaces between larger stones with smaller thinner ones, a structural technique encountered in areas where platy stones were used, for example in south-east Down with the Silurian greywacke, and in parts of the Sperrin mountains in Tyrone with mica-schists.

Good quality ashlar stone-work (Fig. 46) is seldom encountered in vernacular building in the north of Ireland. Improving landlords with an interest in the architectural appearance of their estates sometimes did go to the expense of specifying or supplying ashlar for houses occupied by estate workers, or even tenant farmers, but the design and construction of these houses was usually organised from outside the vernacular tradition. Architectural detailing occasionally found its way into the vernacular tradition, in the use of cut-stone quoins, drip moulds, cornices, dressings, more commonly around door openings than around windows, and occasionally ashlar chimney stacks. Such detailing is uncommon, and in the nineteenth century only dressed window sills, and less commonly quoins, were at all extensively used.

Earth

When the building of mass walls of tempered earth, or 'mud' as it is colloquially known, was introduced to Ireland is not known for certain. There is archaeological evidence for its use in early Christian times, but it is suggested that earth house walls are possibly an Anglo-Norman introduction.[35] Earth walls need elaborate protection in Ireland's moist climate, with rendering and heavy overhanging thatch eaves, so it is unlikely that the practice of building earth walls evolved independently. In the north of Ireland there is no documentation of their existence prior to 1600, after which time references to mud-wall houses are fairly plentiful. However, the illustration of Irish houses fairly uniformly with mass walls on contemporary maps of the period raises the possibility that mud-wall houses may have been known in northern districts in the sixteenth century, if not earlier.[36] Mud-wall

Fig. 49.   Mud-wall dwelling, with ruins of others, Bladon, Belfast, *c*.1900. UM W10/72/1

houses are attested in county Armagh[37] and in county Tyrone[38] about 1700, one of which, a tenant's rather than an under-tenant's house, in Mullabane, county Armagh, was 18.3 m. long, no mean dwelling.[39] Mud building was not confined to rural districts. Arthur Young described Dromore, county Down as 'a miserable nest of dirty mud cabins' in the late 1770s,[40] and Wakefield in 1812, speaking generally of Ireland, mentioned clay-wall houses in urban areas.[41] The Ordnance Survey memoir compilers in the 1830s reported mud houses in Antrim, and at English-town two miles outside Lisburn in Blaris parish. I recall seeing in the 1960s a terrace of clay-wall houses being demolished just north of the railway station in Portadown. The Ordnance Survey memoirs and the evidence of the poor inquiry, both in the 1830s, show that mud-wall houses were widespread, and not only amongst the poor, and Table 5 shows how ubiquitous they were near Charlemont in the following decade. Many mud-wall houses remain occupied today, especially in county Armagh, their real nature successfully concealed behind external rendering and a veneer of modernity which includes new windows, roof tiles, cement-block porches at the front and kitchen extensions at the rear, and rustic-brick chimneys. Nor

were clay-wall houses all of one storey, although the vast majority were; the seventeenth-century Waringstown House in north-west Down, a multi-storeyed small mansion, has some solid earth walls. There is evidence that mud-wall houses were being replaced by stone-built ones in various districts in the nineteenth century, for example in Dunsfort parish in county Down,[42] in the more fertile, lower-lying parts of county Londonderry, where mud building was known as 'cat and clay',[43] and in the Malone district (Fig. 49), now a prosperous suburb of south-west Belfast.[44] Mud-wall had its advocates in the nineteenth century, for the *Dublin Penny Journal* published a suggested improvement to strengthen the angles between walls by inserting timber ties across the angles within the layers of earth.[45] An emigrant to Upper Canada, writing to a brother in Lisbellaw, county Fermanagh in 1848, complains of his dislike of timber houses there because he found them cold in winter and hot in summer. He built himself 'a neat cottage house' with mud walls faced internally with brick. 'It is well thought of in this country (stones is very rare in this place).'[46]

Jonathan Binns described the construction of mud houses in the Richhill area of county Armagh in 1835:

E

Fig. 50.   Detail of mud walling on basal stone courses, Derryadd Td., Co. Armagh. UFTM L 1055.17

There tenants build their own houses of clay and scraw, or rushes. They make the walls solid, raise them two feet at a time with mud and rushes, allowing them ten days to dry between the several layers. The doors and windows are cut out with a spade, and the sides made straight and smooth. These dwellings, including windows, cost the tenant 50s. The landlord frequently finds, in addition, some fir, or poles of other sort of wood, for the roof. They contain two bays or rooms, each 14 feet [4.27 m.] square. Most of the poor people prefer these thatched mud cabins to a house of stone and slate . . . We called on an old man who was having a stone cottage built for him at Lord Gosford's expense; he said, 'I would rather live and die in my old cabin; the mud walls are warm; it is the warmest hut in all Ireland.'[47]

Many older people still claim that the old mud walls are warmer than those built of modern materials, and M'Evoy, writing of houses in Dungannon barony in east Tyrone in 1802, substantiated this, though he considered the houses there inferior to the mud-wall dwellings of county Dublin.[48]

Earth with a suitable clay content had the merit of being readily available in most districts, although in the stony parts of Tyrone and most of county Donegal there is little evidence for its use. The house site was more or less levelled, and usually some stone foundation courses (Fig. 50) were laid down to protect the bottoms of the earth walls from damp and the attentions of burrowing rodents. The earth was prepared by digging in a pit, adding water, tempering the mixture by tramping with either human or animals' feet, adding straw, rushes or other fibres for binding, and perhaps leaving the mixture to 'sour' for a

Fig. 51. Mud gable of derelict house, with four courses of sod topped with brickwork, Gartross Td., Co. Down. UFTM L 1438.17

time. The mud was then laid on in layers as described by Binns, 0.45 to 0.61 m. thick, each layer being covered with straw and allowed to dry sufficiently to become load-bearing before the next was superimposed. In a house I saw in Blunnick townland in west Fermanagh in about 1969 (Fig. 52), thin layers of scraw were used instead of straw as cappings for each layer of mud. Walls were commonly 0.55 m. to 0.62 m. thick, gables often slightly thicker than front and rear walls. Upper triangular parts of gables and partition walls were difficult to achieve, and often were constructed of layers of sod (Fig. 51), but many clay-wall houses with roofs supported only on purlins had clay gables carried the full height. The weight of the roof, transmitted to the points where the ends of the purlins were bedded in the clay, produced a compressive force in the mud walls which helped their stability. Just as door and window openings could either be cut out of the solid, or built up as the successive layers of mud were applied, so it was not difficult to build in chimney flues, or smoke channels to integrate with wattle chimney canopies or hearth walls. For greater stability, M'Evoy recommended in 1802 that mud side walls should taper upwards from about 0.7 m. at the bottom to 0.55 m. at the wall heads,[49] and mud walls with a slight batter on one or both faces are occasionally found, but

many maintained a near constant thickness from bottom to top. Most mud-wall houses were built as described above — a very few, however, were constructed with shuttering, in the same way that concrete walls are poured between shutters today, for the marks left by the junctions between adjacent shutter boards can be seen in the clay once the rendering is stripped away.

Many clay-wall houses are known to have survived since the late seventeenth and early eighteenth centuries. Clay walling was used in some houses with crucks which must date from this period. On the other hand, poorly constructed clay cabins in Aghabog parish, county Monaghan, in 1835 were said to be capable of surviving only fifteen to twenty years.[50]

Three houses may be mentioned in which earth was used in a different manner; one was in Annaloist townland (Fig. 53) on the south shore of Lough Neagh, another in Killyruddan in mid Armagh, and the last in Tirmoneen townland (Fig. 54) in west Fermanagh. In each case large blocks of earth had been cut and used rather like unfired bricks, from which they differed, however, in not having been moulded in any way. Unfired bricks were occasionally used elsewhere in Ireland,[51] but there is little evidence that they were ever used in Ulster, nor is there knowledge as to how

Fig. 52.   Detail of alternating thick layers of mud separated by thin layers of sod, on basal stonework, Blunnick Td.,
Co. Fermanagh. From a transparency. UFTM L 1661.10

widespread use of earth blocks or lumps may have been, for it is undocumented apart from the three cases noted here. The case of the Fermanagh house in particular illustrates the poor quality of this material; the junctions of gables and side walls seem to have been especially weak. Use of this material could not, in any of the three cases, have been discovered until the fabric of the houses started to disintegrate.

Fig. 53.   Earth lumps exposed in house wall, Annaloist Td., Co. Armagh. UFTM L 323.5

Fig. 54.   Earth-lump walling in derelict house, Tirmoneen Td., Co. Fermanagh. UFTM L 530.36

Fig. 55.   Brick farmhouse, Dernalee Td., Co. Armagh. UFTM L 1541.20

Brick

Manufacture of, and building with brick were introduced to northern parts of Ireland about 1600 from England — brick seems not to have been used to any significant extent in Scotland at this time, and so its use could not have been brought to Ulster by Scots settlers, although brick oven linings are known in some Scottish-style planters' castles. Plantation records refer to brick houses, built primarily in the lowland clay areas along the Lagan valley and into north Armagh, to the west and north of Lough Neagh in the Bann basin, and in the Erne basin and central Cavan in the south-west. The various plantation surveyors looked with especial approval on them. Bricks necessary for their construction were usually fired on the spot or nearby.[52] One such house built at this time was referred to later, near Belfast, as 'a fair house, walled with bricks, and a tower slated'.[53]

At this early period bricks used in the north of Ireland were 4.4 to 5.1 × 10.8 × 21.6 to 22.9 cms., marginally thinner than contemporary bricks used in England and North America. By the 1730s, and perhaps a generation earlier, the size had increased to 5.7 to 6.4 × 10.2 × 21.6 cms., in the Downpatrick area. In anticipation of a spate of brick building in Belfast, minimum dimensions of 5.7 × 11.4 × 24 cms. were laid down for brick makers

in 1754,[54] and this was fairly generally maintained until about 1820 in east Ulster, and even later for example in Fermanagh when bricks about 7.0 to 8.3 × 9.5 to 10.8 × 23.0 cms. became fairly general. Standardised machine-moulded bricks were introduced later, but of rather similar sizes. These dimensions provide only the roughest guide to the dating possibilities provided by brick sizes. There was much local variation, remoter small-scale brick fields ignoring changes in the bigger concerns in the Lagan valley and in east Tyrone, apparently for considerable periods. Further militating against imposition of standardised brick sizes throughout the north of Ireland was the common practice, at least until the beginning of the nineteenth century, of firing bricks on site for the construction of individual buildings, and similarly informal and difficult to control was the firing of bricks as a communal activity by rundale joint-tenants on the Abercorn estate in west Tyrone after 1750.[55]

The walls of the earliest brick houses were laid on stone foundations, a feature which, with imperfect knowledge of brick technology at vernacular level, is clearly demonstrated by two houses, one in north county Londonderry in Clooney townland,[56] the other in Rossavally townland south of Belnaleck in west Fermanagh, in which the bricks were not properly bonded. The builders of these two houses used a

Fig. 56. Brick dwelling with some stone in basal courses, roof supported internally on crucks, Kingarrow South Td., Co. Fermanagh. UFTM L 530.25

technique of supporting the roof independently of the house walls, with cruck trusses, so unsure were they of the potentiality of the new material. The Clooney house, traditionally the first in the area built at vernacular level with brick walls, almost certainly originated about 1780, but the Fermanagh building (see Chapter 5; cf. Fig. 56), a small hip-roofed farmhouse built on cut-out bogland, may possibly be later, although earlier than the 1830s when it is shown on the first edition of the six-inch Ordnance Survey map.

Significant adoption of brick building at vernacular level started as late as the second half of the eighteenth century. Bricks of seventeenth-century size have not been found in vernacular houses, and those of the size known in the Downpatrick area in the 1730s are not common. However, brick dwellings are noted in Dromoher and Drumnasollagh in the manor of Castledillon in Armagh about 1700,[57] in Navan townland west of Armagh city, and in Tulledowe in Tyrone about the same time,[58] although the Navan house was built partially of stone. As an alternative to stone, brick was permitted for houses construction of which was stipulated in Tyrone between 1778 and 1805.[59] Three county surveys of the early 1800s mention brick houses. In Monaghan in 1801, in Dartrey barony 'all the houses in

this country are built of brick', perhaps something of an exaggeration, but near Dawson's-grove the landlord had provided two-storey, brick, 'neat and ornamental farmhouses' which 'possess much comfort and convenience within'.[60] Sampson told that by 1802 the better farmhouses in the more fertile areas of county Londonderry were of brick,[61] and ten years later Dubourdieu stated that the mud houses disappearing in the Malone area outside Belfast were being replaced by brick ones.[62]

In the documentation of the 1830s brick houses are noted mainly in the same areas where brick manufacture and construction commenced in the seventeenth century. The Ordnance Survey memoirs authenticate brick farmhouses in north and north-west Antrim, north Londonderry, and east Tyrone, as well as west Fermanagh, and cottages in these areas and in north-west Down and south-west Tyrone. The poor inquiry evidence of 1835 cites parishes only in north Antrim, east Londonderry, near Lisburn in the Lagan valley, and west Fermanagh — brick was obviously too expensive for the housing of the poor, except in the lower Bann valley and the Lagan valley, relatively prosperous areas in any case, and, interestingly, in Killesher parish in west Fermanagh, where bricks were produced very cheaply, but not of very

Fig. 57. Brick walling, mainly Flemish bond, intrusive part-courses of headers, Ballyardel Td., Co. Down. UFTM L 1285.20

good quality.[63] Figures already provided in Table 5 for estates outside the brick-making areas show how closely confined to those areas vernacular use of brick remained in the 1840s. On the three estates where Collis recorded any use of brick, the combined total is only eight houses. Numbers of brick houses anywhere never became large later in the nineteenth century, but they became rather more widespread following improvements in transport that permitted movement of bricks from commercial brick yards to rural areas. Some of the slated two-storey farmhouses (Figs. 53, 55), whether elaborated vernacular forms or designs inspired by earlier Georgian farmhouses, had walls of this mass-produced material.

Rendering and Limewash

Rendering of internal and external wall surfaces with clay or lime plaster was widely practised. Internal clay plastering of the medieval houses at Caherguillamore was noted in Chapter 2, but references before the nineteenth century are few. In the late 1660s houses mentioned in the Brownlow Lease Book in the town of Lurgan were usually roughcast externally, as were at least three houses to be built in the surrounding rural area. Plaster, rather than roughcasting, was applied to some external wall surfaces.[64] A large house built about 1717 at Lismacloskey near Toome Bridge in county Antrim had an external gable rendered with a thick skin of clay plaster which included cow hair as binding. Addition of animal hair to clay or mud when it was to be used in this way was usual in other parts of Ireland also, and other additives were lime and cowdung,[65] the last especially when the plaster was to be applied to wattled chimney canopies. I have found some houses in northern Ireland with whitewashed clay plastering which had a rather uneven surface, overlaid by later thinner plaster of lime and sand, worked to a smooth finish.

Nineteenth-century evidence divides between rather few references to the rendering of cottage walls, and many more to the plastering of farmhouse walls. With the exception of Enniskillen parish in 1834,[66] all of the references to the rough-casting of cottage walls are from east Ulster, mainly parishes in south-east Antrim where there was ready access to lime in the outcrop of the Cretaceous chalk under the basalts. But experience varied widely. A prosperous parish like Glenavy had 'even the houses of the working class roughcast',[67] whereas in Carrickfergus only a few were so treated.[68] In Londonderry in Desertmartin parish, although lime was available it was seldom used for plastering,[69] and in Kildrumferton in Cavan the poor inquiry of 1835 was told the same.[70] By contrast, mud-walled houses in the Monaghan parish of Aghabog were roughcast.[71]

Although there are more references to rendering of farmhouse walls, reflecting the greater prosperity of farmers as compared with cottiers, *in toto* they provide a similar pattern, their preponderance in county Antrim in the 1830s indicating that proximity to a source of lime was important, but perhaps also that south Antrim in particular was a significant centre of building innovation. Indeed a county Antrim house in 1701 at Ballymenoch (Ballymena) was built with 'lyme to plaster the syd wall and gevlles',[72] and it was suggested early in the nineteenth century that many county Antrim houses were usually roughcast.[73] Eighteen parishes in southern parts of Antrim are noted in the Ordnance Survey

Fig. 58. Whitewashed coursed stonework with black-painted dressed quoins, farmhouse and outbuilding, Eshywulligan Td., Co. Fermanagh. UFTM L 324.14

memoirs as having farmhouses with roughcast walls, although in Ballylinny those of the 'less extensive farmers' were 'unadorned' in this way.[74] Outside county Antrim, by contrast, the same source provides evidence on this matter only for Drumcree parish in Armagh,[75] and for Desertoghill in Londonderry where 'comfortable, spacious farmhouses' constituting up to a quarter of the dwellings in some townlands, were 'plastered and whitewashed inside and in some instances outside'.[76] Documentary silence on the matter of rendering must not, however, be taken to imply its absence, certainly in many districts in the nineteenth century. Clay walls were usually rendered in Ireland, for to leave them unprotected in the moist climate would patently have been unwise — nobody wanted walls that would quite literally have melted away if left unprotected on their outer surfaces. However, stone buildings in many districts like the Glens of Antrim, the Sperrin mountains and west Donegal were normally left unrendered (Fig. 58), and many have survived until recently covered only by successive layers of whitewash, which in themselves, of course, ultimately built up to provide what amounted to rendering, so heavy did the accumulation become.

Irish houses with mass walls, probably plastered and certainly lime-washed, either white or some pale tint, are illustrated on a number of the early seventeenth-century cartographic sources for Ulster,[77] and stone houses built by British settlers in county Londonderry at the same time seem to have been similarly treated.[78] Towards the end of the third quarter of the same century a house to be constructed in Balliblagh, on Brownlow property in north Armagh, was to be 'white-lim'd'.[79] Nevertheless, widespread use of whitewash became common only about the end of the eighteenth century. About 1770 very few houses in Magheradrool parish in mid Down were whitewashed, but by 1791 there were 'many neat farmhouses built and whitened'.[80] As has been true of so many building innovations, the change to lime washing came earlier in the east than in the west. Magheradrool was not exceptional. In the linen-rich county of Armagh in 1804 'The meanest hut has something of neatness to recommend it; almost in every one the exterior is whitewashed . . .',[81] and whitewashing was 'general' in the extreme south of Antrim at the same time,[82] while Dubourdieu, writing of the county in general in 1812, claimed that farmhouses were generally whitened.[83] Generally where lime was readily available, as in much of Antrim, it was being used in the early nineteenth century, but in Londonderry it was only in the restricted areas where lime could be acquired easily that the houses of

Fig. 59.   Whitewashed rendered stonework, farmhouse, Relagh Guinness Td., Co. Tyrone. UFTM L 986.15

small farmers were whitened.[84] A writer addressing himself to 'the Patriotic Committee conducting the farming or agricultural society of the County of Down' in 1802 suggested, 'Were the peasantry encouraged by small premiums, to whiten their houses with lime, to keep away dung and stagnated water from their doors, it would tend to prevent fevers and other disorders',[85] and a comparable suggestion was made in an account of Maghera, county Londonderry, in 1814.[86] Landlord encouragement in this matter was evident in the 1830s in a number of places. In Taylorstown townland in west Antrim, near the river Bann, lime was provided gratis by the landlord, but houses were 'anything but neat looking' elsewhere because the people were unable to get lime;[87] the proprietor in Glynn parish near Larne in the same county acted similarly.[88] In the east Londonderry parishes of Kilcronaghan and Lissan the Drapers' company as landlord insisted in leases upon regular whitewashing, in some cases providing the lime free for poor tenants, but requiring others to purchase it and exacting a year's rent in advance from those who refused to keep their houses clean and comfortable.[89] If many parishes in eastern areas displayed much use of whitewash, there were exceptions. People in Aghalee and Aghagallon, Antrim parishes close to the east side of Lough Neagh, used whitewash less regularly than those occupying neighbouring parishes,[90] and similar situations existed in Inver and Templecorran south of Larne.[91]

Whitewashing came later in the west. In a relatively prosperous area like south Donegal, as early as 1821 annual whitewashing was in vogue, seemingly having been introduced as a hygiene measure to combat outbreaks of typhus: 'In some cabins they have their bedsteads whitewashed with lime water'.[92] But at the same time further east in the Tyrone barony of Clogher, only a few houses had their exterior whitened,[93] while later in the 1830s, in the east Donegal parishes of Clonleigh and Desertagney, neither exteriors nor interiors were regularly limewashed.[94] Again in the west, the attitude of a landlord could be vital. Lord George Hill purchased the Gweedore estate in north-west Donegal in 1838 and set about improving it. According to a report in 1843, 'Until lately the people were crowded together in miserable villages, where want of cleanliness and the impure exhalations of dung pits, close to their dwellings, generated disease and misery'. Hill encouraged building of new houses, offering premiums for features like chimneys, plastered walls, and whitewashing internally and externally.[95] However, photographs of houses in the Gweedore area in the 1880s, although it is not known if they were in what had been Hill's estate, show sparing external use of whitewash, about door and window openings mainly,[96] and similar treatment or whitewashing of one end of the dwelling only was seen on houses on Rathlin Island off the north Antrim coast in the 1930s and 1940s.[97] Even in the 1830s, houses in northern parts of county Antrim seem to have been less commonly whitewashed than their counterparts in southern districts of that county, certainly at the level of the cottage rather than the farmhouse.[98]

Reflecting their occupants' lower social standing and at least relative impoverishment, cottages in the 1830s are much less commonly reported as being whitewashed, but the pattern of such reportings as do exist is similar to, if geographically more limited than, that of the farmhouse evidence. The pattern is one of whitewashing of cottages limited to a few parishes in south and south-east Antrim, and its virtual absence in west Ulster. Again there is evidence that the attitude of landlords was crucial, as in the case of the Drapers' company in Desertlyn parish, county Londonderry,[99] the other significant factor being proximity to a source of supply of lime, as in Mallusk in county Antrim.[100]

Caution is needed in associating absence of limewashing, both inside and out, with uncleanliness. Whitewashed stone cottages in the Tyrone parish of Artrea in 1835 were described as being 'for the most part very dirty',[101] and the absence of limewashing gave to cottages in the Antrim parish of Ballylinny in 1839 an 'appearance of neglect and want of attention to cleanliness which they do not altogether deserve'.[102] By the end of the nineteenth century whitewashing of farmhouses was usual (Fig. 59), and of most cottages also. Some landlords continued to insist upon it,[103] and the earliest public authority housing, the 'labourers' cottages' erected by the rural district councils from the 1890s, were often whitewashed.

Tinted limewashes seem to have been rarely used, perhaps until within the present century when occasional cases of external use of a yellow ochre wash have been reported, and rarely of pink or blue on rather socially superior buildings. On examination such examples usually show that colour is a later feature, the earliest layers of limewash being white. An interesting local variant was the addition of a deep red dye for the painting of a dado internally in farmhouses in the Glens of Antrim, using an additive from the interbasaltic horizon in the eastern edge of the Antrim plateau. In part of west Fermanagh also, 'In the past the lower walls [of kitchens] were painted a dark colour, and the bright ornamental upper half was white-washed — often. A decorative border ran between, a stream of stencilled shamrocks at Denis Gilroy's, a pinked horizon of points at Mrs. Keenan's.'[104]

FIVE

The Roof

Form (Figs. 60-68)

ROOFS of vernacular houses in the north of Ireland since at least the nineteenth century have usually been gabled, hip roofs occurring in a minority of thatched houses in parts of Cavan and in south-western parts of Fermanagh, and slated hip roofs in the same districts, but extending further north into mid and north-east Fermanagh, south Tyrone, and eastwards through Monaghan into west Armagh. Wherever hip roofs were found, half-hip roofs also occurred. Occasional vernacular houses with hip roofs have been found elsewhere also. Other roof forms were unknown in vernacular house building in the north of Ireland, indeed in Ireland as a whole.

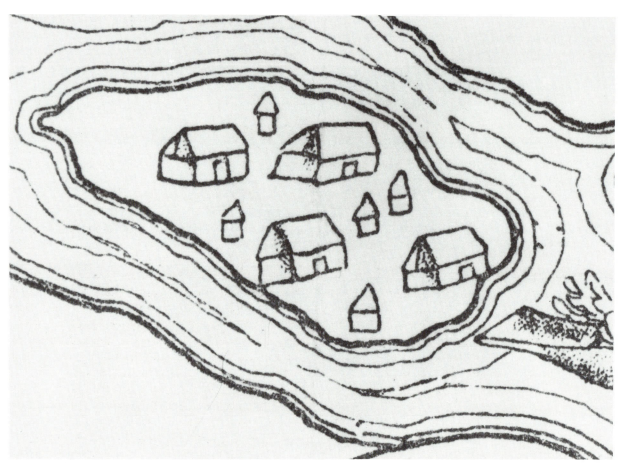

Fig. 60.   Detail from map of siege of Maguire's castle, Enniskillen, Co. Fermanagh, 1593-4, reproduced in *Ulster Journal of Archaeology,* 2nd ser., 2 (1906), showing hip-roof dwellings. The smaller structures are interpreted as straw-rope-wall bins, thatched, for grain storage.

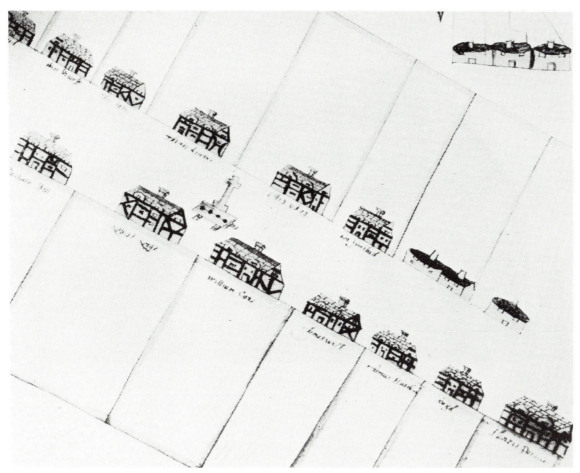

Fig. 61.   Detail showing gabled English timber-framed houses and some hip-roof Irish houses, Bellaghy, Co. Londonderry, 1622, from 'A Plat of the Vintners' Buildings' by Thomas Raven in Chart, *Londonderry and the London Companies, 1609-1629* (Belfast, 1928), Plate 25.

The contrast presented by native housing at the time of the Plantation of Ulster is complete. All the known evidence suggests the ubiquity of the hip roof, and houses with this roof form appear on maps of the late sixteenth and early seventeenth centuries (Fig. 60). The few gabled houses illustrated were inside forts and in towns. The gable was usual only on houses, whether timber-framed or with stone walls, built by British settlers (Fig. 61), as illustrated for example on the maps of county Londonderry towns already referred to. A number of houses dated in recent years by means of dendrochronology to the second half of the seventeenth century, with cruck-supported roofs, are all gabled, and most are known to have been built by British settlers, or at least within districts dominated by them. But it is significant that one of the isolated examples of a hip roof in east Ulster, at Ballinderry in Antrim, is on a house also with crucks with composite blades which perhaps derive

from the norms of native housing about 1600 rather than from carpentry practices introduced by British settlers.

Little documentation exists about roof form at any period after the cartographic evidence of the early seventeenth century. A lease for two Tyrone townlands in 1700 includes an agreement to build a 'large dwelling house of good oak timber with two upright gavells . . .';[1] reference to a gable in a lease for the Ballymena area in county Antrim at the same time has been noted above;[2] and 'a four couple house with mud or stone wall 7 ft. high and two upright gables' was specified to be constructed in Lavehill (now Longfield) townland, Laragh parish, county Cavan in a lease of 1712.[3] A century later, gabled houses were noted as usual throughout Tyrone.[4] Hip roofs are shown on a detail on an estate map of 1800 in north Antrim in the Ballymoney area, where hip roofs were unknown on vernacular houses in more recent times.[5] Late nineteenth- and early twentieth-century

Fig. 62.   Hip-roof farmhouse, Killesher Td., Co. Fermanagh. UFTM L 1378.7

Fig. 63.   Hip-roof farmhouse, Clonosey Td., Co. Cavan. UFTM L 1378.17

Fig. 64.   Rear view of partially cruck-supported hip roof, Ballinderry Td., Co. Antrim. UFTM L 1172.3

Fig. 65.   Slated vernacular house with half-hip roof, Tamlaght Td., Co. Fermanagh. UFTM L 985.13

Fig. 66.   Slated vernacular farmhouse with half-hip roof, entrance slightly left of centre on facade, Derryloman Td., Co. Fermanagh. UFTM L 992.15

Fig. 67.   Formerly thatched, gabled farmhouse, Glenish Td., Co. Monaghan. UFTM L 1437.1

Fig. 68.   Gabled rope-thatch cottage, Inishowen, Co. Donegal, early 20th-century. UFTM WAG 1189

photograph collections almost invariably show gabled houses, but occasional photographs record hip roofs where now there are none, for example in the Clogher valley in county Tyrone.[6] Scanty though the total evidence may be, the general impression is that north Irish vernacular houses changed from having hip roofs in 1600 to being dominated by gable roofs a century or so later. The number of survivals of the hip roof declined rapidly after 1800, the form surviving in significant numbers only in south Ulster (Figs. 62, 63, 64), and transferring through to newer slated roofs which replaced thatch from the second half of the nineteenth century onwards (Figs. 65, 66), thatched hip roofs remaining in only a limited area of Fermanagh and Cavan.

Roof Timber

The nature of the main timbers of the framework that carried the roof covering often provides a valuable guide to the general period within which a vernacular house may have originated. Native oak commonly provided the principal load-bearing members in many areas until about the middle of the eighteenth century. Fossil timber

recovered from peat bogs became increasingly important as a resource for building purposes as the eighteenth century progressed, particularly at lower social levels. Purchased sawn timber of foreign origin was first used by more prosperous owners, became increasingly common in the roofs of better farmhouses towards the end of the eighteenth century, and was being used even for cottage construction in the second half of the nineteenth century. But this is a generalised picture. Social differences were significant; more prestigious, that is usually more expensive, timbers were used at higher social levels; and changes appeared sooner in more easterly and in more low-lying fertile districts than in more westerly and environmentally more marginal localities.

While the seasonal creats associated with use of summer pastures may have been built of a variety of timbers, it is likely that the more substantial native timber-framed, if not cruck-framed, houses of about 1600 utilised oak cut from woods and forests which existed in many parts of Ulster except east Down. Similarly, box-framed houses built by British settlers in the early seventeenth century used locally cut oak. It is significant that all of the houses with cruck trusses datable to the seventeenth century had oak timber in the trusses and purlins.Extensive exploitation of local forest resources,

F

especially oak, in the seventeenth and early eighteenth centuries led to rapid depletion. Replacement planting was not undertaken to any significant extent. The story of this industrial rape of Ireland's woodlands in Tudor times has been told elsewhere.[7] It is sufficient to note that the last native forest advertised for letting for charcoal burning was in about 1750 in the extreme south-east of county Londonderry. Across the Bann, between Toome Bridge and Randalstown in Antrim, a house signified as English by its brick-lined oven and its roof-timbering system was built about 1717 using oak cut in the systematic clearance of native oak woods[8] that had earlier provided timbers for the framing of houses in Antrim town.[9] Roofs known from documentation to be of seventeenth- or early eighteenth-century date invariably have oak timbers, such as those in Waringstown House and the nearby parish church in north-west Down. A lease of 1700 in Tyrone specifies the building of a large dwelling house 'of good oak timber',[10] and another in north Donegal to run from ten years later stipulated oak for the roof.[11]

As the native woods disappeared, increasing use was made of bog timber. Bogs had long been recognised as a resource in Ireland; there is reference to their use for fuel in the Brehon laws.[12] Writing of the early seventeenth century, Fynes Moryson claimed that the Irish in some areas used brushwood for firing, 'but in other parts they burn Turfe . . .'[13] At the end of the century Sir William Petty, stating that turf was the commonly used fuel everywhere, suggested that its use had become so popular that it was preferred even where timber was yet available for burning.[14] So both the knowledge that fossil timber existed in the bogs, and the techniques for its recovery, would have been widespread in rural Ireland by the time native forest timber ceased to be available for building purposes. Use of bog oak and bog fir for building, especially for roofing, became so widespread as early as the eighteenth century that already in some districts in the early nineteenth century even this resource was nearly exhausted, as in the Armagh parish of Ballymyre[15] in 1816, and in the areas around Lough Swilly in north county Donegal in the 1830s.[16] Local variability of the situation has already been mentioned. Timber was in such short supply in the relatively treeless parts of east Down that when a ship carrying cedarwood was wrecked at Tyrella before 1796, that timber was later used in local buildings.[17] On the other hand, cutting-out of the woods of Munterloney was mentioned at about the same time as being the reason for the fairly recent commencement of use of bog timber in parts of county Tyrone,[18] and then also bog timber was used in county Armagh for roofing.[19] In 1816 together with Ballymyre in

Armagh, use of bog timber for roofing was noted in Dungiven (Londonderry),[20] parishes to the east of Lough Neagh in county Antrim,[21] and the barony of Upper Fews in south Armagh.[22] The Ordnance Survey memoirs in the 1830s contain widespread references to the use of bog wood for roofing except, interestingly enough, for county Antrim. Bog oak was particularly prized, and in Inishmacsaint parish in Fermanagh, more so than inported deal.[23] Its use had been so popular in the Monaghan parish of Tedavnet that by the 1830s it was rare and difficult to obtain.[24] Only four Ordnance Survey parish memoirs in Donegal, however, refer to use of bog timber for roofing: Clondavaddog, Donoughmore, Mintiaghs and Tullyaughnish;[25] but oral evidence from west-coast parishes relating to later in the nineteenth century attests its use there.[26]

Evidence of depletion of bog wood for roofing in county Armagh by 1816 has been noted; and it is obvious that is was disappearing earlier in parts of Down even before 1800. Imported timber from Baltic ports was distributed through Downpatrick in the latter part of the eighteenth century, 'Canada timber being at the time unknown in this quarter',[27] and as early as 1760 Swedish timber was imported to Londonderry, together with American and Memel (Prussian) pine later on.[28] In the 1830s three Antrim parishes, Ballynure, Carrickfergus and Layde,[29] all used imported pine for house building, brought in through either Belfast or Larne. Downpatrick continued to import American timber,[30] while Warrenpoint[31] and Newry,[32] also in county Down, imported both American and Baltic wood for building. Imported timber was sent on from the ports to inland parishes also, like Seapatrick in west Down,[33] whither it went by road, and Magherafelt to which it came from Belfast by barge to Ballyronan on the north-west shore of Lough Neagh.[34] Coleraine and Portrush on the north coast were important ports through which American and Baltic timber went to parishes like Maghera, Errigal, and Ballyaghragan.[35] This timber was regarded in the mid-nineteenth century as the best available for building. American black beech and oak were also widely used, being cheaper to purchase, and it was suggested in the Drumachose, county Londonderry parish memoir in the 1830s that Memel pine was preferred by those who held perpetuity leases because, although dearer, it was more durable and so cheaper in the long run.[36] Timber merchants in inland centres like Enniskillen, also bought in foreign timber for resale locally, for example in Ballinamallard.[37] However, remote and impoverished areas like the coasts of west Donegal had to make do with whatever could be found, and driftwood was widely used for roofing there and also on Rathlin Island.[38]

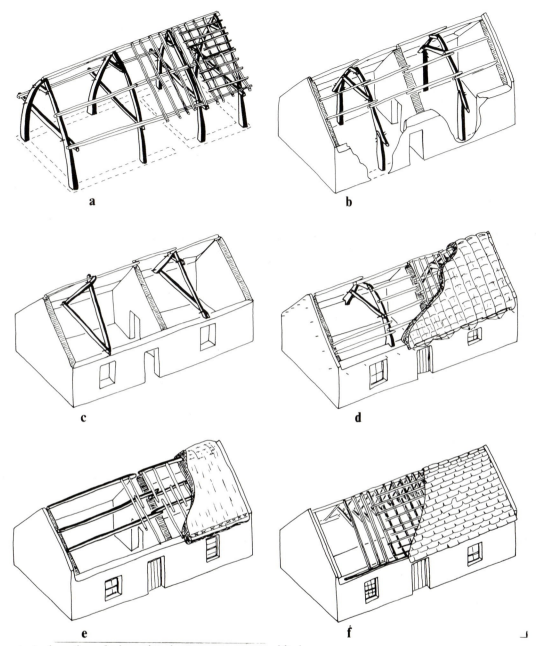

Fig. 69.   The principal northern Irish roof-timbering systems, simplified.
a: cruck trusses (continuous blades), through purlins, and overlying common rafters;
b: cruck trusses (jointed blades) interposed between transverse walls, with through purlins;
c: tie-beam trusses, through purlins (only ridge shown);
d: collar-beam trusses, with through purlins;
e: purlin roof supported on gables and internal transverse wall, with common rafters;
f: common-rafter trusses with ridge piece, for slating.

Timbering Systems

Roofs of vernacular houses in the north of Ireland have normally been carried on one of two apparently different systems of arranging the various timbers to provide support for the roof cover (Fig. 69). A truss consists of side members ('blades', colloquially 'couples') tied by a collar or collars, often a yoke at the apex, and sometimes a tie-beam at wall-head height. Trusses span the dwelling from front to rear, at bay intervals, carrying on their backs longitudinal through purlins, consisting either of jointed timbers providing continuous runs, or purlins of little more than bay length overlapped on the back of the trusses. These trusses provide the more widespread system all over the north of Ireland, as minority forms in central and east-central Ulster, and as the sole forms in a peripheral belt from east Down and most of Antrim, westwards across Londonderry, mid and west Tyrone, into Donegal, and south through north and west Fermanagh and west Cavan. The other basic roof form consists of longitudinal ridge and side purlins alone, their ends borne in the gables and internal walls. Overlying common rafters are often so insubstantial as to be little more than heavy laths. Appearances may deceive, however; it is suggested in this book that the latter form is a late derivative of the former, formed by omitting trusses between gables and internal cross walls, or by substituting internal transverse load-bearing mass walls where formerly there would have been trusses. In describing transverse trusses, it is best to distinguish between 'cruck' trusses and 'collar-beam' and 'tie-beam' trusses; the former are the typological and historical antecedents of the latter.

Examination of roof timbering systems is one of the most important aspects of the study of vernacular architecture. Regrettably it has received least attention in much of Ireland. While the general Irish context of many other vernacular dwelling elements is well known, information on Ulster's roof forms recorded especially since about 1955 has little counterpart in the vernacular housing literature dealing with the remaining three provinces. This is regrettable, because roof carpentry details provide valuable clues as to cultural movements and historical contacts. There is some danger of over-emphasising the parallels, if not also the connections, that exist between circumstances in the north of Ireland and in Britain, merely because of the absence of evidence from the rest of Ireland. Recent discovery of cruck-related forms at the west end of the Dingle peninsula in county Kerry reinforces this view[39] — otherwise, all the Irish buildings with crucks of one kind or another are in northern areas. However, there is some literary evidence which may be interpreted as referring to cruck traditions,[40] in particular one account from county Galway in 1824[41] and oral traditions gathered about the middle of the present century in county Leitrim.[42] Also, a medieval reference to crucks in county Kerry has recently come to light. An extent of the lands of Thomas FitzMaurice in 1298 in the manor of Insula mentions a hall constructed with *furcis*, and also an apparently

decayed chapel of similar construction. From comparable English evidence, *furca* means cruck when it occurs in documents dating from the late twelfth to the fifteenth centuries.[43] English 'fork' had the same meaning in references to buildings in documents of the fifteenth and sixteenth centuries, and indeed was still in colloquial use with this meaning in the north of England at the end of the nineteenth century.[44] So, when in the English plantation documentation of the north of Ireland in the early seventeenth century the same word occurs in building contexts, it must also refer to crucks. For example, in the Moneymore area in south Londonderry about 1615 John Brighton, an English carpenter, cut '10 forks for cabbynes'.[45]

The distinction between a cruck truss and a collar-beam or tie-beam truss is simple; cruck blades spring from ground level or from some position between there and the heads of the side walls of the structure. Tie-beam and collar-beam trusses have shorter blades rising from the wall-heads only. Cruck-truss blades may be continuous or they may consist of a wall-post portion scarfed and pegged at its top end to the lower end of a roof member. There is no essential difference between continuous and composite cruck blades insofar as they support much, if not all, of the burden of the roof independently of the side walls of the structure.

Many of the problems and fascinations of the study of roof timbering systems are best illustrated by describing three houses in some detail, one in Antrim and two in Fermanagh. The first in Knockarevan townland south of Derrylin in south Fermanagh (Fig. 70) was first investigated in 1969, again in 1975 and finally after it was accidentally destroyed in 1977. That so many visits were needed to discover its true structural nature is not unusual. Many details of interesting houses sadly are only revealed as they decay. The building was about 24.3 m. long, almost 5.5 m. from front to rear, with a kitchen extension added outside the original rear door, which was slightly offset from the front entrance. Two outhouses occupied some 7.2 m. of the south end, terminating in an upstanding gable, while the thatched roof had a hip end at the opposite northern extremity of the dwelling portion, which comprised a central kitchen almost 4.3 m. long by 4.6 m. wide internally, flanked by two smaller rooms at each end. None of the internal partitions was keyed into the front and rear walls, which, coupled with their anomalous relationship to the pattern of roof trusses, suggests firstly that the partition walls were inserted after the external walls and roof, supported on its trusses, had been completed, and secondly that the most recent pattern of internal division may not always have existed. Indeed, the presence of a window in the rear wall

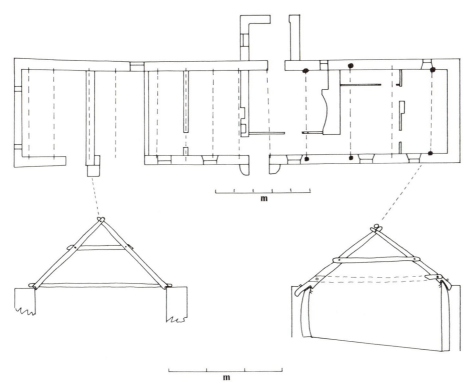

Fig. 70. Cruck house, Knockarevan Td., Co. Fermanagh.

of the innermost of the two outhouses may point to this area at least having once been part of the dwelling. The kitchen probably always occupied its recorded position, although the separation of the front passage-like entrance 'hall' inside the front wall from the kitchen proper was not original.

Three complete scarfed-jointed cruck trusses were finally identified, at the northern hip end of the house, in the room behind the kitchen hearth, and in the kitchen itself. The other kitchen truss had its rear blade scarfed to form part of a jointed cruck-blade, but this could have been a re-used timber, either from a partial rebuilding of the house, or from elsewhere. Apart from the half-size hip bay, bay intervals between these trusses were about 2.1 m. All apparently had been scarfed tie-beam cruck trusses, but the low-level tie-beams had been found inconvenient and had either been removed completely or been cut away leaving their ends pegged to the cruck blades, just above the joints. The other end of the building was roofed with tie-beam trusses resting on the wall-heads, spaced at bay intervals of about 1.35 m. to 1.5 m., except for one bay straddling the division between dwelling and outhouse which was the same size as that within which the kitchen hearth wall had been constructed. This suggests that most of the building from the kitchen southwards was reconstructed at some time, raising the possibility that cruck trusses perhaps were at

first more extensively used to support the roof, some later replaced by tie-beam trusses. Bog oak was used for the wall-post portions of the the cruck blades, and probably also for their upper portions, while some of the collar-beams were of ash. All truss blades crossed at the apex where some were pegged and some not, providing cradles to accommodate the ridge purlin. Use of bog timber suggests that the house probably originated in the eighteenth century, but the standard of construction of the trusses and use of tie beams as well as collar-beams may point to construction early in that century.

The second house was some miles further north in west Fermanagh, in Rossavally townland south of Belnaleck (Figs. 71, 72). It had been constructed on cut-out bog, the road about fifty metres to the east standing up like a causeway a couple of metres above the surface of the fields. Softwood trees had been used throughout in framing the house, which was very small, barely 10 m. by 4.5 m. A small porch of corrugated metal sheeting had been added at the front, and a small brick extension at the rear. External walls were of brick with stone quoins at the south-west corner, with very low wall heads at about 1.5 m. high. The walls varied between 45 and 50 cm. thick, and the brickwork was imperfectly bonded. Brick size throughout was about 21.5 cm. × 10.0 cm. × 6.5 cm.

The kitchen chimney stack was also of brick, joined to

Fig. 71.   Derelict cruck house, Rossavally Td., Co. Fermanagh. UFTM L 1182.3

the rear wall of the house by brickwork a single course thick. Opposite the hearth, the end of the house was closed off by a stud-and-board partition, not an original feature. The trusses were set slightly askew, particularly that closest to the hearth wall which was parallel to it; obviously the hearth wall and chimney were constructed *after* the roof trusses were in position.

The roof was thatched with a full hip at each end, and borne on four open scarfed cruck trusses, with a scarfed cruck blade centrally placed in each hip end. The entire frame was set up before the walls were constructed; this was obvious from the way the brickwork had been worked around the trusses, the blades being concealed within the wall thickness except below the wall-heads where they emerged due to their inward and upward curve. At approximately joint level in one face of each blade there was a hole bored into the wood parallel to the long axis of the house, but not completely through the blade. These holes would have served to secure temporary struts to keep the trusses upright and rigid, together with the purlins, while the walls were constructed. Each truss was tied by means of two collars, the upper only just below the apex where the squared-off ends of the blades met to form a cradle for the ridge purlin.

Like the Knockarevan house, many of the critical features of the Rossavally house only became apparent after it was destroyed by fire. For example, only then was it possible to confirm that the cruck blades sprang from ground level. This house is the most completely cruck-framed building yet discovered in Ireland. Nevertheless all its features, together with its representation on the Ordnance Survey map of 1834, suggest it was probably constructed only at the end of the eighteenth, or possibly in the early nineteenth century. In recent decades its appearance had been severely altered with smooth cement rendering, the tin porch already noted, and insertion of metal-framed windows.

Equally undistinguished looking are the derelict remains of the third cruck house (Figs. 73, 74) referred to as Corcreeny 'B' because a scarfed-cruck house in Corcreeny townland in north-west Down, west of Waringstown and south of Lurgan, was explored in 1972.[46] Corrugated asbestos sheeting covers the roof, concealing earlier thatch, modern pebble-dash covers the front wall of the house, and windows and doors are missing. It measures about 20.7 m. by 6.3 m. externally, being continued beyond its north-west gable by a range of outbuildings providing a back wall continuous with the house totalling 41.3 m. long, but the outhouse, barn, byre, stable and cart-shed, are only 5.2 m. from front to rear. To judge from the many window openings, some

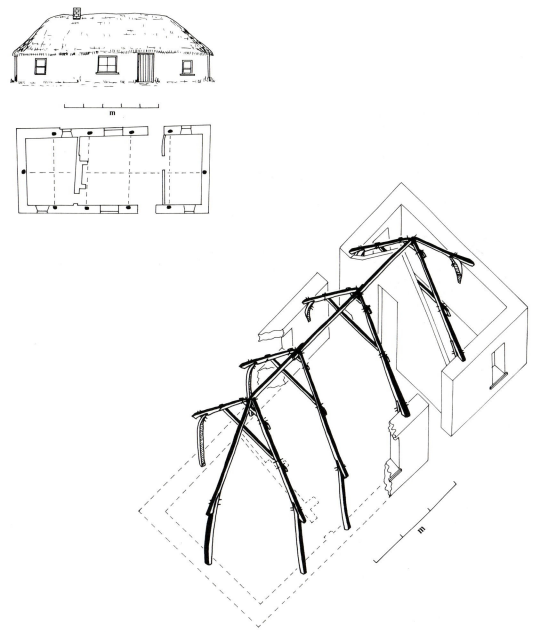

Fig. 72.   Cruck house, Rossavally Td., Co. Fermanagh.

now blocked up, the barn next the house was originally a dwelling, probably originally connecting internally with the byre which has opposite entrances. Passage through from barn to byre to stable was also provided at loft level. The roof of the outhouses is now of corrugated metal sheeting on wall-heads raised above their original height, and there was galleting evident in the mortaring of the front wall of the barn, the former dwelling portion. Clearly the whole building range had a complex developmental history which cannot now be fully interpreted; of prime consideration here is the south-eastern end which had always been a dwelling. It consisted of four units, separated from one another internally by three cruck trusses of various forms, around and within the central one of which the hearth and chimney stack was built. The north-western unit was divided longitudinally, providing a dairy at the rear, a narrow opening having been cut through the stonework of the rear wall, probably in the nineteenth century, to take the drive shaft of a horse-driven churning

Fig. 73.   Derelict cruck house 'B' with outhouses to right, Corcreeny Td., Co. Down. UFTM L 1095.18

mechanism. The same mechanism drove a threshing machine in the barn, a belt drive coming through the gable from the dairy.

Uncoursed field and quarried boulders bonded with lime mortar constitute most of the walls, but some clay walling on basal courses of stone in part of the rear wall suggests that much of the surviving stone walling may be a rebuild. Investigation of the window openings, however, showed that if this was the case, rebuilding took place early. The original openings were wider and lower than the surviving ones, providing shapes not usually encountered in vernacular houses in the north of Ireland. Almost centrally placed in the house, the kitchen hearth was screened from the front wall by a jamb wall. Tongued-and-grooved timber sheeting of nineteenth- or early twentieth-century type had been used to ceil over the entire house at wall-head height, and to sheet the internal surfaces of all walls except in the kitchen. Brick sizes showed that the kitchen chimney and hearth were constructed in the mid or late eighteenth century and that the gable stacks and flues were nineteenth-century additions. Although the roof ridge is approximately horizontal from end to end, the ground level falls away north-westwards so that at the south-east gable the wall-heads are at a height of about 2.75 m. rising to 3.15 m. at the opposite gable.

Separating the dairy end from the kitchen was a truss with one continuous and one composite blade tied by tie-beam and yoke, and originally by a collar which had been cut away to insert a door frame into the truss at loft level, supported on the tie beam. Doors had also been inserted at front and rear below the tie-beam, necessitating notching into the under sides of the blades, very deeply in the case of the rear blade which is elbowed quite high up where it had broken, unlike the almost straight front blade. The truss timbers are all oak, the broken portions of the rear blade being spliced together just above collar level. Perhaps the breaking of this blade necessitated reconstruction of the roof at the north-west end of the house, and at this time the horizontal roof ridge already mentioned was achieved by propping the ridge above the yoke, and also the purlins by means of struts, that on the rear rising vertically from a notch in the back of the cruck blade. The original apex form had the cruck blade ends rising above the yoke, probably to cradle a ridge purlin at a lower level than that recorded.

Only the front blade of the truss in the kitchen hearth wall was discovered — perhaps the rear blade was removed when the roof was reconstructed and the brick chimney stack built. The oak blade was continuous, tied at the apex by a yoke, the ridge cradled by the ends of the blades. No peg holes for tie-beam or collar-beam were seen, but one or both must have been present. Again, a door frame was notched into the underside of the cruck blade.

At the south-east end of the house the truss was of a

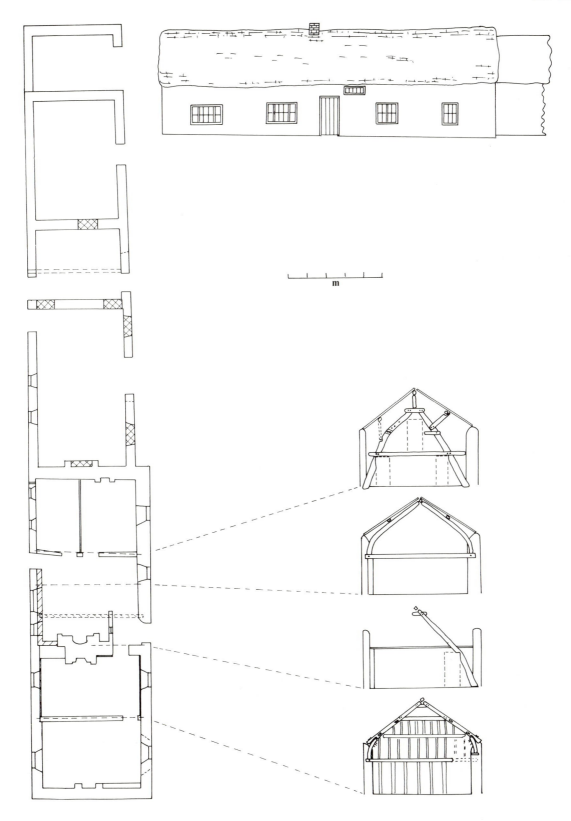

Fig. 74.   Cruck House 'B', Corcreeny Td., Co. Down.

different form. A tie-beam crossed the house, its front end having been later cut through to insert a door frame. Mortices in the ends of the beam accommodated tenons on the ends of short, curved wall-posts, the joints secured by pegs. Pegged scarfed joints secured the upper ends of the wall posts to roof blades tied by collar-beam and yoke, the latter and the ends of the blades cradling the ridge purlin. Also unlike the other trusses, which supported through purlins on their backs, this truss had tenoned ends of the purlins butted into mortices in the blades. The entire space within the truss had originally been framed in to form a partition, but it is not clear if this was originally the gable, or if there had been alternative access to the south-eastern room before the doorway already noted was cut into the partition wall involving removal of the end of the tie-beam.

Finally, a secondary cruck-like truss was added within the kitchen, consisting of continuous elbowed softwood blades pegged into and springing from a tie-beam, the blade ends cradling the ridge purlin but not secured by either collar or yoke.

Corcreeny 'B' stands on property bought in 1658 from a Captain Barrat who had earlier purchased it from Cromwellian soldiers who had obtained it in lieu of pay,[47] and from an enumeration of 1659 it is obvious that only Irish then still inhabited the townland.[48] The nature of the cruck truss with continuous blades is similar to that of trusses in nearby Waringstown which certainly were built by English settlers, and so it may be concluded that Corcreeny 'B' was also built in the second half of the seventeenth century for and possibly by an English family. However, the upper scarfed cruck truss at the south-east end, also of oak timbers, is rare in Ireland in being confirmed as such, although another possibly survives in a nearby two-storey house,[49] while the only others known are in an English house at Crookedstone, county Antrim, dating probably to 1699. It is interesting to see the later persistence of the cruck tradition, using softwood in the truss added in the kitchen perhaps as late as the nineteenth century.

Each of these three houses, Knockarevan, Rossavally and Corcreeny, included trusses with continuous or scarfed-jointed blades which sprang from the ground. A house at Allistragh, north of Armagh city, graphically illustrated the true function of such trusses as it was being demolished about 1970. A substantial portion of the rear wall had been removed, yet the scarfed cruck blade still successfully supported the roof. Obviously upper cruck trusses could not have done this, nor could an entire class of raised crucks, springing from a point between ground and wall-head levels. Like the full crucks, they had continuous or scarfed blades.

The range of roof-frame types so far encountered in the north of Ireland may now be summarised; details of most have been published elsewhere.

A. *Open Cruck Trusses with Continuous Full Blades* (Fig. 75)

Three houses are involved, for the hearth-wall truss in Corcreeny 'B' seems to have lacked a tie-beam. Similarly proportioned oak blades were used in Magherana 'A', also in the Waringstown area; this truss is interesting for the way the collar beam extends beyond the backs of the blades to carry the purlins, which support common rafters from ridge to wall-heads.[50] A third house which may belong to this group is at Turmoyra, Kinnego, north of Lurgan, a few miles from Waringstown (Fig. 76). The true status of the trusses in this house remains to be confirmed, but they appear to have continuous blades, lack a tie-beam, and spring from ground level. Magherana 'A' (Fig. 77) bears resemblances to trusses used in Waringstown which were built late in the seventeenth century, and Corcreeny 'B' seems to belong to the same century. It is likely that the Turmoyra house also belongs to this period.

B. *Open Cruck Trusses with Continuous Raised Blades* (Fig. 78)

A larger group of much less substantially constructed trusses with raised blades is concentrated in districts close to the north coast in Donegal and on Rathlin Island. All have crudely shaped members, of bog wood or various softwoods. Blades include straight, elbowed, continuously curved and ogee shapes, and they never meet at the apex, being tied by a yoke (which in the Rathlin example is bowed slightly upwards, and relatively long) and a collar-beam often set only slightly below the yoke. All these trusses determine rounded roof profiles and are usually associated with roped-thatched roofs. Measured examples spring from as low as 0.75 m. above ground level in the Rathlin example to a truss at Claggan, Moville in the Inishowen peninsula where the blades rise from heights of 1.37 m. and 1.68 m.[51] The trusses illustrated in Fig. 76 are arranged to show a typological progression, from one reported orally from Largatreany, Horn Head, in north Donegal which apparently sprang from a height of 0.6 m. in the side walls of the structure,

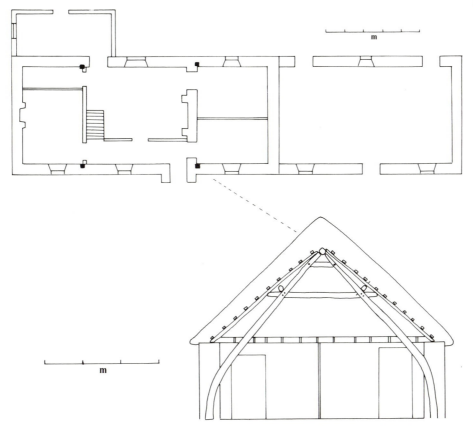

Fig. 75. Open cruck truss (no tie beam) with continuous full blades, house 'A', Magherana Td., Co. Down (after Cooper).

Fig. 76.   Lower portion of continuous cruck blade; projecting peg end below ceiling may betray concealed tie-beam. Internal corner between front wall of house and internal transverse wall indicated by pole marked in feet, Turmoyra Td., Co. Armagh. UFTM L 25.3

Fig. 77.   Apex of cruck truss wth continuous blades in house 'A', Magherana Td., Co. Down (cf. Fig. 75). UFTM L 357.10

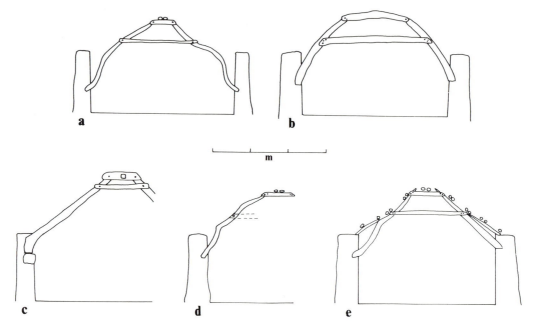

Fig. 78.   Open cruck trusses (no tie beams) with continuous raised blades.
a: Largatreany Td., Co. Donegal (from oral description, after D. McCourt);
b: Rathlin Is., Co. Antrim (after E.E. Evans);
c: Crossconnell Td., Co. Donegal (after D. McCourt);
d: Ballynahowna Td., Co. Donegal (after D. McCourt);
e: Claggan Td., Co. Donegal (after D. McCourt).

to the Claggan house noted above. A logical final stage in this progression is to include the normal 'couple' truss (collar-beam truss) used commonly in vernacular houses in northern and north-western areas from at least the mid-eighteenth century onwards. It is probable that the collar-beam truss developed as the typological progression suggests, indigenously in these areas. In most cases also, the surviving crucks are structurally anachronistic, for the stone walls from which they spring would equally have carried the later collar-beam trusses. As such, the recorded trusses are unlikely to be earlier than the late eighteenth century. Bishop Pococke saw trusses probably of this kind in 1752 in the Letterkenny area, also in north Donegal, but in view of the walling material used — sod — they may have sprung from or very close to ground level, and so represented an earliest stage in the typological series. He referred to the roof being 'fixt on wooden posts within the wall, which is not strong enough to support the roof'.[52] However, his description is ambiguous and could relate to either of the classes of scarfed open cruck trusses. An interesting penultimate degenerate stage in the development of these trusses is provided by examples noted in Tirlayden in the north Donegal Fanad peninsula, again at Scotch Garvagh and Burndennet in county Tyrone, and at Sessiagh, near Belnaleck in west Fermanagh — indeed, these and the noticing of a cruck house near Newtownstewart in 1972, of which details remain unpublished, are the sole traces of crucks and cruck-derived traditions thus far recorded in Tyrone, apart from normal collar-beam trusses. In these cases truss feet are carried on stone pads corbelled out from the inner wall faces at or just below wall-head height.[53]

In county Armagh there is a single cruck blade, in a composite truss, which was continuous but raised. It was of ash probably late in date, and stood within a cross wall in a structure now demolished, in Derrybrughas townland north of Portadown.[54]

C. *Open Cruck Trusses with Scarfed Full Blades* (Fig. 79)

This class of crucks is one of the two largest recognised in northern Irish cruck typology, with cases recorded in counties Antrim, Armagh (Fig. 80), Down, Fermanagh, Londonderry and Monaghan.[55] Examples have been illustrated already in the Rossavally house, the nature of the timber in which betrays a late date; by contrast the massive oak beams in Waringstown 'C' were put together to form cruck trusses just before 1700.

Trusses of this widespread type seem to be involved also in houses in the Myroe area in county Londonderry in 1802:

> Though of mud, the couples rest on perpendicular timbers, called couple-feet — these are of glen-oak, and are in perfect preservation. The old ones [walls] have been occasionally taken down and renewed, the roof still standing on these timbers.[56]

A similar description is on record for Ballycarry in south-east Antrim in 1839. 'The couples of the roof are supported by low wooden knees sunk in the ground within the side walls, which are of mud plastered with mortar . . .'[57] Oral traditions of scarfed cruck-like features reported from Antrim, Fermanagh and Londonderry may refer to this class of cruck, or to open raised scarfed crucks noted below.[58] A roof resting on 'oak columns

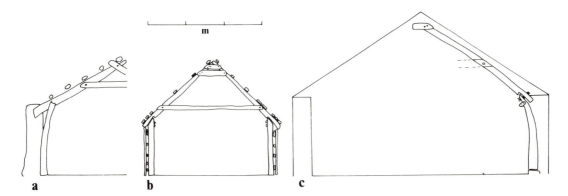

Fig. 79. Open cruck trusses (no tie beams) with scarfed blades.
a: house 'B', Duncrun Td., Co. Londonderry (after D. McCourt);
b: Derryhowlaght Td., Co. Fermanagh (after Glassie);
c: house 'B', Clare Td., Co. Down.

Fig. 80.   Roof supported by scarfed cruck blade after removal of house wall, during demolition of cruck farmhouse, Allistragh Td., Co. Armagh. UFTM L 530.10

which stand in the side walls' was reported at Derriaghy east of Lisburn in 1837,[59] but more importantly, since actual examples have not yet been reported from Cavan, an oral description from that county referring to house building states, 'Apparently, posts were put down first, and the roof put on before they began to build the walls. The posts were about eight feet or ten feet apart'.[60] These words could equally describe the Rossavally house in neighbouring Fermanagh.

D. *Open Cruck Trusses with Scarfed Raised Blades* (Fig. 81)

This other large class of crucks has representatives recorded in Antrim, Armagh, Down, Fermanagh and Londonderry.[61] Most of the blades are of relatively poor workmanship, timbers like ash being normal; all therefore seem to be of late eighteenth-century or even later origin. No oak examples are known. The trusses, like those of the open continuous raised variety, can be arranged in a typological series, from Ballyhenry East, Myroe, in Londonderry, where the scarfed blades spring from stones only 0.2 m. above ground level, to examples in Articlave springing from more than 1.2 m. up from ·ground level, and in Shanvey from even higher, both in

the same county.[62] The Gortmore, Magilligan truss is especially interesting, for it has a scarfed cruck blade on one side, and a normal straight continuous blade supported high up in the opposite wall-head. This single truss seems to support the idea of derivation of the couple or collar-beam truss through degeneration of a cruck tradition, following a change from non-load-bearing walls to mass walls, usually of stone.

E. *Tie-beam Cruck Trusses with Continuous Blades* (Fig. 82)

Four houses have been recorded with crucks that belong to this class: in Waringstown village, 'A' and 'B', Corcreeny 'B' to the west of the village, and not many miles to the east in Trummery townland, east of Moira, in county Antrim. All have or had blades of oak, and the Waringstown examples were constructed in the second half of the seventeenth century. They can be of no later than 1703, but stood in a continuous row of houses, another in which originated about 1660 and was raised by addition of an upper storey in about 1693.[63] The Trummery house, discovered in the autumn of 1981, is at least as old but may pre-date the rebellion of 1641, for a portion of a date stone from the site hints at an origin in

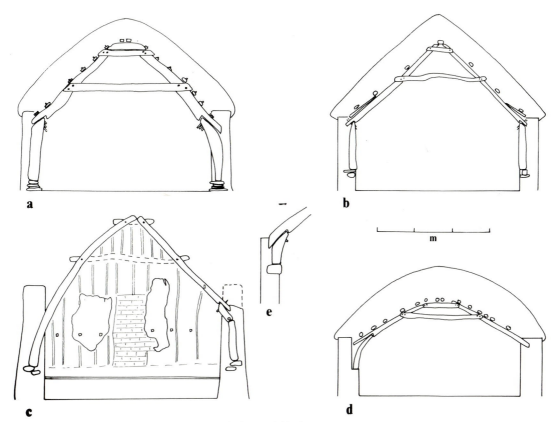

Fig. 81.   Open cruck trusses (no tie beams) with scarfed raised blades.
a: Rathfad Td., Co. Londonderry (after D. McCourt);
b: house 'A', Clare Td., Co. Down;
c: Derrybrughas Td., Co. Armagh (after E.E. Evans);
d: Gortmore Td., Co. Londonderry;
e: Shanvey Td., Co. Londonderry (after D. McCourt).

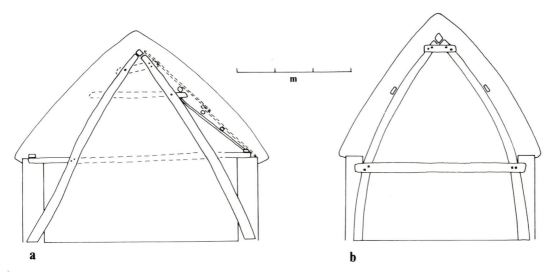

Fig. 82.   Tie-beam cruck trusses with continuous blades.
a: house 'A';
b: house 'B', Waringstown village, Co. Down.

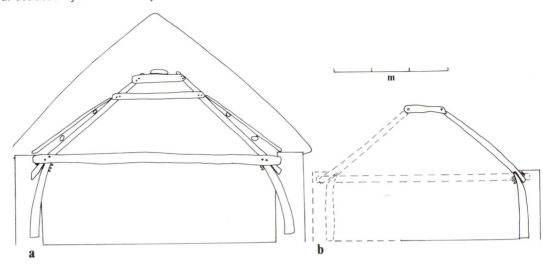

Fig. 83.   Tie-beam cruck trusses with scarfed blades.
a: Liffock Td., Co. Londonderry (after D. McCourt and Evans);
b: Pottagh Td., Co. Londonderry (after Baillie).

1629.[64] All of these trusses displayed a massiveness of construction unknown in other Irish crucks, and typologically they have many counterparts in sixteenth-century and later crucks in some parts of England; it seems certain they were built into houses by and/or for English people. An oral tradition of similar trusses was collected about a mile to the south of Waringstown village also.[65]

F. *Tie-beam Cruck Trusses with Scarfed Blades* (Fig. 83)

Four houses with scarfed tie-beam trusses have been recorded. That at Seacash in Antrim from dendrochronological evidence appears to date to the 1650s,[66] and the house at Pottagh in north Londonderry was built about 1665,[67] a date also known from dendrochronology. Truss timbers in both were of oak, but the nature of the jointing at wall-head height of the tie-beam to the blades is unknown. The two portions of each of the blades were also scarfed and pegged at about this height. Also in north Londonderry, at Liffock near Castlerock, is a house with finely carpentered oak trusses. It has a dendrochronologically determined felling date for some roof timber of 1690, corroborating a documentary date of 1691 for construction of the house.[68] The tie beams in at least two of the trusses were pegged to the cruck blades at about wall-head height, just above the pegged scarfed joints of the two parts of each of the blades. The fourth house was at Knockarevan in Fermanagh, already

described in detail — the bog timber used for its blades, rather than the native oak as used in the other three houses, suggests that the Knockarevan house may have been the last of the four to be constructed. Low-level tie-beams had been removed from some of its trusses.

G. *Upper Cruck Trusses* (Fig. 84)

The existence of two trusses of this class in Corcreeny 'B' in Down has already been described; one had scarfed blades of oak tenoned into a tie-beam, the other had continuous elbowed softwood blades similarly connected and springing from a tie-beam, but not linked in any way at any higher level. The latter is obviously a late degenerate form. The other presumed example is in the two-storey house, Magherana 'B', west of Waringstown village, but because the truss is concealed behind wall surfaces and ceilings, its true nature cannot be determined; particularly there is some doubt whether it springs from a tie beam or not. However, it certainly appears to relate only to the upper storey of the house and to have jointed blades, and like the jointed upper crucks in Corcreeny 'B' (Fig. 85), butt purlins rather than through purlins seem to be involved.[69]

A fine, well-preserved two-storey thatched house in Crookedstone townland, near Belfast Airport in county Antrim, has three impressive upper-cruck oak trusses carrying through purlins. Its 1699 date-stone may relate to an enlargement of an earlier house on the site, to judge from the family history involved, but the upper crucks

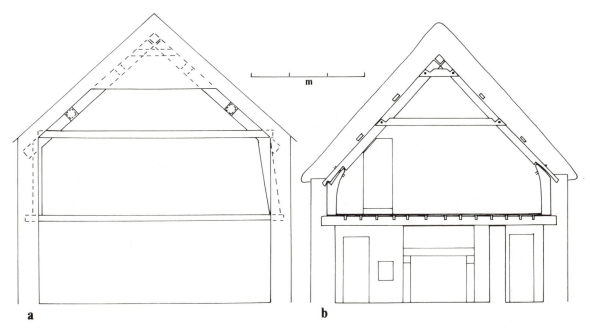

Fig. 84. Upper cruck trusses.
a: house 'B', Magherana Td., Co. Down;
b: Crookedstone Td., Co. Antrim (after unpublished survey by P. Robinson).

Fig. 85. Doorway (at right) cut through tie-beam from which springs scarfed upper cruck truss, house 'B', Corcreeny Td., Co. Down. UFTM L 1115.1

G

would date to this alteration at the latest. The house plan and the trusses point to English vernacular architectural influences, yet enigmatically, the family connections of the house are with Ayrshire in Scotland in the early seventeenth century. The Crookedstone house roof contains a feature so far discovered elsewhere only in the late seventeenth-century two-storey thatched house at Horsepark, to the west of Lisburn further south in county Antrim. Light diagonal braces were pegged on to the backs of the truss blades and to the purlin backs below. They served to keep the trusses and purlins in correct position while construction work proceeded. Similar light braces were included in at least two of the bays of the cruck house at Liffock, county Londonderry, but rising from the backs of the truss blades to the ridge purlin halfway between adjacent trusses.

As a whole, evidence for crucks in northern Ireland progresses from use of oak to use of bogwood and softwoods, and suggests that the distinction between continuous and scarfed blades may not be very important in Ireland, possibly relating more to availability of suitable timber than to distinctions of carpentry tradition. The same may be said of the distinction between full and raised trusses. Derivation of collar-beam, and indeed tie-beam trusses, from cruck origins has also been suggested on the basis of evidence in Britain and in western France. Almost certainly this development evolved independently in each country, associated with changes towards use of mass materials in walling, particularly stonework, perhaps influenced also by the problem of declining timber resources in Ireland at least.

Two houses, one outside Derry city, the other in east county Londonderry, had collar-beam trusses of normal type for their areas, although in the case of the former, at Shantallow, the collars had been removed from the trusses. But both at Shantallow[70] and at Lislea the truss blades had been scarfed and provided with peg holes to secure joints to earlier wall members of scarfed cruck blades. These houses with reused portions of scarfed cruck blades support the idea of precedence of cruck traditions in areas later dominated by collar-beam trussed roofs.

A number of examples call for particular comment. The scarfed full crucks of the Liffock house are historically intriguing. There is little doubt of an English ancestry for the house, yet associated with regions in England where scarfed crucks are unrecorded. Built about 1691, oak substantial enough for continuous blades could still have been easily acquired, albeit rather further away in the south of the county than would have been the case half a century earlier. The good standard of carpentry in the

Liffock crucks argues for competent craftsmen, but were they influenced by already existing traditions of scarfed crucks elsewhere in the north of Ireland? The Derrybrughas truss in county Armagh with members of ash is obviously late but, having one continuous raised blade and one jointed raised blade, it supports the idea that so long as a blade fulfilled its function, its jointed or continuous status was unimportant. The Knockarevan hip-end truss shows that the presence of a tie beam served no real purpose; its removal did not affect the stability of the roof at that end of the house. The Pottagh truss in north Londonderry showed the same thing. Lastly it should be noted that the cruck frame is not inconsistent with a hipped roof form; Knockarevan had a tie-beam scarfed truss closest to its hip end, hip cruck blades were discovered in other Fermanagh examples at Sessiagh East (an outhouse) and Corry (a dwelling), and of course the most convincing evidence for the compatibility of hipped roof and crucks is provided by the Rossavally house. The cruck survival in the Ballinderry 'A' house in county Antrim, too, is in a hip-roof house, one of the few survivals of this roof form outside Fermanagh and Cavan.

Obviously hip cruck blades could only survive where hip roofs remained, especially concentrated in south-west Fermanagh; perhaps they may be discovered also in Cavan. However, given that native housing about 1600 seems to have had a hip roof in most of the north of Ireland, and that the 'couples' with which this housing was roofed may well have been crucks, hip-end cruck blades may formerly have been much more common.

H. *Collar-Beam Trusses* (Fig. 86)

Crucks of the different kinds described are relict features, mostly surviving in technically anachronistic circumstances. Their place was taken in northern Irish vernacular building by couple trusses, most commonly in the form of frames lacking tie beams at wall-head height. Usually straight, sloping continuous blades spring from the wall-heads, or especially in Donegal and west Tyrone from within the wall-heads. They are tied by a collar beam, occasionally by two, the ends of which may project beyond the blade backs to seat side purlins.

The apex of the truss is commonly formed in one of four ways. In the north and west, a more or less extended yoke is scarfed and pegged to the upper ends of the blades (Fig. 87): if short, it supports only the ridge purlin, and a reasonably sharp roof ridge can be achieved. A longer yoke may carry the ridge purlin, and a side purlin at each of its ends, achieving a rounded roof profile

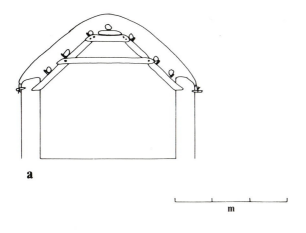
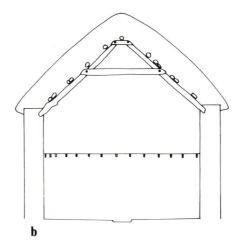

Fig. 86. Collar-beam roof trusses.
a: byre-dwelling, Co. Donegal (after Evans);
b: dwelling with bedroom over byre, Cruckaclady Td., Co. Tyrone.

Fig. 87. Driftwood collar-beam trusses, with blades tied at apex by short yokes, pegged joints, in derelict byre-dwelling, Magheragallan Td., Co. Donegal, now reconstructed at UFTM. UFTM L 818.8

Fig. 88. Collar-beam truss with blades cradling ridge purlin at apex, in bedroom of house with byre under bedroom, Cruckaclady Td., Co. Tyrone, now reconstructed at UFTM. UFTM L 620.7

commonly associated with roped thatch in coastal areas. In eastern and southern parts of the north of Ireland the yoke is short, the ends of the blades projecting above it to clasp the ridge purlin resting on the yoke (Fig. 88). Central, southern and south-western districts have a similar apex form, varying only in that the yoke is dropped to a position where it no longer supports the ridge purlin. Lastly, a minority of roofs in all districts, except apparently Donegal, had an apex cradle to carry the ridge purlin, formed simply by overlapping the ends of the blades in a scarfed and pegged joint. All of these apex forms are common to all classes of roof trusses, collar-beam, tie-beam, and cruck. All, too, display the same straightforward carpentry techniques of scarfed and pegged joints, mortices and tenons being rare. All roofs are of the through-purlin type, that is the trusses support longitudinal ridge and side purlins on their backs. Usually purlins span single bays, those of adjacent bays overlapping on the back of the truss separating them. A few examples of early oak-timbered roofs have been discovered where the purlins are in continuous runs from end to end of the house, consisting of lap-jointed pieces pegged together. An example on what seems to have been a tie-beam trussed roof was discovered at Derriaghy, near Lisburn in south Antrim, and others survive in the roof of the late seventeenth-century two-storey house at Horsepark, west of Lisburn.

I. *Tie-beam Trusses*

A tie beam spans a building, its ends resting on or built into its side walls. Truss blades rise from the ends of the tie beam, to which they are usually pegged. Sometimes the truss was braced by a collar beam placed some distance below the apex of the truss. The commonest apex form has the truss blades crossed to form a cradle for the ridge purlin. In one case near Waringstown a tie-beam truss was supported on upright posts placed close to the inner faces of the side walls.[71] Almost as few examples of tie-beam trusses have been discovered as of tie-beam crucks, and the fact that they have been located in the same areas in south Antrim, north-west Down, north Armagh, and south-west Fermanagh perhaps indicates derivation of the former from the latter.

J. *Purlin Roofs* (Fig. 89)

A unique method of roofing a house, with longitudinal heavy purlins with their ends bedded in gables and internal partition wall, without the interposing of any

transverse beams, was widespread in much of the Bann and Lough Neagh lowlands, extending south-westwards along the Clogher valley into east Fermanagh and southwards into Monaghan. Such roofs were often on mud-walled houses. The purlins bore much of the weight and thrust of the roof, which was then concentrated into downward forces where the purlin ends were carried in transverse walls, and downward compressive forces are most suitable in mud walls once they have dried out. However, some stone-walled houses had purlin roofs.

Various suggestions as to the origins of this roof form, unknown elsewhere in Ireland, have been advanced: that it derives ultimately from Scandinavian antecedents,[72] or that it developed from English box-frame carpentry traditions,[73] or that it arose in response to a need for a roof space unencumbered by tie beams and collar beams to accommodate the height of linen looms after damask weaving was introduced in the early nineteenth century.[74] Plain-linen looms are about 2 m. high, but addition of the jacquard machine on top to achieve the woven pattern in double damask increased the height substantially. In a weaving shop with up to four damask looms a clear roof space was obviously an advantage. However, while the purlin roof was found in the damask-weaving districts, it was also used beyond them, and in individual buildings its use was not confined to the weaving shops but extended throughout kitchens and bedrooms also, whether these apartments had looms in them or not.

All purlin roofs in vernacular houses so far examined are clearly not early, and are usually ascribable to the late eighteenth century or later. The purlins invariably consist either of bogwood or of imported, squared softwood. A purlin roof of native 'green' oak has yet to be reported. Whether or not the need for absence of cross members in damask-weaving areas was an additional factor, the purlin roof seems most logically to relate to two things. The transition from early traditions of houses without load-bearing walls, to those with mass walls, meant that the gables and internal walls could now take on the function of roof trusses; they quite literally served as stone or mud 'couples'. Bays now became defined in terms of separation by walls and not roof frames. Associated with this, by the middle of the eighteenth century poverty of timber resources made the emergence of the purlin roof almost inevitable, for it minimised the amount of heavy timbers required to roof a house. Especially where longer purlins were used, problems were caused by the weight that gradually built up on a roof due to regular re-thatching; later, purlin roofs commonly had various kinds of props and supports rising either from the ground or from inserted secondary tie beams.

Fig. 89. Purlin-supported roofs.
a: Derryinver Td., Co. Armagh (after Evans);
b: Derrytresk Td., Co. Tyrone (after McCourt).

In a small area on the north bank of the Arney River in west Fermanagh, evidence gathered in the 1970s from local informants suggests a sequence of roof-framing techniques. Many of the changes of roofing and wall construction involved were late, towards the end of the nineteenth century or even later, but they mirror changes elsewhere in northern Ireland at earlier times. Jointed open cruck trusses, locally called 'building on knees', were once usual, and evidence more widely in west Fermanagh quoted in this book attests this. The collar-beam truss, carried on load-bearing mass walls often built of brick, superseded the cruck, in a few cases with vestigial cruck corbels retained. Growing familiarity with the structural potentialities of mass materials like brick brought the discovery that internal partition walls could suitably replace roof trusses altogether, leaving a purlin-supported roof. In areas like the Ballymenone district north of the Arney River, where brick was locally made and widely pressed into vernacular use late in the nineteenth century, imperfect knowledge of brick bonding and use of collar-beam rather than tie-beam trusses both contributed to house walls tending to bulge outwards as roof weights increased with continual re-thatching. Thus there was a local need to develop the building on internal walls to serve in place of roof trusses.[75]

This kind of sequence has been suggested in other areas. Local circumstances may always have produced an initiative to develop solutions as in Ballymenone; on the other hand, they took place within a broader context of change in building technology, and a heavy reliance on modern local oral testimony, as in the case of the west Fermanagh study, may underplay the possibility that what are presented as indigenous solutions to technological problems are, in fact, the application of more generally known solutions, present and having been seen elsewhere by local people, and applied in their own districts when social and economic circumstances were appropriate.

K. *Other Roof Systems* (Fig. 90)

Individual cases of other roof forms have occasionally been reported. Some, like the post-supported tie-beam truss already noted near Waringstown, may be isolated examples of true roof-truss forms in their own right, perhaps imported from Britain in the seventeenth century. A cruck-like truss reported at Maghery in north Armagh is more difficult to explain. Raised wall posts supported horizontal spurs sticking out of the side walls, which in turn carried a collar-beam truss with blades crossed at the apex. Details of the joints between wall posts, spurs and blade ends are not available. The spurs seem not to have been the remains of a cut-out tie-beam. It is impossible to classify this roof frame, it is so unlike any others seen in Ireland or elsewhere. Another cruck-like feature was observed in a house in Drumbargy townland in west Fermanagh where, in a brick-walled house, the blade ends of a roof truss were carried on keyed-in brick buttresses on the insides of front and rear walls, rather like brick substitutes for timber wall posts in scarfed crucks; they might be thought of as cruck corbels carried down to ground level.

Other forms are best seen as attempts to put right, or to prevent, faults developing in crudely constructed truss forms already described. Some involving posts underpinning truss blades may be distinguished from

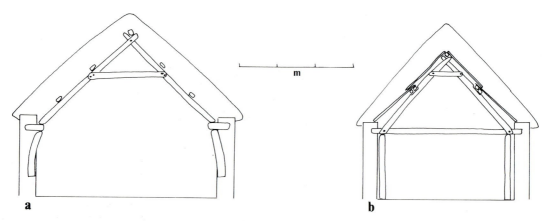

Fig. 90. Other roof-support systems.
a: Maghery Td., Co. Armagh (after Evans);
b: Tullyheron Td., Co. Down.

crucks because of the unscarfed and unpegged joints involved, if not because of the obviously secondary nature of the posts themselves. Other props, for example underneath collars and purlins, are obviously not original, and the nature of the re-used cruck truss in the Corcreeny 'B' house described earlier should be borne in mind here, with its secondary ridge and purlin props springing from the back of the truss.

Trussed roofs were overlain by longitudinal purlins, including the ridge. Depending on the nature of the available timber, there might be as few as two or three runs of purlins on each side of the roof, but where poor, insubstantial timber was the only wood available, there might be six or eight. The ubiquitous word throughout most of Ulster for these timbers is the dialect form 'purloin', but especially where a large number of lighter purlins were used, they were formerly known as 'ribberies' in some places. Such ribberies were often overlain only by light brushwood, indeed occasionally by nothing at all, to provide the base on which the underthatch was placed. On better roofs with fewer heavier purlins, closely spaced timbers overlap the purlins, parallel to the trusses underneath Occasionally these were continuous common rafters rising from wall-head to ridge, but shorter lengths overlapped on the back of a purlin half-way up the roof slope were common. These timbers often consisted of riven bogwood, or earlier of oak, but many late eighteenth- and nineteenth-century roofs made use of unbarked branches. Usually this framework sufficed to take the underthatch, but sometimes a top layer of brushwood was added. Untrussed purlin roofs were finished off in much the same manner as roofs with trusses.

Purlins on late roofs often simply lay on the underlying trusses or were tied to them with twisted straw or bog-fir ropes. Older roofs sometimes had the purlins pegged to the backs of the trusses, or pegs or blocks attached to the backs of the blades acted as stops against and above which the purlins rested. Only occasionally have notches or trenching been discovered in the backs of truss blades to provide purlin seatings.

L. *Framing of Slated Roofs*

The earliest slated roofs at vernacular level were based upon adaptations of timbering systems intended to bear the usual sod underthatch and straw covering. Such roofs are rarely encountered, and it seems that together with the spread of slates went a fairly standardised roof-timbering system derived in the first instance probably from current practice in town-house building in the north of Ireland, but descended ultimately perhaps from common-rafter trussed roofs in England. At first, the regularly spaced horizontal lathing needed for hanging slates was borne on common-rafter trusses with collars, or simply on common rafters alone, carried on a single purlin on each side of the roof. Usually these purlins were of imported softwood, but sometimes an unhewn softwood tree trunk, or long straight branch, or occasionally even lengths of bogwood are seen. Later roofs sometimes omitted purlins, common-rafter trusses at about 0.3 m. to 0.4 m. centres being sufficient to bear the slating laths. The rarity with which collar-beam or tie-beam trusses are seen in slated roofs suggests that introduction of slating and the development of the purlin

Fig. 91.   House with sod-covered roof, Gweedore, Co. Donegal, *c*.1880s. UFTM L 440.19

roof may have been at least contemporaneous if not related events. The apex of a vernacular slated roof is always achieved without the presence of a substantial ridge purlin, indicating that the origins of slated roof-timbering systems in the north of Ireland do not proceed from through-purlin systems of roof carpentry. Add to this the common presence of timber wall plates on the wall-heads, to which the ends of the common rafters are fixed, and a non-indigenous origin seems certain, for wall plates are found only on northern Irish vernacular houses known to be of English origin.

Roof Covering
A. *Scraws*

Throughout the north of Ireland, a layer of thin tough sods lies on the framework of roof timbers to serve as an underthatch. Many thatchers in recent times have claimed this was technically necessary to provide a bed into which the wooden pins (scollops) were driven to keep the thatch material in place; but a layer of sods was always used also where the thatch was held in place by an external network of ropes (Fig. 92). The scraws were cut in lengths about 0.6 m. wide, long enough to overlap at the roof ridge, or shorter ones were used which overlapped also halfway up the roof slopes.

Occasionally, also, some houses have been observed where the scraws consisted of large rectangular overlapping 'tiles' about 0.6 m. by 0.75 m. or 0.8 m. Scraws were laid so that they overlapped at both top and bottom ends, and also at both sides, and they were often tied to the underlying timbers with twisted straw or bog-wood ropes. They were commonly laid with their vegetation sides uppermost, but not invariably so.

Occasionally other forms of underthatch have been reported, most significantly in the early English-settled barony of Lecale in south-east Down, where use of a prepared underthatch of straw ropes[76] and a woven straw mat[77] have both been reported. Possibly another alternative is recorded in a report of a house in north-east Londonderry demolished in about 1745, of which 'The entire roof was lined beneath the thatch with oak basketwork'.[78] I have only once seen an alternative underthatch, on the roof of a farm outbuilding near the Armagh/Louth border. A layer of straw was tied to the roof timbers with straw ropes, and the outer layers of bundles of thatch were simply thrust direct into this, without added pinning with scollops.

In view of the fact that alternative forms of underthatch were known, albeit rarely in the north of Ireland, the thatchers' argument for the technical need for the presence of an underthatch of scraws does not convince. It is best to regard it as evidence of an old tradition of the

Fig. 92.   Scraw underthatch on rope-thatch cottier's dwelling, after removal of thatch, Duncrun Td., Co. Londonderry, before removal and reconstruction at UFTM. UFTM L 38.7

regular use of sod as a building material, an older form of sod-covered roof surviving as it were underneath a later one of thatch. Sod is reported as the sole covering of houses of the poor in various districts in the 1830s, and a few such houses survived long enough to be photographed at the end of the century (Fig. 91). Two were in Gweedore in north-west Donegal. Sods constituted the walling at an end in one, and the roofing scraws were here and there weighted down with stones. Smoke issuing from the door betrayed the absence of both chimney and smoke hole. The other was probably a combined dwelling and byre (Fig. 91), the living end roofed with thatch, the smaller byre end only by strips of sod running from the wall-head across the roof ridge. We have already seen, in an earlier chapter dealing with wattle-work, that about 1615 in the Moneymore area of south Londonderry an account was paid by the Drapers' company for construction of a 'grett cabbyne' covered with sod, absence of reference to a further coat of thatch implying that the sod was the sole roof covering.

B. *Thatch*

Vegetable roof covering was ubiquitous throughout the north of Ireland from the early seventeenth century until late in the nineteenth in some areas, and even into the present century in others. Nor was its use confined to middle and lower social levels. Kilclief Castle in east Down in 1744 was roofed with thatch,[79] and twenty years earlier 'all the houses in one of the principal streets [in Belfast] are thatched with straw'.[80] Thatch was the normal roof covering in towns as well as in rural areas; Bangor in north Down in 1752 consisted of about 200 houses, all thatched, despite the presence of a slate quarry nearby.[81] Downpatrick in 1708 contained 136 dwellings, of which only four were slated and one tiled;[82] at the end of the eighteenth century three-quarters of the houses in the town were still thatched.[83] Between 1835 and 1840 a sample of towns across Ulster shows that circumstances had changed little; percentages of thatched dwellings were as follows: Ballynure in Antrim and Keady in Armagh, 56% and 57% respectively, Gilford in west Down 70%, Trillick in south Tyrone 68%, and Dromore further west in the same county 74%. The influence of a landlord in improving conditions was obvious in Glasslough in Monaghan, where only 35% of the houses were still thatched.[84] Apart from Glasslough, these figures display a slight progressive westwards increase. Presence of slate quarries nearby and progressive attitudes on the Londonderry family's estate were responsible for the very low percentages of thatched houses, 2.7% and 1.6% respectively, in the north Down towns of Comber and Newtownards in 1848; but at the same time on this estate 75% of all the rural houses were still thatched,[85] and this was the common experience throughout rural districts;

evidence on this point from Collis's surveys (Table 6) of estates across the north of Ireland in the 1840s is unequivocal.[86]

TABLE 6.   PERCENTAGES OF TOTAL RURAL HOUSES BY ROOF COVERING IN 1840s

Estate	Thatched	Slated	Total Rural Houses
North Down	75.1	24.9	1863
Lecale, Down	95.8	4.2	118
Charlemont, Armagh	98.4	1.6	378
Killylea-Keady, Armagh	88.2	11.8	2122
Rosslea, Fermanagh	97.1	2.9	828
Bundoran, Donegal	99.0	1.0	294
Ballintra, Donegal	90.2	9.8	1530
Kilmacrenan, Donegal	97.8	2.2	1336

Alongside this documentation of numbers of thatched houses, there is much more which records merely the presence of thatch, for example in the Ordnance Survey memoirs and in the evidence given before the poor inquiry in the 1830s. By contrast, almost none of the historical documentation records details of thatching techniques and their regional distributions, and there is surprisingly little reference even to the different vegetable materials used as thatch. Specialist craftsmen thatchers are barely attested, and until within the present century it is likely that such as there were plied their craft mainly in the towns, for ability to patch and rethatch a roof was widespread in rural districts. Major work may well have been undertaken on a co-operative neighbourly basis; oral traditions of this have been collected in Donegal.[87] Need for occasional patching was naturally attended to, usually sooner than later, since along with the necessary skills, materials were always to hand. The contrast with the circumstances of today could not be more marked. Only a couple of thatchers remain to work throughout east Ulster, and suitable materials are scarce and extremely expensive when they can be found.

If historical documentation of thatch materials and techniques is poor, there was thorough postal questionnaire-based study of this topic for Ireland as a whole in the 1940s,[88] and extensive field study of surviving thatch in northern areas in the 1950s.[89] Continued field study has modified some of the conclusions of the latter, particularly so far as distributions of the various techniques are concerned.

Choice of thatch material aimed towards durability and was fundamentally influenced by what was environmentally available locally. Available materials often changed over time as economic factors altered one crop's position relative to another. The durability of any thatched roof depended on many things. Aspect,

exposure to moisture-laden winds, shelter, quality of thatching technique, and pitch of the roof were all important. So at the local level there was wide divergence of view as to what was suitable, individuals often arguing merely for whatever happened to be currently in use in their district.

Wheat straw was widely preferred and survives as the most commonly sought-after thatch. It has become very scarce, however, for modern strains of wheat with short straw developed for combine harvesting are unsuitable. A few farmers, for example near Moira and to the west of Strangford Lough, still grow wheat of the older strains and harvest it by older techniques specially for thatching. So the former pattern of availability of wheat straw as a by-product of normal agricultural activity has gone. Wheat straw has long been used in south-east Down, which in the early and mid-nineteenth century was an important grain production area, exporting wheat; wheat straw thatch was applied in Lecale in the 1830s even to the dwellings of the poor.[90] It was popular because of its fairly constant quality and its clean straw, therefore requiring less preparation than other material. *Oat straw*, by contrast, was a poor material, rather soft, and apparently avoided where possible for house thatching, though sometimes used on farm buildings, although in west Fermanagh it was reckoned to provide a bright, attractive-looking roof.[91]

Rye straw was preferred in a number of places. It has been recorded on roofs around the southern margins of Lough Neagh, and was, and still is, grown in parts of Fermanagh specifically for thatch. *Barley straw* was rarely used, although together with oat straw it was noted in the barony of Dungannon in east Tyrone in 1802.[92]

Reeds from Lough Neagh were used in areas close to the lake shores, especially in south-east Antrim. In north Armagh about The Birches the reeds which grew in profusion in Ballybeg townland near Washing Bay and on Scaddy Island in Lough Neagh were treated almost like wheat or corn, as a crop to be harvested and sold to those requiring it for their roofs.[93] Similar reeds were used in the Carrigallen area of county Leitrim,[94] but it is puzzling why they were not similarly used in parts of south Fermanagh where they grew in Upper Lough Erne, thatched house owners preferring to grow rye for their roofs. The same reeds were used widely in England for thatching, and it is difficult to explain why they were not more extensively used in Ireland — moister climate, lower roof pitch and a different thatching technique may have been contributory factors.

Rushes (juncus species) cut from ill-drained land were used widely, for example in Fermanagh, south Armagh, marginal hill areas in general, and also in the Bann valley.

Fig. 93.   Scollop thatching. Completed new coat at right; spars in progress, centre left; old thatch coat, centre and centre right; scraw underthatch at right. Note scollops exposed at ridge only, and concealed by overlying thatch.

Commonly used for thatching hay, corn and turf (peat) stacks, and on farm outbuildings, it was most widely used on houses as a fall-back material in times of shortage of the better straws. It rotted quickly and needed constant attention. Rushes and mountain grass were used in inland parts of Gweedore, and rushes used for thatch were regarded in the Randalstown area of Antrim as a sign of 'ill doing' or extreme poverty.[95] *Heather* was only occasionally used on dwellings in recent times, for example as a bottom 'filler' layer of thatch showing sometimes at the eaves on some north-west Donegal houses, to be covered by 'bent' grass. The only consistent former use made of it for roofing was for thatching some churches in the eighteenth century.

In coastal districts where supplies could be had from local sandhills, *marram grass* ('bent') was used for thatching, for example near Kilkeel in south Down.[96] In the Magilligan district of north Londonderry where it was pulled, it was laid on the roof in bundles roots uppermost, but in west Donegal where it was cut just above the roots, the cut ends were placed downwards to prevent rain draining into the hollow centres of the straws and so rotting them. Bent is not a long-lasting material. Roofs thatched with it require attention at least every two or three years, and where used it was always secured on the roof by a network of ropes, formerly twisted of the same

material. Its use is not a late expedient as other materials became difficult to obtain. In 1752 Bishop Pococke recorded roped bent thatching in parts of north county Donegal.[97]

A widely used material for thatching in the north of Ireland was *flax*, although to what extent this could be said of the seventeenth and eighteenth centuries is unknown. Its use has been noted in most Ulster counties, but especially in northern districts from north Antrim in the east to Inishowen in north Donegal in the west. Indeed in Inishowen and elsewhere in Donegal many farmers grew, and some still grow, a small plot of flax solely for thatching. Flax was widely believed to provide the longest-lasting roof, fifteen to twenty years being frequently quoted as its life; seven to twelve years was commonly claimed for wheat, and shorter periods for the other materials.

Substitute materials have been widely reported in use in times of want and on the dwellings of the very poor: bracken, potato haulms, even hay. A cottier house dismantled in the early 1960s in the Magilligan area had a thickness of almost 1.25 m. of thatch on its ridge, tapering to 0.3 m. to 0.5 m. at the eaves — at various levels oat and rye straw, bracken fronds, flax waste from a flax mill, rushes and bent had been used, the last being the most recent material, but used also at other levels.[98]

Fig. 94. Re-thatching farmhouse roof with rushes. The thatcher is working part-way up a spar, to right of the ladder. On completed roof, note exposed scollops only at ridge and eave, Eshywulligan Td., Co.Fermanagh. UFTM L 324.17

Fig. 95. Scollop-thatch roof, without added scollops above eave level, Drumsillagh Td., Co. Fermanagh. UFTM L 986.5

Fig. 96.   Scollop-thatch roof, with a new spar patched in below the chimney stack, Edentiroory Td., Co. Down. UFTM L 969.19

Fig. 97.   Detail of additional decorative scolloping above eaves, Dergalt Td., Co. Tyrone. UFTM L 322.21

Fig. 98.   Heavily patched thatch with scollops exposed over most of roof surface, Ards peninsula, Co. Down, early 20th century. UFTM WAG 292

Whatever the material, it required some preparation before being taken onto the roof. It was 'drawn' by hand to remove the smallest straws and any grain or seeds remaining in the heads. Bundles of approximately uniform size were made up, and sometimes grain straw was treated at this stage with powdered copper sulphate which acted as a preservative. 'Bluestone' also inhibited the activities of insects upon which birds would feed and thereby, seeking the insects, pull holes in the roof. Application of the bluestone was usually done on a damp day after thatching was completed, and repeated at regular intervals, preferably annually.

No less than five thatching techniques were used in the north of Ireland, but only one was very widespread. *Scollop (or pinned) thatch* takes its name from the use of scollops, or 'scobes' in county Down, to secure each bundle of straw in place on the roof (Fig. 93). A widespread thatching technique in many parts of Ireland, it was also used in some districts alongside other methods, examples having been seen on Rathlin Island where roped thatch was usual.[99] The thatcher worked in 'spars', the width of each of which could conveniently be reached from his ladder (Fig. 94), usually two bundles of straw wide. Starting at eave level, the straw was laid cut

end downwards, the upper end of the bundle being secured with a scollop bent 'staple'-like across it, secured with one or more scollops twisted into a hairpin shape and drawn down across the first into the underlying straw and scraw. Subsequent bundles of straw placed on the roof above concealed the scollops of the bundles below, so that it was only at the ridge that the scollops of necessity were exposed on the roof surface (Fig. 95). A spar completed, the ladder was moved to work on the adjacent one, so that the thatcher gradually worked from one end of the roof to the other. The ridge was completed by overlapping it with bundles of straw, scolloped in place. A decorative finish of a row of bobbins was sometimes added at the ridge; in parts of Cavan this was achieved by working the bobbins into a woven straw mat, prepared on the ground, and then fixed to the ridge.[100]

The surfaces of the finished roof were trimmed using a sharp knife, often a portion of an old scythe blade hafted into a piece of wood, which was used also to prepare the scollops and to trim the eaves, though even sheep-shears were used for this. Other thatchers' tools were a hand-leather or mallet to drive the scollops, a rake made of some large nails in a piece of wood to smooth the thatch

Fig. 99.   Cluster of rope-thatch houses, some with bed outshots, Dunargus Head, Co. Donegal, early 20th century. UFTM WAG 2395

and remove loose straws, known in the Cullybackey area of west Antrim as a 'spaldrick',[101] a long thatching needle sometimes used with straw rope to tie down the first layer of straw through the scraws to the roof timbers below, and a 'spurtle' or thatching fork for thrusting bundles of straw into a worn roof when patching it. Inevitably, scollops securing such patching remained exposed on the roof surface (Fig. 98), and a heavily patched roof was often almost completely covered with exposed scollops. It could be difficult to distinguish visually between a heavily patched roof and one where an inferior technique was used which left all the scollops exposed. Exposed-scollop thatch may have been fairly widespread towards the end of the nineteenth century, to judge from photographic evidence, for example in east Down. At Garrison in west Fermanagh a scollop exposed on the roof surface was called a 'stretcher', and it was held in place by hairpin-shaped 'keepers' driven over it into the thatch below.[102]

The commonest scollops used were of osier (willow), but other suitably pliable woods were used, like briar, hazel, snowberry and occasionally split bog-deal. In an area in south-east Antrim wire scollops were used, at least since early in the present century; the wire was that

cut away from bales of material brought to mills in Larne for paper-making.

Roped thatch was the second most widespread type in the north of Ireland, found in recent times in the coastlands of west and north Donegal (Figs. 99, 100), in the Magilligan area in north county Londonderry, and on Rathlin Island further east (Fig. 101). Its distribution was formerly more widespread. I discovered a ruined house at Stoneybatter near Cushendun in the Glens of Antrim in the 1960s which had animal bones projecting at eaves level to which thatch ropes were tied, and some miles further south, near Cushendall in Coshkib townland, a house to which in the early 1900s upper bedrooms were added, now at the Ulster Folk and Transport Museum, originated in the 1850s as a one-storey, two-roomed farmhouse with roped thatch. Photographic evidence of about 1900 shows that roped thatch existed then near Cushendall,[103] and at Bushmills and Portstewart on the north Antrim coast (cf. Fig. 102);[104] a sketch of Quintin Castle in the Ards Peninsula in east Down in the 1840s shows roped thatch there;[105] photographs taken around 1900[106] and also more than a decade later[107] illustrate roped thatch in south Down (Fig. 103), where Professor Evans also described it in his classic study, *Mourne*

Fig. 100.   Rope-thatch one-room farmhouse and outhouses (note differences in roping technique), Rosguill, Co. Donegal, early 20th century. UFTM WAG 2590

Fig. 101.   Rope-thatch houses with ridge coping of sods. Note whitewash around windows only, Rathlin Is., Co. Antrim, *c.*1900. UM WO1/83/5

Fig. 102.   Rope-thatch houses near Giant's Causeway, Co. Antrim, *c*.1900. UM WO1/47/5

Fig. 103.   Rope-thatch houses at Annalong, Co. Down, early 20th century. UFTM WAG 1796

Fig. 104. Pegged thatch. A lath placed on the thatch above the eaves prevents some added transverse wires cutting back into the thatch above the wall head, Bushfoot, Co. Antrim. UFTM L 893.0

Country,[108] although no examples survive today; half a dozen roped-thatch houses existed until the 1950s in east Lecale also.[109] Roped thatch is historically authenticated in the Donegal parishes of Clondavaddog, Clonmany, Desertagney, Mevagh and Mintiaghs in the Ordnance Survey memoirs of the 1830s, and Bishop Pococke saw it in the parish of Ray in 1752.[110]

Roped thatch from Inishowen eastwards usually involved a close grid of ropes spaced about 15 cm. to 25 cm. apart, both horizontally and vertically, the ends of the ropes tied to pegs in the wall-heads and gables. In north-west Donegal and down the west coast of that county, few horizontal ropes were used, and while the rope ends most recently have been tied to pegs in the wall-heads (often stone pegs), formerly stones were tied to the ends of the ropes, a technique reported in the 1930s on the roofs of summer-pasture dwellings in the Errigal Mountain district, where the ropes were of twisted fibres of bog-wood, spaced about 50 cm. apart, keeping heather thatch in place.[111] In more recent times the ropes used were an imported sisal two-ply cord, widely known as 'Hairy Ned', but the older tradition was to twist ropes of the thatch material, although longer-lasting ropes of

twisted bog-wood fibres were sometimes used in north Londonderry and parts of county Donegal.[112] With the thatch material placed fairly loosely on the roof, a particular problem with roped thatch was to avoid the ropes cutting into the roof at ridge and eaves. This could be countered at the eaves (cf. Fig. 104) by introducing osiers or laths placed on the thatched surface over which the ropes passed before being tied to the pegs. At the ridge, a thin horizontal layer of thatch material or of rushes or even flax might be placed under the ropes,[113] or a ridging of scraws might be used (Fig. 101).[114] Such expedients were usually unnecessary where there was a close network of both horizontal and vertical ropes.

Pegged thatch is a hybrid method used in a restricted area in north county Antrim, and westwards into north-east Londonderry (Figs. 104-107). Some early photographs confirm the pegged thatch in this area at Portstewart about 1900 and twenty years earlier in Coleraine,[115] while others from the Glens of Antrim show that the distribution of pegged thatch in the nineteenth century was more extensive than that reported in recent times.[116] The thatch was laid in overlapping bundles like scollop thatch, but without the scollops. Two-ply ropes,

H

Fig. 105. Pegged thatch, using ropes only at eave, ridge, and roof slope mid point, Glenshesk, Co. Antrim, early 20th century. UFTM WAG 1943

Fig. 106. Pegs prepared for thatching, Cozies Td., Co. Antrim. UFTM L 1182.10

Fig. 107. Possible variant of pegged-thatch roof. It is difficult to tell if the laths or rods pegged to the thatch should be considered a variant of pegged thatch, or of exposed scollop thatch, near Cushendall, Co. Antrim, early 20th century. UFTM WAG 259

often of twisted bog-fir slivers which tightened as they expanded due to damp, were laid end to end on the thatch about 60 cm. apart. These ropes were then pinned in place at close intervals of 10 cm. to 15 cm. by means of bog-wood pegs driven at a slight upward slant, to shed water, between the plys of the rope into the underthatch; occasionally hairpin scollops were used over the ropes.

Thrust thatch has been mentioned when discussing underthatch. Recent survivals are located only along the extreme south-east boundary of Ulster, but the technique may formerly have been more widespread in Down and Antrim,[117] although oral reports there may refer to the thrusting of patching bundles of straw into an old roof to repair it, rather than to the technique common throughout much of Leinster.

Finally, a very interesting method was used in the barony of Lecale in south-east Down where occasional examples survive, now almost always in a state of disrepair. *Stapple thatch* (Figs. 108, 109) made use of mud rather than scollops to secure the bundles of straw ('stapples') to the roof. The upper ends of the bundles were knotted and then laid in rows, from eaves to ridge, working in spars as in scollop thatch. Sometimes the heads of each layer of stapples were bedded in mud, but often mud was used only along the eaves, about midway up the roof slopes, and at the ridge. The ridge was capped with unknotted straw secured with scollops, and a coping of mud was added, later occasionally replaced by cement. A similar coping was sometimes added up the gable skews, effectively sealing the thatched roof in place at each end.[118] The technique, or something like it, may have been known in south-west Ulster also. Oral information gathered in the Lisnaskea area of Fermanagh tells of the use of blue clay instead of scollops in house thatching,[119] and in 1945 stapple thatching was observed in Kilbride parish in county Cavan.[120]

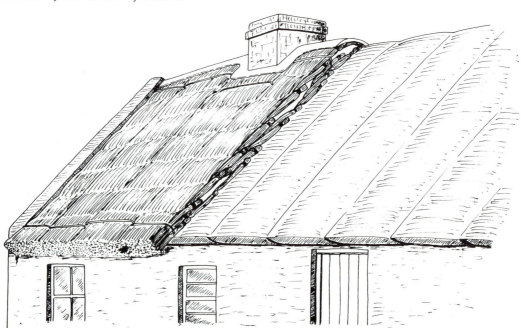

Fig. 108.   Stapple thatching. Scraw underthatch at right; stapples (knotted bundles of straw) held in position on the roof by lenses of mud at three positions on the roof, together with ridge coping and chimney-stack flashing of mud.

Fig. 109.   Remains of staple-thatch roof, which survived under corrugated-metal sheeting. Smooth lenses of dried mud are seen mixed through the thatch material, Sheepland Beg Td., Co. Down. UFTM L 1429.3

C. *Shingles*

Although roof detailing of the representation of the Temple of Jerusalem in the Book of Kells has been interpreted as shingling, and the texturing of the roofs of the little skeuomorphs of timber buildings on the heads of some high crosses may be similarly interpreted, there is no evidence for any roof covering other than thatch for native houses of about A.D. 1600. Documentation of British settlement in the early seventeenth century makes it clear, however, that many planters' houses were covered with oak shingles, and in 1641 Boate referred to their use on both dwellings and churches, but added that though they gave a tight enough roof to start with, they soon required replacement, presumably because the thin oak shingles rapidly warped.[121] In county Londonderry shingled roofs were built on the estates of the ironmongers, mercers, vintners and salters. Shingles were used in Dungannon and at Castle Balfour in Fermanagh, and also in the English-settled areas of north Armagh and the Lagan valley, on both mass-walled and timber-framed houses. Lisburn lost its shingled roofs when it was burned accidentally in 1707, and there are references to use of shingling in other towns; perhaps the last two shingled roofs survived in Lurgan in the 1830s.[122]

There are only rare references to shingled roofs outside the towns. On the Brownlow estate in north Armagh between the late 1660s and the 1690s, shingled roofs were specified in leases for at least nine urban dwellings, but only for two in the rural area.[123] Not far away, Waringstown House was built in 1666 and covered with oak shingles, removed in 1834.[124] A house at New-forge on the Lagan, in north Down, had its shingles 'raised or ruffled' when it was struck by lightning on 9 August, 1707.[125] Usually these houses seem to have been occupied by well-off people. Sir Robert Staples's big house in Lissan parish, county Tyrone about 1700 was shingled,[126] as was one built by a Mr. Robert Usher in Aghagallon parish, county Antrim, perhaps in the second half of the eighteenth century, but the shingles were later replaced with thatch.[127]

This imported tradition of shingling had little influence outside the towns, and appears to have had no influence on north Irish vernacular building in general.

D. *Tiles*

Fire-clay tiles are mentioned in only a few instances in the northern Irish documentation of the early seventeenth century. Ten timber-framed houses on vintners' lands in Londonderry were tiled, and tiles were made at Enniskillen and in county Cavan;[128] almost certainly these tiles were flat. Curved interlocking pantiles were being imported into Dublin as early as 1641,[129] and a century later imported pantiles were advertised for sale in Belfast.[130] Pantiles, together with floor tiles, were manufactured during the first half of the nineteenth century in Londonderry city,[131] but whether they were made there earlier, or indeed anywhere else in the north of Ireland is unknown. Like shingles, roof tiles played no significant part in northern Irish vernacular building traditions.

I have seen pantiles on three roofs. Remains of a small one-room house near Kilkeel, with granite walls, are roofed with pantiles (Fig. 110), probably imported through Kilkeel; possibly they formed part of a speculative ballast cargo on a boat working into the harbour to take away either granite or seed potatoes. Another pantiled roof was on a small farmyard building in the lower Bann valley, while the third is on a rear wing added to a former schoolhouse, later used as a dwelling, built in the first half of the nineteenth century close to Florence Court in west Fermanagh (Fig. 111). Significantly, these two cases are in areas where bricks, drainage tiles and floor tiles were made locally, and they may survive as the outcome of unsuccessful local attempts to introduce pantiles in the nineteenth century.

E. *Slates*

Of the roofing materials introduced to northern Irish vernacular house building about or soon after 1600, only slate became commonly used; but if its introduction was in the early seventeenth century, on houses of better quality,[132] its widespread adoption was in the second half of the nineteenth century, and in many areas the transition from thatch to slate was made only recently.

There are occasional later seventeenth-century references to slated houses lived in by gentry. One was some miles upstream on the river Lagan, probably near Shaw's Bridge in 1635,[133] and another looked across the North Channel from south of Donaghadee in 1683. It had been built close to slate quarries which served east and north Down and south Antrim at that time.[134] In fact the Ards peninsula with its small-size, coarse, locally quarried slates was the first area in the north of Ireland where use of slate became common at vernacular level. Further south in the peninsula at the same time, in the parishes of Ballywalter and Ballyhalbert (where again there was a slate quarry), there were 'handsome slated

Fig. 110.   Pantiles on a derelict one-room house, Dunnaman Td., Co. Down. UFTM L 1285.17

Fig. 111.   Pantiles on extension at rear of a dwelling, Lisdivrick Td., Co. Fermanagh. UFTM L 1550.0

Fig. 112. Derelict farmhouse with remains of locally quarried slate roof, laid in diminishing courses towards the ridge, patched with imported Welsh slates, Carnacally Td., Co. Down (cf. Fig. 235). UFTM L 891.9

houses built by John Bayly, Hugh Montgomery, and Hugh Hamill, Esqrs. Justices of the Peace . . .'[135] In 1743 a glebe house in Seapatrick parish in north-west Down was roofed with slates, carried on Norway fir wood; this is the earliest known reference to importation of north European softwood for roofing a northern Irish house.[136] At the end of the eighteenth century slating of houses both in the parish of Magheradrool[137] and in county Down generally[138] was being advocated as a means of saving straw to increase quantities of manure for agriculture; the writer told of 'many slate Quarries in this part of the country [Ballynahinch area], superior in quality and colour to either English or Scotch'. Initiative in the introduction of slating long lay with the landlords, and earliest bore fruit in the towns. Ballymoney in north Antrim was described in 1806 as 'a neat little town, well built with stone and slated roofs'.[139] In 1802 larger dwellings on better-off farms in county Down were being slated as older houses were being replaced,[140] and in Tyrone there were slated houses in some districts, but in advocating extension of slating, M'Evoy sought an improvement in the quantities of manure, for he estimated that still, one third of the straw produced annually in the county went to thatching.[141] 'In many

instances the houses are slated': thus a description of county Antrim in 1816.[142] Then also we learn that 'many new houses are slated' in the mid-Down parish of Annahilt,[143] but only 'sometimes' were they slated in the Antrim parishes of Glenavy, Camlin and Tullyrusk.[144] About the same time on the county Armagh estates surveyed by William Greig, no more than three houses from a total of 162 on the Drumbanagher estate,[145] and forty-eight of a total of 622 on the larger Gosford estates[146] had slate on them. By the second half of the 1830s the Ordnance Survey memoirs attest the use of slating on farmhouses in most parishes throughout south Antrim, and in a scatter of isolated parishes elsewhere. Even at the level of cottages, slates were in use in many of the south Antrim parishes as well as those in the Ards peninsula in east Down. Thus the general picture is of earliest acceptance of slating in east Ulster and first of all on farmhouse roofs, the application spreading geographically westwards and socially downwards as the nineteenth century progressed. However, the fairly low percentages of rural houses with slate roofs quoted in Table 6 urge caution in assuming that the evidence noted here implies large numbers of houses.

In the middle of the century, individual landlords

Fig. 113.   Hip-roof, lobby-entry farmhouse with roof of imported slates, probably Welsh, Lisslanly Td., Co. Armagh. UFTM L 1376.13

remained locally influential in promoting slating. One was the proprietor of the Glenravel estate in east Antrim about 1830, who generally provided both slate and timber;[147] in the 1840s the Grocers' company made allowances to their tenants for slates and other materials when constructing approved houses, or carrying out agreed improvements;[148] and on Sir Arthur Brooke's estate in Magherastephana barony in east Fermanagh, within ten years the number of slated houses had risen from six to 114, a significant factor being the ease of transporting the heavy slates by canal;[149] it was said about 1883 that in the two decades prior to 1875 'A very marked improvement was manifest in the homesteads . . .' on the estate of the Mercers' company in Ireland, that a number of two-storey slated houses were built, and that 'The Company were in the habit of giving slates to the tenants who wished to build decent houses . . .'[150] However, a landlord in the Clogher area of east Tyrone discontinued this practice after the passing of Gladstone's Land Act, one of the consequences of which was to transfer the interest in building improvements from the landlord to the tenant, and probably this was not a unique case.[151]

As well as the local slates of east Down (Fig. 112), slates were quarried occasionally elsewhere, especially in the vicinity of Londonderry city, both in the county itself, and in adjacent parts of east Donegal, for example near Saint Johnstown[152] where the two grades were known as 'blues' costing 37 shillings per thousand, and 'tops' at 28 shillings per thousand, sold by a Mr. Alexander of Trentagh on the Marquis of Abercorn's estate and a Mr. Marshall of Tubber. But once transport improvements allowed, imported slates, especially Welsh ones (Fig. 113), became the most widely used. They came in through Newry, Belfast, Larne, Portrush, Coleraine, Londonderry and Ballyshannon, and an important inland distribution centre was Ballyronan on the north-western shores of Lough Neagh, whither the slates were brought by canal and lake from Belfast and Newry. Slates were also brought by water to Enniskillen for distribution in south-west Ulster. Competition in selling slates was intense. In a letter of 1841 a general merchant in Moy, county Tyrone, who had interests in grocery, linen and woollen goods, ironmongery and shipping (and Moy is an inland town on the river Blackwater!), wrote, 'I import my own slate from the quarries in Wales direct, so that no man in either Newry or Belfast can undersell me'; he had customers in parts of Tyrone and Armagh near Moy, but even as far away as Ballymoney in north Antrim.[153] Welsh slates were sold in a variety of sizes and qualities, of which the most widely used seem to have been 'Countesses', sold usually by the thousand, measuring about 60 cm. by 25 cm. 'Ladies' were smaller, also sold by number. Large-size slates, 'Mills', 'Imperials', 'Kings' and 'Queens' were usually sold by weight, averaging perhaps 170 to the ton for Mills. Other denominations mentioned in the Ordnance Survey memoirs, which list these and other building materials for a variety of parishes across the north of Ireland in the 1830s, were 'Cardigans', cheap slates sold by the thousand, and 'Rags', also cheaper slates sold by weight.

SIX

Hearth and Chimney

TYPOLOGICAL stages in the evolution of the hearth and chimney can be documented in the north of Ireland (Fig. 114), and for some there is abundant evidence, both documentary and in the form of observed examples. In some places, too, the series is an historical one, and evidence for more than one stage can sometimes be discovered in individual houses. But stages in the series were often missed out, some families even moving from the earliest, free-standing hearth lying on the floor somewhere between the ends of the house, to the latest, a properly built stone or brick chimney with a fire in a grate below, when in the nineteenth century they moved from the rural slums of the landless poor to terraced factory houses in urban areas. Superimposed on the geographical variations are those of social class, for the changes in hearth position and in ways of dealing with smoke usually started at upper social levels, their introduction being long-delayed amongst the landless rural poor. Lastly, it is impossible to say with certainty if some or all of the impetus for change was inspired by external contacts, particularly following the Plantation of Ulster or due to influences spreading elsewhere in Ireland, or if change developed indigenously. These interlocking factors meant that from the early or mid-eighteenth century onwards, almost all of the typological stages involved co-existed within quite limited districts.

The medieval houses at Caherguillamore in the south of Ireland (Chapter 2) each had a free-standing hearth situated between the ends of the house, and set some distance away from the entrance, and the Tildarg house recently excavated in county Antrim seems to have been similar. Northern houses at the end of the sixteenth century were probably of this kind, although a minority of the cartographic representations of the time show chimneys. By contrast, both documents and contemporary maps show that in the early seventeenth century British undertakers, servitors and wealthier tenants were constructing houses with chimneys, usually more or less centrally placed.[1] It is likely, too, that in Donegal Walter McLaghlin McSwine was following British exemplars when he had 'build 3 new Irish houses, well timbered and large, one of them with a double chimney of stone . . .'[2] Unfortunately we know almost nothing of the housing of the lesser British tenants and cottagers in the early seventeenth century. Hearth-tax and poll-tax figures gathered later in the century are suggestive. A great number of British settlers in Ulster in the 1660s were living in chimneyless houses, especially the poorer elements amongst them; their living conditions can hardly have differed significantly from those of the Irish. The initiative of landlords of British origin in insisting on the building of stone or brick chimneys at this time is illustrated by the leases of the Brownlow property in north Armagh, but it is interesting that while leases for town houses usually contain a covenant to this effect, only rarely is this covered in leases for rural tenancies.[3] Later documents also show insistence on the building of chimneys. A lease from the Lord Bishop of Derry to a local merchant for a plot of land on the east side of the river Foyle in 1694 laid down that within seven years John Cunningham was to build a good house two storeys high with floors, walls, a stone chimney and oven.[4] About 1700 the tenant of Grange in the manor of Castledillon in Armagh had a house with a kitchen chimney,[5] and in Drumoher one under-tenant lived in 'a good stone and clay house with a brick chimney' and another in a mud-wall cabin similarly provided. Rather than continue citation of the documentation on the evolution of hearth and chimney historically, the following discussion of the evidence, documentary and observed, is arranged according to the evolutionary development it represents. In fact, two interlocked strands of development are involved, that of hearth position, and that of the chimney canopy or flue and stack above the hearth.

Free-Standing Hearth, without Chimney

We have already seen that this medieval arrangement was usual in Irish housing about A.D. 1600. The

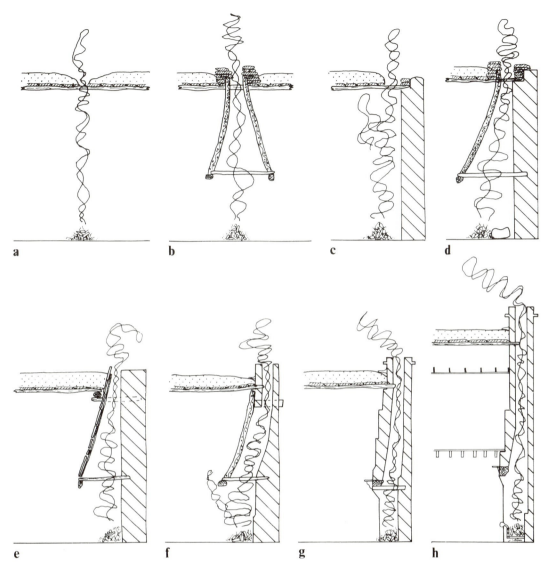

Fig. 114.   Evolution of hearth and chimney.
a: free-standing hearth with smokehole;
b: free-standing hearth with suspended wattle canopy;
c: wall hearth, with smokehole;
d: wall hearth, suspended wattle canopy, note backstone or 'dais' and external sod chimney;
e: wall hearth, wooden canopy protruding above roof ridge;
f: wall hearth, wattle canopy leading into stone chimney;
g: wall hearth with stone or brick canopy and chimney:
h: wall hearth, fire in raised grate, stone or brick flue and chimney, chimney breast disappears in upper storey.

presence of central, external chimneys on a minority of Irish houses illustrated on maps of the period is difficult to interpret, for they may have been no more than external shields around smoke holes. Lucas has interpreted features on the ridges of eighth-century bronze house-shaped shrines as representations of shielded smoke holes, and plausibly linked them with documentary references to the *forlés* dating from the eleventh century and later, some of which hark back to ninth-century origins. This word has hitherto been translated by literary scholars as 'skylight', but Lucas's translation as 'smoke hole' (as distinct from 'chimney') is convincing.

Furthermore, there is the survival in modern Scottish Gaelic of the same word with this meaning.[6] So the representation of external chimneys on maps of the early seventeenth century in the north of Ireland need not *necessarily* involve anything more than smoke holes, but their central locations on the ridges of the house representations does suggest hearths placed well away from the end walls of the houses. However, I doubt if the centrally located doors shown on these houses imply precise alignment of hearth and door; rather, I suspect that the arrangement was comparable to that in the Caherguillamore and Tildarg houses. In each, the hearth was well to one side of a line transversely across the house through the entrance. There is no evidence for substantial chimney stacks rising from floor level in contemporary Irish houses and in their absence, a hearth in line with the entrance would be inconvenient, indeed improbable. There is a multitude of later references from all over Ireland to chimneyless houses, but their general context argues that they refer to the third stage described below. However, an account from the coast of Gweedore in north-west Donegal, from a modern observer, suggests there may have been occasional later instances of the type which survived even into the present century and in some of the Scottish islands:

> I saw in Donegal, on the shores below Gweedore, the ruins of foundations of a rectangular stone house, with the hearth in the centre of the room. This hearth consists of two more or less semi-circular flags laid side by side. There was no indication of a hearth or fireplace anywhere else in the room.[7]

It is pertinent to set alongside this the description of houses in the same area in 1753–4, which tells that they were 'chiefly of one room with the fire in the middle of it'.[8] Perhaps the later common practice of suspending the pot chain over the fire from a beam set high in the chimney, or even from the ridge purlin itself which was often carried through the chimney, harks back to the circumstances of these early houses, where the pot hung over the open fire from a roof timber.[9] Memories of free-standing kitchen hearths were also gathered in west Fermanagh in the 1970s.[10]

Free-Standing Hearth, with Suspended Chimney Canopy

The chimney canopy of wood or wickerwork suspended over a free-standing hearth has been reported from other parts of the British Isles, including Tuosist in county Kerry.[11] There is no evidence for it in the north of Ireland unless the ruins of a house in Ballyvaston townland in south-east Down accidentally discovered in about 1735

can be thus interpreted. A strong south wind eroded a sandy rabbit warren, 'by which the vestiges of several Cabbins were discovered, and the Hearth-stones, and wooden Chimney Frames surrounding them appeared';[12] but this description is amenable to alternative interpretations.

Wall Hearth, no Chimney, with or without Smoke Hole

Removal of the hearth, away from its position closer to the entrance, to a position close to[13] (Fig. 115) or at the foot of a wall (often a gable, but possibly also against the foot of an internal partition wall when such was introduced) was a logical re-arrangement of the vernacular interior. It left the remainder of the interior free of any encumbrances. An informant in 1961 recalled an arrangement in Racavan in county Antrim where the fireplace was built about a metre out from the wall, the smoke ascending freely to a hole in the roof, there being no chimney canopy, although externally there might either be a chimney of 'moss sods', that is peat, or a wooden barrel might be built into the smoke hole to provide the same effect.[14] There is also an account from county Antrim in the 1850s of kitchens wherein hearths

> were generally a square pavement of broad flat stones, on which the fire rested; the square from three to ten feet on the side. Very frequently the fire was a 'round-about-fire'; implying that persons could sit in a circle entirely round it. In such circumstances a large undressed log of bogwood, called the *dais*, lay 'beyond the fire', that is, between the fire and the gable. Three or four of the cold-rife, or the worst clad, by some instinct always discovered the dais, and occupied it. . . .
>
> When the fire was so near the wall as not to admit the dais, a 'back-stone' became an indispensable requisite. This was a stone not less than two feet high, a foot and a half broad, and one thick. Against this stone the huge turf fire was raised; the result was that any one became able, by its colour, wear and tear, to recognise a back-stone.[15]

Many of the abundant references to chimneyless houses relate to this or similar arrangements; a few samples will suffice. A house excavated recently at Camphill, near Newtownstewart in north-west Tyrone, was arranged similarly to the county Antrim description above, and additionally there was decorative cobbling of the floor area in front of the fire.[16] Smoke tracing its way up the inside of a chimneyless gable to a smoke hole is recorded from the Ballygawley area in south-east Tyrone,[17] while the trace it left on the wall surface was known in the Cushendall area of the Glens of Antrim as the 'smoke walk'.[18] Before Lord George Hill commenced improvements in Gweedore in north-west Donegal about 1840,

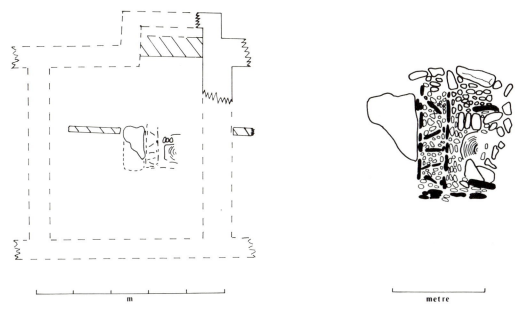

Fig. 115.   Excavated free-standing hearth in late 18th-century dwelling, Castletown Td., Co. Tyrone (after Brannon).

the dwellings there were chimneyless,[19] as were those on the nearby island of Aranmore,[20] and in the Inishowen parish of Culdaff in 1816.[21] Windowless, chimneyless cottages existed in the Omagh district of county Tyrone in the mid-1830s,[22] and in the Fermanagh/Cavan border parish of Tomregan,[23] in the barony of Upper Dundalk in north Louth in the south-east of our area,[24] and across Carlingford Lough in the Hilltown-Rostrevor district in south county Down.[25] Want of chimneys in Rathlin Island houses was blamed for the prevalence of respiratory and eye complaints.[26] Some accounts describe chimneyless houses resembling vapour-issuing dunghills. It is worth noting that old enumerations of dwellings counted 'smoakes' instead of buildings. However, some of these descriptions do not distinguish between chimneyless houses with and without smoke holes in their roofs. Nevertheless, in the more progressive east of Ulster, as late as 1848 on the north Down estate of the Londonderry family there were still thirty-one houses without even a smoke hole, 1.7% of the rural houses on that estate.[27] Also on the Londonderry estate in 1848 there were forty-eight rural houses (2.6%) with only a hole in the roof to allow smoke escape.[28] In the mid-1830s houses with smoke holes existed in county Donegal[29] and in Tartaraghan parish in north Armagh in sod-walled houses.[30] In the parish of Enniskillen in Fermanagh, in sod or mud-wall cottages in the higher districts, 'The fire is burned against one of the gables, above which is a hole in the roof to emit the smoke,

which more frequently escapes by the door.'[31] Most of the houses of the poor in 1835 in north Louth had only a smoke hole,[32] and similar dwellings were also reported from the Drapers' company estates in the Moneymore and Ballinascreen areas of Londonderry just after 1820.[33]

Wattle or Timber Chimney Canopy

The earliest chimney forms observed in recent times in the north of Ireland consist of large canopies, fixed over a fire on the ground at the foot of a wall. The canopy was fixed to that wall with its outer bottom edge supported on a heavy bressumer, or 'brace' beam which spanned the house at a position up to almost 2 m. from the hearth wall (Figs. 116-118). 'Brace' is often applied in historical descriptions, and still colloquially, to the canopy itself, occasionally also called a 'flake'. Another word applied in both ways was 'balk' (also 'bock' and 'back'). The canopies usually consist of wattling, or basket-work, sometimes worked around a rigid timber frame. They took the shape of a truncated rectangular pyramid, or of three sides of such, the fourth being the wall itself to which the canopy was fixed or against which it rested. The wattling was plastered with mud, tempered with chopped straw, rushes or hair, sometimes with an admixture of animal dung, and when it had dried out it was usually limewashed. Usually also the upright frame members and wattles protruded above the roof ridge

Fig. 116.   Clay-plastered wattle canopy over open hearth, front carried on a 'brace' beam, near Cooneen, Co. Fermanagh. UFTM L 290.29

where they were capped by a chimney of sods, or the thatch was continued up around them, perhaps on a base provided by an old bottomless bucket or further basketwork. These external chimneys and their interior wattled canopies caught the imagination of many travellers and other observers of domestic conditions in the first half of the nineteenth century; consequently this is the most completely documented traditional type of chimney. The descriptions refer to all parts of the north of Ireland and so need not be quoted *in extenso*; only some representative examples are provided. Jonathan Binns, the poor inquiry commissioner, quotes external chimneys as described above, indicative of internal wattled canopies, in north Monaghan;[34] the Ordnance Survey memoirs provide other examples for the Antrim parishes

of Donegore, Kilroot and Grange of Shilvodan, and the Londonderry parishes of Banagher and Faughanvale, and describe farmhouses with wattled chimneys smeared with clay in Clondermot parish in the same county.[35] In Raloo in south-east Antrim 'a very wide chimney Brace impends over a spacious paved hearth', according to the memoir of 1840.[36] The same source for the same county reports that in Racavan parish farmhouses 'The fire is lit upon a paved hearth, and the chimney "Brace" the front of which does not come within 6 or 7 feet [about 2 m.] of the floor is usually from 5 to 6 feet wide at the bottom, but becomes gradually narrower as it approaches the top.'[37]

Comparable descriptions for Templecorran in county Antrim in the memoirs relate to farmhouses and cottages, but in the case of the latter, report a development. The

Fig. 117.   Thatched chimney, probably above wattle canopy inside, near Cushendall, Co. Antrim, *c.*1900. UM WO1/50/29

Fig. 118.   Chimney canopy borne on framework supported by 'brace' beam spanning a bed-outshot kitchen, Lisnamuck Td., Co. Londonderry (after McCourt).

brace beam is dispensed with. 'A wide chimney supported by a sort of springing or machicolation, rises at some distance above a paved hearth, backed by a large whin stone, which it is alleged, assists in preventing smokiness, but more probably was originally continued for the purpose of retaining and throwing out heat.'[38] Such canopies, supported on wooden or stone brackets cantilevered out of the hearth wall, have been recorded in various parts of the north of Ireland in recent times; there are examples on wooden brackets in cottier houses from counties Londonderry and Tyrone now reconstructed at the Ulster Folk and Transport Museum.

One of the finest examples of a wattled chimney canopy supported by a brace beam I have seen survived in north county Armagh in the early 1960s. It was fully 2 m. wide and projected from the hearth wall about 1.5 m. A similar but smaller example, later replaced by a brick canopy of more modest dimension, had existed in a ruined house near Knockarevan in south Fermanagh, and this was clearly the original arrangement also in a cruck-framed house at Trummery, Megaberry in south Antrim, certainly of the seventeenth century. Many canopies supported on a brace beam were flanked on each side by a small loft known as a 'skeagh', 'flake', or 'thallage'. Examples and reports of these small lofts and their terminology have come principally from Armagh, Monaghan[39] and Cavan,[40] but an example in Lisnamuck townland in Londonderry has been illustrated (Fig. 118).[41] In the Lisnamuck house, however, the front of the canopy no longer extends out to the brace beam, but rests on two side supports the outer ends of which are borne by the brace. This house clearly documented development away from the very wide canopy, presaging its translation into a more restricted flue built of stone or brick.

The earliest chimney canopies introduced into Irish vernacular houses at the end of the sixteenth century were of this wattled canopied form, perhaps supported on a brace beam or bressumer, with or without the small lateral lofts. They were fitted in urban houses in Dublin and some other Leinster towns and were known as 'forest chimneys'. From contemporary evidence it is obvious that they were constructed neither of stone nor of brick, and they were obviously generally regarded as a significant fire hazard. It is impossible to tell if they were sixteenth-century introductions from Britain, or if they were developed from ideas seen in earlier buildings of the monastic orders like the Augustinians or Cistercians after the twelfth century. In a lay context the earliest stone chimneys were in castles erected by the Anglo-Normans, but it is questionable if these socially superior buildings would have provided significant exemplars for developments at vernacular level.[42] It should be recalled that wattling was a common building material throughout the medieval period, and in the sixteenth century some Irish house builders perhaps worked out for themselves how to construct these smoke canopies, possibly spurred on to emulate English fashions for having lofts, if not upper storeys, in their houses. If the upper part of the volume of a house is to be usable, some kind of smoke canopy is esssential. But the English were at the same time introducing stone and brick chimneys in their own houses in the north of Ireland, as well as lofts and upper floors, and it has been suggested that the Irish wattled smoke canopies were poor attempts to copy these English stone or brick constructions.[43] If so, the Irish were merely basing their ideas on the outcome of the same evolution from wattled antecedents, the development having taken place in the sixteenth century in England.

Some other developments besides the diminution in its size in evidence in the Lisnamuck house, took place before the wattled canopy was dispensed with. Sometimes an external chimney of brick or stone was built, cantilevered out of the apex of the hearth wall, into the bottom of which the wattled smoke hood fitted. Furthermore a smoke channel could be modelled into the face of the hearth wall itself, compensating to a degree for the decrease in the size of the canopy. This was done both in stone-walled houses, for example in Donegal in the nineteenth century, and in mud-walled houses in Lecale in south-east Down, as in Lisoid townland, perhaps built in the eighteenth century. Finally, once suitable timber became more easily available, the entire canopy was sometimes translated into a wooden framework covered in flat softwood boards.

A house examined in the late 1960s in Dullaghan townland in south-west Tyrone neatly illustrates a number of these changes.[44] Solidly built with stone walls having well worked corners, it probably belongs to the early nineteenth century; it existed already in 1833 when the first six-inch Ordnance Survey map was published. The chimney canopy consisted of a funnel of boards, its wider bottom resting on a long, heavy brace beam that spanned the kitchen end of the two-roomed house about 1 m. from the gable (Fig. 119). This supported the outer ends of side members, the other ends of which were embedded in the gable stonework. The upper narrow end of the canopy butted against the bottom of a stone chimney at the apex of the gable which was carried on two stones cantilevered out of the gable internal face. Additionally, and unusually, there was a timber screen carried down from the underside of the left-hand canopy support to the ground, parallel to the front wall of the house, so that the hearth on the ground below the

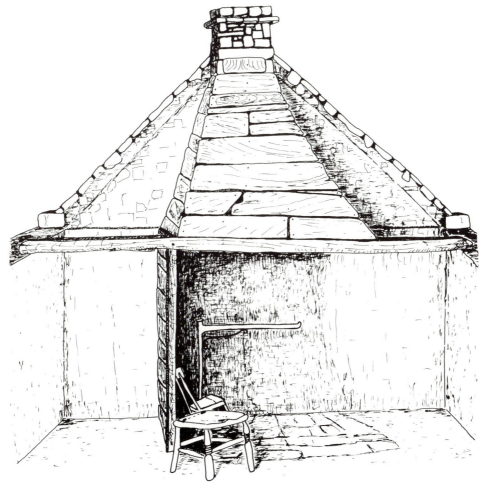

Fig. 119. Boarded chimney canopy supported on 'brace' beam in a derelict farmhouse. Note screen to one side of hearth below, Dullaghan Td., Co. Tyrone.

canopy was lighted more from a window in the rear wall than from the opposite window in the front. The externally visible chimney continued only slightly above roof-ridge level where it was capped by a thin, stone string course and a top course of stone.

There is mid-nineteenth-century evidence from county Antrim at least, that the wide wattled or boarded smoke canopy served as a means of meat preservation by smoking: 'it had its large, ponderous, yellow, toothful flitches; its quarters of hard and dry hung beef; its tasty mutton; and its strings of long puddings, both black and white'.[45] Almost certainly this observation holds true for other periods and places throughout the north of Ireland.

Stone or Brick Chimney Canopy

A proportion, perhaps many, of the chimneys built into their houses by better-off English settlers in the north of

Ireland in the early seventeenth century were constructed in either stone or brick. They would have been fairly direct translations of the form of older wattled canopies into more permanent materials. Stone and brick chimneys were insisted upon in leases later in the seventeenth century, as we have already seen for example on the Brownlow estate in north Armagh. An eighteenth-century house, perhaps originating fairly early in the century, at Cockhill, Drumanphy townland in north Armagh (Fig. 120), derelict but still fairly complete when examined in 1981, but having a later slated roof, had a fine example of a brick-built smoke canopy of very large size supported on an oak bressumer placed about 1.37 m. away from the kitchen hearth wall, which is in the centre of the house. Other examples seen have usually been smaller, and it is obvious that the transition from wattling to brick or stone accompanied constriction of the canopy until it became a narrow chimney flue,

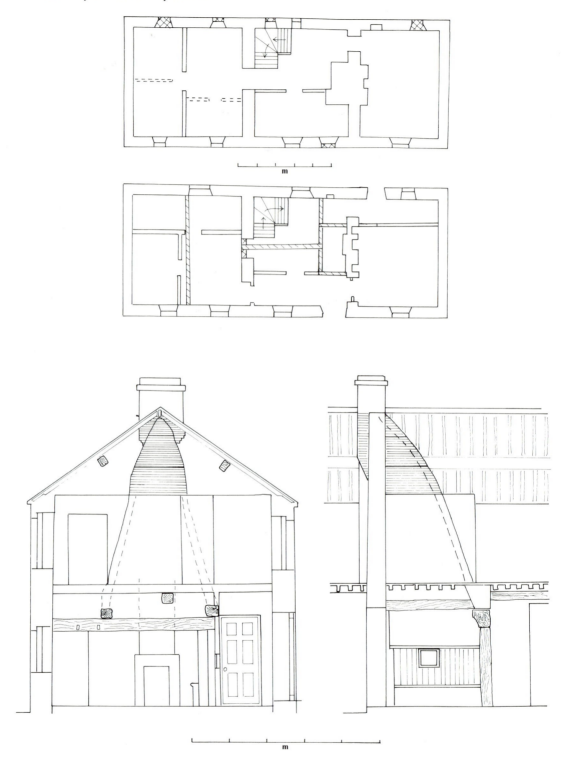

Fig. 120.   Brick chimney canopy supported by oak bressumer resting on end of jamb wall, in derelict farmhouse, Drumanphy Td., Co. Armagh (from unpublished survey by R. Oram).

Fig. 121. Cantilevered restricted canopy, apparently of brick, inside a jamb wall, Co. Antrim, early 20th century.
UFTM WAG 1163

Fig. 122. Stone chimney canopy carried on masonry jambs. Note cobbled hearth area before the fire, Inishowen, Co. Donegal, early 20th century.
UFTM WAG 1185.

Fig. 123.   Restricted canopy carried over fire in raised grate. Glendun, Co. Antrim, early 20th century. UFTM WAG 1953

earlier examples still expressed as a breastwork keyed into the hearth wall, and carried on a hearth lintel or bressumer placed 25 cm. to 40 cm. out from the face of that wall but spanning a hearth that was still up to 2 m. wide from side to side (Figs. 121, 122). Later examples dispensed even with the breastwork, the flue being completely accommodated within the wall thickness. This change often also accompanied other alterations made in response to the need for more efficient draught to burn coal rather than turf (peat) in the second half of the nineteenth century. Many better, slated, two-storey farmhouses built in the early nineteenth century in south Antrim, reported in the Ordnance Survey memoirs, had chimneys of this description, and the memoir for the Londonderry parishes of Banagher, Dungiven and Boveva reported that in 1821 'Particular attention is now paid to construction of the chimneys and fireplaces, so that the eyes of the inhabitants are no longer spoiled, nor the furniture blackened, with the eternal volumes of smoke that used to float in the upper regions of the buildings'.[46] Even cottiers' houses in the vicinity of Enniskillen town in 1834 'have regular built chimneys and chimney places'.[47] In 1835 some poorer houses, but not those of labourers, in Monaghan barony had brick chimneys, a few poor houses in north Louth had either stone or brick chimneys, and the housing of the poor in Lecale in south-east Down usually had brick chimneys reflecting greater prosperity there.[48] Some of the smaller farmers at the same time in Ardkeen parish in the Ards peninsula had houses with brick chimneys.[49]

Late Developments

There were two principal late developments, both manifested to a significant extent in the nineteenth century. Although it is clear from hearth-tax records that a minority of houses in earlier periods had more than one hearth, in the latter part of the eighteenth century most rural vernacular houses had only a kitchen hearth and chimney. Thus in 1791 the return showed that 71.4% of the houses in Ulster had only one hearth, but another 15.2% were exempted pauper houses and about 20% were exempted new houses. Most of the rest were in the towns.[50] These are the conditions noted also in the 1830s in the Londonderry parish of Tamlaght Finlagan when we read, 'As to their interior arrangements, the house of

Fig. 124. Constricted flue within an older open-hearth chimney, fire in raised grate, Co. Antrim, early 20th century. UFTM WAG 1963

the small farmer consists of two apartments — one called the "kitchen", and the other by way of distinction the "room". This "room" is always close and damp, having no chimney'.[51] But by then things were changing elsewhere. In the east of the same county, in Aghadowey parish, 'twenty years ago the occurrence of a fireplace in their "parlour" or best room was comparatively rare, but now it is always to be found'.[52] Already the rural parts of the Londonderry family's estate around Newtownards and Comber in north Down in 1848 have been quoted to show survivals of numbers of chimneyless houses and others having only a smoke hole. The numbers quoted, however, must be seen against the facts that 831 houses (44.6% of the rural houses concerned) had one chimney, and 953 (51.2%) had two or more. The mid-nineteenth-century revolution in rural housing standards was under way. The second half of the century saw proliferation of domestic fireplaces, inserted not only in parlours, their flues often opening into those serving kitchen fires, but also in bedrooms. So, most of the multi-chimneyed houses we now regard as traditional rural dwellings are in reality either late houses, or they were lately altered. To this period also must belong most of the dummy chimneys added to roof lines, usually for the

sake of an approach towards symmetry (see Chapter 9).

The other major late change was due to the move away from burning peat to coal, within the nineteenth century, and especially in the eastern counties of Down and Antrim. To burn successfully, coal requires a stronger draught than peat, and it was not suited to an open fire at floor level. So the nineteenth century saw the introduction of hand-turned rotary fans built into the hearth area to deliver draught to the fire from below, made especially in the foundry of Pierce Bros. in Wexford and sent north. Others were made in local foundries, for example by Scott of Belfast. Fixed fan bellows were fitted to hearths only in Monaghan, Down, Armagh, east Tyrone and south Antrim, but portable equivalents, adapted to blow a draught into fires in grates raised off the floor were used in these same areas and also further north, into south Londonderry and mid Antrim, and westward into east Fermanagh. They were a response to the other change, that of lifting the fire into a grate. In 1835 in Lecale we are told that 'All the cabins have grates; "for 2s 6d" said one of the witnesses, "you may buy a grate that would boil a dinner fit for a man of a hundred a year" ':[53] thus Jonathan Binns, the poor inquiry commissioner. Introduction of grates, of course, accompanied restriction of the width of the hearth and of the flue above (Figs. 123, 124). Many kitchen hearths were altered in the mid-nineteenth century simply by building closely set hobs, one to either side of the new grate and firebars, the new narrow flue being built between the jambs and below the lintel or bressumer of the older open hearth. In a few instances a cast-iron oven or water boiler, or both, might be built in at the sides, but these were really individual elements inspired by integrated ranges and stoves, mass produced by northern Irish and other foundries, changes which were hardly vernacular by any definition.

SEVEN

Floors and Piercing

Floors and Lofts

REMARKABLY little documentation exists as to the nature of floors in vernacular houses in Ireland. What little there is tells of housing of the poor and of the small farmers which excited comment from travellers in the first half of the nineteenth century, or takes the form of generalised brief comments in some of the Ordnance Survey memoirs, principally in county Antrim parishes, photographs of the end of the nineteenth century and early in the present one, and observations made in houses studied in the field. Caution is needed in arguing backwards from any of these sources, for flooring is one of the most easily altered parts of a house.

Two references in the Ordnance Survey memoirs for county Antrim hint that oak floors might occasionally have been laid in ground-floor rooms. Moore Grove, a prosperous house in Killead parish was 'floored with oak',[1] and in nearby Glenavy some of the oldest houses, built probably in the seventeenth century, were similarly provided.[2] Both descriptions are ambiguous and particularly the Glenavy one may refer to upper-storey floors. Oak flooring was also originally provided in Waringstown House in north-west Down, built in 1666.[3]

Clay or mud floors were commonest at vernacular level in the first half of the nineteenth century. They are noticed in the Ordnance Survey memoirs, widely in Antrim and Londonderry in farmhouses, and in these

Fig. 125. Earth floor and cobbled hearth area in farmhouse kitchen from Cruckaclady Td., Co. Tyrone, reconstructed at UFTM. UFTM L 1627.15.

125

Fig. 126.   Stone-flagged kitchen floor, Drumaghlis Td., Co. Down, *c.*1900. UM W05/10/3

counties together with Fermanagh in cottages. They were also seen in much of Donegal in the 1840s.[4] Poor inquiry evidence extends the range to Armagh, Down and Monaghan; especially in the cottiers' houses earth floors were often damp. In Tomregan on the Fermanagh/Cavan border houses of cottiers never had paved or flagged surfaces.[5] In some the floor level inside was lower than the exterior ground level, perhaps due to removal of earth for building the house itself.[6] To improve earth floors, lime was added in a number of places in greater or lesser quantities; evidence is from Lecale in south-east Down where smithy ashes were also used and where road mud sometimes provided an alternative;[7] the Monaghan-Tydavnet area in north Monaghan where the ground was dug up, lime mixed, and the floor trampled;[8] and in the Londonderry parishes of Banagher, Dungiven and Boveva.[9] In the barony of Lower Fews in mid Armagh, earth floors were made by digging up the ground where the house was to be erected and it was then trampled. 'When this is to be done, they sometimes have a dance for that purpose.'[10]

Areas on earth floors particularly vulnerable to wear, at the entrance, and especially at the hearth were often paved or cobbled (Fig. 125). The small cottier house moved from the Magilligan area in north Londonderry to the Ulster Folk and Transport Museum originally had a cobbled hearth, later upgraded with a schistose flagstone brought across Lough Foyle from Inishowen in county Donegal.[11]

An account of Islandmagee in south-east Antrim in 1839 tells that with few exceptions ground floors were of earth, with the hearth and entrance areas 'all neatly paved with small white stones from the seashore'.[12] The cruck-framed house in Carravindoon townland on Rathlin Island, already abandoned when examined about 1940, provided an elaboration of this cobbling, in a rectangular area at the door decorated with a lozenge inset with black and white shore pebbles of basalt and chalk.[13] This calls to mind decoration of Scottish doorsteps,[14] but even more, the decorative 'pitched paving' of some Welsh[15] and similar cobbling in some southern Irish houses.[16] How often have such delights been lost in the north of Ireland under the layers of concrete commonly laid on kitchen floors in the twentieth

Fig. 127. 'Caledonia' imported cream, and dark grey tiles on kitchen floor of house from Lismacloskey Td., Co. Antrim, reconstructed at UFTM. UFTM L 1627.6

century? The only surviving examples of decorative black and white cobbling known to me are in The Square in Comber, and on the footpath on the east side of Scotch Street, Downpatrick. Recent excavation of an outshot house at Camphill, county Tyrone revealed black and white patterned cobbling in front of the hearth, probably dating to the late eighteenth or early nineteenth century (Fig. 115).[17]

Where suitable stone could be had, there must for long have been some better farmhouses with flagged or paved floors. In 1825 in Clogher barony in east Tyrone there were some,[18] and in Desertlyn parish, county Londonderry in 1836.[19] Flags were in use in house building, but even more so in field drainage, before 1790 in Redford Glebe townland, county Donegal;[20] in the Cushendall area of the Glens of Antrim flags quarried in 'some good quarries of coarse freestone' were noted in 1819;[21] and in 1835 'Flags of large dimensions and of a good quality for various purposes in building' were to be had in Drumagusker townland, Balteagh parish, county Londonderry.[22] At the end of the century flagged kitchen floors are shown in photographs of some kitchen interiors, for example in county Down (Fig. 126).[23] Other hard floors inserted in kitchens from the second half of the nineteenth century onwards involved various kinds of

tiles. Both yellow, and dark blue/grey or black square 'Caledonia' tiles, with sides either 23 cm. or 30 cm. approximately, were imported from Scotland (Fig. 127), but red ones of the same sizes were likely made in local brickyards in the north of Ireland. Interesting local tiles of a reddish/yellow colour, about 5 cm. thick, had parallel hollows running through them, providing some insulation in the floor once they were laid. They were made at Florence Court in west Fermanagh from the early 1850s and laid in farm kitchens in south and east Fermanagh (Fig. 128), west Monaghan and south and east Tyrone.

Boarded floors of imported softwood, carried on joists, began to be laid in parlours in Ulster farms, apparently first in the east. In 1816 one or two rooms might be thus floored in better county Antrim houses,[24] particularly in the parishes of Glenavy, Camlin and Tullyrusk.[25] By the mid-1830s floors of this description, invariably laid first in parlours in better-class farmhouses, were reported in the Ordnance Survey memoirs for Carrickfergus, Glynn, Islandmagee, Kilroot, Templecorran, and Raloo, parishes clustered in south-east Antrim, beyond which they were noted only in east Londonderry (Desertlyn, Ballinascreen, Kilcronaghan and Desertmartin) in a few instances. However, the patchiness of the cover provided by these memoirs probably conceals the fact that parlours

Fig. 128.   Mid 19th-century hollow clay tiles fired at Florence Court, Co. Fermanagh in kitchen of farmhouse from Corradreenan West Td., Co. Fermanagh nearby, reconstructed at UFTM. UFTM L 1627.14

with boarded floors graced county Down farmhouses also, especially in the north and in the Lagan valley. Data on floors in rural houses in the north Down estates of the Londonderry family in 1848 are so generalised as to be difficult to interpret in respect of timber floors, but the figures are worth quoting, for they provide a view of the continuing prevalence of earth floors in a prosperous area, and of the minor role played by stone flags which were readily available near Newtownards. Of 1863 rural houses, 1470 (74.9%) had earth floors, 165 (8.9%) had timber floors, 100 (5.4%) had earth and timber floors, and 128 (6.9%) had stone flags.[26]

Upper floors in multi-storey houses, the generalised spread of which has already been described in Chapter 3, were constructed mostly of imported softwoods. At first butted boards were laid on joists, and when the boards dried fully and contracted, spaces opened up between them. This was often counteracted by pinning ceiling material to the undersides of the joists, use of tongued-and-grooved flooring boards not becoming widespread until the second half of the nineteenth century. Of course there was a minority of two-storey houses of earlier origin. One was an English house built at Lismacloskey, near Toome Bridge in west Antrim, apparently erected in

1717. Its upper floor is carried on a system of heavy oak beams which support oak joists (Fig. 129). Probably the original flooring was of oak planks, but when first examined in the 1960s softwood boards had been substituted.[27] We have already seen the possibility that houses in the 1830s in Killead and Glenavy, further south in county Antrim, may have been comparable, and another early house that probably originally had an oak floor for an upper half storey survives at Carrickreagh in west Fermanagh.[28] Others with early loft or upper-storey floors, perhaps of oak, are the cruck-framed house now preserved by the National Trust at Liffock, near Castlerock in north Londonderry, built in 1691,[29] and a two-storey house of the same period west of Waringstown in Magherana townland. This last seems to have an upper cruck truss, and while its floor boards are of softwood, the nature of the supporting joists is unknown.[30] Houses like the Carrickreagh one, built in the 1650s, were described and illustrated in the documentation of the English settlement of county Londonderry in the early seventeenth century as having 'garrets', although as illustrated on the contemporary maps they had the additional feature of dormer windows lighting rooms in the roof spaces.[31] They were sited

Fig. 129. Heavy oak beams and joists carry the upper floor of a large 'English' house of *c.*1717 from Lismacloskey Td., Co. Antrim (cf. Fig. 127) reconstructed at UFTM. UFTM L 1627.4

mainly in the plantation towns, but some were built in rural areas too. A few, for example in Ballykelly, had gable chimneys but most, like the Carrickreagh one, had axially located stone chimney stacks situated near the centre of the house.

It is important to recognise that use of the upper part of the volume of a house is only realistic once a chimney canopy is provided to take smoke away through the roof. We have already seen that introduction of chimneys to northern Irish vernacular houses was, at least in part, stimulated by English exemplars like the Londonderry ones. In other contexts in this chapter evidence for houses with upper storeys and garrets has been cited. One was in Mucklagh, county Armagh, about 1700, clearly a superior house, for in addition to 'good Chambers and Garrots' it had a 'handsome Parlor' and 'Sellars'.[32] Possession of cellars usually betrays socially superior housing, often with English connections, and houses with cellars like those in the Quaker community about Ballyhagan in Armagh in the second quarter of the eighteenth century are rare, for in other respects the Ballyhagan dwellings have been interpreted as belonging to the local vernacular tradition.[33] But the fact that they were Quaker houses betrays English family origins in the

second half of the seventeenth century. The Ballyhagan houses were interesting for another reason. They had lofts, the boarded floors of which belonged to the tenants, the boards being listed as inheritable property in probate inventories included in the community's will-book.

Spread of lofts throughout northern Irish vernacular housing was slow, probably because introduction of wattled, brick or stone chimney canopies was equally slow. The northern Irish county statistical surveys of the early 1800s do not mention lofts, and thereafter only a handful of house descriptions include reference to them. Lofts in which servants slept are noted in the 1830s in farmhouses in the county Antrim parishes of Grange of Ballywalter, Carrickfergus, and Islandmagee where access to the floors over parlour and ground-floor bedrooms was by ladder from, presumably, either end of the kitchen.[34] Similar lofts similarly used were in the Londonderry parishes of Desertlyn (where, however, they extended over parlour and kitchen), Desertoghill, and Clondermot where storage rather then sleeping is stated as their use.[35] Lofts are also noted in Cappagh, county Tyrone in the 1830s.[36] A decade later on the Glenfin estate in Donegal, tenants refused to put lofts into improved houses for fear of becoming liable to pay poor

Fig. 130.   Loft over hearth area in weaver's house in Ballydugan Td., Co. Down, reproduced in UFTM. UFTM L 344.7

rate, even though all they contributed to the building costs was their own labour.[37] We have already noted in other contexts how older vernacular architectural traditions sometimes survived in the housing of the poorest people in the first half of the nineteenth century; it is significant that no northern Irish references to lofts are to hand either from the evidence given before the poor inquiry, or in the descriptions of cottages in the Ordnance Survey memoirs, both in the 1830s. Lofts were obviously an innovation.

Hearth-area lofts built around the chimney have already been mentioned. They were particularly common in central and south Ulster (Fig. 130). Elsewhere, half-lofts over the end of the kitchen were more usual, their outer edges supported on a beam which spanned the kitchen, its ends resting on the front and rear wall-heads. These lofts were always open to the kitchen, and access was usually by ladder. Lofts over other rooms were often lighted by small gable windows. In a few houses with three or more units, the centre lofts were occasionally lighted. In a 'Georgianised' early nineteenth-century house in Carnacally townland near Crossgar in county Down, the top part of a fanlight over

the front entrance to the house lights the loft above. In some older houses, like the seventeenth-century cruck houses in Corcreeny, north-west Down and Trummery, south Antrim, low eaves-level windows in or on the wall-heads served the same purpose. Many vernacular farmhouses of the mid and later nineteenth century were built with lofts, a development being provision of proper stairs in place of ladders to give access to the upper spaces, always used as bedrooms; a brick-walled farmhouse, with half-hipped thatched roof, of mid-nineteenth-century origin in Drumduff townland, west Fermanagh, is a good example.[38]

Doors and Windows

There is no evidence, nor are there surviving examples, to tell what seventeenth-century doors may have looked like in vernacular houses. The earliest surviving door is from Berwick Hall, a large two-storey thatched house with English connections near Moira in county Down, which dates from about 1700. It is a fairly thin panelled door; the panels have raised fields the uppermost two of

Fig. 131.   Farmhouse door surrounded by 'Georgian'-style fanlight and ¾-sidelights, Dinnahorra Td., Co. Armagh. UFTM L 1541.12

Fig. 132.   Vertically divided early 19th-century door with raised-field panels and decorative door-head light, Balloolymore Td., Co. Down. UFTM L 975.8

which are shouldered with curved tops.[39] Occasionally one sees later eighteenth-century doors (Fig. 132), more commonly inside farmhouses than on the facade. I saw one on a derelict two-unit, two-storey slated farmhouse in 1981, near Roscor in north Fermanagh; but although the raised-field panels betray an earlier style, the house itself perhaps dates only from the early nineteenth century. Most panelled doors on farmhouses that survive are Victorian: usually four panels bordered with moulding. An interesting vernacular house, greatly elaborated with formal architectural detailing in Tullykenneye townland in the Clogher valley in east Tyrone has two long panels with semi-circular heads (see Chapter 8), a style in use in Befast about the 1880s.

Most rural houses had simple boarded doors. Earlier examples have broad boards (sometimes false-beaded to suggest narrower ones) with lapped joints, secured on the back usually by three transverse battens. Later doors of this type, from the second half of the nineteenth century on, have narrow, tongued-and-grooved boards with bevelled edges, sometimes with beading as well, and these are superseded mostly in the twentieth century by framed doors with an infill of boards.

The smallest rural houses usually had no doorhead light or fanlight, and from the later part of last century a windbreak built around the outer side of the door opening, often of brick, became widespread throughout the north of Ireland. Houses earlier than about 1860 always show these windbreaks to have been added. Sometimes they were roofed separately; but especially with thatch, the house roof was merely extended down over the windbreak. Late examples on slated houses often have a minuscule pitched slated roof, perhaps with decorative barge boards matching barges on the gables.

Fig. 133.   Victorian-style panelled door with simple rectangular door-head light, Clough Td., Co. Down. UFTM L 1147.5

Fig. 134.   Victorian-style farmhouse door with decorative fanlight and sidelights, Killartry Td., Co. Fermanagh. UFTM L 1029.5

Fig. 135.   Rectangular door-head light above folding door of framed mock panelling constructed of timber sheeting, crudely grained for superior appearance, Caldrum Td., Co. Tyrone. UFTM L 1263.11

Fig. 136. Hurdle door, apparently bound by ropes of twisted withes, for setting into door opening. Note half-door also. Farmhouse in Clogher district, Co. Tyrone, *c.*1910. UFTM L 919.3.

Some better-standard rural houses had a rectangular light accommodated above the door in an upward extension of the door frame (Figs. 132, 133, 134); it could be left plain or decoratively treated. Many of the best farmhouses from the early nineteenth century onwards borrowed detailing from formally designed modest Georgian farmhouses (Figs. 131, 133), either of contemporary or slightly earlier construction. The commonest features taken over into the vernacular tradition were window and door styles. Examples all over the north of Ireland of fanlights of various forms and decorative styles could be quoted. They were not confined to the newer two-storey slated farmhouses becoming widespread at that time. Good examples are known in single-storey thatched houses, even there occasionally supported by half or three-quarter side lights. Decorative pilasters, however, seldom flanked the door frames. In Fermanagh, parts of Cavan, Monaghan, west Armagh, south Tyrone and south Donegal, a distinctive and practical variant type of door frame was used; the earliest example I have seen is perhaps of late eighteenth-century date. Instead of the frame side members extending to ground level, they rest on blocks

of stone (occasionally brick) which rise to a height of as much as 25 cms. Treated thus, the bottoms of the wooden frames were protected from wet rot.

It is paradoxical that an element most popularly associated with traditional rural Irish houses is undocumented: the half-door. By no means all farmhouses and cottages were provided with one, but they occurred in all districts, mostly amongst smaller farmers and landless folk. Always fitted in the front door opening, hinged outside a full-length door so arranged that both opened inwards, the half-door is probably a nineteenth-century feature inspired from the bottom halves of horizontally divided stable doors seen in landlords' planned farmyards dating from the period of agricultural improvement from about 1790 onwards. Perhaps the popularity of the half-door first related to the expense of providing glazed windows in poorer homes, where it maintained the barrier of the full door so far as wandering animals in the farmyard were concerned, yet it admitted light. Only domestic fowl overcame it as a barrier, and only the man of the house leaning over it for contemplation or conversation with a neighbour minimised its light-admitting capacity. It was important, too, in controlling draught to the turf-burning open hearth.

An early tradition of doors, harking back to use of wattling more generally, survived in mid and west Ulster until the middle of the nineteenth century. Oral traditions of these doors were collected in west Donegal during the 1940s. Writing in 1818 John Donaldson described houses in south Armagh:

> The houses were generally built in clachons or clusters and had two doors or entrances which were closed up with bundles of sticks or hurdles, alternately, or as it answered to keep out the wind and rain.[40]

A more elaborate account is by Thomas Reid, who described such doors in the Ballygawley area in south-east Tyrone (cf. Fig. 136) four years later:

> The doors of these huts if doors they can be called, are framed by two perpendicular sticks, and five cross ones, somewhat resembling a gate of rude workmanship, having the interstices filled with ropes made of straw, worked in after the manner of a basket. Persons desirous of *extra* comfort plaster these doors with a substance composed of tenacious clay and cowdung, which renders them impermeable to the severe winds of winter . . .[41]

Ordnance Survey memoirs of 1834 for three east Fermanagh parishes describe doors like the Ballygawley ones, those in the highest parts of Enniskillen parish being simply hinged to the door post 'by a gad at top and bottom',[42] while in Derryvullen[43] and Trory South[44] the thick, twisted straw ropes, packed very close together, were bound vertically around the door framework. These memoir descriptions may be added to seventeen accounts of similar doors from Armagh, Donegal, Fermanagh and Tyrone in Ulster, and one in Leitrim and one in Sligo are on the southern margins of our area. All are cited in a study of this tradition published by Dr. A.T. Lucas in 1956.[45] A fourth addition to his citations shows that 'hurdle' doors were known earlier further east in Ulster, about 1759, in the mountainous parts of south Down; they are mentioned in a letter from Edward Willes, Chief Baron of the Irish Exchequer written, while he was on circuit in Ireland, to the Earl of Warwick.[46] We have already, of course, had later eighteenth-century confirmation of such doors in county Down, in the description of communal house building quoted in full at the beginning of chapter 3. Lucas has shown that doors, in the form of wicker hurdles, sometimes supplemented by woven straw mats hung on the inside of the door or door opening, or in the form of the straw-rope doors, belong to a consistent tradition which included use of wattling for chimneys, chimney lofts, and internal house partitions. This tradition goes back to a house type in construction of which wattling was extensively employed, and for which there is adequate documentation in early Christian and medieval sources.

In no respect are the social variations in vernacular housing more marked than in the matter of windows. Houses of the poor in the first half of the nineteenth century were often windowless or at most had one or two openings, usually unglazed. Indeed, cheap ready-made windows were still sold in local markets in the early part of the twentieth century for setting into poorer houses so that they could be improved. By contrast comfortable, well-constructed farmhouses in south Antrim parishes in the 1830s had sliding-sash windows, and if these were then an innovation there, farmhouses elsewhere usually had fixed leaded or lattice windows. Sash windows were noted in Glenavy parish as early as 1816.[47] As we have already seen in other contexts, the pattern of social differences was complicated by geographical variations; this is obvious from the data gathered by Maurice Collis in his estate surveys in the 1840s (Table 7).[48] If the number of windows in the facade of a house is generally indicative of the standard of accommodation involved, then the north Down estate of the Londonderry family in 1848 stands out from the others in having a low proportion of windowless houses, and a relatively high proportion with four or more windows. However, it seems to have been the west Armagh Killylea-Keady estate which had the lowest proportion of single-room houses. Furthermore, the very high proportion of windowless houses in the Charlemont estate must be set alongside a proportion of about 15% of the houses there that were of one room. Absence of windows was not confined to the very smallest, poorest houses. This is evident in the Kilmacrenan estate in north Donegal also, where more than 46% of the rural houses were windowless in their facades, yet the proportion of houses consisting of a single undivided room was lower, at 35%. In general, however, the standards of lighting seem to have been highest in north Down, followed by the south Donegal estates in the Bundoran and Ballintra areas; then west Armagh represented by Killylea-Keady and south Fermanagh by Rosslea display similarities, while the worst circumstances were endured by the rural populations in the Charlemont estate in north-west Armagh and the Kilmacrenan area in north Donegal.[49]

No mention is made in the early seventeenth-century documentation of the nature of windows in Irish housing, although some representations of Irish houses on maps of the period show small rectangular openings, sometimes placed high in walls just below thatch eaves. The houses of the English in county Londonderry, on the other hand,

TABLE 7. PERCENTAGES OF TOTAL RURAL HOUSES BY
NUMBER OF FACADE WINDOWS IN 1840s

Estate	0	1	2/3	4+	Total Rural Houses
North Down	4.3	25.6	55.1	15.0	1863
Lecale, Down	25.4	31.4	37.3	5.9	118
Charlemont, Armagh	67.7	13.5	15.1	3.7	378
Killylea-Keady, Armagh	26.3	26.3	40.8	6.6	2122
Rosslea, Fermanagh	42.7	21.4	33.5	2.4	828
Bundoran, Donegal	13.3	16.3	65.3	5.1	294
Ballintra, Donegal	23.2	17.2	55.0	4.6	1530
Kilmacrenan, Donegal	46.6	23.6	27.8	2.1	1336

had well-proportioned windows lighting ground-floor rooms. They were usually drawn wider than high, and similarly proportioned, but smaller windows are shown in dormers lighting roof-space rooms. Gable windows are also sometimes shown.

Windows were easily altered, and therefore few early window openings survive. Two houses studied in detail in east Ulster give some clues as to the nature of seventeenth-century and early eighteenth-century window shapes. Wide, not very high windows were the earliest form in the cruck-framed house, Corcreeney 'B', south of Lurgan, but the openings had been altered to upright shapes possibly as early as the late eighteenth century. This house retained internal evidence in its wall-heads of wide eaves windows, about 15 cm. high, a type also recorded in the seventeenth-century cruck house in Trummery townland in south Antrim. The early eighteenth-century house at Gloverstown, in Lismaclos-key townland in west Antrim, now at the Ulster Folk and Transport Museum, first had small narrow window openings, each apparently glazed with four fixed panes. A blocked-up opening was found with remains of its original heavy oak frame *in situ*. Most of these windows were later replaced by larger Georgian-style fenestration of sliding-sash type in enlarged openings.[50]

A few houses have been examined, apparently of mid-eighteenth century origin, with tall narrow windows in their facades. One is a thatched farmhouse in Moneydarragh Beg townland (Fig. 137) south of Annalong in south Down. Its window panes are arranged in two vertical rows. Also perhaps belonging to this period are a few houses with single vertical rows of panes, usually four in number, flanking the front door but, unlike Georgian side-lights, set a little distance from the door frame. I have seen examples in west Fermanagh.

The most widespread window forms show Georgian and later influences from the formal end of the building continuum. Sliding-sash windows with one or both sashes hung and sometimes weighted, having commonly six (Figs. 138, 139), sometimes eight, panes aranged in two horizontal rows in each sash, appeared first in formally designed farmhouses and in rectories of the established church. By the early nineteenth century they were being built into more modest houses. Earlier examples are without a parting bead or slip between sashes, a feature that did not become common, at vernacular level, until after 1850. A minority of vernacular houses had larger windows divided by vertical timber mullions (Fig. 140) having a single row of panes in two sashes on the outer sides, with usually a three-pane-wide window between. Upper floors often display reduction of the window height by a row of panes (Fig. 139), and windows with the remaining three rows of panes divided in sashes one up, two down, or two up, one down, occurred widely.

Later nineteenth-century development of windows saw removal of the vertical glazing bars, leaving two sashes each with two horizontally rectangular panes, a form that had developed earlier in Regency formal architecture. As glass became cheaper towards the end of the nineteenth century, single-pane sashes became common.

There is a widely held belief in many parts of the north of Ireland that imposition of window tax led to blocking up of windows in older houses of the late eighteenth and early nineteenth centuries. Where significant numbers of blocked-up windows have been encountered, they have usually been in larger houses, obviously the homes of better-off folk. An example may be a blocked window in the Lismacloskey house mentioned above, additional to one closed up because stairs were placed inside it.

K

Fig. 137.   Narrow 18th-century style sash windows, Moneydarragh Beg Td., Co. Down. UFTM L 1066.0

Fig. 138.   Small-pane sash windows (top sash, single row of panes), one replaced by later sash window, Cranfield Td., Co. Antrim. UFTM L 899.4A

Fig. 139.   'Georgian'-style sash windows in a 19th-century farmhouse, Ballynagarrick Td., Co. Down. UFTM L 1104.5

Fig. 140.   Timber-mullioned 'Georgian'-style windows of late 19th-century date, Scarva Td., Co. Down. UFTM L 969.5

Fig. 141.   Late 19th-century margined sash windows in derelict farmhouse, Ballykeel Artifinny Td., Co. Down. UFTM L 932.27

Fig. 142.   Cast-iron swivel opening lattice window, in vernacular cottage, Magirr Td., Co. Tyrone. UFTM L 1055.12

Blocked windows ascribable to window-tax avoidance are difficult to find at vernacular level, for the houses were too small to have been liable to the tax in the first place. In the northern Irish area in 1810 almost 12,000 houses were taxable, about half of which were paying on between one and nine windows.[51] Two facts put these figures in context. First, the northern Irish total represented only 23.3% of all Irish dwellings liable to payment of window tax in 1810. By comparison, the hearth-tax figures for 1791 showed that Ulster houses constituted 31.9% of all Irish dwellings in that year. So we may safely conclude that the tax bore less heavily in northern areas than elsewhere in Ireland. Second, the 1791 hearth-tax figures showed that, including exempted new and pauper houses, there were almost 233,000 houses in Ulster.[52] Population was rising steadily about the turn of the century, therefore the 1791 total represents a conservative estimate of the total for 1810. So northern houses liable to window tax in 1810 constituted less than 5.3% of total northern dwellings.

Houses liable to the tax were landlords' and other wealthy people's homes, and mainly middle-class urban houses. In fact, writing in 1812, Edward Wakefield categorically stated that window tax 'seldom affects a farmhouse in Ireland'.[53] His opinion was reiterated in 1817 in the report of a deputation which visited the Grocers' Company's estate in south Londonderry. 'The King's Taxes consist of the Hearth Tax and Window Tax; and, so far as respects by much the majority of the tenants, their habitations do not contain hearths or windows enough to be rateable at all, and therefore they have nothing to pay.'[54] When blocked-up windows are encountered in rural houses, a more significant explanation may lie in the relatively high cost of window glass until late in the nineteenth century. In cases where a window was accidentally broken, especially if it was an older small one, it was sometimes more economic to put up with the inconvenience of a loss of internal illumination by closing up the opening, than to pay for replacement glass.

EIGHT

Vernacular House Types

I. THE BASIS OF CLASSIFICATION

THUS far, materials and modes of house construction have been examined, and parameters noted for traditional house construction: construction in bays or structural units stretching from front to rear, axially placed hearths and absence of end piercing at ground-floor level. These are not sufficient conditions to provide a set of ground rules for house building; in particular, the position must be known of the entrance from outside, which in the Irish house is almost universally directly into the unit used as the principal living space or kitchen. Entrance position must be considered relative to the location of the other universal feature of houses in Ireland, the hearth.

In Chapter 1 the pioneering dichotomy drawn between houses with central hearth and those with gable hearth was noted. It was early recognised that discrimination between house types on the basis of hearth position presented problems.[1] Åke Campbell's definition of central-chimney and gable-chimney houses was made on the basis of two-roomed (two-unit) structures (cf. houses A1 and 2 and B2 in Fig. 143). At that level the classification works. But when a third room is added to the gable-hearth house behind the hearth, it becomes a central-hearth house. In the case of some three-unit houses this is what happened. Others were built *ab initio* as three-unit structures. Must we, then, distinguish between three-unit houses that started as gable-hearth types and became central-hearth ones by accretion of a third unit, and others which were always three-unit central-hearth buildings? Their final ground plans are identical.

Brief diagrammatic consideration of plan types encountered in the countryside shows that the situation is even more difficult if the hearth (chimney) position is to be maintained as the basis for classification, whereas there is a relatively simple way forward. Fig. 143 identifies the observed one-storey arrangements. Two simple points are made here. Multi-storey vernacular houses merely impose a further floor over these plan types, and extension in length adds additional units at one or both ends. For purposes of classification these enlargements do not constitute separate types, they only multiply the members in the basic plan-form families. Secondly, chimneys and fireplaces in units other than the kitchen have been omitted. From what is outlined in a previous chapter about the history of multiple hearths in northern Irish houses, it will be appreciated that only the kitchen hearth/chimney complex is of fundamental significance in vernacular house typology.

Fig. 143 may be read in vertical columns to accord with the chimney-position dichotomy. At the left are gable-hearth houses. House A2, with a central door, represents a common type all over Ireland, although the added feature of the outshot (A1) at the rear corner was confined to northern and western districts. House D represents a minority form recognised in Down, Armagh, Monaghan, east Tyrone and south Antrim; further south an example has recently been noted in county Dublin.[2] On the right are houses having their hearths more or less centrally positioned, located at one or other end of the central unit in a three-unit house. Here it is essential to take notice of the entrance position. House B1 (of three units) and house B2 (of two units) both have entrance and hearth adjacent to one another, a screen wall (the 'jamb wall') which separates them forming a lobby immediately inside the entrance. This set of relationships also characterises house D. Houses D, B1 and B2 together form a class which we may refer to as *hearth-lobby* houses, meaning that they all have the jamb wall between entrance and hearth.

Ignoring for the present the outshot on house A, if a third unit is added behind the hearth, the form C1 results, bringing about conversion from gable-hearth to central-hearth type. However, if one reads Fig. 143 horizontally across the top, houses A, C1 and C2 (a minority form) share the same kitchen layout, with hearth at one end, entrance at the other end leading *directly* into the living space, no lobby being *essential* since entrance and hearth

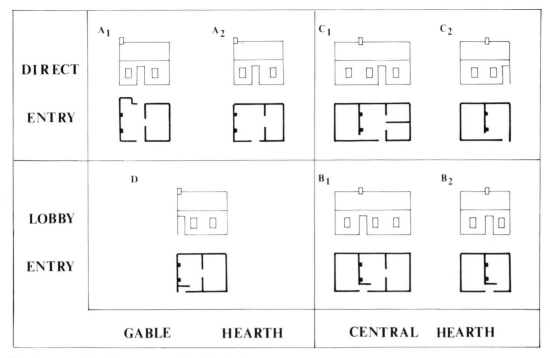

Fig. 143. Classification of Irish house types by plan form.

are no longer adjacent to one another. Whether there is only a single entrance, or opposed entrances as in A1, is unimportant for purposes of classification. We may refer to these houses in the upper part of Fig. 1 as being of *direct-entry* type.

Two things support classification of Irish vernacular housing on the basis of horizontal rather than vertical reading of Fig. 143. As will be seen later in this chapter, distributional evidence for hearth-lobby houses is consistent, whereas that for central-chimney or central-hearth houses is not. Secondly, since Åke Campbell's 'Notes on the Irish House' in the 1930s,[3] the jamb wall and the bed outshot have commonly been regarded as fundamentally opposed features.[4] The fact is that the bed outshot in the districts where it occurs may be a minority feature in direct-entry houses, not encountered in houses with a jamb wall (except in a tiny number of hybrid houses at the distributional limit of the hearth-lobby type).[5] Furthermore, regarding the jamb wall as a fundamental feature obviously did not accord with associating it exclusively with central-hearth houses, because of the existence of the minority form represented by D in Fig. 143 (cf. Figs. 179, 180).

All of the vernacular house types commonly encountered in rural parts are illustrated in Fig. 143, or may be derived from them by processes of enlargement mentioned above. Obviously these types do not exhaust

all the theoretically possible relationships between entrance and principal hearth. A variant is where, in the kitchen unit of A, the entrance is not actually alongside the partition wall between the units, but removed some way from it; this variation also occasionally occurs in C1 and C2 houses.

The four basic layouts, A-D, are represented in Fig. 144 which sets out most of the possible door/hearth relationships theoretically possible. Of the three possible entrances in the front wall into the unit adjacent to the kitchen, I have found only two houses which can be assigned to each of two of the options. Houses with an entry leading in onto the rear side of the hearth wall (H1) are a fundamental British vernacular form, represented in Ireland only by a house, now demolished (see Fig. 210), to the north of Derry city,[6] and a miller's house, perhaps of eighteenth-century origin in county Louth, just south of the area with which this book deals. Two further houses, one in Armagh in Tullyah townland (see Fig. 5), the other in Kilsob townland in Cavan, have an entrance into the unit next the kitchen alongside the wall separating the two units (H2). The first of these has been included in Chapter 1 in discussion of the building continuum where it is assigned to the middle 'grey' area between the vernacular and formal architectural extremes. The Cavan house lies further in the direction of the truly vernacular, is a late, nineteenth-century

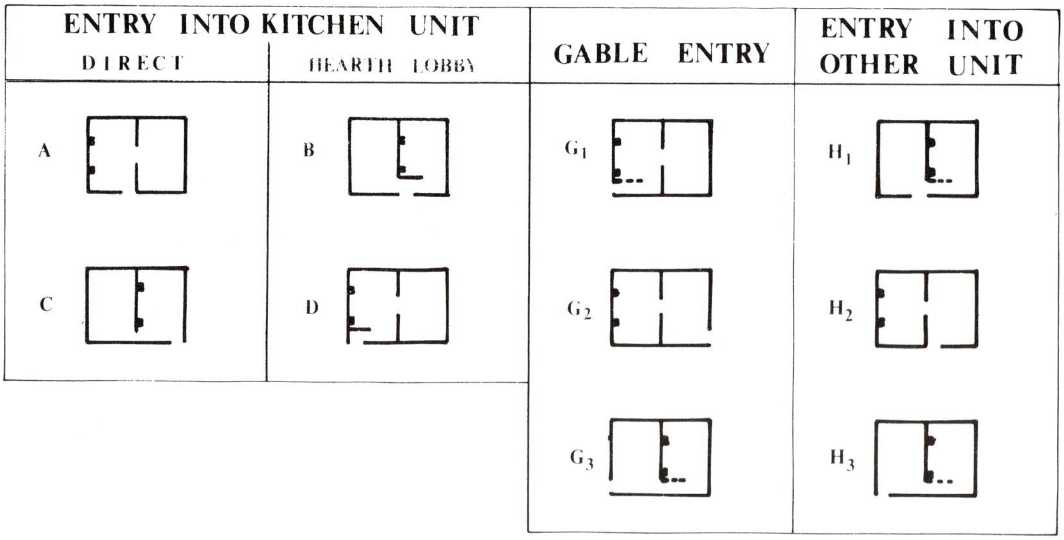

Fig. 144.   Observed, and some theoretically possible, two-unit house plan forms, within the norms of Irish vernacular house construction.

dwelling, and the displacement of its front door out of the kitchen (there is a rear one also leading directly in) was probably associated with desire for greater family privacy within the house, for it stands on the roadside at a road junction. Type H3 in Fig. 2 is so far unrecorded in the field.

It has not been considered necessary to add to Fig. 144 the various possibilities of house forms with lateral hearths and chimneys. Vernacular houses with lateral chimneys are known in Wales[7] and south-west England;[8] the only examples in Ireland known to me appear in early photographs of the Claddagh, the fishing village across the river Corrib from the walled city of Galway.[9]

Northern Irish, indeed all Irish vernacular housing may be discussed within the formal categories of *direct-entry* and *hearth-lobby* plan types. Entry into the dwelling is invariably into the unit containing the kitchen and living area, although lobbies of various kinds, including those in the hearth-lobby itself, may be constructed inside the entrance. Houses with an entrance lobby or hallway wholly occupying a structural unit, usually centrally located in the building, invariably indicate formal architectural planning either directly or as derivatives. The Scottish form of but-and-ben house, with an entrance opening onto a small closet contained between two main units and backing onto a hearth wall in each, is unknown in Ireland.

II. DIRECT-ENTRY HOUSES

Byre-Dwellings

The most archaic-seeming houses of which there are survivals are combinations of quarters for people and cattle in which there is no physical separation between the byre and house ends. The mildness of the climate over most of Ireland permits keeping of animals like sheep and dry cattle outdoors at most times, but milk cattle need housing in winter and during the night in spring and autumn. On the relatively small peasant farms in much of Ulster in the past many farmers had only four or five milk cows at most which could easily be accommodated in one end of a byre-dwelling. Additional or alternative space was obviously essential on farms with more cows.

The byre-dwelling was used widely in Donegal in the early nineteenth century.[10] In 1814 it was seen as far east as Culdaff in Inishowen,[11] but by mid-century had retreated mainly to the west coast and inland mountainous districts, where, in Gweedore (Fig. 145), in a district occupied by several hundred families, there were only six houses with separate byres.[12] Byre-dwellings were common elsewhere in the west, for example in the north part of county Leitrim.[13]

Typically, the byre-dwelling was about 9 m. long, 5 to 5.5 m. wide, and solidly constructed with stone walls 0.6 m. thick, sometimes built dry, sometimes mortared. Opposite doors were usually placed nearer the end away

Fig. 145.   Small byre-dwelling with bed outshot, *c.*1880s, Gweedore, Co. Donegal. The byre is at the low end, to the right of the door. UFTM L 440.1

Fig. 146.   Byre end of a byre-dwelling from Magheragallan Td., Co. Donegal, reconstructed at UFTM. The bucket stands on the farther side of the drain separating the cows' accommodation beyond from the living accommodation in the foreground.

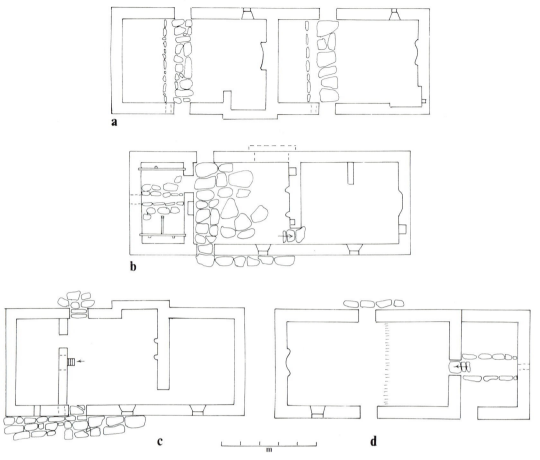

Fig. 147. Plans of byre-dwellings.
a: Magheragallan Td. (cf. Fig. 146, house to right);
b: Croaghnashallog Td.;
c: Lunniagh Td.;
d: Meenmore Td.
All Co. Donegal (after McCourt).

from a gable hearth, a walk-way between them that was often flagged separating the larger living end from the smaller byre end, a stone-lined drain usually running along the byre side of this walk-way and out through the base of front or rear wall according to slope (Figs. 145, 146). Some byre-houses had no drainage to the exterior. Animal urine was absorbed in turf (peat) mould spread in the internal drain, which was forked out regularly and replaced. Some larger examples had another unit, used for sleeping, behind and 'above' the hearth wall, and in some examples seen in the 1930s this had been abandoned as families contracted due to emigration.[14] It is obvious that this additional sleeping unit was regarded as an element that could conveniently be added to or subtracted from the byre-dwelling as the needs of family size dictated, for many byre-dwellings known from the

nineteenth century onwards had a bed accommodated in a corner of the living end, close to the hearth.

Opposite doors seem to have been an essential element in the use of these byre-dwellings, for once the cattle were removed to separate accommodation, the rear door was often blocked up.[15] Opposite doors at the end of the living quarters away from the hearth therefore perhaps betray the existence, or former existence, of byre-dwellings; they were commented on in north Donegal in 1752,[16] and in recent survivals of vernacular houses were not uncommon even in east Ulster. Traditions of common accommodation of people and cattle in byre-dwellings have been reported also from the Carrickmore area in Tyrone and from south Armagh, where 'Parents of people still alive remembered having seen houses with the hearth at one end and the cattle at the lower end. A drain called a "group" or "trinket" ran across the floor behind the cows which were tethered with their heads to the end wall.'[17]

In the nineteenth century there were growing pressures of hygiene standards and domestic convenience, so in some instances the byre end was partitioned off from the living quarters, though cattle still came in and out using the same doors as the human occupants. Construction of this partition may have been facilitated, even prompted, by the existence of a storage or sleeping loft over the cattle; it was easy to screen the space between the floor and the underside of the beam that carried the front edge of the loft, as in a house at Croaghnashallog in west Donegal (Fig. 147). The next stage in the diversification of the direct-entry plan-form family is seen in another house in the same district, at Lunniagh, where the loft was also partitioned by boards from the living space and access provided by means of wooden stairs. An abandoned byre-dwelling on Gola Island, off the west coast of Donegal, illustrates this stage also, but the partition between byre with loft above, and living end is now a stone wall, and separate external entrance into the byre is provided in the rear wall, the internal access having been blocked up. This house had a third, sleeping unit beyond the kitchen hearth.[18] Most late survivals of this arrangement had the byre end itself converted for sleeping, but the former function was usually betrayed by evidence of the byre drain. Further separation of man and beast was achieved by building a separate byre with its own external entrance onto the end of the house, but internal access from house to byre was maintained. Finally, internal communication between byre and house was omitted, and in the nineteenth century two- and three-unit houses with a byre added at one gable became common.

Evidence for this development is not confined to county Donegal (Fig. 148).[19] In the Ballinamore area of Leitrim some farmhouses were arranged similarly to the Croaghnashallog one, and other evidence is from north Louth and south Armagh.[20] Late persistence of the type in Donegal was documented by an officer of the Congested Districts Board at about the end of the nineteenth century,[21] and a century earlier some examples probably existed in north Antrim and north Londonderry.[22] There are hints also that byre-dwellings were still in use in the 1830s amongst poorer farmers in Longfield East parish in Tyrone,[23] and in Ematris parish in Monaghan.[24] However, documentation of the keeping of animals in their dwellings by the poor is difficult to assess. The practice is widely commented upon, for example in the evidence given to the poor inquiry in the 1830s. In the west Tyrone parish of Camus, near Strabane, in low, two-unit cottages the kitchen was occupied at night by the younger members of the family and the pig, and 'a room' by the parents and the cow;[25] it is unlikely that this was truly the byre-end of a byre-dwelling. And what are we to make of the comment in a report on conditions in the dwellings of cottiers on the Drapers' Company's lands in the Moneymore and Ballinascreen divisions of their

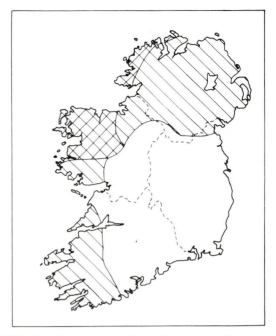

Fig. 148.   Distribution of evidence for byre-dwellings in Ireland in recent times (after Ó Danachair). Single shading: traditions of the house type; double shading: standing remains of byre-dwellings.

property in county Londonderry in the period 1817 to 1827: 'there is a partition between that part of the cabin which is devoted to the use of the family and that part which is applied to the use of the horse, the cow or goat, and the pigs'.[26] In the overcrowded social circumstances of rural Ireland in the late eighteenth and first half of the nineteenth centuries, the poor undoubtedly sometimes kept their few animals at night in the houses with them, houses neither traditionally intended nor laid out to accommodate beasts, unlike the byre-dwellings. Nevertheless there is more than adequate evidence, a little of it quoted here, to show that the tradition of the byre-dwelling was formerly widespread throughout the north of Ireland.[27]

An interesting localised development of the byre-dwelling happened in parts of the north of Ireland. As population pressure forced construction of houses into physically difficult terrain and onto slopes, byre-dwellings were sometimes put up where it was possible to accommodate a full bedroom over the byre, as it were a development from the loft arrangement in the Croaghnashallog or Lunniagh houses. The floor of the byre was now at a lower level than that of the living end, and so a separate external byre entrance was essential for the cattle, although in some cases, for example in a house at Dore (Fig. 151) in west Donegal, internal access

Fig. 149.   Farmhouse with bedroom over byre, Crolly Td., Co. Donegal. Byre entrance is at right-hand end. UM WO4/23/13.

Fig. 150.   Rear of farmhouse with byre under bedroom, showing byre entrance and kitchen bed outshot at upper end. Note mucking-out hole in gable. House from Cruckaclady Td., Co. Tyrone, reconstructed at UFTM. UFTM L 695.6

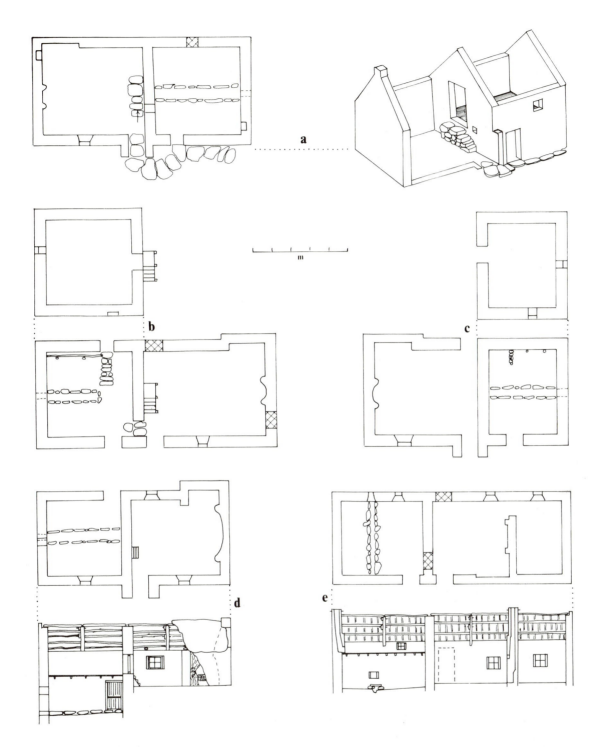

Fig. 151. Plans of houses with bedroom over byre.
a: Dore Td., Co. Donegal;
b: Meenacung Td., Co. Donegal;
c: Crolly Td., Co. Donegal (all after McCourt);
d: Cruckaclady Td., Co. Tyrone, reconstructed at UFTM (cf. Fig. 150).
Blocked openings cross-shaded.

from the kitchen, stepping down into the byre, was still provided for keeping an eye on the cattle in bad weather. Houses without this internal access, and with a bedroom over the byre, have been recorded in Donegal (Meenacung and Crolly), Tyrone (Cruckaclady, now at the Ulster Folk and Transport Museum)[28] (Figs. 149, 150) and Armagh (Tullyah) (Fig. 5), although the internal layout of the last does not conform to either of the basic Irish vernacular house types, and in Chapter 1 it has been assigned to the middle of the building continuum. Comparable houses may have been known also in south Down.[29]

Byre-Dwelling Derivatives

Removal of cattle from the 'low' end of a byre-dwelling, either to a byre attached at one end of the house or to a separate building, released the animals' end of the byre-dwelling to domestic use. As elsewhere in the west of Ireland, this end may at first have been divided off by use of larger pieces of furniture: dresser and larger presses. Two of these could even be arranged to leave a space between them into which a door was fitted. They provided a partition that approximated to the heights of the front and rear wall-heads, or to the transverse beam that carried the front of a half-loft. Few northern Irish traditions of this arrangement have been recorded, and it

seems that the idea of inserting a solid partition wall was readily taken up. Immediately, a simple byre-dwelling became a two-unit house, the position of the former byre now taken by a bedroom (Figs. 152, 153). Where a bedroom already existed beyond the kitchen hearth, a three-unit house came about (Figs. 154—157) and the possibility of devoting space to a 'room' or more or less formal parlour could be entertained. In the nineteenth century especially, even earlier in eastern districts, many vernacular houses were built in these two- and three-unit forms, and simple reduction of the house to the kitchen unit alone provided the cabins which accommodated many poor families during the period of massive population growth from about 1750 until the potato famine period in the 1840s (Figs. 27-29). As living standards rose, provision of lofts was common over units other than the kitchen, but insertion of an upper floor continuous from one end of the house to the other was rare until late in the nineteenth century.

Two-unit and three-unit houses became the norm, although larger dwellings were not unknown (Fig. 158). More than four units have rarely been seen in surviving houses, and thus the great majority of rural houses in 1841, as we have already seen, were classified in the census in Class IV (one unit) or Class III (two to four units). We have seen, too, that at the beginning of the nineteenth century more than one hearth was unusual in a vernacular house, but by Victorian times fireplaces to

Fig. 152.   Two-unit direct-entry farmhouse, Brackenagh Td., Co. Down. UFTM 1218.3

Fig. 153.   Two-unit direct-entry cottage, Drumgare Td., Co. Armagh. UFTM L 1541.14

Fig. 154.   Three-unit direct-entry farmhouse, Scaffag Td., Co. Fermanagh. UFTM L 986.1

Fig. 155.   Three-unit direct-entry farmhouse, Drumsillagh Td., Co. Fermanagh. UFTM L 986.5

Fig. 156.   Three-unit direct-entry house, Clough Td., Co. Down. UFTM L 1147.3

Fig. 157. Three-unit direct-entry farmhouse, Mullan Td., Co. Londonderry. UFTM L 899.14A

heat other units, and later loft rooms and attics, were coming into favour. So the two-chimney vernacular houses familiar amongst the survivals came into being. Two-unit houses with two gable chimneys became almost symmetrically arranged (Fig. 152), but in east and north Ulster three-unit houses with two chimneys often maintained a rather lopsided look (Figs. 156, 157). Not so, however, in the south-west in Fermanagh, Monaghan and Cavan, where the three-unit house commonly carried its two chimneys on the internal cross walls separating the units (Fig. 155), and so only the door, contrasting with the windows, broke the symmetry of facade piercing. This particular form of the three-unit vernacular house became widespread across Ireland into county Galway and southwards from there; but it must be distinguished from another type with a similar external appearance but different internal arrangement (cf. Fig. 181), described below.

The Bed Outshot

A distinctive element in many north and west Irish vernacular houses is the 'outshot' (also *cúilteach*, *cailleach* and various English renderings of these Irish terms, e.g. 'cooltyee', and 'hag' or 'haggard') which accommodated a bed in a corner of the kitchen beside the hearth (Fig. 159), usually on the rear wall. Expressed externally as a projection outside the rectangle of the dwelling (Figs. 160—163), varying from 15 cm. to about 80 cm. deep, internally it enlarged the living space so that the bed it accommodated impinged as little as possible, if at all, on the kitchen floor area (Figs. 159, 164). It is as long only as the bed it accommodated, in which traditionally the senior occupants of the house slept. The bed in many shallower outshots, especially in Tyrone, had its projecting end protected by a wall sticking out into the kitchen space. By contrast, some kitchen-corner beds, especially in Donegal and Tyrone, were recessed only a few centimetres into the wall thickness, no externally expressed outshot being created. Most outshots were roofed externally merely by continuing the house roof outwards, but in a few cases a small separate roof was necessary where the house wall-head was appreciably higher than normal. A few examples have been seen where the outshot was carried into an upper storey, as at Straw in east county Londonderry,[30] and others where the outshot was carried across behind the kitchen hearth wall into the next unit, either as a second outshot, or as a widening of the full length of that unit, as in a thatched farmhouse in Bodoney in south-west Tyrone which I saw in the 1960s.

Internally, the outshot bed was usually screened from

L

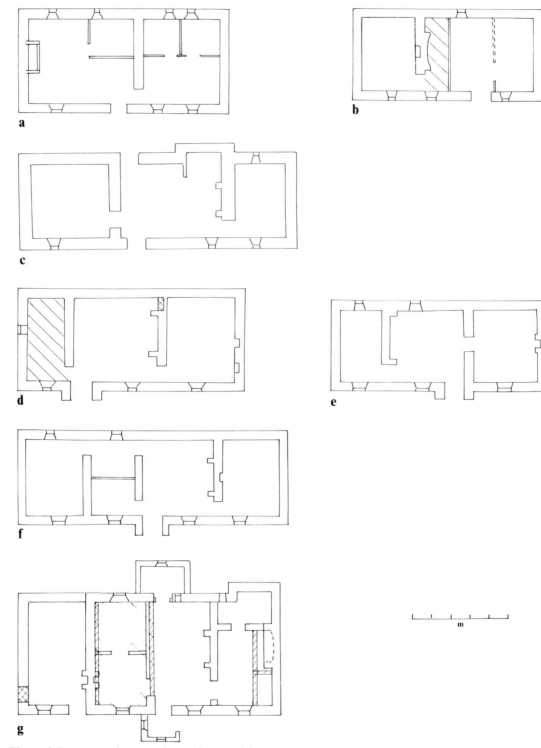

Fig. 158.   Plans of direct-entry houses of two, three and four units.
a: Clooney Td., Co. Londonderry (after McCourt);
b: Dragh Td., Co. Fermanagh;
c: Glencolumbkille, Co. Donegal (after Ó Danachair);
d: Drumskinny Td., Co. Fermanagh;
e: Corliss Td., Co. Armagh;
f: Legnahorna Td., Co. Fermanagh;
g: Newtownstewart Td., Co. Tyrone.
Floor beams and loft areas shaded, blocked openings cross-shaded.

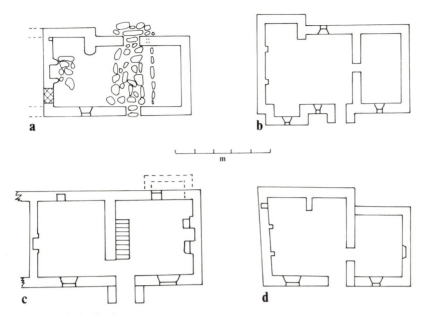

Fig. 159.   Plans of houses with outshots.
a: bed outshot at rear of byre-dwelling, Meenacreevagh Td., Co. Dongal (after Evans);
b: weaver's house with rear bed outshot and front work outshot, Glengomna Td., Co. Londonderry (after McCourt);
c: outshot closed off and removed following addition of upstairs bedrooms, Coshkib Td., Co. Antrim, reconstructed at UFTM;
d: double outshot at rear of original one-room dwelling, Beagh Td., Co. Tyrone.

Fig. 160.   Bed outshot with small window, Fawney Td., Co. Tyrone. UFTM L 933.16

Fig. 161.   Bed outshot at rear of two-unit dwelling, Binn TD., Co. Londonderry. UFTM L 933.17

Fig. 162.   Outshot at rear of slated farmhouse, Cavanakill Td., Co. Armagh. UFTM L 1376.2

Fig. 163.   Outshot at rear of a large three-unit farmhouse carried through from kitchen (left part of outshot) into unit behind the kitchen hearth, Lisnacreaght Td., Co. Tyrone. UFTM L 933.3

Fig. 164.   Kitchen interior, *c.*1900, with bed outshot closed off behind timber-sheeted doors, between dresser and hearth, Teelin, Co. Donegal. UM W04/13/36

view, commonly by means of curtains draped across its kitchen side and any exposed part of its end, but in some cases, especially along the north coast and in county Donegal, the outshot was encased behind timber doors (Fig. 164). Something similar was seen by John Gamble in 1818 in the Fintona area in south Tyrone:

> I had not walked far, when a shower forced me to take shelter in a little cabin. A woman was busily occupied at her wheel; another was in her bed, which as is customary here, was a little boarded place at the side of the fire.[31]

Evidence from the west of Ireland shows that formerly the bed was screened from the kitchen by means of straw mats,[32] and perhaps only poverty of documentation obscures this practice in the north.

The bed outshot is clearly described in Racavan parish in mid Antrim in the 1830s[33] and also in east Londonderry parishes in the Slieve Gallion area,[34] but it is difficult to tell if '. . . the many little "outshots" or new bedrooms now building . . .'[35] in Kilrea parish also in east Londonderry were actually true outshots, which hardly could realistically be described as bedrooms. Only two other descriptions are known to me. One is for west Fermanagh and neighbouring parts of Cavan, a district in which I have been unable to find surviving examples; it is a fictional account telling of the early eighteenth century, but drawn on the author's experience of houses in the second half of the nineteenth century.[36] The other is in the documentation of the Congested Districts Board at the end of the nineteenth century describing conditions in The Rosses on the west Donegal seaboard. Like the Kilrea reference, it is not definitive, for it merely refers to a situation 'where there are only two rooms in a house, the father and mother sleep near the fire in the day room . . .'[37]

The outshot was found in houses in Donegal, Londonderry, Antrim, Tyrone and north Fermanagh, as well as north Leitrim and Sligo (Fig. 165). I have also discovered three examples in the south-east of our area, one between Newtownhamilton and Belleek in south Armagh and two just south of the Armagh border in north Louth.[38] Perhaps outshots may have existed also in the eighteenth century in east and south Down, for these areas were and are dominated by direct-entry houses of byre-dwelling derivative type. This is the vernacular context to which the outshot obviously belongs. Yet it must be stressed that the outshot was not a universal feature of housing within its distribution area. In many districts only a minority of houses had outshots, so the presence of the outshot should not be regarded as sufficient basis to define a separate house type. On the other hand, the consistency of its distribution coupled

Fig. 165.   Distribution of houses with bed outshot in Ireland. Main distribution, shaded; northern Irish outliers to east of main distribution, dots (cf. also Fig. 201).

with the albeit meagre documentation confirming its existence back at least to the beginning of the nineteenth century suffices to confirm the outshot as a genuine, traditional element in the housing of northern and western Ireland. It was not a late expedient introduced to ease overcrowding.

Outshots on the fronts of houses, sometimes with windows, have been noticed in a few places, in county Londonderry for example, which were used to provide a sitting-out area, well-lighted, for women working at linen embroidery and drawn-thread work, and on the rear perhaps to provide added space for a linen loom in a few cases in Waringstown in north-west Down. The recorded examples are so few that they are best regarded as an adaptation of the bed-outshot tradition, perhaps arising in the eighteenth century or even later.

Enlargement and Elaboration of Direct-Entry Houses

Just as the three-unit direct-entry house may be considered a lengthening of the two-unit dwelling by simple extension at one or other end, so the three-unit

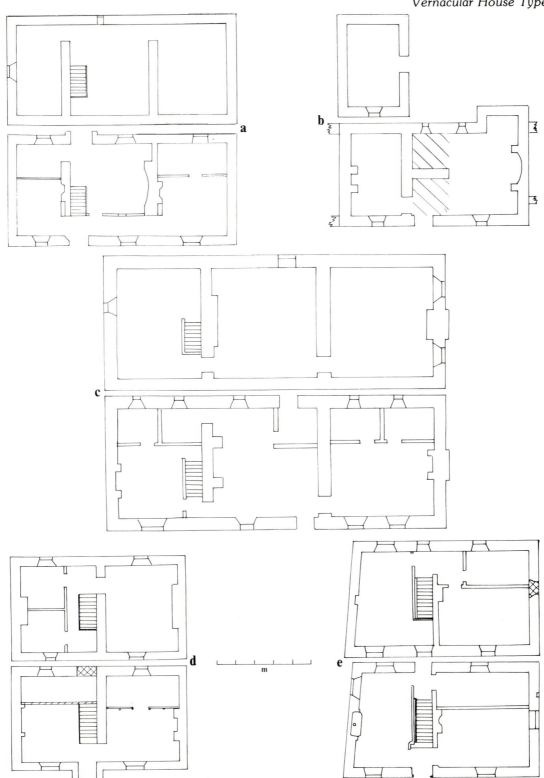

Fig. 166. Plans of developed and enlarged direct-entry houses.
a: Druminiskill Td., Co. Fermanagh;
b: Dergalt Td., Co. Tyrone (cf. figs. 170, 259);
c: Dunglady Td., Co. Londonderry;
d: Dreenan Td., Co. Fermanagh;
e: Ballyskeagh Td., Co. Down.
Loft area in Dergalt house shaded; blocked openings cross-shaded.

Fig. 167.   Direct-entry farmhouse, Terrydreen Td., co. Londonderry. UFTM L 1066.6

Fig. 168.   Direct-entry farmhouse, near Cloghan, Co. Donegal. UFM L 933.6

Fig. 169.   'Formalised' three-unit farmhouse; note soot on kitchen chimney which, with door position, betrays direct-entry layout, Ballyferris Td., Co. Down. UFTM L 1146.1

Fig. 170.   One unit of farmhouse raised and slated, Dergalt Td., Co. Tyrone (cf. Fig. 166 for plan). UFTM L 322.19

Fig. 171.   Two units of direct-entry farmhouse of two storeys, remainder single-storey, Carrickmaddyroe Td., Co. Down. UFTM L 977.11A

house itself could be enlarged, although single-storey houses with more than four units are unusual. In this way a family of house forms is generated having in common the direct-entry kitchen layout with single or opposite doors at the end of the unit away from the principal hearth in the house. Once the house has achieved a size of three or more units, the kitchen unit is commonly placed away from the gable ends.

Many enlarged houses had lofts or attic rooms contained within the roof space, sometimes with half a metre or so of side wall (Fig. 166). Lighting the end units posed no difficulty. Small windows could easily be placed in the tops of gables. Lighting lofts over other units presented a problem. Skylights let into thatch were difficult to keep watertight, and if lighting was provided it usually came from small eaves-level windows, sometimes placed only at the rear of the house, or in the nineteenth century a fanlight above the front door might be used, the attic floor level coinciding with the top of the door frame, or even with a horizontal glazing bar placed halfway up the fanlight itself.

In more prosperous farmhouses from the late eighteenth century, permanently fixed stairs rather than ladders began to be installed, but they seem to have become a widespread feature only in the second half of the nineteenth century. Stairs usually rose from a position inside the front door and were fixed to the wall opposite

the kitchen hearth; occasional houses reversed the stairs, to rise from inside the rear wall.

Coinciding with these adaptations, full upper storeys (Figs. 167-169) were often provided in newly constructed dwellings and by removing the roofs of existing houses, building up the walls sufficiently, and applying a new roof. When the latter was done, usually in the second half of the nineteenth century or even later, a slate roof was commonly substituted for the earlier thatch. Ground-floor outshots were closed off also, or at least their beds removed, adjustments were made to the hearth to burn coal, and a windbreak was added around the outside of the front door, and sometimes of a rear one also. Yet in spite of these changes the true vernacular basis of the house plan survived, even to be detected externally from the off-centred door in a two- or three-unit house, its position relative to the smoke blackened kitchen chimney betraying the internal layout.

Some country houses added only partial upper storeys (Figs. 166, 170). Often only one unit was carried upwards in a two-unit house, or sometimes two units in a three-unit house. In many places when this happened, the last unit retaining its single-storey status and thatch cover was the kitchen, testimony to the regard paid to the insulating quality of the old roofing. Many houses in all districts may be seen in which stage-by-stage development can be clearly traced, by means of breaks-

Fig. 172. Modest two-unit two-storey farmhouse, of a type common throughout the north of Ireland, Parishagh Td., Co. Antrim. UFTM L 1095.9

in-build in walls and variations in roof covering: first extension in length at ground-floor level, then provision of the upper floor piece by piece, until a fully two-storeyed house was achieved. It is pointless to quote individual cases. These changes took place everywhere, although commencing earlier in the east than in the west, but by the end of the nineteenth century modifications and enlargements of direct-entry houses were ubiquitous.

A final adjustment led ultimately to development of a house form whose vernacular origins are difficult to trace, for a similar form emerged also by gradual degeneration from simple but formally planned Georgian farmhouses, the remaining distinction possibly being that the latter were rather deeper from front to rear (perhaps in the range 7 m. to 8.5 m.) than the narrower vernacular norms. When stairs were first introduced rising from inside the front door of a direct-entry house, they remained open to the kitchen hearth along one side. Some remain occupied like this today. As demands for increased privacy and specialisation in the use of internal space developed, mainly after 1850, the staircase was commonly sheeted off from the kitchen, and a small lobby developed inside the front entrance from which the kitchen was entered through a newly provided door. Sometimes the timber sheeting was replaced by a stud-and-plaster or brick wall, but its thickness, usually no more than 25 cms., showed that it served no purpose in supporting the roof, and that it was an insertion into the kitchen unit of the house, often resulting in cramping the proportions of the kitchen itself. It was but a step from this layout to widen the stair lobby to allow a passage along its side, forming a central 'hallway' running through the house, either to a closet at the rear under the stairs, or to a rear door. This usually late nineteenth-century arrangement was often accompanied by building both walls flanking the hallway of similar thickness, repositioning the front door to provide a symmetrical facade, and the use of much Victorian detailing, in window and door styles, and smooth rendering of the outer wall surfaces. So long as the kitchen unit running through from front to rear survived, vernacular design antecedents are detectable; but a well-proportioned kitchen backed by a rear pantry or other room may more suitably be regarded as a decline from the arrangement of four rooms around a centrally placed formal hall and rear stair-well, typical of some formal Georgian farmhouses in Ulster.

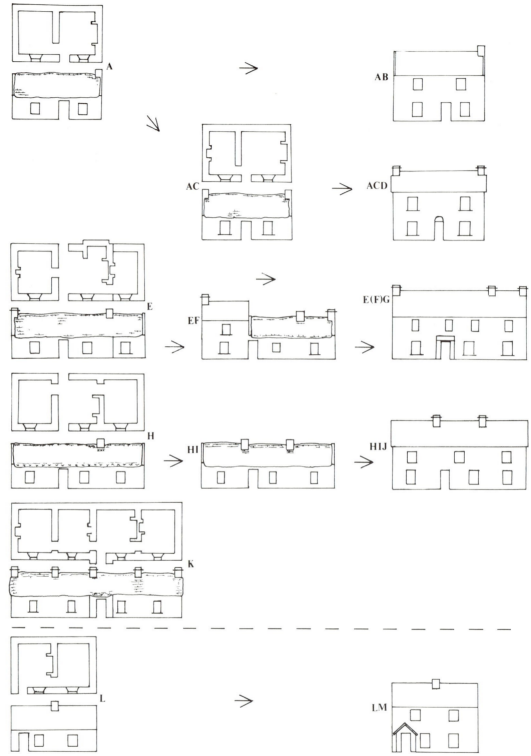

Fig. 173. The 'family' of direct-entry house forms. Simpler one-storey forms down left side of diagram; houses partially heightened, and tending towards symmetry in centre; two-storey forms at right. Arrows suggest directions of development. The diagram may simply be extended to encompass other forms not included; e.g. the Dergalt house (cf. Figs. 166, 170) is a two-unit version of EF. A, E, H were common. K less common. AC became a common north-east Ulster form in the 19th century, infrequently leading to ACD. AB, often with two chimney stacks, is perhaps the commonest small northern Irish farmhouse of traditional type today. EF (and in its two-unit form) was widespread in hill-farm areas. E(F)G, more usually probably EG, is a widespread larger farmhouse type. HI and HIJ are commonest in southern and south-western parts of the north of Ireland. Minority forms are below the dotted line; L occurs as a cottage type sporadically, and LM is found commonly only in the Mourne area of south Co. Down.

Summary

The family of direct-entry house types may conveniently be summarised diagrammatically (Fig. 173). All share a kitchen layout with hearth at one end and entrance(s) at the other. It is easily seen how one form is generated from another by accretion of additional space, which happened in individual cases, but of course new houses were also built in the enlarged forms. Reading the diagram, it must be borne in mind that innumerable permutations were possible: single or opposite entrances; windbreak absent or present on front and rear doors; slate or corrugated metal sheeting replacing thatch; variations in window styling, rendering, presence or absence of cut-stone window sills and quoins; presence or absence of whitewash; possession and arrangement of chimneys as more or fewer rooms were provided with heating; the 'drive' towards facade symmetry more or less achieved by adjustment to front door position and provision of dummy chimneys. Inevitably, therefore, the diagram is a simplification of reality, but as such it helps identify the essential unity of this family of house forms.

Origins

We may speculate as to the probable origins of the direct-entry house type so far as the north of Ireland is concerned. It was almost the only type represented in the nineteenth century and probably from the late seventeenth century, the whole way around the periphery of the north of Ireland, from south Armagh and south and east Down, through east and north Antrim and westward through much of Londonderry into Donegal and southward to include mid and west Tyrone, north Fermanagh, the Cavan 'panhandle', and so on into north Connacht. Direct-entry houses co-existed with hearth-lobby ones over the same period in the remainder of the north of Ireland, although many there are nineteenth-century houses built when it seems that the hearth-lobby house type was no longer widely favoured, especially amongst more comfortably-off farmers. Perhaps the direct-entry house, more nearly approaching a symmetrical form when built in two units of two storeys with gable chimneys, was perceived as acceptable at a time when urban and upper-class attitudes to accommodation spread into rural areas.

The family of direct-entry houses may safely be regarded as byre-dwelling derivatives, so the origins of the byre-dwelling layout must be explored. Combination of quarters for people and cattle was not confined to Ireland. Since medieval times Highland Scotland, Wales,

parts of England and western France have all been characterised by houses of this type, although the exact forms differed in the different countries. Medieval and earlier evidence extends the distribution of byre-dwellings backwards in time, and more widely in space, in southern England and on the continent, for example in Denmark. It appears therefore that the tradition is an ancient one, and it is understandable that regionally divergent forms should have developed. A recent summary of much of the European evidence on the byre-dwelling[39] associates it with traditions of cruck roof support, but while in Ireland crucks have been found in byre-dwelling derivatives, they occur also in hearth-lobby houses. However, as housing traditions spread and influenced one another, it should not be expected that all elements appeared and disappeared at the same rates. If crucks originally belonged to a byre-dwelling tradition, there is no reason why they should not have persisted as a new house type displaced the byre-dwelling, so long as the need remained to support the roof independently of the walls. Crucks must first be related to building materials and techniques, and only thereafter can a possible connection with house types be contemplated.

Similar reasoning explains why the bed outshot, a minority feature of the direct-entry house type, persisted in many areas but seems largely to have disappeared from the south-east of our area, to judge from the failure to discover examples in east and south Down. On the other hand the outshot may be a marker of the antiquity of the byre-dwelling family of house types. Dr. A.T. Lucas has examined early and medieval documentary sources that tell of domestic conditions.[40] He suggests that the outshot may be an attenuated survival of an early tradition of a rear annexe to the house, originally devoted to storage, although in emergency it could be used for private retiral, for example in cases of childbirth or illness. It is at least intriguing that the commonest Irish term for the outshot in Ulster and Connacht was *cúilteach*, the term descriptive of the rear annexe in the documents back as far as the tenth century.[41] Interestingly also, the outshot is not restricted to Ireland; it has been well described from many of the same districts of the British Isles and the western European mainland[42] where byre-dwellings were also found, whereas in Ireland it seems to have been a minority feature usually associated with sleeping, and commonly placed on the rear of the house close to the main hearth.

As the various members of the direct-entry house type have been defined, the hearth is always against a wall at the opposite end of the kitchen/living unit from the entrance(s). Evidence on the evolution of the hearth quoted in Chapter 6 shows that in earlier byre-dwellings it was not located there, but was free-standing on the floor, and perhaps there was no substantial wall separating a living area about the hearth from the further end of the house, used presumably for sleeping. The hearth would have been located nearer to the entrance, yet not opposite it; this is the layout of the excavated medieval houses at Caherguillamore and Tildarg. Such dwellings could almost be regarded as the prototypes of three-unit houses, but without structural partitions between the units, and in these circumstances internal separation could have been identified with roof (cruck?) trusses, and the units with bays. A byre-end would have existed to one side of the entrance, probably the smaller end of the structure, consisting of perhaps one or two bays. To the other side of the entrance, or opposite entrances, was a living space again perhaps of one or two bays' extent, with a free-standing hearth more or less centrally located. Beyond, perhaps only a single bay would have been reserved for sleeping and storage. To judge from the documentary evidence, some of these houses may have had some kind of rear annexe. It is likely that in medieval times they would have had hipped roofs, and thus an end position for the hearth would have been inhibited. So when internal partition walls dividing the house into units began to be inserted, perhaps in the early seventeenth

century, three-unit houses would have been usual. Only following the change to a gabled roof form, which apparently happened between 1600 and 1700, would the two-unit gable-hearth byre-dwelling and its derivative with a bedroom in the former byre location have become possible.[43]

III. HEARTH-LOBBY HOUSES

Since at least the end of the eighteenth century hearth-lobby houses in the north of Ireland have been distributed throughout Monaghan and most of Cavan, all of Armagh except the mountainous south of the county, south and mid Fermanagh, and the extreme south of Tyrone, the Clogher Valley and east Tyrone, west and north-west Down and south Antrim. Isolated outliers lie beyond the frontier of this distribution, detailed consideration of the significance of which follows later.

The Jamb Wall

The type is defined by the fact that the front entrance to the kitchen unit is adjacent to the hearth position, and the

Fig. 174.   Interior of a Co. Armagh house, early 20th century. Note jamb wall, with seat on its inner face, separating the entrance to extreme right, from open hearth under a large wattle, clay-plastered canopy supported on a bressumer which rests on the end of the jamb wall. UFTM WAG 282

Fig. 175. Jamb wall of brick separating entrance (left) from hearth (right). Note the lobby formed by the jamb wall, out of which a further door leads to the unit behind the hearth wall; farmhouse from Corradreenan West Td., Co. Fermanagh, reconstructed at UFTM. UFTM L 609.1

two are separated by a 'jamb wall', also known in parts of Armagh and Monaghan as the 'hollan' or 'hallan' wall (Figs. 174–176). Typically, but as we saw at the start of this chapter not invariably, there is a unit behind the kitchen hearth, entry to which is through a door in the hearth wall between the jamb wall and the front of the house. In many cases, and in all early houses of the type, a 'brace beam' stretches from the end of the jamb wall to the rear wall of the kitchen, often indeed spanning the kitchen from front to rear and resting on the end of the jamb wall. It is obvious that the original function of this beam was to support the front of a wattled and plastered, stone or brick chimney canopy, to which the word 'brace' also sometimes applied. The spaces between the sides of the chimney canopy and the front and rear walls of the house were often lofted over; such a loft was called a 'skeagh', 'flake', 'thallage' or 'farray' in the southern parts of our area. As the chimney canopy developed into a constricted flue in a modestly proportioned breastwork, the brace beam sometimes remained to support an extended loft over the hearth area (Fig. 130), and in a few cases survived as a transverse beam without any structural purpose.

The jamb wall was sometimes constructed of the same materials as the house walls, but more commonly it was of brick once the chimney had been built of this material, or it comprised studs and planking. It seems that the jamb wall was considered to belong with the chimney. Usually there was a small window in it, the 'spy' hole or window, or 'logie hole', allowing light into the hearth area from the door when it was open, but it also permitted a view out to the door from the fireside. Light was provided for the inglenook in many early houses through a small window in the rear wall, positioned between the hearth wall and the brace beam.

Most commonly the lobby inside the front door remained as described above, but it was sometimes closed off by a door between its end and the front wall of the house; so where a door opened into the unit behind the kitchen hearth, the jamb wall itself became the only one of the four sides of the lobby without a door. Unlike the direct-entry house before the development of the transverse hallway with its stairs, the lobby provided a clearly defined 'reception' area inside the front door, but now within the living space proper. More significantly, the confined space of the lobby and the abrupt changes in

Fig. 176.   Hearth-lobby kitchen interior, Derrytrasna Td:, Co. Armagh (after Evans).

direction necessary to enter the units leading off it meant that it was unsuited to admit large animals like cows. The hearth-lobby plan could not therefore be associated with byre-dwelling combinations, and on farms wherever the house type is found a separately entered byre is usual.

Hearth-lobby houses were of various sizes (Fig. 177), lengthening being possible at either end of the kitchen unit simply by adding further structural units. By far the commonest arrangements were of two units (Figs. 182–184) with the hearth placed almost centrally, and of three units with a central kitchen (Figs. 178, 180, 181). The three-unit gabled hearth-lobby house achieves an external facade appearance very like the similar-sized direct-entry house when both have chimneys located on the internal walls separating the units (Fig. 181). Only internal inspection or external observation of a smoking or smoke-blackened chimney almost in line with the front door betrays the hearth-lobby interior configuration. A few houses throughout the geographical distribution of the type have the kitchen hearth at a gable-end (Fig. 182). Usually these are two-unit houses, often but not always cottiers', craftsmen's or labourers' dwellings rather than farmhouses, sometimes single-storeyed, although

there was a small farmhouse of this kind with attic bedrooms lighted by gable windows in Ballykeel Artifinny townland near Hillsborough in county Down.

Houses with a jamb wall at the gable are not recent innovations. The house of Thomas Beggs, the mid-Antrim-born poet who lived at Mallusk between Antrim and Belfast in the early 1840s, was a two-unit thatched house which obviously, from a drawing of it published in 1902 (Fig. 183), had this arrangement.[44] Cartographic representations of about 1800 of tenant farmers' houses near Ballymoney, county Antrim include one with this configuration also, although when another seems to have a gable entry above which is a loft window and a smoking chimney, the detailed accuracy of these particular representations may be questioned.[45]

In the north of Ireland the hearth-lobby house usually has gables rather than a hipped roof, but the latter was common in Leinster to the south, and both forms are seen in south Fermanagh and Cavan. An end hearth and chimney were difficult to arrange in a hipped roof, so inevitably in these cases the minimal size of house was of two units. In the north of Ireland where the gable predominated, a single-unit hearth-lobby house was

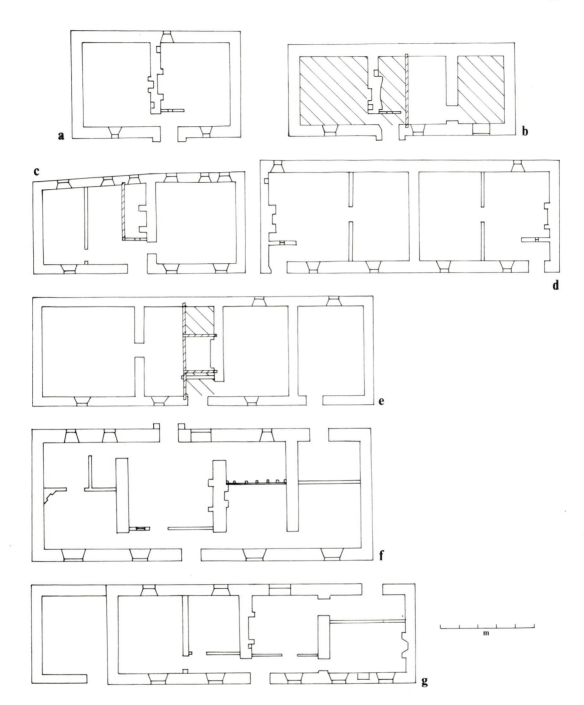

Fig. 177.   Plans of hearth-lobby houses of two, three and four units.
a: Kilnamaddy Td., Co. Monaghan;
b: Gortalughany Td., Co. Fermanagh;
c: Tullyheron Td., Co. Down;
d; cruck house 'A', left of pair of cottages, Corcreeny Td., Co. Down;
e: Derrytresk Td., Co. Tyrone (after McCourt);
f: Killycolpy Td., Co. Tyrone;
g: Ballysessy Td., Co. Antrrim.
Loft areas, bressumers, and loft beams shaded.

M

Fig. 178.   Two-unit dwelling and byre, Annahugh Td., Co. Armagh. UFTM L 969.14

Fig. 179.   Three-unit dwelling and outhouse, Ballyvarley Td., Co. Down. UFTM L 969.6

Fig. 180.   Three-unit lobby-entry farmhouse, lived in by William Carleton, the novelist, when a boy, Springtown Td., Co. Tyrone. UFTM L 1006.14

Fig. 181.   Three-unit lobby-entry farmhouse with loft floor, Croaghrim Td., Co. Fermanagh. UFTM L 1550.7

Fig. 182.   Hearth-lobby entry at gable end of cottage, Drumdellum Td., Co. Armagh. UFTM L 1287.14

Fig. 183.   The gable-side entry, hearth-lobby cottage occupied by Thomas Beggs, vernacular poet, *c.*1840, at Mallusk, Co. Antrim (after *Ulster Journal of Archaeology*, 2nd ser., 8 (1902)).

possible, but I have never seen one survive, and the only record I know is the case of the sod house near Toome Bridge in county Antrim photographed early this century (Fig. 34). The great change in rural housing standards after 1845–48 inevitably swept away other examples, yet it is possible that proportionally there never were as many one-unit hearth-lobby houses as there were of the direct-entry layout.

Extension in length beyond four units seems from the survivals to have been rare, but many three-unit dwellings had their roof lines continued over separately entered stores and outhouses (Fig. 179). In the linen-weaving areas of west Down, Armagh, south-east Tyrone, south Antrim and north Monaghan, two- and three-unit houses often had a loom 'shop' added at one end. Sometimes the shop had a fireplace, and often there was internal access from the dwelling, but others had a separate door from outside. Always there was better provision of light from windows for work at the looms than was provided for the dwelling. Usually, too, simply by using longer purlins for roofing, the weaving-shop unit was appreciably larger than the other parts of the house.

Hearth-area lofts were often supplemented by lofting over the structural units either side of the kitchen, access

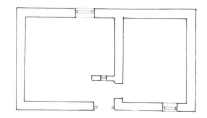

Fig. 184. The 'common cottage or cabin' illustrated by William Greig in his reports on the Co. Armagh estates of Gosford and Drumbanagher *c*.1820. Redrawn from plan in PRONI T 3097.

being gained by ladder. These lofts are referred to in the inventories of the Ballyhagan Quaker community in mid Armagh in the first half of the eighteenth century, but we can only infer that their houses must have been of hearth-lobby type.[46] Documentary evidence on hearth-lobby houses is unfortunately sparse. The only northern Irish references known to me are two, in addition to the gable-entry references quoted above. One is the illustration of the common rural house type of about 1820 included by William Greig in his surveys of the Drumbanagher[47] and Gosford[48] estates in Armagh — a two-unit, gabled house with central hearth (Fig. 184). It is interesting that in advocating improved domestic conditions Greig based his plans for new dwellings (never built) on the hearth-lobby arrangement. The essential difference he was making between the 'common cottage or cabin' and his improved houses was in provision of more, smaller bedrooms, a clear assumption that segregated sleeping for parents and children, and between boys and girls was not only desirable but essential. Secondly, many of the houses represented by Raven on his maps of the Londonderry plantation in the early seventeenth century are of hearth-lobby type.[49] The only written description of a jamb-wall arrangement anywhere in Ireland that I have seen refers to county Kilkenny in Leinster in the early nineteenth century.[50]

Enlargement and Elaboration

Provision of a full upper floor in hearth-lobby houses was a nineteenth-century phenomenon so far as the great bulk of such housing was concerned, but from at least the early eighteenth century there was a minority of larger farmhouses of two storeys (Figs. 185–189). A derelict example with a fine wide brick chimney canopy supported on a brace beam remains at Cockhill, in Drumanphy townland in Armagh (Fig. 120). West of Waringstown, the farmhouse in Magherana townland

with supposed upper cruck truss is a county Down example,[51] and the farmhouse in Carrickreagh townland in west Fermanagh believed to date to the 1650s is another.[52] The earliest evidence for houses of lobby-entry type with upper floors lighted by dormer windows is on the early seventeenth-century maps by Thomas Raven of the London companies' building operations in county Londonderry (Fig. 217).[53]

Proper provision of an upper floor raised the problem of access from below (Fig. 190). So long as lofts over other units entered from an unlofted kitchen were involved, access by movable ladder was inevitable. Insertion of separate stairs to both sides of the kitchen unit, still less within the kitchen, would have been unrealistic in, for example, a three-unit dwelling. But once the loft floor was continuous from above the kitchen unit into one or more others, fixed stairs could be inserted. The earliest arrangement, seen in the Carrickreagh house in Fermanagh in its original form (Fig. 191), and probably present in the houses represented on Raven's county Londonderry maps, was to carry the stairs on the rear of the chimney stack, between it and the back wall of the house. This was the position for stairs in many English hearth-lobby houses of the seventeenth century, but it never became common in the north of Ireland. The reason may be that by the late eighteenth and first half of the nineteenth centuries, when upper floors were becoming numerous, the massive chimney stack necessary for stairs in this position had given way to more restricted wattled or brick chimney flues supported on the hearth wall, and so the stairs were seen to obtrude excessively into the kitchen.

So long as there was no great desire for privacy necessitating increased specialisation in the use of internal spaces, stairs could rise around the angle in a corner of the kitchen opposite the hearth, or even in the rear corner alongside the hearth. However, I have seen only one example of the latter arrangement, obviously of nineteenth-century date, in a house in Clogher townland in north Down near Lisburn; the former provision I have

Fig. 185.   Lobby-entry farmhouse with two units raised and slated, Drumnahare Td., Co. Down. UFTM L 966.9

Fig. 186.   Small lobby-entry farmhouse, of type common throughout west Armagh, Monaghan and Cavan, Cargaghbane Td., Co. Monaghan. UFTM L 1413.20a

Fig. 187.   Three-unit thatched two-storey farmhouse of lobby-entry plan, probably 18th-century, Edenballycoggill Td., Co. Down. UFTM L 1114.13

Fig. 188.   Lobby-entry farmhouse, Killcurry Td., Co. Antrim. UFTM L 1206.1

Fig. 189.   Lobby-entry farmhouse, Lisslanly Td., Co. Armagh. UFTM L 1376.13

noted in a few places, for example in Drumnahunshin townland in south Armagh in a farmhouse now removed to the Ulster Folk and Transport Museum, and in Legge townland in west Fermanagh.

Much the commonest position for stairs in the hearth-lobby house relates to extension of the jamb wall the whole way along the front of the kitchen unit, forming a 'hallway' parallel to the long axis of the house. Access to the kitchen is through a door in this extended jamb wall. Stairs rise from this hallway and are carried on the kitchen side of the wall opposite the hearth. The stairs are always at least sheeted in from the remainder of the kitchen unit with timber, but sometimes they are enclosed by a thin wall of brick or stud-and-plaster. They often rise to a landing at the back of the house which parallels the ground-floor hallway, giving entry to rooms over the kitchen and adjacent units. This configuration became the standard enlargement or elaboration of the hearth-lobby house after about 1850.

Finally, as ideas of symmetry percolated socially downwards from formal Georgian architecure, it was a simple matter to rearrange the facade of the hearth-lobby in front of the extended jamb-wall hallway across the front of the kitchen unit (Figs. 192–195). Re-arrangement entailed omission of the front window in the kitchen unit, often compensated for by a fanlight or sidelights around the door, sometimes by both. Especially in Fermanagh and Cavan there arose a nineteenth-century hearth-lobby form, still being constructed in the first half of the twentieth century, with central door flanked by sidelights, above which a dormer window lighted the central-unit loft in a three-unit house, the end lofts being lighted by gable windows. A farmhouse in Coolbeg townland in Fermanagh, which originated perhaps in the mid-seventeenth century, was converted to this developed symmetrical form as late as the 1940s according to the memory of the occupant, a daughter-in-law of the owner who carried out the alterations (Figs. 196, 197). She married a descendant of the family which had come into the property in the Cromwellian period.[54] Symmetrically arranged facades on fully two-storeyed houses also arose in the nineteenth century, especially in Fermanagh, and only internal inspection reveals their vernacular layout; a good example is the Tamlaght house in Fermanagh (Fig. 65), while the Edenordinary house in Down (Fig. 195) lacks only a fourth, dummy chimney to achieve complete symmetry, its formality enhanced by a sophisticated Georgian-style doorcase.

At this stage of development it can be difficult to distinguish between houses developed from the vernacular tradition, and others which represent degeneration from formal architecture. The point is best

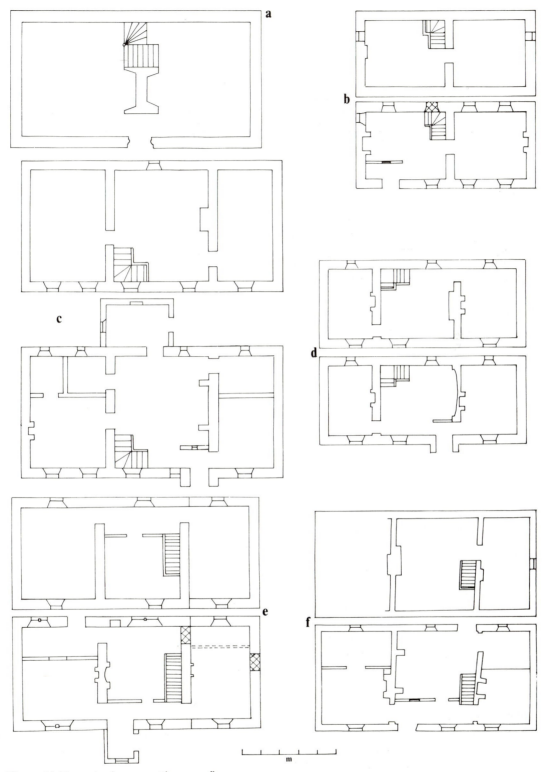

Fig. 190.   Plans of lobby-entry houses with upper floors.

a: house proposed for construction at Moneymore, Co. Londonderry, 1615, by Drapers' Company (redrawn, to scale, from Fig. 207 below);

b: Ballykeel Artifinny Td., Co. Down;

c: Carrowmannan Td., Co. Armagh;

d: near Kingscourt, Co. Cavan;

e: Feumore Td., Co. Antrim;

f: Drumduff Td., Co. Fermanagh.

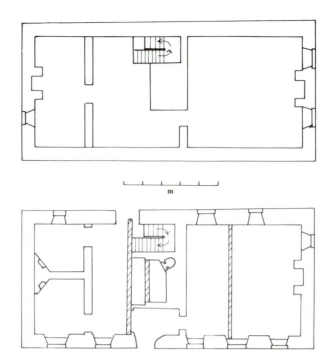

Fig. 191.   Plans of Cromwellian-period farmhouse with built-in oven, Carrickreagh Td., Co. Fermanagh.

Fig. 192.   Formalised hearth-lobby farmhouse, 'Bloomvale', Bleary Td., Co. Down. UFTM L 969.15

Fig. 193. Fully symmetrical facade with heavy 'architectural' detailing on a hearth-lobby farmhouse, Tullykenneye Td., Co. Fermanagh. UFTM L 992.18

Fig. 194. Formal facade of a hearth-lobby farmhouse, formality enhanced by small pavilion-like rooms at each end. Dark creeper covers wall, Rossigh Td., Co. Fermanagh. UFTM L 991.0

Fig. 195.   Only a chimney stack is needed to complete the symmetry of the facade of this hearth-lobby farmhouse, Edenordinary Td., Co. Down. UFTM L 975.1

Fig. 196.   Three-unit hearth-lobby 18th-century farmhouse (chimney stack almost hidden by tree to right of door), Coolbeg Td., Co. Fermanagh, from Trimble, *History of Enniskillen*, III (Enniskillin, 1921). UFTM L 1661.7

Fig. 197.   The same house today, 'modernised' out of recognition, Coolbeg Td., Co. Fermanagh. UFTM L 991.7

Fig. 198.   Thatched farmhouse ultimately of formal architectural inspiration, Drummal Td., Co. Fermanagh. From a transparency, UFTM L 1661.12

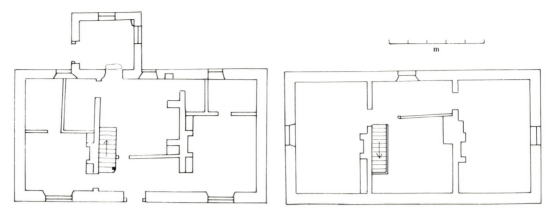

Fig. 199.   Floor plans of the house in Drummal Td., Co. Fermanagh, Fig. 198.

illustrated by considering a house at Lisnarick in Fermanagh (Figs. 198, 199). It has an almost symmetrically arranged facade behind which is a deeper-than-usual longitudinal hallway from which stairs rise to an upper half-storey; its formal inspiration is betrayed by a greater dimension from front to rear than usual in vernacular houses, which permits front and rear rooms in both end structural units. This is an eighteenth-century house, according to local tradition built by a local landowner as one of two or three similar dwellings for friends. The fact of a thatched roof does not prove vernacular design origins.

Summary

As in the case of direct-entry houses, the family of hearth-lobby house forms may conveniently be summarised diagrammatically (Fig. 200). A kitchen layout with jamb wall, or its extension to form a longitudinal 'hallway', is common to all. Generation of the larger more complex forms is easily visualised simply by addition in length and/or upward provision of lofts or a full upper storey. If most of the recognised houses of this type are of 'central-hearth' nature in terms of the older classification of the Irish vernacular architecture literature, it is obvious that the gable-hearth houses with jamb wall belong in this family of plan types. Many visual variations developed historically, depending on the nature of external finish, provision of porches or windbreaks around the front door, changes in roof covering and provision of additional fireplaces leading to multiplication of chimneys on the roof ridge, and the outcome of what I have already referred to as the 'drive' towards symmetry in the arrangement of piercing of the facade.

Lastly, while definition of this family of house forms depends on consideration of the front entrance alone, and in many earlier one-storey houses this was the sole entrance, some also had a rear door, usually in the kitchen unit placed alongside the wall opposite the hearth at the 'low' end. In many instances this door is demonstrably an added feature, but towards the limit of the distribution of the hearth-lobby house type, a rear entrance was commoner than in much of Armagh and Monaghan.

Origins

It is theoretically possible to generate a basic hearth-lobby house within Ireland by assuming an evolution which moved the fire in a Caherguillamore-like house to a position in line with the front entrance. F.H.A. Aalen in an analysis of evidence from western Ireland, favours this view;[55] but it is based at best on circumstantial evidence. No house has been located anywhere in Ireland to substantiate this proposed development of plan forms. More cautiously, Caoimhin Ó Danachair does not suggest that this line of development actually took place in Ireland,[56] whereas both Campbell in the 1930s[57] and most recently Evans and Glassie[58] have unequivocally linked its appearance in Ireland with introduction from England. Desmond McCourt regarded the house with jamb wall as an innovation and applied innovation-diffusion theory to explain its distribution in the north of Ireland,[59] suggesting that the type spread into Ulster from southern and eastern directions. His conclusions are based on personal field experience in north-west Ireland together with published data drawn especially from analysis of returns made to a postal questionnaire enquiry

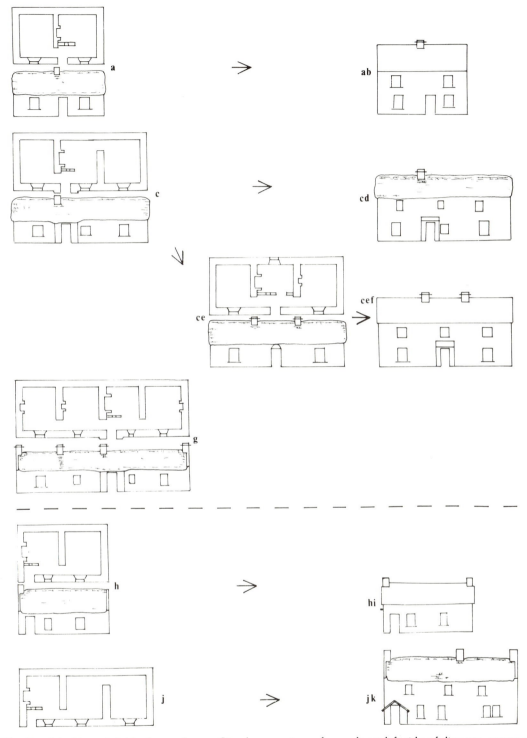

Fig. 200.   The 'family' of hearth-lobby house forms. Simpler one-storey forms down left side of diagram, symmetry imposed on facade in centre, and two-storey forms at right. Arrows suggest directions of development. a, c and g were very common forms. ab and cef are common forms of vernacular farmhouses surviving across south Ulster from west Armagh to Cavan; cd, often with further chimney stacks, commoner in Down, Antrim and Tyrone. Minority forms are shown below the dotted line. j has rarely been encountered, but jk is based on 'Horsepark', Horsepark Td., Co. Antrim, in existence in this form in 1690. The diagram may simply be extended to encompass forms like that illustrated in Fig. 185.

carried out in 1960/61.[60] The weakness in his procedure was to base an argument on an amalgam of field observation and unverified postal questionnaire returns. Subsequent field and documentary work makes necessary some re-assessment of his conclusions.

The Detailed Distribution of the Hearth-Lobby House in the North of Ireland

Fig. 201 illustrates in detail the distribution of the hearth-lobby house type, taking into account all its forms, and is based on data gathered in the field over the past twenty

years or so, and especially since 1976. Only a sample of houses have been recorded in the core of the distribution area, but approaching the distributional frontier where the numbers of hearth-lobby houses are fewer and farther between, as many as reasonably possible have been located. Isolated outliers beyond what has been interpreted as the frontier have also been found. No particular attempt has been made to segregate earlier from later houses, but a number which were built in the late eighteenth century have been discovered fairly near the margins of the distribution.

The one-and-a-half-storey slated house, now ruinous in Moyheeland townland in south-east Londonderry (Fig. 202), has a datestone reading 1791; Moyheeland is

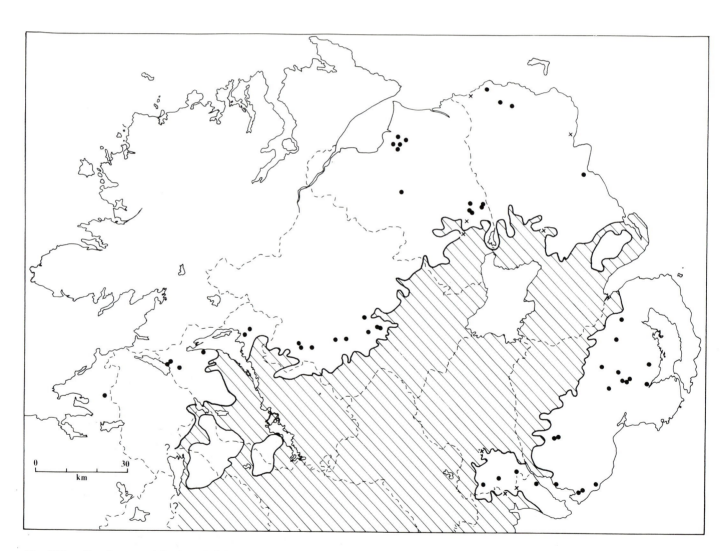

Fig. 201.   Distribution of the hearth-lobby house type in the north of Ireland. Main distribution, shaded; outliers beyond the main distributional limit, dots; locations of isolated bed-outshot houses, × (cf. Fig. 165). The hearth-lobby distribution has not been investigated west of Lough Allen, in north Leitrim and in north Sligo.

virtually at the upstream limit in the Moyola valley reached by the hearth-lobby house type. Similarly located at the frontier in north-west Fermanagh, another derelict hearth-lobby farmhouse overlooks Lower Lough Erne. Trimble, the Fermanagh historian, associated it with a British family settling there and suggested that it was built before 1744.[61] Fermanagh has two other early hearth-lobby houses, in Coolbeg (Fig. 196) and Carrickreagh (Fig. 199) townlands, already mentioned. In Down a late eighteenth-century substantial farmhouse, known as 'Sylvan Hill', in Greenoge townland, hides a vernacular hearth-lobby interior behind its formalised facade,[62] and south of Moira, in Lurganville townland a large farmhouse sadly mishandled in being modernised bears a datestone recording 1772 (Fig. 203). Probably there are many other hearth-lobby houses of similar late eighteenth-century or earlier date awaiting discovery; these few examples located close to or on the distributional frontier of the type suffice to confirm that the distribution mapped recently existed before 1800. If McCourt's thesis that the distribution resulted from an historical innovation diffusion process is correct, then that process seems to have been largely arrested before the nineteenth century. It is interesting that some of the outliers beyond the distributional frontier are nineteenth-century buildings, for example the two-storey slated

farmhouse of perhaps 1876 in Islandboy townland in north Antrim (Fig. 204), although the one-storey thatched farmhouse in Drummanmore townland near Kilkeel in south Down perhaps dated to about 1800 (Fig. 205). Such cases may be regarded as forward-leaping innovators. Had the spread of the hearth-lobby house continued according to the model of innovation diffusion used by McCourt, one would have expected the areas between these advanced locations and the distributional frontier proper to have been taken up by similar houses.

In the extreme south-west of our area this process may have persisted later than in other regions. Most of the remaining hearth-lobby dwellings I have been able to locate in mid Cavan and in the Ballinamore-Drumshanbo part of mid Leitrim, and all those in a cluster of outliers in the extreme north-west part of the Cavan 'panhandle', are two-storey, slated two-unit farmhouses of obvious nineteenth-century date — indeed some may be post-1850 — although possibly slightly older three-unit two-storey slated examples are at Rantoge Glebe between Ballinamore and Drumshanbo, and at Mully, a mile or so north-west of Glengavlen. Failure to find eighteenth-century hearth-lobby houses in this south-western area may therefore be due to late spread of the type in this direction; but it is noticeable that late nineteenth-century and early twentieth-century overall

Fig. 202. Ruins of large hearth-lobby farmhouse, of 1791, Moyheeland Td., Co. Londonderry. UFTM L 1252.6

Fig. 203.   Modernised hearth-lobby farmhouse, of 1772, Lurganville Td., Co. Down. UFTM L 1362.16

Fig. 204.   Three-unit lobby-entry farmhouse (jamb-wall window may be glimpsed through open door), Islandboy Td., north Co. Antrim. UFTM L 1491.6

Fig. 205.　Three-unit hearth-lobby farmhouse, Drummanmore Td., south Co. Down. UFTM L 1132.17

renewal of housing was much more complete in marginal areas like this dissected limestone plateau between the Lough Erne basin and Sligo, and in the difficult terrain of the drumlin belt to the south, than in more favoured areas to the east and north-east.

Elsewhere, for example in mid Down, most of the outliers were cottier dwellings rather than farmhouses, dating mainly from the early nineteenth century. Perhaps by that time this landless class was better able to provide folk to move from time to time carrying their vernacular traditions with them. Evidence from the southern parts of Antrim suggests a reason why advance of the hearth-lobby house may have come to a halt in the first half of the nineteenth century. Hearth-lobby houses mapped in the field in parishes about Antrim town and eastward towards Ballyclare are few in number and usually not dwellings to which land attaches. Ordnance Survey memoirs for the parishes in this same area and southwards reveal that to the east of Lough Neagh in the 1830s many more prosperous farmers were replacing their older vernacular houses with modern two-storey dwellings which, from surviving examples, clearly drew their inspiration from the formal end of the building continuum — they had symmetrical facades, and were deep enough from front to rear to accommodate a four-square arrangement of ground-floor rooms about a

central hallway and staircase. Some such houses were perhaps built in south Antrim as early as the end of the Napoleonic wars.[63] We have already seen that this part of the north of Ireland was early to adopt building innovations, but it is likely that similar changes in their attitudes to housing were taking place elsewhere amongst wealthier farmers.

There is some evidence positively supporting the idea of innovation diffusion put forward by McCourt. A small number of direct-entry houses with bed outshots have been located which must be seen as implying survivals within the hearth-lobby distribution. Outshot inliers have been found in south Londonderry between Slieve Gallion and Lough Neagh,[64] and the two houses in north Louth recently discovered to have outshots are further examples.[65] Almost the most convincing evidence for the spread of the hearth-lobby house over areas formerly dominated by the direct-entry type or its antecedent forms is the fact that the former is almost never an exclusive form; a minority of direct-entry houses are usually also present, perhaps representing persistence of an older tradition.

Little reflection is needed to realise that the jamb wall and the bed outshot are not easily compatible elements in the one house. Both encroach upon space around the kitchen hearth. Yet a few 'hybrid' houses have been

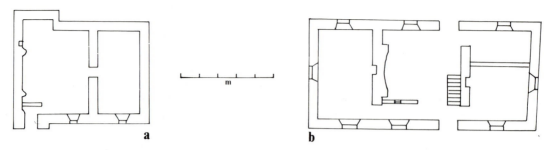

Fig. 206.   Plans of hybrid house forms.
a: hearth-lobby gable entry and rear bed outshot, Ballybriest Td., Co. Londonderry (after McCourt);
b: jamb wall screening hearth from window, Corrakelly Td., Co. Fermanagh (cf. the screen to one side of the Dullaghan house hearth, Fig. 119).

discovered (Fig. 206). Some have bed outshots added to hearth-lobby houses. One was in Muntober townland, west of Cookstown in Tyrone, a small two-unit house with gable hearth. This type of hybrid has only been found very close to the distributional limit of the hearth-lobby house type.[66] Another mixed house form has a screen like a jamb wall added to one side of the hearth in a direct-entry house, between the fireplace and a window. Thus placed it serves no obvious purpose and, indeed, diminishes light reaching the hearth from the front-wall window. Examples I have seen are in Fermanagh and south Tyrone, like the Dullaghan house described in the previous chapter, and Professor Evans reports one seen by him in Cavan in the 1940s.[67] The

most singular hybrid kitchen layout I have seen is in a large three-unit, formerly thatched farmhouse with a continuous loft floor. It is in Caldrum townland near Aughnacloy in Tyrone, and is used now as an outhouse. Indications are that it was built perhaps in the early eighteenth century, but was subjected to many modifications. A more or less symmetrically arranged front had a jamb wall continued to form a longitudinally placed hall inside the front wall from which stairs rose to the loft floor in the usual way. In the rear wall of the central kitchen unit there is a door in the common position, at the 'low' end opposite the hearth, but the hearth is screened from a rear-wall window by a second screen wall. As Professor Evans suggested in the case of

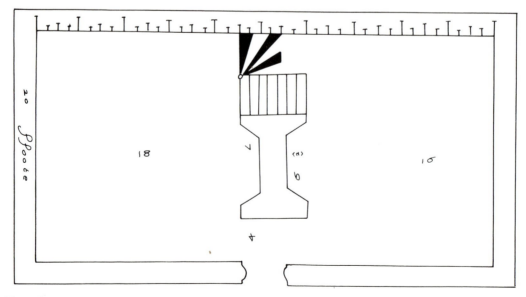

Fig. 207.   Plan of house proposed for construction by the Draper's company, 1615, at Moneymore, Co. Londonderry. Redrawn from original in Drapers' Company records, Ma.Dr.b.1858, published in *Post-Medieval Archaeology* 17 (1983).

the Cavan house he reported, this arrangement perhaps resulted from adaptation of an earlier house; but equally it may have resulted from idiosyncratic experimentation within the limitations of the direct-entry and hearth-lobby house types. The possibility of such individuality must always be allowed for. What is so impressive, nevertheless, is the overall consistency observed within the northern Irish vernacular housing traditions.

There is no Irish evidence for development of the hearth-lobby house type from anything older, and its distributional characteristics accord with its having been introduced historically. Suggestions can be made as to when it was introduced and whence it came. In the first place the recent distribution correlates broadly with areas in which cultural characteristics of recognisably English origin have been found, as Professor Evans suggested in 1955,[68] in particular dialects.[69] Secondly, documentary proof has now been discovered which confirms recent interpretation of the houses represented on Raven's early seventeenth-century maps of county Londonderry.[70] There survives in the records of the Drapers' Company in London a ground plan for a house to be built at Moneymore in the second decade of the seventeenth century.[71] It shows the contemporary lowland English small-house plan, with massive chimney stack in line with the entrance and stairway climbing to an upper floor between it and the rear wall (Fig. 207), the very arrangement observed in the Carrickreagh house in Fermanagh which originated four decades later (Fig. 191). Taken with the British settlement context of other early hearth-lobby houses in Fermanagh, this evidence points to England as the source of the hearth-lobby plan family, and to the early seventeenth century as being the earliest period for which we have unequivocal evidence of its introduction.

It is virtually impossible that the lobby-entry configuration could have come to the north of Ireland with seventeenth-century Scots settlers. The only Scottish evidence available for this house type consists of illustrations of a couple of cottages in Roxburghshire of late eighteenth- or early nineteenth-century date,[72] while West Lothian farm cottages of seemingly hearth-lobby form are only of early nineteenth-century date, and they were not a particularly popular form even then, not being found after about 1850.[73]

Thomas Raven's maps of the county Londonderry building enterprises of the London companies suggest that the hearth-lobby house type may have been introduced into some districts in which it did not take root, thereby possibly explaining some of the outliers in the distribution (Fig. 201). A number of innovation centres must be visualised in the early seventeenth century from which the type subsequently spread. Some were northern but others lay elsewhere in Ireland. The hearth-lobby house type became widespread in Leinster, east and north Munster and east Connacht. Caoimhín Ó Danachair has suggested that the type had already reached its western limit in parts of south-western Ireland by about the same time as the maximum distribution was attained in Ulster, the late eighteenth century.[74]

The similarity with the northern evidence goes further, however. A house excavated at Knockadoon, Lough Gur, in county Limerick, ascribed to the early seventeenth century on the basis of the occupation material, had a layout remarkably similar to that of the Moneymore plan, with a massive double chimney stack, except that no evidence for stairs was found and there was a door leading to a rear wing (Fig. 208).[75] A similar double chimney stack heated a small house, but with an end entrance, on Inishcealtra, an island close to where the Galway-Clare county boundary meets the west shore of Lough Derg.[76]

The closeness of Moneymore, one centre from which this innovation spread, to the ultimate distributional limit

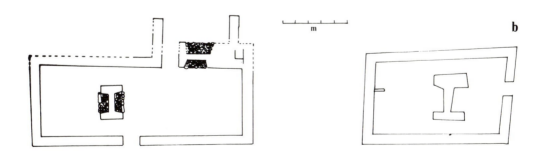

Fig. 208. 17th-century house plans.
a: Site J, Knockadoon, Lough Gur, Co. Limerick (after Ó Ríordáin and Ó Danachair), excavated;
b: Inis Cealtra (after Macalister), surface survey.

of the house type shows that the nature of the innovation diffusion was far from simple. It was probably fundamentally influenced by relationships that obtained in different places between British settlers and the Irish amongst whom they came, and it is unlikley that the fine detail of the nature of the diffusion of this historical innovation can ever be fully known.

It remains to be said that if the hearth-lobby house was introduced from England to the north of Ireland, this could hardly have happened much before 1600, for the type only emerged by insertion of a massive chimney stack in the cross passage of a sub-medieval English vernacular house form towards the end of the sixteenth century.[77] It is eminently understandable that, as a recently evolved small house form, it was the perceived 'modern' house type brought with them by contemporary English settlers in Ireland, as it was brought also to some Tidewater settlements in America, as along the James River in Virginia, and also in Massachusetts. A suggestion made some years ago based upon linguistic analysis of the English loan word 'thallage' which refers to the loft over the hearth area of a hearth-lobby house in south Ulster, that the thallage, and perhaps the house type it belongs to also, were earlier medieval introductions to Ireland, must now be revised.[78]

Following its introduction to the north of Ireland, the development of the hearth-lobby house type is simply explained. The early massive chimney stack placed in line with the front door effectively divided the house into two units. It gave way to a wicker chimney canopy carried on the kitchen side of a mass wall separating the kitchen from its adjacent structural unit, the door opening into the house on the kitchen side of this wall. The inconvenience of this arrangement in controlling draught and smoke at the hearth necessitated perpetuating the door-side jamb of the old stone stack in the form of the jamb wall. Information from an informant in Lisnoe townland in county Down, near Lisburn, who found that having removed a jamb wall the fire became excessively smoky, confirms its practical utility if not also the sheer necessity for it.[79] Later development replaced the canopy in brick or stone and diminished its size. Replacement of the early central brick or stone chimney stack by the wattled chimney canopy may, paradoxically, in parts of Londonderry at least, have accompanied replacement of the early seventeenth-century timber-framed houses by later ones with mass walls. This line of development resulted in a version of the hearth-lobby house that differed in detail from many built in England. In particular the double stack that was found extensively there, seen in the Moneymore plan, never became common in the north of Ireland. So the hearth-lobby house in Ulster may

justifiably be considered an *Irish* house type, despite its imported origins, unlike a few northern Irish representatives of other British house types, including some few survivals of the earliest imported hearth-lobby houses themselves.

IV. BRITISH VERNACULAR HOUSES AND BUILDING FEATURES IN THE NORTH OF IRELAND

If imported hearth-lobby houses developed into an Irish form, the earliest built in the north of Ireland undeniably were cases of transplanted British vernacular forms. None survive from the early seventeenth century, and the earliest remaining may be the cruck house at Trummery in south Antrim of perhaps 1629, but a few larger houses built in the second half of that century and in the first decades of the eighteenth may be the last whose direct English ancestry is obvious. Two are in county Antrim. One dated 1699 is at Crookedstone near Belfast's airport at Aldergrove, and in Ballyelough townland to the west of Lisburn in the extreme south of the county there is the large house known as 'Horsepark', reputedly in existence before 1690 (Fig. 209). Another is the Cromwellian-period house in Carrickreagh townland in west Fermanagh already discussed from a number of points of view. Other large early houses of probable British origin, but not of hearth-lobby plan, are Berwick Hall, close to Moira in north-west Down, a two-storey thatched house of about 1700;[80] Rosscor House in west Fermanagh (Fig. 210), originally a large thatched building with an attic floor, cellar below the west end, and kitchen with built-in oven in a separate building, according to Trimble built before 1690;[81] nearby, a four-unit, two-storey originally thatched house in Farrancassidy townland may be a late example;[82] the earliest house at The Argory near Charlemont in west Armagh, built in 1698, has an L-plan and is built of brick on a one-metre-high stone plinth; and a four-unit one-storey house in Ballyoan townland east of Derry city which has a kitchen hearth at one gable, the kitchen being entered out of a transverse passageway through a metre-thick wall which carries a late dummy chimney. The Ballyoan house is roofed with collar-beam trusses and one tie-beam truss, carrying through purlins, and only its plan, deviant in Irish terms, perhaps suggests direct British inspiration possibly during the eighteenth century. An interesting, seemingly Georgian large house at Chrome Hill, Lambeg in north Down developed from a two-unit, probably two-storeyed or lofted thatched

Fig. 209.   Hearth-lobby farmhouse with original gable-side entry, of two storeys, believed to have been in existence in 1690, 'Horsepark', Ballyelough Td., Co., Antrim. UFTM L 1237.20

Fig. 210.   17th-century farmhouse, Rosscor Td., Co. Fermanagh, from Trimble, *History of Enniskillen*, III (Enniskillen, 1921). UFTM L 1661.2

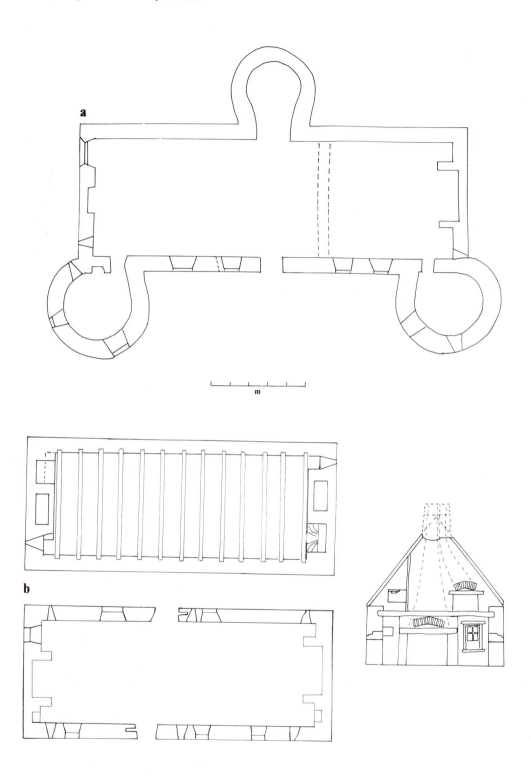

Fig. 211.   a: early 17th-century (? late 16th-century) defended house (note pistol loops as well as windows), Whitehouse, Co. Antrim (after Jope); b: early 17th-century defended two-storey house, The White House, Ballyspurge Td., Co. Down (after *Archaeological Survey of Co. Down*).

house which may have existed before 1690.[83] There is evidence of two hearth-lobby configurations within it, but I am inclined to think that the hearth at the original east gable, with its more massive chimney stack, may be the earlier.

Two houses of the earlier part of the seventeenth century may also be mentioned here. One is at White House (Fig. 211) on the north shore of Belfast Lough,[84] now greatly altered and in use as a gospel hall. It was a three-unit two-storey house with gable hearths, squat circular towers at the front at each end, and a rear round-ended stair projection. Pistol loops in the towers and the small number of ground-floor window openings indicate the builder's concern with defence. Similarly defended with pistol-loops in both sides at ground-floor level, and in both gables at upper-floor height, The White House in Ballyspurge townland in the Ards Peninsula in east Down (Fig. 211) has been ascribed to about 1630.[85] Also with gable hearths, on both floors, it was only slightly shorter than the county Antrim house but lacked the towers and rear stair projection. Its internal arrangement is not known, but in view of the built-in keeping places, window and pistol-loops flanking the gable fireplaces, it is unlikely that access to the upper floor was at either end of the house. The White House bears some resemblances to one end of a planter's defended house which survives at Doohat in Fermanagh,[86] and is reminiscent even of some of the simpler medieval tower houses, looking almost as if the latter were lowered and lengthened. At about 20.6 m. by 8 m. and 17 m. by 7.1 m. respectively, with walls about 0.75 to 0.8 m. thick, the proportions of these two houses do not relate to the norms of northern Irish vernacular housing, and they are most realistically regarded as non-vernacular structures built by and lived in by landed or wealthy people.

Near the south-west shore of Lough Neagh stands the derelict slated 'Belleville House', in Gortnaglogh townland, county Tyrone. On its front is a datestone reading 'IMF 1682', with an unidentified achievement above it. The house measures 15 m. by 8 m., with a rear outshut, 9.5 m. long and 4 m. deep, now roofed under a continuation downwards of the rear slope of the main roof; the pattern of slating, however, shows that originally there was an asymmetrically pitched roof over a smaller central rear outshut, which may have been a stair projection. The outside walls of the main part of the house are massively constructed of random rubble with some brick (18.2 cm. × 4.5-5 cm. × 9-11 cm.). Thin partition walls divided the ground floor into an off-centre hallway with possibly later stairs rising from front to rear, a large almost square room with fireplace occupying the left-hand end, and a kitchen with small pantry (?) behind

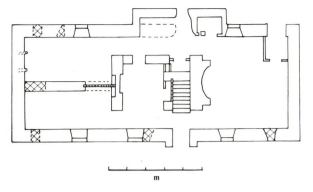

Fig. 212. Plan of farmhouse with entry giving onto back of kitchen-hearth wall, stairs later inserted in original cross passage between front and rear doors, original kitchen outshot enlarged presumably after stairs inserted blocking cross passage, Shantallow Td., Co. Londonderry (after McCourt and Evans).

in the right-hand end, with its hearth on the gable. Only the partition wall separating the stairs from the kitchen carries into the first floor space to the wall-head level of the outer house walls. Above the kitchen are front and rear rooms. Over the entrance hall the stairs rise to a landing area partitioned from a large room at the left-hand end of the house by a light stud-and-timber-sheeted wall. This upper floor is borne on oak joists carried on heavy oak beams with chamfered bottom edges. The house was lofted at wall-head height to provide attics, again carried on heavy oak beams. All of the oak beams and the brick size are consistent with the 1682 date. What identifies the house as of British provenance is the gabled three-bay roof. Unlike the usual Irish practice already described, of carrying load-bearing internal mass walls to the roof ridge, here the only supports between the gables are two enormous pine tie-beam trusses. A single continuous heavy through purlin rests on each truss blade halfway up the roof, and the truss is braced from the tie-beam diagonally up to the underside of each blade below the purlin. A second 'skin' of squared, sawn softwood, common rafters clamping a flat ridge piece at the apex rises from wall plates on the stone wall-heads. The slated roof, common rafters and pine trusses are possibly late eighteenth-century replacements for an older roof, but its design, carried on trusses rather than on internal load-bearing walls, may reflect the nature of an original thatched roof with oak timbering.

At the outset of this chapter a plan type with the entry giving onto the rear of the kitchen hearth was noted as a possibility. The *entry backing on the hearth* was the conventional configuration of many Welsh and English

Fig. 213.   Two-storey thatched house of *c*.1717, with unit added at left end 1800–1825, entrance shown probably not original, from Lismacloskey Td., Co. Antrim, reconstructed at UFTM. UFTM L 898.2

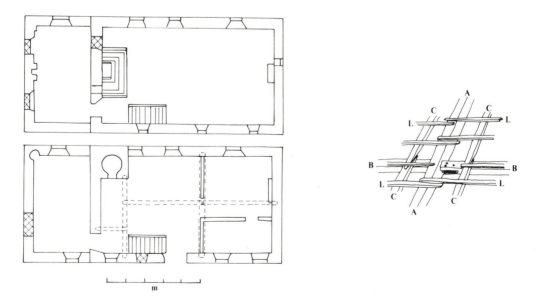

Fig. 214.   Plans of house of *c*.1717 from Lismacloskey Td., Co. Antrim. Note oven beside and under massive stone chimney canopy. Detail, not to scale, showing purlins (B) butted into faces of principal rafters (A) so that the backs of the principal rafters and the common rafters (C) lie in one plane. Beams supporting first floor, and bressumer, dotted; blocked openings, cross-shaded.

Fig. 215.   Raised oven in corner of hearth of Cromwellian-period farmhouse, Carrickreagh Td., Co. Fermanagh (cf. Fig. 191). Note curved oak bressumer. Pole at left marked in feet. UFTM L 83.8.

versions of the byre-dwelling,[87] and some houses with this layout have also been found in Scotland.[88] Only one has yet been identified in Ulster, at Shantallow north of Derry city (Fig. 212); it was demolished some years ago. There was some evidence both for a cross passage with an external door at each end, located behind the kitchen hearth, and for the keeping of cattle in the portion to the other side of the cross passage. The house was lofted with a unique ceiling pinned to roof timbers over at least part of the roof, consisting of plaited bands of marram grass, mentioned in the following chapter. Re-used portions of scarfed cruck blades served as truss blades in the roof. Dr. McCourt and Professor Evans published details of this house, associating its construction with plantation settlers from south-west England in the seventeenth century.[89] The only possibly comparable house I have seen in Ireland belonged to a miller and is perhaps of the eighteenth century. It is in Milltown townland, east of Castle Bellingham in county Louth, immediately south of our area.

If one visualises a plan of the Shantallow type, from which the byre-end and cross passage are removed, a house with external entry in the gable alongside the kitchen hearth results. This derivative form is widely attested in England and Wales[90] but has possibly been encountered only once in the north of Ireland, in a two-storey thatched house formerly at Gloverstown, Lismacloskey, in west Antrim (Figs. 213, 214) and now reconstructed at the Ulster Folk and Transport Museum.[91] No documentation survives to tell of its origin but dendrochronology provides a probable building date of 1717. It has a massive stone chimney stack carried on an oak bressumer, built against what was originally a gable wall, beyond which another unit was added between 1800 and 1825; it is suggested that the original entrance was through this gable beside the hearth, the opening being that which now gives entry to the added unit, a new outside door having been provided in the present position. Access upstairs was by ladder through a trap door near the rear wall, stairs later provided inside the front wall necessitating the blocking of a ground-floor window.

Apart from interpretation of its ground plan, two features of this house assign it to an English context, and both were repeated elsewhere in Ulster, providing constructional evidence of influences from English vernacular architecture. The *roof timbering* system in the Lismacloskey house consisted of two principal-rafter trusses of heavy scantling, carrying butt purlins tenoned into the faces of the principals so that the backs of the principals and the backs of the common rafters carried by the purlins all lie in a single plane. Butt-purlin roofing systems have been located in two other vernacular houses, one rural, the other urban. The latter has been dated dendrochronologically to about 1674/5 and is one of only three roofs seen in our area having longitudinal bracing between purlins and principal rafters. It is on a derelict stone-wall house in New Row, Coleraine; its future is uncertain in spite of its constituting the only recognised urban seventeenth-century roof carpentry in Ulster.[92] An English architectural context for it is certain; Coleraine was developed by The Hon. the Irish Society of London. The second house has already been discussed by virtue of its supposed upper cruck truss; but whatever the nature of the crucks in the two-storey formerly thatched house in Magherana townland, west of Waringstown in north-west Down, the purlins are obviously butted into the blade faces. The Waring lands were settled in the second half of the seventeenth century by English settlers (cf. the Corcreeny 'B' cruck house described in Chapter 3), and again a late seventeenth-century dating and British context seem assured. Butt-purlin systems with principal-rafter trusses relate to English traditions of box-frame carpentry, such as may have been built in the first half of the seventeenth century to judge from Raven's representations of houses on the properties of the various London companies. They have also been discovered covering the two National Trust properties at Springhill, Moneymore, in south Londonderry (*c.* 1680) and at Ardress in north Armagh (*c.* 1660) as well as in the roof of Waringstown House in north-west Down (*c.* 1666).

It is worth recalling here that certain classes of *cruck trusses* found in northern Irish houses betoken English influence; tie-beam cruck trusses with continuous blades, and upper cruck, are the categories involved (classes E and G in the discussion of roof timbering systems in Chapter 5).

A built-in *oven* to the right-hand side of the kitchen hearth is the other feature in the Lismacloskey house that identifies it with an English historical context. It is brick-lined, hemispherical in shape, and originally would

Fig. 216.   Enlarged drawing based on an English timber-framed house drawn by Thomas Raven whose maps were included in the Phillips survey of Co. Londonderry and published in Chart, *Londonderry and the London Companies* (Belfast, 1928).

perhaps have had a wooden or slate door, a later cast-iron one from a range having been fitted (Fig. 128). It was heated by lighting a fire inside it using fuel that produced as little smoke and soot as possible. The oven's location underneath the stone chimney canopy of the kitchen hearth meant that a separate flue was unnecessary. Similar ovens have been found, notably in the Carrickreagh house (Fig. 215) of the 1650s discussed in other contexts, and built by or for a Cromwellian soldier,[93] and in Newlands cottage in Erganagh Glebe townland north of Omagh in Tyrone, a house built on land owned by the established church perhaps as an early glebe house or rectory.[94] Another house with church associations that may have had an oven in an analogous position to the Lismacloskey one is the cruck house at Liffock in north Londonderry.[95] There was much English influence in Lecale barony in south-east Down from medieval times, and an account of life there in the last two decades of the eighteenth century tells that 'Ovens were built in the respectable houses especially through the "ten towns" in the wall near to the kitchen fire they were built of small size many of them remain to the present day' (1854).[96] Larger, probably non-vernacular houses with ovens have been noted in both Tyrone and Armagh, and again the historic settlement contexts are English. Two brick-lined ovens built into the sides of kitchen hearths were found in the excavation of a pair of urban houses of possibly early seventeenth-century date within the walls of the English-built city of Derry.[97] Lastly, early seventeenth-century references exist to ovens built upon three plantation estates in county Fermanagh,[98] and at the end of the century a Derry lease specified inclusion of an oven in a house on the east side of the River Foyle.[99]

Provision of *cellars* was exceptional in northern Irish vernacular housing, yet their existence in some houses in the Ballyhagan Quaker community in mid Armagh after 1715 again suggests English influence. Other references to cellars are in Thomas Ashe's 'View of the Archbishopric of Armagh' of 1703, but in houses in Tulledowe, county Tyrone, and Mucklagh, county Armagh which were so large as to rule them out as examples of indigenous vernacular architecture; once again British imports are involved.[100]

A final element present in the early seventeenth-century English building in county Londonderry did not become a significant feature in local building, although it appeared in the late nineteenth and twentieth centuries, apparently inspired by renewed outside influence — the *dormer window*. Raven's maps of towns in county Londonderry *c.* 1620 show widespread use of dormers to light attic rooms. They appear on facades as a continuation upwards of the wall face above eaves level in a sort of gablet, rather than as dormers contained wholly within the roof. Both timber-frame and mass-wall houses are shown with these windows, usually one to each side of a more or less centrally placed entrance and chimney (Fig. 216). Dormers may now be seen to any significant extent in two areas only. In south Fermanagh, adjacent parts of south Tyrone and west Monaghan, and in Cavan, a hearth-lobby house development (already commented upon) produced a symmetrical facade with a dormer window above the entrance (Fig. 193). In houses examined with these dormers, the windows always appear to be of late nineteenth-century character at the earliest, and the insertion of one example in modernisation of an early house in Coolbeg townland, county Fermanagh (Fig. 197) was carried out as late as about 1940. What outside influences were at work to generate this distinctive regional feature so late are unknown. Scottish influences, however, are likely in the appearance of some houses in east Down with dormers, and in some towns in the area the characteristically Scottish five-sided dormer occurs occasionally.

V. THE RELATIONSHIP BETWEEN IRISH AND BRITISH VERNACULAR HOUSING

Northern Irish vernacular architecture, of course, does not exist, nor did it evolve historically, isolated from what happened elsewhere in Ireland and Britain. Already an English origin for the hearth-lobby house plan has been suggested; the general point may be suitably illustrated by considering little more than the distributional aspects of

that plan-type and of a few other features of northern Ireland's traditional housing.

Housing with jamb walls was distributed in Ireland widely in the province of Leinster, north and east Munster and east Connacht. Although this feature has not yet been reported in the literature at the Atlantic coast, the westernmost outliers of its northern distribution in the Garrison area of Fermanagh are only a dozen miles from the coast; an early twentieth-century photograph of Falls Cottage in Glencar, county Sligo is similarly placed;[101] and comparable houses were reported by Caoimhín Ó Danachair in the eastern parts of county Limerick not far from the Shannon estuary.[102] The type is almost unknown in Scotland, but in England (Fig. 217), as we have seen, variants lie in a broad area south from Lancashire through Cheshire and Staffordshire and then west into Montgomeryshire almost to the Welsh coast, and again everywhere south-east of a line joining the Tees and the Severn.[103] The earliest historical evidence for development of this house plan is from south-east England in the sixteenth century, and it must be more than coincidental that its distribution in Ireland encompasses all those areas most thoroughly anglicised in post-medieval times.

If an impression has been gained that the direct-entry house plan evolved from a 'native' type, 'native' must be

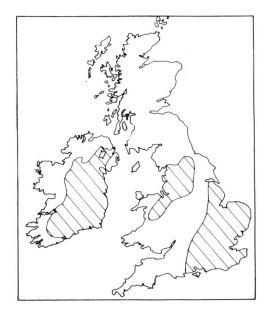

Fig. 217. Principal distributional concentrations of hearth-lobby houses in Ireland and Britain (after Ó Danachair: central and southern Ireland; Smith and Brunskill: Great Britain).

defined principally in terms of what existed before the hearth-lobby arrangement was introduced; but this merely pushes the search for origins and external influences back to earlier periods. Combinations of quarters for people and their cattle existed in Scotland, much of Wales, and south-west England, and there were comparable forms also in Cumbria, the Pennines and the north-east, south as far as the Humber.[104] For Ireland, Ó Danachair has summarised evidence showing late survivals of the type in the north and north-west especially, but oral traditions of byre-dwellings existed more widely, while distribution of the apparently related feature of opposite entrances excludes only most of Leinster (except parts of Longford, Meath and Louth) and east Munster (except west Clare, west Limerick, most of Cork, and Kerry).[105] The latest functioning survivals of byre-dwellings were in the western and northern islands of Scotland.[106] I recall one in Fivepenny Borve in north Lewis in the late 1950s, entry to which for both humans and cows was by the one door, and in which there was not even a smoke-hole. We have already seen, too, that the related minority elements the bed outshot, occurred in Scotland, parts of Wales and south-west England, and possibly related wall-bed types were known in the north of England.[107]

From the material discussed in Chapter 5 two features suffice to illustrate the point. The commonest northern thatching technique, scollop thatch, was also the commonest technique over most of Ireland; comparable techniques were widespread in England. Norfolk reed thatching is one variant. This type is known in Europe eastward at least as far as Hungary. The distributionally contrasting coastal roped thatch was not a northern Irish expedient. Roped thatch was used all along the west Irish seaboard, and also in the Isle of Man and western Scotland. Common environmental problems demanded similar responses fairly widely.

Irish cruck forms are obviously related to British ones, and the English provenance of some is historically certain. The fact that almost all of the Irish evidence is northern reflects only the greater detail of field investigations carried out there. Related roof timbering forms have recently been reported from south-west Kerry,[108] and there is reasonably clear nineteenth-century literary evidence for cruck forms in county Galway,[109] and more recently oral testimony of scarfed crucks in Leitrim.[110] Related scarfed-cruck forms survive in westen parts of Britain, from south-west England to Highland Scotland. It is particularly interesting that the sole survivals of end crucks, known from fourteenth-century documents and excavation of twelfth-century structures in England, are distributed from Devon to Inverness, even in Brittany and Limousin in France, and in northern Ireland.[111] If to this we add that the dominant roof-truss apex forms in northern Ireland, whether with crucks or not, are those adjudged to be amongst the earliest forms recognised in Britain,[112] the importance of considering the northern Irish evidence in as wide a context as possible is obvious. Alcock wrote, 'It is ironic that because end-crucks have not survived from the area where they are recorded in documents, we must go either to Scotland or to Corèze, France for the best idea of the prototype of the properly carpentered English cruck building'.[113] He quoted a barn in Inverness-shire as coming closest to the form this prototype could have taken, but the Rossavally house in west Fermanagh is just as quotable, with its end-crucks, non-load-bearing brick walls and an old apex form (Figs. 71, 72). As is true of so many aspects of northern Irish vernacular housing, in the case of crucks it is essential to distinguish between the possible late date of survivals (the Rossavally house may be of early nineteenth-century origin) and the antiquity of the building traditions they represent. So it is with house types. Many of the surviving direct-entry and hearth-lobby houses in the north of Ireland were built as late as the nineteenth century, even after 1850. Yet the vernacular traditions within which they were constructed are much older, recognisable at least as early as the second decade of the seventeenth century in the case of the hearth-lobby house in the north of Ireland, and in medieval times in the case of the antecedents of the direct-entry plan form.

NINE

The House and Society

MAINLY structural and constructional aspects of the northern Irish vernacular house have been the concern of this book thus far, but a house above all is lived in by some people, and commonly passed by on the outside by many others. A central purpose of ethnological enquiry is to explore the attitudes of both to the dwellings surrounding them. Vernacular architecture studies of Irish housing have concentrated on a rather 'archaeological' approach, in spite of some pioneering contributions dealing with the use of the house,[1] as a 'machine for living'. This chapter introduces this aspect of the subject. Relatively little historical documentation exists in this field, and in view of the present rapid disappearance of truly vernacular houses, and even more of the former life-styles to which they belonged, comprehensive studies in this field can now be based only on oral tradition. Three broad areas will be explored briefly: attitudes to housing, expressed particularly through the words used to describe dwellings; family use of the dwelling and some ways in which this has changed; and the symbolic value of the house within local society.

Creats, Cabins and Cottages

A variety of words denote dwellings in the early seventeenth-century northern Irish documentation of the plantation, and indeed the same usages occur more widely in descriptions of Irish circumstances at that time, mostly by outsiders. We have earlier seen that there was common survival in the early 1600s of small flimsily constructed huts, circular in shape, chimneyless, built mainly of wattle and thatch. Contemporary English commentators were confused between the Irish name for these impermanent dwellings, *creata* (a timber framework; the ribs of a house or roof), and the agrarian system of which they were a part involving the practice of and human participants in seasonal migrations of cattle exploiting summer pastures, *caoraidheacht* (a foray party; cattle and their caretaker). A variety of

anglicisations was applied to these distinct Irish words, including 'creaght', 'creat', 'creet', and 'crate'. Examination of the contexts in which these English forms occur is therefore vital to determining whether it was the dwellings, or the system of which they were a part, that was at issue.[2] 'Crate' continued in use through the seventeenth century until at least as late as 1703, when Thomas Ashe noted 'some Crates or Cabbins' at Plaister in Tyrone.[3] Equation of these two words seems to have been going on for almost a century when Ashe was writing, for in 1617 Fynes Moryson, in perhaps the most widely known quotation of creaghting, described those involved as being 'Like the Nomads removing their dwelling according to the commodity of pastures for their cows', and their dwellings as 'cabins wattled and covered with turf'.[4]

Some contemporary houses in the north of Ireland differed structurally from these seasonal dwellings and were less obviously connected with creaghting. Wattled houses are shown on the map of Armagh c. 1600 by Richard Barthelet,[5] and it was probably these which were noted by Camden as '. . . a few small wattle cottages . . .'[6] Thus there were three different words in use in the first half of the seventeenth century, all apparently describing similar structures, having in common a smaller size and perhaps less permanent nature than what were being described at the same period as 'houses'. Then, to make confusion worse confounded, there was an Act passed by the Irish Parliament in 1705 forbidding the use '. . . in wattling the walls of houses or cabins, or out-buildings, [of] any kind of gadd or gadds, wyth or wyths, of oak, ash, birch, hazel or other tree whatsoever . . .'[7] The same equation was made much earlier too. In north-west Tyrone Sir George Hamilton in 1611 had already built 'good timber houses',[8] which only two years later were described as 'Irish cabins'[9] and in 1619 as a village of 'Irish coupled houses'.[10] Similarly in east Tyrone 'Irish coupled houses' noted in 1611 were referred to as 'small cabins' in 1619.[11] However, the distinction between creats and houses was clear enough in a survey of the city of Armagh in 1618. Seventy of the 120 houses were listed as creats: including thirty-one 'Little Creetes', nineteen 'Creetes', and one 'little creete', four 'coupled creetes', one 'long coupled creete' and one 'old coupled creete'. Fifty dwellings were listed as 'houses', of which fourteen were 'forked houses', two were 'stone houses' and twenty-nine were 'copled houses' — one each 'fair', 'good', 'great', 'long' and 'little'.[12] 'Houses' were more substantial buildings than 'creetes', probably having walls of clay, earth, or earth and wattle, rather than flimsy wattlework, but as yet stone walls were uncommon.

In spite of Ashes's use of 'Crate' in 1703, the word mostly dropped out of use during the seventeenth century, 'cabin' apparently replacing it as the distinction from 'house'. Its disappearance almost certainly relates to discontinuance of constructing dwellings with mainly wattled walls. Between 1667 and 1670 in townlands to the south of Lough Neagh near Lurgan, leases quoted labour requirements due from 'every house or cabbin'.[13] About 1700 on Turkarry and Drumnasolagh in the county Armagh manor of Castledillon, there was a good sod-wall house 40 ft. long and 13 ft. broad and two cabins.[14] Obviously the nature of materials used did not distinguish a house from a cabin, and so size probably was the definitive criterion. On the same property two of three undertenants occupied 'a little sod-wall cabin', 'a small wattled wall house', and the undertenants had 'three good cabins for their cottagers'.[15] So it is impossible to relate the terms specifically to tenurial status. In Grange in the same manor, three undertenants occupied 'a small sod wall cabin', 'a small sod wall house' and 'a small sod stone and clay house', while in Mullynasillagh and Legavilly one undertenant lived in 'a small mud wall cabin'.[16] In Drumnasolagh, there were numerous undertenants who lived in 'ordinary little cabins', 'a small mud wall cabin', 'a good stone and clay wall house with a brick chimney', 'a small mud wall cabin', and 'a small walled-wall [sic] cabin'[17] — obviously by the time he had reached the listing of the last of these, the surveyor himself was very confused!

Reference in this Castledillon survey to the existence of a brick chimney in both a stone-and-clay-wall house and a mud-wall cabin is interesting. In the early seventeenth-century documentation it is impossible to assume that use of the word 'house' presupposes existence of a substantial chimney, but whenever such a chimney is noted, invariably it occurs in a 'house' rather than a cabin or a creat. This is true whether the buildings concerned were occupied by Irish or by British settlers.[18] By the end of the seventeenth century this distinction was breaking down, and throughout the eighteenth century and later these words relate more to ill-defined conceptions of size and of

inferior/superior dwellings than to any clear-cut criteria like construction methods, wall materials, or the nature of the hearth and the presence or absence of a chimney canopy or flue.

In his account of Fermanagh in 1759, Rev. Mr. Henry referred to farmers living in 'neat little stone cabbins',[19] and if the interpretation of the farmhouse from Corradreenan West townland in that county, now at the Ulster Folk and Transport Musuem, is correct, then such small 'cabbins' had wattled chimney canopies. In 1752 Bishop Pococke saw 'cabbins' having two doors (presumably opposite doors) in the Donegal parish of Ray,[20] and these certainly would have been byre-dwelling farmhouses, though probably without chimneys. Edward Willes, Chief Baron to the Irish Exchequer, when on circuit in the Castlewellan area of county Down in 1759, saw comparable 'cabins', the doors of which were 'crowded with little naked boys and girls'.[21] Ten years later a glebe house at Culdaff in the Diocese of Derry consisted of 'two ranges of thatched cabbins . . . the whole new sashed and glazed. The barn, stable, and cow-house are low, insufficient cabins, built without lime; and near the glebe house are the remains of some other cabins, which were cottages for labourers, but now not one of them habitable.'[22] Here, 'cabin' can only mean what was regarded as some inferior kind of building, for the word is applied indiscriminately to a glebe house, labourers' dwellings and outhouses. Arthur Young's tour in Ireland in the 1770s was undertaken to explore the extent of, and to advocate, agricultural improvement. Inevitably he largely ignored the circumstances of the mass of the population, but occasionally he referred to the building costs of a 'cabbin', for example £5 for a stone one in Clonleigh parish in east Donegal and £5.5s. for one on the Farnham estate in Cavan.[23]

In the nineteenth century 'cabin' was extensively used, as in the Ordnance Survey memoirs and in the evidence given before the poor inquiry of the 1830s, to refer to the housing of the poor, the landless, and even of small farmers. The usage was so widespread as to make it pointless to quote individual instances. Some writers used 'cabin' more indiscriminately. A clergyman describing housing in the north Armagh parish of Seagoe in 1816 used it,[24] and in 1844 the medical man, James Johnson, travelling northwards towards Enniskillen, wrote, 'We see as we enter Ulster that the cabins become more substantial, comfortable and water-tight'.[25] By this he meant nothing more definitive than single-storey thatched houses, of whatever size, with or without chimneys.

Denoting a small dwelling of inferior construction, 'cabin' lacked any tenurial connotation, and so it is understandable that its use should have been commoner before the nineteenth century than that of 'cottage'. A 'cottager' ('cottar', 'cotter', in Ireland 'cottier') was someone occupying a cottage belonging to a farm, and the subsidiary status of the cottage was thus usually fairly clear. In England, cottages were, like cabins, nevertheless small dwellings, and it is readily understandable how the word came to be applied rather loosely by English observers in seventeenth-century Ireland. As already noted, Camden described houses in Armagh c.1600 as 'small wattle cottages', and small temporary dwellings erected after their arrival in east Down in the early 1600s by Scottish settlers were described as 'cottages or booths'.[26] Even earlier, new stone and lime houses were replacing what were described in 1593 as 'rotten and ruinous clay houses and cottages' in Carrickfergus.[27] 'Cottage' was used occasionally by other writers describing circumstances either elsewhere in Ireland or generally in the island[28] during the seventeenth century, equating it with 'cabin' or some other description of a small dwelling. In 1700, however, we have already seen that the tenurial connotation was implicit in the description referring to undertenants on the manor of Castledillon in Armagh, in Turkarry and Drumnasolagh, who had 'three good cabins for their cottagers'.[29] Perhaps the problems presented by seventeenth-century usage are best illustrated in the English translation of 1652 of Gerard Boate's original Latin description of 1641 of the dwellings generally of the Irish in his time as being 'very poor and contemptible cottages'.[30] In the eighteenth- and early nineteenth-century documentation 'cottage' was less commonly used than 'cabin' by most writers, and it was not until after 1830, when concern for the living conditions of the Irish rural poor was growing, that use of 'cottage' became common, for example in the poor inquiry evidence of the 1830s and in the contemporary Ordnance Survey memoirs. Then, 'cottage' was generally used in contexts that show it meant a house to which either little or no land attached, but to which the occupant usually had some tenurial or customary rights.

It was the mid-nineteenth century before this usage became general. Still about 1820 in his surveys of the Drumbanagher estate[31] and of the Gosford estates in east Armagh,[32] William Greig described and illustrated the 'Common Cottage or Cabin' (Fig. 184), obviously a house that could be occupied by a tenant farmer or a landless weaver, and his usage contrasted with his plans for 'Improved Cottages' (Fig. 218) for weavers and other landless people, and for an 'Improved Farm house & Yard' (see Chapter 10).

The reader will by now have determined that use of 'creat', 'cabin' and 'cottage' in the documentation of northern Irish housing before the middle of the nineteenth century is so imprecise that only one approach to interpretation is possible. Whenever any of these words occurs, the neutral 'dwelling' must be substituted, at least mentally, and the context examined to determine the nature of the structure and the status of its occupants. This has been the procedure underlying a recent successful analysis of the northern Irish early seventeenth-century documentation on housing.[33] So far as attitudes are concerned, however, use of 'cabin' and 'cottage' by mainly English observers of Irish housing is revealing. Before the start of the seventeenth century a quite clear size distinction existed in many parts of England between yeomen's and other peasant farmers' houses, and the homes of landless cottagers and labourers, a distinction that accorded with a literal meaning of 'cottage'. Arrived in Ireland, English observers naturally applied the terms 'cottage' and 'cabin' to the houses they saw because these were small, and ignored any tenurial connotations the words may then have normally held. However, in Britain, the landless poor were looked down upon and application of a word like 'cottage', or 'cabin' even more so, was reinforced by the socially, even racially superior way in which the native population were regarded. It was not until a social conscience stirred amongst some Irish landlords and others in the nineteenth century that the disparagement implicit in descriptions of Irish rural houses as 'cabins' and

Fig. 218.   Improved cottage advocated by William Greig for Gosford and Drumbanagher estates, Co. Armagh, c.1820. Redrawn from plan in PRONI T 3097.

'cottages' began to disappear. Sir William Petty summed this attitude up neatly for us in 1672 when he claimed that many of 'the Irish live in brutish, nasty conditions, as in cabins with neither chimney, door, stairs nor window'.[34]

The attitudes of landlords in regard to rural housing take on significance in the nineteenth century. Until after 1700 they had been concerned to establish a prosperous and, as they saw it, a loyal tenantry on their estates. Long leases at favourable terms were granted, which of course militated against landlord improvement or investment in rural housing. Building and repair of farmhouses and cottages were left to the tenantry themselves. Undoubtedly there were examples of concerned landlords, and their influence was seen in the landscape. Good houses surrounded by planting in the Waringstown area in the 1740s were '. . . all owing to the Encouragement and Long Tenures and kind Landlords living on their Estates among their Tenants'.[35] There was, too, the 'Ulster custom' of tenant right whereby a tenant on leaving a property was recompensed for any improvements, including buildings, he had carried out during his tenancy. An incoming tenant had to buy the tenant right from his predecessor, either at the end of the tenancy or when a sitting tenant sold the remaining portion of his lease. Obviously the custom took on greater significance as the early long leases on favourable terms fell in during the late eighteenth and early nineteenth centuries. James Johnson's comment in 1844 that he observed a better standard of housing as he came north through Enniskillen must be seen in this context.[36] Similar comments might be quoted from the early nineteenth century onwards. Existence of the custom must have encouraged many tenant farmers and cottiers to maintain their houses, especially in more prosperous districts. Nevertheless little evidence exists that its operation encouraged people to build themselves larger houses of improved design, or to depart from the parameters of vernacular building.

Once landlords had short-term control over their properties, after the long leases had finally expired, it was at least theoretically in their interests to invest in their land and buildings. More prosperous, more highly capitalised tenancies could be expected to be more profitable to the tenants and to return higher rents to the landlords. Some landlords simply did not bother about conditions on their estates. Others operated practices that today seem harsh or exploitative. In the 1830s in Enniskillen parish in Fermanagh, for example, sod and mud cabins were built in mountain areas, and colonised free of rent for three-year periods during which their builders broke in and cultivated the ground. The landlord then took the ground back into his own hands, and the cabin builders had to

move on to another patch to repeat the process. The landlord could take what crop he could from the improved land and lay it out to pasture, or he could set it out at rent to a tenant.[37] He certainly was profiting at no outlay to himself, but it should be remembered that the poor man who supported his family by breaking in waste land in this way at least was paying no rent, and to that extent was incomparably better off than many of his contemporaries elsewhere in Ireland at this time of very severe population pressure on rural resources, just before the Great Famine.

It had been widely believed that only long tenancies would encourage tenants to maintain standards on their holdings. By the 1830s, when many tenancies had been renewed for short terms, or the land-holders had become tenants at will, experience was already showing this was not necessarily the case. In the county Antrim parish of Templepatrick good modern housing standards enjoyed by the tenantry in the late 1830s were attributed to

> encouragement given by Lord Templetown, for instead of being injured as they expected to have been by his system of not granting leases, they have so far evinced a proof of their being benefited by the improvements which they have made in their places since their farms fell out of leases.
>
> Previous to that period almost all the houses had been but one storey high, but since then many have been raised a story. Some have been thrown down and rebuilt on a better plan, and many have been roofed [with] slates, almost all having previously been thatched.[38]

In Fermanagh in Killesher parish Lord Enniskillen maintained farmhouses on his property for tenants at will, but leaseholders were responsible for their own houses, although they could get timber from the landlord for housebuilding and repairs as required. This was in 1835 when as yet the farmhouses were only 'in a few instances good and commodious, but the generality are far otherwise, they are however improving'.[39] Generalisation for the whole of the north of Ireland is impossible in this matter. Conditions varied from estate to estate, and even the personalities and preferences of landlords and of tenants were significant. In eastern parts of Killinchy parish in east Down, perpetuity leases were reported in 1833 as responsible for a good standard of housing, 'many of them being 2 story houses and the farm offices are good', whereas in the western part of the same parish, leases for three lives, thirty-one years, twenty-one years and tenancies at will were regarded as responsible for a lower standard of housing.[40] Lease holding was probably still prevalent on the Crom estate of Mr. Creighton in the Derrylin end of Kinawley parish in south Fermanagh at this time; tenants were expected to keep their houses in repair themselves, but the landlord to promote neatness and comfort among his tenantry, at his own expense, slates the roofs of those among them who will erect decent farm houses. This in many instances has had a good effect and there are already several neat commodious dwellings on the estate.[41]

Close to a landlord's demesne formally designed buildings were sometimes provided by the landlord himself as part of a broad concept of landscape development. A good example, of which survivals can still be seen, was on Lord Caledon's property in south-east Tyrone close to the Monaghan border, where the cottages were described as 'extremely neat and ornamental'.[42] In the Monaghan parish of Muckno,

Lord Blayney's tenantry have lately built some good two story houses in their farms for which his Lordship has made some allowance. Lord Templeton supplies his tenantry with timber and slates, to build good farmhouses and offices.[43]

Other landlords who at the same time were behaving similarly were Mr. Law who had property in Bovevagh parish in Londonderry,[44] and Mr. Thompson who owned Taylorstown townland in the west Antrim parish of Grange of Ballyscullion.[45] Some landlords went further. Lord George Hill carried out a radical reformation of his newly acquired Gweedore estate in north-west Donegal about 1840, insisting on the building of new houses. Premiums were to be awarded for housing improvements; he offered eight in 1852, four for new houses built on the old farms since 1843, and four for houses in respect of which premiums had already been awarded in earlier years, obviously an encouragement to maintenance of improved standards. Hill's tenants were also eligible for four premiums offered by the Irish Peasantry Improvement Society of London.[46] About 1829, premiums of 'small sums of money or consisting of utensils of a domestic and useful nature were given to cottagers whose dwellings etc. evinced the greatest regard to or taste for comfort and cleanliness' in the east Fermanagh parish of Magheraculmoney, but as so often happened with such well-meaning schemes, initial enthusiasm by a landlord rapidly evaporated, even though as in the Magheraculmoney case 'it was attended with success in its results'.[47] Lord George Hill lost his improving zeal in north-west Donegal. It was one thing for a landlord to have improving ideas; it was another for a tenantry to agree to be 'improved'.[48]

As already mentioned, not all landlords were interested in improving their estates or concerned with the social conditions of those living on their property. Of the thirteen townlands in the south-east Antrim parish of Glynn, ten were included in the Magheramourne estate of Mr. Irving in 1840. He encouraged 'the industrious and improving tenant' by supplying materials for flooring and roofing provided he would build a two-storey farmhouse, and slate and lime to others who preferred to retain a single-storey dwelling. 'The consequence is that very few thatched houses are to be seen on the estate. Lime is also given gratuitously to whitewash the houses . . .' Mr. Irving also built twelve double cottages of an improved design to accommodate labourers.[49] The remaining three townlands in Glynn were owned by Mr. Johnston, who did not encourage his tenantry as Mr. Irving did. As a result the farmhouses remained single-storeyed, mostly thatched, rather small dwellings maintained in indifferent repair with ill-designed outhouses that were too small. These farms were characterised by that mark of indifference that came in for so much disapproval from the compilers of the Ordnance Survey memoirs — manure heaps in front of the houses.[50] If some individual landlords could actively encourage their tenantry to improvement of their living conditions, so too could some institutional ones. The Drapers' Company in mid-nineteenth-century county Londonderry was a case in point. The Ordnance Survey memoirs for the parishes of Ballinascreen,[51] Lissan[52] and Desertlyn[53] all testify to this, as does the return made to the North-West of Ireland Farming Society in 1821 preserved in the Ordnance Survey memoir for the parishes of Ballinascreen, Kilcronaghan and Desertmartin.[54] In Ballinascreen, cottages on the Drapers' estate were superior to those on properties of other landowners; the evidence from Desertlyn suggests that cottagers were required to whitewash their houses regularly; in Lissan, the Drapers' agent provided lime *gratis* to poor tenants, although those with the means to do so had to purchase it, but he exacted a year's rent *in advance* from recalcitrant tenants refusing to keep their houses clean and comfortable. Already in 1821 the Company had erected a model farm at Gortnaskeagh 'with suitable buildings in the English style, all slated', and 'a respectable tenant' had been encouraged to emulate it. The hope was that 'miniature copies' would soon be more generally built, firstly throughout the Company's estates, and then that they would spread to adjoining properties.

All of this evidence points to a growing concern for the living conditions of the rural classes in the nineteenth century. The government inquiry into the circumstances of the poor in Ireland in the 1830s was part of it. As Greig's reports in county Armagh about 1820 show, improved housing was even then being advocated. But as the Drapers' Company found, while landlords might encourage, householders did not necessarily respond in the expected manner. Perhaps as Maurice Collis's survey of Lord Londonderry's north Down estate in 1848 shows, tenantry attitudes were crucial. This was a progressive estate in which in the preceding century no less than 5000 acres had been reclaimed from waste. The fact that 25% of the rural houses on the estate had slate roofs was attributable to the existence of local slate quarries. That only just over 5% of the rural houses had more than four rooms is much more significant, and less than this proportion had more than one storey; the traditional one-storey two-, three- or four-room house was still usual. Almost 80% had earth floors, and another 7% had flagstones. The probability of there being a parlour is suggested by the 9% only with timber floors, together with just over 5% which had some combination of earth and timber floors. These two categories add up remarkably closely to the 15% of the rural houses on the estate with more than three windows; introduction of a parlour went with provision of better standards of lighting and ventilation. Few houses were without at least one proper chimney. Thirty-one had no chimney, and forty-eight had only a hole in the roof, yet more than 700 of the rural houses on this estate were occupied by cottiers; even they seem to have been fairly comfortably accommodated.

The prosperity of this estate is perhaps illustrated in the literacy rates of the tenantry. More than half could read and write, and only 18% were wholly illiterate; since about 15% were aged under five years, clearly almost all could read, and 65% of the population over five years could also write. If these figures reflect prosperity, why was it not more manifest in the housing standards? It was a peaceful estate where the Ulster custom prevailed, and security of tenure was available to tenants who conducted themselves in a reasonable manner. About a third of all the rural houses had been occupied by the families resident at the time of Collis's survey for between one and three generations, and almost a tenth for more than a century. In all of these circumstances it is tempting to argue that the value system predominating amongst the mainly Presbyterian tenants of this estate in the middle of the nineteenth century did not include extensive acceptance of building innovations or social ostentation in their housing.[55] Let us recall, too, the Clogher Valley comment of the 1830s quoted from the Ordnance Survey memoirs, that a farmer living apparently in abject poverty, to judge from his material standard of living, yet could provide sizeable money dowries for his daughters at marriage.[56]

It is important to keep this matter of attitudes in mind when considering some comments regarding the state of housing in the north of Ireland. It was suggested that the housing of Protestants, sometimes of Presbyterians in particular, was of a better standard and better maintained than that of Roman Catholics. One may note, too, the colloquialism still current in north-east Ireland that something neat and tidy is 'Protestant looking'. In the Londonderry parish of Lissan in 1836 'In Roman Catholic districts there is more poverty and the houses consequently not kept as clean as in the Protestant and presbyterian districts.'[57] Similar comments were made by compilers of the parish memoirs in the 1830s of Dunaghy and Templepatrick in Antrim,[58] of Tullyniskan in Tyrone,[59] and of Ballinascreen, Banagher, Bovevagh, Upper Cumber, and Maghera all in Londonderry.[60] The relationship with poverty mentioned in Lissan is more clearly illustrated in reverse a century earlier, in the Waringstown district of north-west Down, where prosperous farmhouses were '. . . all inhabited by industrious Protestants, many of whom are engaged in the Linen business . . .'[61] A consequence of the pattern of British settlement in the north of Ireland in the seventeenth and early eighteenth centuries was that, at least in some districts, better land was settled by British people, predominantly Protestant, the mainly Roman Catholic native folk congregating in poorer areas.[62] This environmental poverty of the Roman Catholic householders was commented upon by a number of the Ordnance Survey memoir compilers, and obviously is another factor to set alongside the question of value systems. It is much too simple to ascribe differences in housing conditions and maintenance merely to differences in religion and attendant value systems.

Landlords' concern for the housing conditions of their tenantry resulted occasionally in relatively high expenditures by them. The Earl of Erne agreed an elaborate specification for five cottages to be built 'in the mountains' in Carrickawick townland in Fermanagh, and signed an agreement to build them at a cost of £68 each, a substantial sum for building a cottage in 1839. Their specification was so elaborate as to remove them from the norms of vernacular building. Cut stone was provided for quoins, chimneys, and fireplaces. Roofs were of slate carried on the best timber, to be used for floors, doors and window frames also.[63] A proposal survives for the erection of two labourers' cottages on Myroe level, near Limavady in county Londonderry in 1866,[64] and there is a specification for the erection of labourers' cottages at Glassmullen in county Antrim in 1887.[65] Concern for housing conditions was expressed too by organisations like agricultural societies which in the second half of the nineteenth century were no longer the preserve of their landlord patrons that they had been at the start of the century; there is a prize design of 1861 for labourers' cottages by T. Ross Darlington.[66]

Political pressure was building in the second half of the nineteenth century to improve rural housing in Ireland, especially for the landless labourer, following the evidence of the poor inquiry of the 1830s and the catastrophe of the Great Famine in the 1840s which wrought greatest havoc amongst the landless poor. Acts were passed to encourage the building of labourers' cottages in 1856[67] and 1860,[68] but being only permissive they had little effect. The Land Act of 1870[69] allowed a landlord to repossess a portion of a tenancy to build a labourer's cottage, and a further act of 1872[70] permitted sub-letting for the same purpose. Again permissive, these acts were of little consequence in Ulster. Tenants were able to ignore building provisions in the Land Act of 1881,[71] and because they were difficult to collect, a system of fines enacted a year later[72] to try to bring tenants to a realisation of their social responsibility failed also. An attempt to change from permissive to mandatory legislation came in 1883 when responsibility for building labourers' cottages was imposed on local Boards of Guardians, but it foundered because the Boards were fearful of generating rises in local rates demands.[73] It was a decade later before many of the deficiencies of the 1883 legislation were put right, and at last, in various parts of Ireland, local authorities started to build labourers' cottages. Throughout much of Ireland the word 'cottage' still specifically refers to these houses, which gave adequate standardised conditions to the rural landless classes for the first time. To each cottage a small portion of land was added to permit the growing of vegetables and even the keeping of a pig. Inadequacies in the 1883 legislation were such that, up to March 1892 in the whole of the north-east of Ireland, only Ballycastle and Ballymena Poor Law Unions had authorised schemes, for eighteen cottages in the latter and eight in the former. The Ballymena cottages were built in pairs, each having four rooms, a privy, porch and a half-acre garden, and they were erected at a cost of £126 each. Early building of these labourers' cottages, later carried out by the Rural District Councils, proceeded slowly in the north and west of Ireland, whereas substantial numbers were built in Munster and Leinster. In March 1904 the situation was that Ulster had by then built only just over 5% of the all-Ireland total (Table 8) and even at just over 12% of the cottages then building, the prospect for the immediate future was only slowly improving. However, in the nineteenth century the problem of the landless labourer and his accommodation was less pressing in Ulster than elsewhere; the even poorer start in building cottages in Connacht was much more marked, and that province had not enjoyed the relative rural prosperity, and the alternative of a move to urban,

TABLE 8. LABOURERS' COTTAGES BUILT IN IRELAND, TO MARCH 1904

Province	Built	Building
Ulster	905	255
Connacht	247	76
Munster	9254	1149
Leinster	7005	583
All Ireland	17411	2063

industrialised social conditions, which had prevailed in the north.

In 1906 the powers of the local authorities in Ireland were extended, resulting in simplification of the procedures for building labourers' cottages and provision of suitable financial arrangements and resources. The Local Government Board in Dublin arranged a prize competition for cottage plans, the cottages to be subject to a cost limit of £130, which in the opinion of some was rather low. Nearly 400 designs were submitted. Those considered most meritorious were made available for use by any Rural District Council. At the Home Industries Section of Dublin's Irish International Exhibition in 1907 examples of the first and second prize-winning cottages were constructed.[74] These particular designs had incurred the wrath of the well-known Francis Joseph Bigger, whose nationalist sympathies led him to condemn the award of Irish prizes to English designers.[75] The designs he criticised had no basis in Irish tradition, and seem not to have been widely used by the local authorities, whereas others were taken up which incorporated kitchen layouts of Irish vernacular inspiration. Alongside these may be set the contemporary view of Bigger, and another critic Robert Brown, both of whom, like William Greig about 1820 in county Armagh as we have seen, produced vernacularly inspired designs drawn up for them by the Irish architect, W.J. Fennell. Brown's design (Fig. 219) was based on a hearth-lobby plan, adapted only by having cased-in stairs on the back wall leading to two attic bedrooms, a rear door leading out of the closed-off area at the foot of the stairs. His view was that this arrangement meant that 'Bedroom slops do not need to be carried through the kitchen . . .',[76] but perhaps his concern was influenced as much by a legacy of Victorian prudery as by concern for hygiene. Bigger typically was more forthright. His designs were based on a direct-entry plan (Fig. 220) and did not close off the stairs which wound around the kitchen corner at the rear, opposite the entrance to each of his two designs with upper floors, and he viewed a kitchen sink as 'unwholesome'. He advocated that washing up should continue to be done in a bucket or basin placed on a stool or table, its contents

Fig. 219.   Interior of labourer's cottage advocated by Robert Brown.

Fig. 220.   Interior of labourer's cottage advocated by F.J. Bigger.

thrown out of the door when the chore was completed. Not in the least concerned about 'bedroom slops', he suggested that 'In small cottages there is no occasion for two doors — one is quite ample to prevent draughts, and can easily be kept quite clean, and as a rule always open'.[77] Bigger's ethnocentric nativism carried little sway. Labourers' cottages based mainly on some of the competition designs became distinctive architectural markers of the areas served by local government authorities in rural Ireland (Figs. 221-223). In some instances cottage plans were chosen which did not accord with the local vernacular housing tradition, notably in the

Cooley peninsula in north Louth, and in Larne Rural District Council (Fig. 221) area in east Antrim, where lobby-entry cottages were built. Some in the Glens of Antrim in turn led to the adoption of this plan form in at least one other house in the area. Similarly, hearth-lobby cottages of this period spread northwards from the vernacular hearth-lobby area around Ballinamallard and Irvinestown into south Tyrone in the Fintona and Dromore area. But the labourers' cottages are easily recognisable, both from the distinctive way they were laid out along roadsides, often in groups, sometimes in semi-detached pairs, and also by the use of architectural

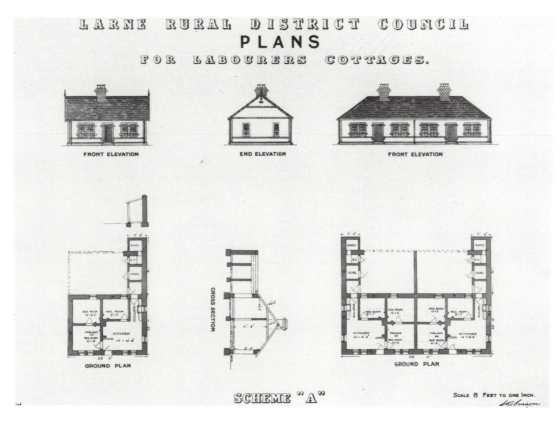

Fig. 221. Larne RDC, Co. Antrim, labourers' cottages plans, 1907. UFTM L 1682.2

detailing like door canopies, mullioned windows, even bay windows in north Armagh, and in some designs the liberal use of contrastive brick detailing around doors, windows and in false quoins. These labourers' cottages provide, nevertheless, an interesting tailpiece to the vernacular tradition, and an equally interesting forerunner of the development of public authority housing in the present century.

A Machine for Living

Some general points may be made about the effectiveness of the northern Irish vernacular house in providing acceptable accommodation. The meagre early evidence in this regard is difficult to interpret; mostly it was gathered by people accustomed to contemporary standards of urban comfort. Either they were travellers to Ireland, and so inevitably from wealthier backgrounds than those whom they were observing; or they were professionally involved in moves to ameliorate the formidable problems of rural Ireland in the first half of the nineteenth century, and so tended to come from educated, if not also wealthy backgrounds, and by virtue of their work they were concentrating on the worst social conditions. Another problem is that although almost everyone passed opinions about living conditions in rural Ireland, few did so with first-hand experience of interior circumstances. Mostly they passed by outside or relied on verbal evidence. Notable exceptions were Jonathan Binns, the poor inquiry commissioner, a Quaker with a social conscience, and some of the staff of the Ordnance Survey who spent years 'in the field'. Many must have sheltered from the rain in country kitchens while others, collecting historical traditions, could often only do so from elderly folk at their firesides.

Particularly with regard to poor houses, we have seen that sometimes they were constructed so that their interior floor level was below the outside ground level. As was sometimes suggested, perhaps this was because earth was removed to serve as mortar, or perhaps it accrued from the process of preparing the beaten earth floor; an observer in 1818 wrote that in his opinion the ground surface was 'not infrequently reduced a foot or more, to save the expense of so much outer walling'.[78] It is, however, noticeable that descriptions of such conditions refer to the housing of cottiers and of the poor. Farmers'

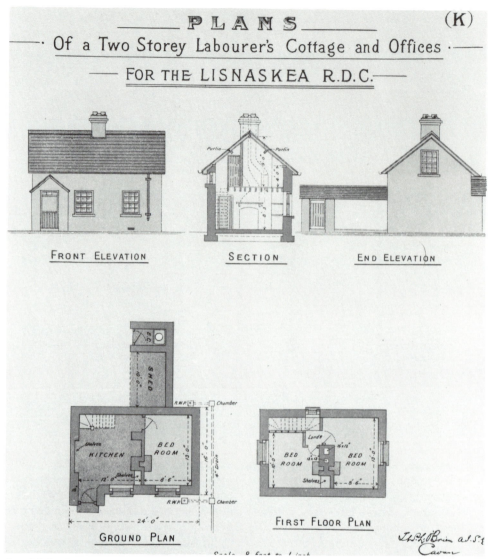

Fig. 222.   Lisnaskea RDC, Co. Fermanagh, labourers' cottages plans, *c*.1907. UFTM L 1682.1

houses were better sited and more solidly constructed. Having reached Enniskillen in county Fermanagh, a medical doctor travelling north in 1844 wrote, 'We see, as we enter Ulster, that the cabins become more substantial, comfortable and water-tight'.[79]

Care was taken in some places to align the long axis of the house relative to prevalent winds; in the Londonderry parish of Tamlaght Finlagan in 1835, 'Near Roe Park all the farm houses make an angle with the road and have their backs turned towards the south-west wind'.[80] Exposure to wind meant that sometimes additional precautions were needed. Stones on the roof to weigh down the thatch were seen in Tamlaght Finlagan, Banagher and Faughanvale, all in the same county,[81] and

ropes were occasionally used also to tie down thatch in inland districts in Londonderry,[82] in addition to their consistent rather than expedient use in coastal areas. Usually, however, normal thatching techniques sufficed, except in exceptional circumstances like 'The Big Wind' of January 6, 1839, memories of the depredations of which remained alive in oral tradition throughout most of the north of Ireland until recently.

Protection afforded by the roof against wet was just as important. Traditional roofing served well provided always that it was properly constructed and regularly maintained. There are many nineteenth-century accounts of people in Ireland living under leaky roofs, but in the north almost all relate to houses of the poor, and in

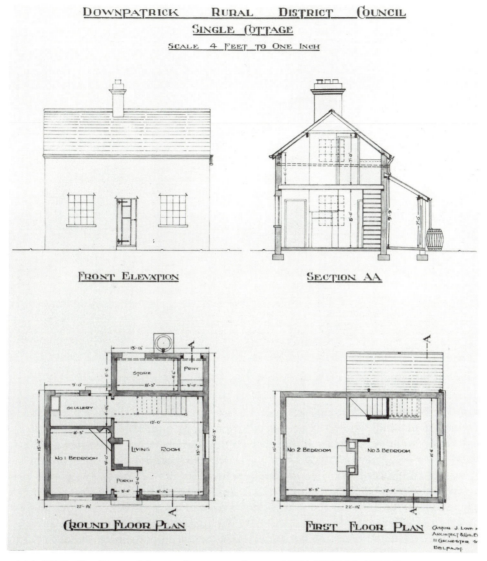

DOWNPATRICK   RURAL   DISTRICT   COUNCIL
SINGLE COTTAGE
SCALE   4 FEET TO ONE INCH

FRONT ELEVATION   SECTION AA

GROUND FLOOR PLAN   FIRST FLOOR PLAN

Fig. 223.   Downpatrick RDC, Co. Down, labourers' cottages plans, c.1907. UFTM L 1682.3

some areas like Lecale in south-east Down even the poor lived in well-thatched houses.

There is little evidence, either, that a vegetable roof constituted an appreciable fire hazard in country districts, although in and about a town the risk was greater, simply because buildings were more closely packed together. Lisburn burned in the early eighteenth century, and later in that century fire risk seems to have been appreciable about Downpatrick.[83] In 1791 it was suggested that slate would make a better roof than thatch in the Ballynahinch area of county Down, for the houses would look better and be safer from fire, and straw would be saved for agricultural purposes.[84] The writer was an advocate of agricultural improvement, and the last of his reasons was

the real basis for his recommending slate roofs. So long as chimneys were wide without any forced draught, and turf was burned, producing few hot sparks to be carried upwards, fire was not a hazard — witness the prevalence of carrying the roof-ridge purlin *through* the chimney, often fixing a chain from it to suspend pots over the hearth below. Furthermore, the outer surface of a thatched roof was seldom really dry in the moistness of the northern Irish climate. For much of the time thatch was therefore rather difficult to burn. Most reports of the fire hazard it represented are recent, correlating with the change from burning turf to burning coal, with the necessary alterations in chimneys to provide the greater draught that coal needs to burn properly, and with the

Fig. 224.   House leek growing on dwelling gable, Ballysessy Td., Co. Antrim. UFTM L 965.4

facts that coal burns with greater heat than turf and is more likely to produce sparks that would still be hot by the time they had been carried to roof level. Another factor was the introduction of corrugated metal sheeting on roofs. Thatch was often covered with this material, and so in time the vegetable material became tinder-dry. Thatch was usually retained under 'tin' for the sake of its other inherent quality, insulation.

Inevitably, of course, thatch in very dry weather added to the fire hazard inherent in any roof carried on a timber framework, and some traditional recognition of this fact is seen in the occasional houses remaining in the countryside where a 'house-leek' still grows either on the thatch, or in a gable (Fig. 224). It is a succulent plant with a bright flame-coloured flower in summer. Besides protecting the house against fire, it is also regarded as a protection against lightning (Castledawson, Londonderry),[85] and is sometimes believed to have curative properties, particularly for eye complaints. I have seen house-leeks growing on thatched houses in counties Antrim and Fermanagh, and reports are to hand for Ballyscullion[86] as well as Castledawson in Londonderry, and for Magheracross and Garrison in Fermanagh.[87]

Many who still live in thatched houses argue that their homes are warm in cold weather, and cool during the rare hot spells experienced in Ireland. The thermal efficiency of thatch is high; scientific measurements are

not needed as a basis for this statement. Given the ubiquitous underthatch of scraws, the vernacular roof is doubly effective as an insulator. The Ordnance Survey memoirs consistently report warmth and dryness as characteristics of thatched houses, exceptions being in east Donegal parishes in one of which it is explained the reason is want of fuel,[88] not the inadequacy of the roof. The almost monotonous regularity of such reports in south Antrim parishes gives way in some degree as one moves westward, and down the social scale from farmhouses to dwellings of cottiers, labourers and the poor. Effectiveness of the thatched roof was seen, too, in how few reports there are of dampness being a serious problem; what little evidence exists refers mainly to floors, especially in wet weather.

A particular problem occurred inside thatched houses, although the only historical reference to it is from the south-western limit of our area, about Sligo in 1835. The poor inquiry commissioners discovered that none of the cabins there had ceilings, 'and the dirt and cobwebs that were continually falling from the roof was a serious inconvenience in a district devoted to the making of butter for exportation'.[89] Unceiled roofs were common in vernacular houses until late in the nineteenth century, and in kitchens especially for long after. Particularly in the linen-weaving areas, coarse home-made cloth or old sacks were sometimes pinned to the undersides of roof

Fig. 225. Ceiling of whitewashed sacking and paper inside cottier's house, Duncrun Td., Co. Londonderry, c.1950. From an original photograph by D. McCourt. UFTM L 11.4

timbers, and whitewashed (Fig. 225); cardboard and paper were similarly used and soon, with repeated whitening, the accumulated layers of whitewash were thicker than the paper. Rigid ceilings were inserted into many farmhouses towards the latter part of the nineteenth century and later, especially making use of timber sheeting, but occasionally lath-and-plaster ceilings are found. The latter came first to larger farmhouses in the first half of the nineteenth century, but remained uncommon in many smaller dwellings even long after 1900.

A woven ceiling of lengths of braided marram grass stitched together and pinned to roof timbers over an attic bed discovered in a house at Shantallow, north of Londonderry city (Fig. 226), remains a rare material record.[90] Marram grass matting made of braids stitched together longitudinally was made by women and children in the Magilligan area in north Londonderry, and as many as about fifty families were involved in this work in the 1830s. This matting was apparently widely used as a kind of carpeting in houses and even in churches. 'It has for these purposes been introduced not only in Derry and

Belfast and in most all the towns of Ulster but of late into the metropolis', but whether this means Dublin or London is not obvious.[91] In Cornwall in the early seventeenth century similar marram matting was made and exported as far as London. 'These bents grow in sandy fields and are knit from over the head in narrow bredths after a strange fashion.'[92] It is interesting that a West Country connection in regard to construction of the house at Shantallow in the seventeenth century has been speculated.[93] Straw rather than marram mats used as ceilings have been noted also in Lecale in south-east Down earlier in the present century,[94] and in the 1830s 'a little screen of straw, which they sometimes put over the bed to keep off the soot' was reported in evidence to the poor inquiry from mid Armagh.[95]

Although Dubourdieu commented adversely on the lack of ventilation in early nineteenth-century farmhouse bedrooms due to the absence of chimneys, as he concluded in response to the levying of hearth tax, the fact is that there is little evidence for any chimneys and hearths other than in the kitchen before his time. Ventilation was not regarded as a problem, apart from

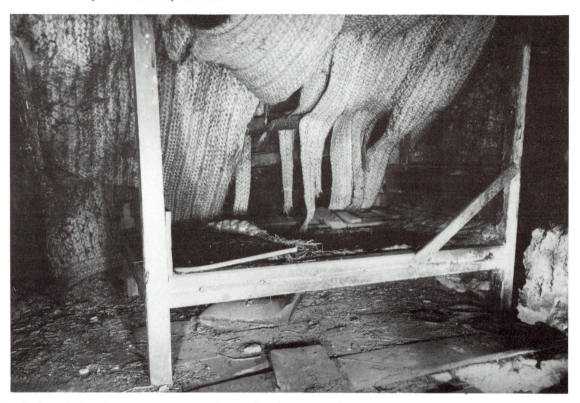

Fig. 226.   Ceiling of plaited marram grass pinned to roof timbers over loft-space bed, Shantallow Td., Co. Londonderry. UFTM L 352.2

smokiness in many of the houses of the poor because of lack of chimney canopies, or use of only imperfectly constructed ones. Social weighting of condemnation of smoky interiors towards cottages in the Ordnance Survey memoirs is obvious. Amongst farmhouses in Antrim this problem is noted only in the environmentally poor western parish of Duneane,[96] and elsewhere in the parishes of Banagher, Dungiven and Bovevagh improvement is noted in this regard already in 1821, wrought by the introduction of improved chimneys.[97]

As in the parish of Tamlaght Finlagan in Londonderry in the 1830s, so in nearby Magilligan 'in the lowlands nearly all the houses are built with one end towards the uplands, and the other towards Lough Foyle, old experience having taught them that by this mode they were best protected from injurious winds'. Interpretation of poor houses in the same district is rather equivocal as regards their efficiency; if as dwellings they soon failed, then they served other less obvious purposes. They were constructed of bog sods or mud (cf. Fig. 35):

> These bog houses last only two or three years before they begin to fail, but they are warmer than stone, cost only two or three pounds, and sometimes less, and when the indweller has no

other resource for fuel, he has in many instances resorted to part of his own house walls. When they are no longer habitable, more fuel is had and the residue forms good manure. The landlords are endeavouring to lessen the number of such habitations.[98]

The comment most frequently passed about housing in the Ordnance Survey memoirs is that the dwellings of the people, farmhouses and cottages, either are or are not 'clean and comfortable'. The reporter on Templecairne parish in Donegal in 1835 was unique in seeing the problem such generalised comment raises. He recognises various degrees of such attributes, 'and what in one district would be considered clean in another is looked upon as unclean'.[99] Alongside we may set the comment made in 1825 about houses in Clogher barony in east Tyrone. Within them

> no order is visible, you may see pigs and fowl feeding in the kitchen, and everything dirty and confused; the furniture a few pots and noggins, a stool, or a broken chair; the potatoes at meals are thrown out in a basket, and so laid on the table, or on a stool, and the whole family gather round . . . in a mass, and eat out of the basket without knife, fork or any other appendage at meals. A man who can give his daughter in marriage £50 or £100, will live in this manner.[100]

Fig. 227. Baking on flat griddle over open fire, Ballyblack Td., Co. Down. UFTM L 1159.1

The contrast could hardly be more marked with the relative opulence and concern with material possessions evinced in many parish accounts also in the Ordnance Survey memoirs, especially in southern and south-eastern parts of Antrim. Attitudes varied widely as to what constituted a habitable home, and were fundamentally affected by a variety of influences like the value systems of local rural communities, or the approaches of landlords to many administrative procedures affecting tenants such as leases and to concepts of 'improvement'. A peasantry without inducement to improve, as in the barony of Tullyhaw in Cavan in the early 1800s, were unlikely to live in neat, good-looking houses:

> Yet it is not poverty that occasions this dreary prospect, for the peasantry, though poor in appearance, are not without means and capability, but they have no inducement to improve, and they have yet sources of wealth in their own industry, were their landlords emulous in promoting their civilization, or active in instructing them in useful and desirable pursuits.[101]

But as the improving landlord, Lord George Hill, was to discover in Gweedore in north-west Donegal, 'improvement' was difficult to impose on a peasantry, simply because those to be improved had their attitudes too. So the social *effectiveness* of the dwelling is difficult to assess, particularly in the light of historical documentation that almost always views the house and its occupants from outside.

The social focus of family life in the vernacular house was, until late in the nineteenth century, and to a degree remains, the kitchen hearth. To understand this situation it is necessary to think of the northern Irish kitchen as having more in common with the 'hall' in medieval English houses than with the more specialised area we know as a kitchen in our modern homes. It was a relatively large space, readily adaptable for a variety of functions. A social history of Irish housing might be constructed solely around the kitchen, tracing its realtionships with other parts of the house, and charting the gradual removal of various functions as they came to be accommodated within specialised parts of the house. It has often been noted that when country houses were enlarged in the nineteenth and early twentieth centuries, the last area to lose its thatched roof and single-storey status was the kitchen unit. This was no accident. The insulation advantage thatch had over any other roof covering meant that it was longest preferred for covering

Fig. 228.   Round-bottom boiling pot over open hearth, early 20th-century, Corrymeela, Co. Antrim. UFTM WAG 1961

the area wherein most of indoor life was lived. A parlour was almost a ritual corner of the dwelling, seldom used, a room to which all the 'best' things were sent to get them out of the way of the bangs and knocks inevitable in daily activities elsewhere. Bedrooms were places to sleep in and not much more, often ill-lighted and poorly ventilated until quite late historically. The kitchen was warm, with its best insulated roof and a permanently burning fire on the hearth; the largest space in the house, its roominess was enhanced by the invariable practice of placing all the furniture around its sides. Here food was eaten, everyday callers entertained, business concluded, domestic chores carried out, and even craft work carried on either by members of the family or by outsiders like the visiting tailor. Stories were told around the fire, and dancing if not outdoors or in a barn was on the kitchen floor.

The centrality of the kitchen in traditional life is evident in folklore. There is a wealth of tradition associated with activities carried out there, especially with churning and other dairying activities, and the domestic emphasis of much of Irish seasonal custom and observance, for example on the quarter days and their eves like May Eve and Hallowe'en, was centred on the kitchen and its hearth.[102] Even yet in modern industrialised, urbanised

society the old Hallowe'en games are played, which belonged around the open hearth of the traditional kitchen: like the roasting of nuts to see which way they moved, indicators of the future happiness of unmarried young folk. What amounted almost to sacredness surrounded the fire on the kitchen hearth — it must never be allowed to burn out, for a cold hearth was equated with ill fortune if not even with death. Fire must not be borrowed at certain times, for to let it leave the house was to let the luck of the house go with it. And in Ireland's rich oral tradition of legend and tale, the social significance of the kitchen and its hearth are ever present; ancient kings and heroes answered callers at the kitchen door and bade them to a seat at the fireside; princesses prepared the meal at the hearth; honoured guests were given precedence there, not at the table.

To understand all of this it is necessary only to think of the simplicity of plan of the byre-dwelling and its antecedent form represented by the excavated dwellings at Caherguillamore and Tildarg. The living space was undifferentiated, a fire burned in the middle of the floor, life revolved around it and people slept within range of its heat. Cows at the other end of the building were similarly given sight of the fire, so the connection between dairying folklore and the hearth is easily explained. Sleeping in the

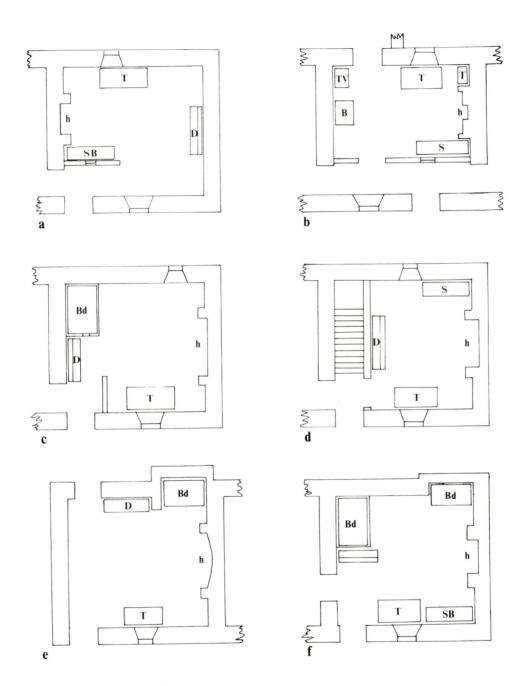

Fig. 229.   Arrangements of kitchen furnishings;
a: Drumbanagher, Co. Armagh;
b: Ballymenone, Co. Fermanagh (after Glassie);
c: Magilligan, Co. Londonderry;
d: Keady More, Co. Armagh;
e: Gweedore, Co. Donegal;
f: Glenswilly, Co. Donegal.
B: bureau; Bd: bed; D: dresser; h: hearth; S: settle or long seat; SB: settle-bed; T: table; TV: television.

Fig. 230.   Bed in outshot curtained off from rest of hearth-side, early 20th-century, Dunlewey, Co. Donegal. UFTM WAG 3395

kitchen survived late, of course, in the byre-dwelling derivative houses with outshots; but the manifold nineteenth-century references to poor people sleeping in the kitchen, even on its floor, reflect not only the endemic poverty of the period leading to the Great Famine in the 1840s, but also something of an older way of life. The physical circumstances of life in older undifferentiated houses are perpetuated verbally in northern Irish colloquial speech, even in urban-living families whose rural roots may be a number of generations back. 'Up' and 'down' in the home are often used with reference to the fireside, and rooms 'above' and 'below' until recently referred to locations relative to the kitchen rather than to positions on different floors of a storeyed house. Particularly in byre dwellings there was much sense in ensuring that cattle were kept literally to the low end, and that one moved upslope to the hearth and beyond it; it was preferable that liquid manure would drain away from the fire, not towards it.

Aspects of older attitudes to the importance of the kitchen hearth linger on in two respects: northern Irish baking traditions and the treatment of visitors. An open, ovenless hearth persisted in the traditional kitchen where bread-baking was done on a flat griddle or in a pot-oven set into the fire or suspended over it (Fig. 227). On some hearths, flat hearth stones were heated by the fire which was then pushed aside, leaving the heated stone as a hot-plate or built-in griddle. Griddle farls of leavened bread and thin oatcake were traditional bread types. They were frequently toasted off to finish baking in an upright position before the fire, supported against bread sticks or hardening ('harnen') stands. Even when in the nineteenth century the developments already traced took place in the hearth/chimney complex, adaptations of this hearth equipment attached griddles and toasters to fire bars, and so the traditional baking techniques persisted. They remain in our own time when the variety of breads still available from commercial bakeries owes much to the older tradition.

Roasting, stewing, and other cooking techniques were carried out either in round-bottomed pots (Fig. 228), or in the highly adaptable flat-bottomed 'pot-oven' ('oven-pot' in some places) suspended over or set into the fire. A crane was usually made by the local blacksmith and swung at one side of the hearth for hanging pots over the heat. Looking at a traditional hearth, one still sees if the housewife was left-handed, for this is betrayed by a crane swinging at the right-hand side of the hearth.

Fig. 231. Table hinged to inside of rear wall of kitchen, farmhouse near Cooneen, Co. Fermanagh. UFTM L 290.29

Occasionally a house is found where the crane was obviously changed from one side to the other, as a left-handed daughter-in-law succeeded her husband's right-handed mother. A few early hearth cranes of oak or other timber have been found, but by their very nature they are unlikely to survive in large numbers. It should be remembered, too, that not all traditional kitchens had the luxury of a hearth crane. It was not only poor cottier houses in which the pot hung over the fire suspended from a chain wrapped around a 'rantle-tree' set across the inside of the chimney canopy, or even around the roof-ridge purlin where it passed through the top of the chimney. These arrangements echo the hanging of pots from roof timbers over the free-standing open hearths of medieval and sub-medieval houses, and they persisted widely until finally rendered redundant by the introduction of ranges and enclosed stoves. Even though the old open hearths were then closed off, the hearth crane often remained unused at one side, although the other equipment that went with it — griddle, harnen stand, 'links' to connect the pot to the crane, and the 'brander' for grilling fish in coastal areas — all disappeared.

There is appreciable evidence from many districts that the seats nearest the fire were the prerogative of the older occupants of the household, and occasionally one finds the left side was 'hers' and the right side 'his'. Food prepared at the open hearth was often eaten around the fire. In 1839 in Templecorran parish in east Antrim,

Most of the farmhouses have but one door, which opens into a large kitchen with an earthen floor and without any ceiling. It is occupied during the day by the family who usually sit around a large paved hearth above which is a very wide chimney with a brace from 5 to 6 feet from the ground.[103]

Similar accounts in the Ordnance Survey memoirs remain for other parishes in south Antrim — Carrickfergus, Islandmagee, Kilroot, Templepatrick, and Raloo — and for Desertlyn in Londonderry. It is widely known, too, that visitors were asked to have a seat by the fire, the ultimate honour being accorded 'his' or 'her' special place.

This focusing of social and domestic life around the hearth was reflected in the locating of furniture within the kitchen (Fig. 229), particularly of the larger pieces, difficult to move.[104] Obviously in kitchens with a bed outshot in the rear corner next the hearth there was an immediate and immovable element (Fig. 230). But it is interesting that in houses without an outshot a settle bed often occupied this same position. The origins of the settle bed are unknown. It was found in kitchens all over northern and western Ireland and also in north-eastern North America, but it seems that it was largely unknown in Britain. A bench-seat with a fairly high back by day, the box seat opened out to make up a bed if required at night. As a heavy piece of furniture needing an opening-out space in front of it, inevitably it usually went with its back to the wall. Likewise, the dresser was commonly set opposite the fire in two-storey houses often with its back to the stairs rising to the upper floor. Its lower position held larger pots and pans, and even geese sitting on eggs. Earlier examples are without cupboard doors in this lower part. On the broad shelf above, delph bowls were 'whammelled'; set out pyramid-wise on top of each other. On the shallower shelves above, plates, cups and mugs were arranged. Poorer houses without a dresser had a 'tin rail' where tinware mugs were hung against the wall. There is much evidence, too, that the nineteenth-century displays of china and delph on the dressers replaced pewter and wooden wares of the eighteenth century. Extensive use of folk pottery in the seventeenth and eighteenth centuries is not well authenticated.

The table was the third significant piece of furniture in the kitchen. Invariably it was placed against the front or rear wall, and often it was not especially large (Figs. 126, 128). It was seldom moved far from the wall, even at mealtimes. Some houses had no table; others across south Ulster had a small table hinged to the wall (Fig. 231), occasionally in such a way that it could be set up at night to double as a shutter in front of a window opening. Relegation of the table to this peripheral position relates to the importance of the hearth area, and of course it preserved kitchen space that could be used for a variety of social activities like dancing. In the overcrowded circumstances of some linen weavers' houses, where a loom might be accommodated in the kitchen as well as there being others in the 'shop' and in the bedroom, even less space could be afforded for a table.

Seats in the kitchen were usually small and light, easily moved about, readily stored away around the periphery of the kitchen when not in use. Chairs were often rope-seated with perhaps one or two solid wooden ones maybe with arms, these supplemented with 'creepie' and other stools. Some kitchens had long benches which remained against a wall, rather than many individual seats. What many earlier seats usually had in common, however, was short legs, a response to the smokiness of older kitchens. Widespread appearance of full-height chairs roughly correlates with the adoption of developed hearths designed to burn coal, whether coal was used or not. These were efficiently burning fires with forced draughts which drew most of the smoke away, and so the desirability of sitting below the smokiness of the kitchen soon disappeared. Until it did, the visitor asked to sit by the fire in a place of honour found that privilege somewhat reduced by being offered the most imposing looking, highest chair in the household.

Kitchens other than those with bed outshots were regularly used as sleeping places. There are many descriptions from the late eighteenth century and the first half of the nineteenth century which demonstrate this. Obviously in smaller two- and three-unit houses, the kitchen had to be so used where the family was large, and the spatially undifferentiated functions of the single-unit dwellings of the poor are self-evident; in the Londonderry parish of Clondermot in the 1830s,

> In internal accommodation there is yet ample room for improvement for though in the houses of the small farmers the rooms are separated, in those of the poor cottiers one contains everything, the bed of the young couple being planted perhaps close to the fireside [in an outshot?] and supported by the rudest framework, while those required by the family as it increases are crammed together in some other corner being separated by what may be called wooden curtains, a state of things inconsistent with proper delicacy or cleanliness. The mud floor is also a serious evil, but if its abandonment does not precede, it will in all probability follow the growing taste for good clothes which is spreading amongst the rural belles, finery and filth being mutually inconvenient.[105]

'Proper delicacy' rather than desire for cleanliness had much to do with the growth of specialised use of internal space in the northern Irish vernacular house in the nineteenth century. Cleanliness and material comfort as we know it were not very highly regarded in 1825 amongst even fairly prosperous farmers in Clogher barony in Tyrone, as we have already noted.[106]

Prior to the introduction of the lobby-entry house, an undifferentiated internal space was common. Internal partitions in early byre-dwellings were flimsy at best, and as we know from the late survivals and oral traditions, they must often have been absent. The hearth-lobby house, however, usually if not invariably introduced with a massive chimney stack placed between its ends, was automatically divided into two units, so that separation of sleeping or retiral space from other domestic functions was probable for some of the family if not for all. Three-unit houses, common by the eighteenth century if not earlier, increased the possibilities of separate sleeping accommodation, whether in enlarged lobby-entry houses, or in byre-dwellings or their derivative forms from which the cattle had been removed. Houses attested in the Ballyhagan inventories in the period between 1716 and 1740 in mid Armagh were of between two and four units in extent, some of the units divided into front and rear rooms. 'Kitchens' are specifically mentioned, as are 'shops' for weaving. To judge from their contents, the other rooms, identified simply as 'room', 'low roome', 'back roome', 'upper roome' or 'fore roome', were usually bedrooms, though some may have doubled as sitting rooms also, as the parlours doubled as bedrooms in Ballyaghragan and Macosquin parishes in Londonderry a century later.[107] In the Ballyhagan community, however, parlours denominated as such were missing even in the houses of relatively prosperous, even wealthy individuals, although one of Robert Greer's rooms in his house in Altnavannog served as a parlour.[108]

By the 1830s, particularly in east Ulster, specially identified parlours were widespread in farmhouses, but not in cottages. They ranged from the simpler parlours doubling as bedrooms, mentioned above, to veritable shrines, ostentatious, indeed status symbols of their time. In Killead parish, county Antrim,

> A handsome parlour, with marble mantel piece and good sized windows, carpet, and furniture of modern description is to be found in most of them. Some of them have a second sitting room . . .[109]

In Grange of Ballywalter parish, also in Antrim,

> Many of their parlours are carpeted, furnished with modern chairs and tables of mahogany, a cupboard well stocked with china, delf, glass, and some silver spoons, and each of them has a clock.[110]

Carpeting, mahogany furniture and clocks were mentioned as parlour furnishing in a number of parish memoirs in south Antrim and east Londonderry, and possession of a clock was a status symbol of considerable potency at this period, when imported American mantel clocks were rapidly coming into favour at the expense of the local craft of longcase clockmaking. Almost all local longcase clockmakers had disappeared by the 1840s. In Racavan parish in Antrim 'Their great ambition is a clock . . . It is always termed "she" and there is [in] general a carousal or merrymaking at the "setting up of *her*" '.[111] Across the River Bann in the Londonderry parish of Aghadowey, 'every farmer's house is provided with a clock',[112] and in Desertoghill parish in the same county 'There is . . . general fondness for clocks and they may be heard striking in houses in which there is hardly a chair to sit upon or a table to eat their food off . . .'[113] In this context the unevenness of coverage of the Ordnance Survey memoirs is to be borne in mind. In general, the eastern emphasis they display in the matter of clocks is probably correct, but comfortably placed farmers in many other parts of the north of Ireland, for example in parts of Down, Armagh, Fermanagh and east Tyrone, probably shared the attitudes and range of possessions quoted above for their contemporaries in Antrim and Londonderry, in the matter of clocks and probably also in the furnishing of their parlours. On the other hand such

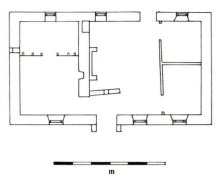

Fig. 232. Plan of farmhouse, Corradreenan West, Co. Fermanagh, reconstructed at UFTM (cf. Fig. 268).

comforts, if not limited ostentation, had not yet spread to the poorer hill and mountain areas and to the far west.

We have seen in an earlier chapter that ground-level boarded floors carried on wooden joists first appeared in parlours, and later spread to bedrooms. Introduction of formal parlours, too, was likely a significant factor in bringing about changes in window styles and sizes, and the desire to have a parlour sometimes led to the dividing of a bedroom unit to form one at the front, with a small sleeping space off it at the rear; even into the present century many small farmhouses survived simply with one or two beds set end to end along the back wall of the parlour screened off merely by curtains, while in other instances box beds were used.

Individual houses demonstrate, in their evolution, the outcome of the changing atitudes to use of domestic space and the development of the parlour. An example is the farmhouse from Corradreenan West townland in west Fermanagh, reconstructed at the Ulster Folk and Transport Museum (Fig. 232, 175, see Chapter 11). It is of two units with hipped scollop-thatched roof, of simple lobby-entry type and has a (? secondary) rear door into the kitchen. The house originated perhaps in the second half of the eighteenth century, and certainly existed in the 1830s when it was identified on the first edition of the six-inch Ordnance Survey map. From structural details discovered during its dismantling it is apparent that originally its two units represented a large kitchen and a smaller bedroom. Towards the middle of the nineteenth century, to judge from the brick size involved, the jamb wall was rebuilt, an original probably wattled chimney canopy was replaced by a more constricted brick flue in a shallower breastwork, and the 'low' end of the kitchen opposite the hearth was closed off to form two small bedrooms, the partition walls again being locally made brick. Perhaps there had early been beds accommodated under a half-loft in this position, prompting creation of these tiny bedrooms. Later, towards the end of the nineteenth century, a stud-and-board partition was set into the bedroom and its front portion was converted for use as a formal parlour, and at this time a boarded floor and a small fireplace breaking into the rear of the kitchen hearth chimney were added together with a sheeted ceiling. So, a house that had originated with two rooms became one of five rooms within the same floor area. The initial impetus obviously was to provide closed-off sleeping accommodation, addition of a separate parlour coming last. Although this house does not show it, many lobby-entry houses also developed to include extension of the jamb wall across the front of the kitchen, and if lofts existed, then stairs were provided rising out of the hallway created by the extended jamb wall. Of course, contemporaneously with these adaptations to existing structures, new houses were being built which incorporated these developments.

Evolution of the vernacular house in the north of Ireland from the earliest stages described in this book, where size was reckoned in roof bays and internal subdivision either did not exist or consisted of the flimsiest of partitions, to division into structural units separated from each other by mass walls, marked the first stage in specialisation of the use of internal space. So long as the interior remained open from end to end in the simplest byre-dwellings, space could be used flexibly according to need. Introduction of the lobby-entry house was part of this process of permanent internal subdivision. All the available evidence points to provision of closed-off bedrooms being the first function separated from the earlier communal single-space interior. As the Ballyhagan inventories in county Armagh show, by the first half of the eighteenth century other functions also were being provided with discrete internal spaces: loom shops, occasionally 'butteries' for the storage of butts and other wooden vessels, perhaps even a parlour.[114]

Appearance of the lobby-entry house in Ireland introduced another most significant feature, for the lobby created by the jamb wall between the door and the hearth provided, apparently for the first time, a 'reception' area inside the house interposed between 'outside' and 'inside'. So long as the lobby remained open, without a door between the end of the jamb wall and the front wall, the reception-area function of the lobby was only partial. When the lobby was fully closed off, as happened in many instances from the mid-nineteenth century onwards, formal 'reception' became a separately identified function within the house. Extension of the jamb wall along the front of the kitchen unit to provide a longitudinal 'hallway' attained the same end, but in a more spacious manner. Development of the direct-entry house was slower to provide for this same reception function, and although closed-off lobbies inside the front doors of such kitchens in one-storey houses were sometimes constructed, usually a distinct entrance lobby only emerged at the foot of closed-off stairs rising from inside the door to give access to upper bedrooms. Sometimes a large piece of furniture, usually the dresser, was placed parallel to the long axis of the house inside the door of a direct-entry kitchen, separating off an entry area from the space behind, often used for a bed; but the entry area always remained open to the kitchen, and its mediation between 'outside' and 'inside' was at best incomplete. Examples have been recorded in northern coastal areas from the Glens of Antrim in the east to Glenswilly in Donegal in the west.[115] Another expedient was introduced into some small houses especially in north Londonderry, for example in Mobuy and Duncrun townlands,[116] apparently to control draughts at the hearth. This was a short screen wall set transversely across the house from within one side of the front door. It had the effect of forming a small lobby area, but open to the remainder of the kitchen, and so its 'reception' function was minimal on account of the short length of the screen itself.

Development of the reception area, whether by extension of the jamb wall in the lobby-entry house, or by elaboration of the cased-off stairs into a transverse hallway with ground level passage from front to rear alongside the stairs in the direct-entry house, had the effect of distinguishing space reserved solely for circulation; and at upper-floor level, parallel developments of landings at the stairheads, off which bedrooms opened, had the same effect. Apart from within some larger houses, like the English vernacular dwelling of 1682 in Gortnaglogh townland in east Tyrone, separation of space reserved for circulation and little else was a late phenomenon in northern Irish vernacular housing, unlike the development of the internal cross-passage, especially in the form backing on the main hearth, in many vernacular houses in England. Cross-passage houses in England were common by the first half of the seventeenth century; the northern Irish development mentioned above belongs mainly to the nineteenth century.

Provision of separate sleeping space in one-storey houses has already been noted and was of course an early stage in the specialisation of internal space use. What led, however, to final removal of beds from the kitchen was the development of upper-level sleeping, first in half-lofts, then in loft floors and attics leading to full upper storeys. Upper sleeping floors were first introduced by English settlers, to judge from the Londonderry evidence, in particular the illustrations provided by Thomas Raven's maps of the early seventeenth century.[117] Few early houses survived the seventeenth century to influence the development of northern Irish vernacular housing, although of course upper floors used largely for sleeping were well known in formal architecture at higher social levels then and later. The later, mainly nineteenth-century development of two-storey vernacular housing has been traced in a previous chapter, and it was this that led ultimately to the closing off of bed outshots in some modest-size country houses. Universal separation of the various functions of the traditional kitchen has only been achieved within the past generation. I recall at least one house occupied in the older form in Glenvar in the north Donegal Fanad peninsula in the mid-1950s; houses usually occupied by elderly folk survive yet with undifferentiated kitchens.

A specialised aspect of sleeping arrangements calls for particular comment: accommodation of farm and domestic servants. Farms large enough to have required the services of large numbers of servants usually involved non-vernacular houses, like those lived in by landlords. Most farms of medium size where numbers of servants were employed usually had cottier houses to accommodate them. Ulster, however, was characterised by small farms, certainly from the late eighteenth century onwards, and so servants to be accommodated were few, although even a small hill farm of only six acres and with rights in common hill grazing in the Sperrin mountains had a Donegal servant girl at the beginning of the twentieth century, because it was occupied by an elderly couple without family. Its dwelling, of bedroom-over-byre type, was removed some years ago from Cruckaclady townland and is now at the Ulster Folk and Transport Museum. The elderly couple occupied the bed in the kitchen outshot while the Donegal girl slept in the bedroom, the sound and warmth of the cattle below coming up to her through the boarded floor. This case was typical of earlier periods in the nineteenth century, in small-farm districts. On the county Armagh Gosford estates in 1821, 'servants can be seen as filling gaps left in the family, due to the age or extreme youth of the holder or his children, or when the holder was unmarried or childless'.[118] Of a total population on the estates of 3,009 individuals in 622 houses, only 119 were noted as servants, sixty male and fifty-nine female.[119] At the same time on the nearby Drumbanagher estate, there were only forty-six servants, eighteen men and twenty-eight maids, in a population of 717 individuals living in 162 dwellings.[120] Many houses had only either a man or a female servant; a few more prosperous farms rose to one of each; but more than this was rare. In these

circumstances, other than cottiers living in their own cottages, servants often lived almost *en famille*, especially on smaller farms. Evidence from more recent times, in the late nineteenth and early twentieth centuries, does not differ fundamentally from that of the earlier parts of the nineteenth century. It shows that much depended on individual circumstances, including the attitude of the farmer hiring servants, the size of his farm and the size of his family. Patrick Campbell's memories of 'Growing up in Donegal' in the 1920s contrast his experience of one farm near Donegal town where as a hired servant he endured accommodation

> not fit for a human being. This was a low structure built off the dwelling-house, with corugated galvanized roof, which both dripped water from condensation and let in rain. At the back of this apartment was a high bank of marl clay which was continually weeping water, so that my bedclothes were usually damp,[121]

with another farm in the same county, near Pettigo, where he was well treated and learned much that stood him in good stead in later years. Later he hired with two aged brothers and their sister near Rossnowlagh in south Donegal where he also did well.[122] A large farm allowed employers greater opportunity to separate themselves spatially from their servants. There is in Ulster no evidence for a bothy system similar to that in parts of Scotland, almost certainly reflecting the small average farm size in the north of Ireland. While servant girls usually slept inside the farmhouse, men often slept in an outhouse or in a loft. Some servants shared rooms or even beds with their employer's children or other relations, others slept in a settle bed in the kitchen. There were similar variations in the extent of social intercourse between the hirers and hired, extending even to eating arrangements. Some servants sat at the same table, and ate the same food as their master's family; others were required to eat separately, at a different time or in a separate room having different and usually inferior food. It seems that the most influential factor here was the greater opportunities for spatial separation available in a large establishment.[123]

Earlier evidence from the Ordnance Survey memoirs of the 1830s accords with much of the foregoing, but is available only from Antrim and Londonderry. In Desertlyn in Londonderry,[124] and Grange of Bally-walter,[125] Carrickfergus,[126] Islandmagee,[127] Raloo[128] and Kilroot[129] in Antrim, lofts are mentioned as servants' sleeping places, while settle beds in kitchens are mentioned also in Raloo and in Templecorran.[130] In Islandmagee 'There is no distinction made between master and servant in eating or drinking, as all, except in

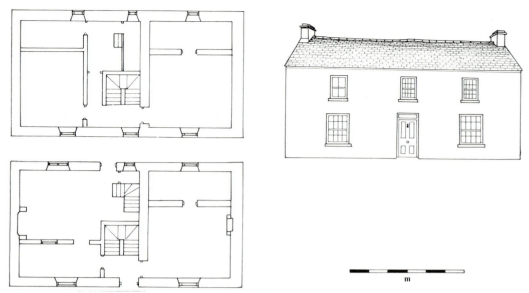

Fig. 233.   Farmhouse in Upper Tully Td., Co. Londonderry, adapted for having servants living in.

a few of the more wealthy farmers, eat at the same table'.[131] There can be no doubt that servants' experience must have been similar elsewhere in the north of Ireland at this period.

Evidence gathered recently relating to circumstances early this century shows that attic rooms occupied by servants in their masters' farmhouses might be uninviting places. An informant from Clogher, county Tyrone:

> I myself was hired in a place and the first night I got a surprize as there were not furniture in the room except one bed and it was that old it must have come from Noah's Ark and the bedclothes were nothing only rags.[132]

Hired at the fair in Strabane in the west of the same county, somewhat earlier the county Donegal man Patrick Magill found that his room, comfortable enough in good weather, had a leaky roof in the wet when his blankets became soaked.[133] If the house was large enough attics occupied by servants might be approached by a staircase discreetly tucked away at the back of the house, while the family used stairs rising from inside the front door.[134] Adaptations of this kind were rare, and I have examined only one vernacular house laid out in this way (Fig. 233). It is now derelict, fronting an extensive farmyard on a roadside in Upper Tully townland, which overlooks the Foyle valley from the east in county Londonderry. This was an area that attracted many servants from county Donegal to the west, hired especially in the hiring fairs at Strabane. It is a two-unit, two-storey slated house with a rear door to the kitchen which is not in line with the front one. To achieve the almost central front door, one unit is larger than the other, the larger containing the kitchen, with a squarish

reception hall inside the front door. Around the rear angle of the hall winds a staircase to a landing above, from which access is gained to the front large bedrooms, and the rear bedroom in the smaller unit opens out of the front one. A door opens off this landing onto a cramped unlighted rear landing, off which is a small servant's room at the rear of this unit, and a second small bedroom set over rear stairs which lead down into the large kitchen just inside the back door of the house. The front of the kitchen unit was partitioned off, serving as a family dining area from which a door opened into the reception hall. The parlour opening off the other side of the hall occupied the ground-floor unit, with another room at the rear used as a bedroom. This house was probably built in the mid-nineteenth century and it functioned as a family dwelling at the front and within the smaller unit, while the servants were kept to the rear, the meeting place between the two being confined to the domestic work environment of the kitchen. Servants and family ate separately although their food was prepared and cooked at the same kitchen hearth. It is interesting that such a level of separation could be achieved within a house whose external ground-plan measurements are only 12.2 m. by 6.7 m. Alongside the details of this west Londonderry house may be set the following account, reported in the 1960s from Tydavnet in Monaghan:

> My grandfather's house was a long thatched house with two windows each side of the front door. There were two bedroom windows upstairs in each gable, one bedroom being reached by stairs from the kitchen for servants' use, the other by stairs leading from a back bedroom, so steep as to be more like a ladder.[135]

Farmers' attitudes to the space requirements for everyday living are evident from the arrangements they made for accommodation of their survivors, especially their widows, following their own deaths. Although until the end of the nineteenth century the great majority of farmers were tenants, yet traditional attitudes coupled with operation of the 'Ulster custom' of tenant right in respect of inheritable outstanding portions of leases, and therefore of the use of dwellings, insisted on the right of a farmer to provide in this way. Widespread knowledge remains in the north of Ireland of the practice of leaving to a widow exclusive right to the use of a room, often in addition to other rights such as the benefit of a cow in the byre with grass to feed her. Implicit in this was an assumption by the farmer so providing that what remained of the house, perhaps two or three units at most, was sufficient for a son or son-in-law to establish a household of his own. This practice is as yet largely undocumented, widespread though it was. A recent study shows that, judging from wills proved in Ireland in 1865, 'the great bulk of farm inheritances were administered outside the law entirely, relying on customary practice not only for their terms but for their enforcement'; an estimate of one will or administration for every six farmer deaths per annum is made.[136] It is interesting that in all-Ireland terms, in 1865 there was a marked concentration of proved wills in Ulster — approximately 61% of the total — but their average value was markedly lower than those in Leinster and Munster, and slightly lower even than the Connacht ones. These circumstances show that operation of the tenant-right custom made it realistic for even small farmers to draw up wills. Inevitably some of these wills specified accommodation of the widow in the house, like one of 1895 of a farmer at Aghnaloo, county Fermanagh, who had left his farm to his son, but saw need to protect the interests of his second wife:

> Should said Thomas Chartres marry during his step-mother's lifetime, I will that she his stepmother occupy the two apartments in the west end of the house in which she now lives with the rent payable to me out of Drumcoo during her natural life, also Turbary and a cow's keep winter and summer for her manure and ground for same.[137]

Similarly, an agreement made some years earlier by a widower farmer near Straid in west Antrim with his son to whom he was handing over the farm specified retention of use of a room and his keep for himself during his declining years.[138] Such provisions existed also in the eighteenth century. There is an entry in the inventory of Joseph Pearson of Drumard townland, one of the Ballyhagan Quakers in mid Armagh, which noted:

> Their [rect. There] being some boards in Joshua's house as lofting which his mother acquitts her half of them and also promises to give him ten shillings towards makeing his end of the dwelling-house as good as hers.[139]

Unfortunately the survival of Irish wills before 1858 is so patchy that full documentation of this practice and of the attitudes to use of domestic space which it enshrines will be impossible.

The House as Symbol

A dwelling is more than simply a shelter, a satisfaction of physical need. Its form owes much to socio-cultural factors as we have seen and changes over time in response to developing pressures of various kinds. As a cultural expression it reflects norms and allegiances, it makes a cultural statement, albeit often a subtle one. Within those limits set by the surrounding culture the householder furthermore imparts a distinctive identity to the dwelling that says much about his place in society. The house has symbolic value, two facets of which are introduced here.

As a family home, the house inevitably reflects individual social self-evaluation. So long as building remained tied to vernacular norms, scope for externally visible individual statement was limited, but this in itself tells of the individual's and the family's role in the community. However, we saw at the outset of this book that the vernacular house developed within a peasant society in which there was interplay between the 'Great' and the 'little' traditions. Consequently, some ideas of social status were borrowed from groups perceived to be socially superior.

External manifestations of status symbolism developed from the late eighteenth century onwards. Window and door styles borrowed from classical formalism are an example, but the overall concept of visual symmetry took longer to manifest itself on the facades of vernacular houses and, in accord with the pattern of individual innovation adoptions, developed first in the east, spread west, and was regarded as socially desirable earliest amongst relatively more prosperous farmers, spreading ultimately even to the housing of the rural landless, as seen in some of the labourers' cottages. Individual elements in achieving this symmetry have been commented upon: adjustments in door position in lobby-entry houses, for example. The most striking manifestation must of course be the placing of dummy chimneys on roof ridges to achieve balanced facades.

Fig. 234.   Farmhouse of three units and four chimney stacks, dummy chimney behind tree, Loughriscouse Td., Co. Down. UFTM L 1068.8

Fig. 235.   Reconstruction of farmhouse facade, Carnacally Td., Co. Down. Three-unit interior, dummy chimney to right of entrance. Based on UFTM L 891.9 (cf. Fig. 112).

This happened in most parts of the north of Ireland, although I have not seen examples in the far west. It was mainly a phenomenon of the second half of the nineteenth century, but some houses have dummy chimneys that seem earlier, if brick sizes involved are a reliable guide. One of the problems in this regard is that brick is a material often readily re-usable, and the quantities involved in adding a dummy chimney on top of an already existing wall between two house units are small, remembering that no flue need be constructed below. I have seen numbers of three-unit single-storey houses without lofts which have four chimney stacks, one on each gable and one on each internal wall. An example is in Loughriscouse townland near Newtownards in north

Fig. 236.   House at roadside in Castlenavan Td., Co. Down. Dummy chimney second from left. UFTM L 1147.9.

Down (Fig. 234), a formerly thatched three-unit small farmhouse, otherwise unelaborated. A 'Georgianised' farmhouse stands derelict and semi-ruinous in Carnacally townland (Fig. 235), also in Down, dating from the early nineteenth century, and another example is alongside the main Belfast-Newcastle road in Castlenavan townland (Fig. 236). In east Tyrone there is a now derelict four-unit thatched farmhouse in Killycolpy townland which had a dummy chimney added to one gable for visual balance. Perhaps the most striking example of all is the fine thatched three-unit farmhouse with fully symmetrical facade in Rossigh townland in Fermanagh (Fig. 194), on the east shore of Lower Lough Erne, its symmetry enhanced by the addition of a small pavilion-like unit at each end. A two-storey example is the eighteenth-century house of three structural units in Drumanphy townland in Armagh, which has two chimneys, one dummy, added probably some time in the nineteenth century.

The symbolic, status function of dummy chimneys is undeniable, as is the achievement of facade symmetry in a house like the Rossigh one and the near-symmetry in Carnacally. Examples of both can be multiplied all over the north of Ireland, and this aspect became a less consciously sought-after symbolic statement as time went on. Along with adoption of various window styles, which always at first were matters of minority adoption which later became accepted forms, a symbolic status element was certainly involved with many of the earliest adopters of new types of roof-covering, rendering and 'false' detailing, like rusticated quoins worked in smooth plaster which bear no relation to underlying random stonework. The latest version of the latter has become almost a folk-art form in the present century, with elaborate three-dimensional painting of quoins in two or three colours on flat plaster finish. Probably also some concepts of status may have been involved in the addition of lighted porches which attained even the proportions of separate rooms around front entrances in the present century, but it is more difficult to argue similarly for the shallower windbreaks around doors added to vernacular houses in the nineteenth century. They undoubtedly fulfilled two valuable practical purposes, in regard to draught control at the kitchen hearth, and in protecting doors from rain.

Symbolic value is fairly easily recognisable in these externally visible elements, but certain internal developments in the house also may have elements of status statement about them. The dummy chimney externally is saying that an additional hearth apparently exists internally, and the presence of the heated, well ventilated, relatively luxuriously furnished parlours with boarded floors, attested in the county Antrim Ordnance Survey memoirs as appearing in the better farmhouses in the 1830s, certainly carry the same connotation. But as

Fig. 237.   Cluster of farmhouses of byre-dwelling type, with bed outshots, *c*.1900, Teelin, Co. Donegal. UM W04/13/34

well as saying something to the outside world, these parlours were self-assuring symbols for the farm families concerned, community recognition of these symbols of wealth and self-esteem being restricted mainly to opening of these 'shrines' on occasions like christenings, weddings and, particularly, funerals and visits of clergy. Particular elements of this have already been mentioned; the clock as an object of ambition was quoted for Racavan parish in county Antrim in 1835,[140] and in Magherafelt parish in east Londonderry at the same time it was mentioned as 'indispensable' for the same reason.[141] Change to burning coal and consequent alterations to fireplaces and chimneys provides another example, particularly when one finds these changes having occurred in houses which remained turf-burning. Provision of a forced draught in a raised grate or fire-basket necessary for coal makes little sense with turf, which demands slow burning for greatest economy. Other changes that betokened ostentatious expenditure of resources included facing of parlour and bedroom walls with timber sheeting, in imitation perhaps of panelling in landlords' houses of earlier periods. Sheeted ceilings, replacement of older jamb walls and lofts, and kitchen floor tiling also had status connotations, but it must also be said that these were part of general practical improvements in the second half of the nineteenth century.

Attitudes to sleeping, however, and their influence on the house, betray very obviously some concern for what the outside world thinks of the family and its behaviour.

Upstairs sleeping was immediately obvious externally, whereas the vernacular tradition had earlier insisted on lengthwise extension of the dwelling at ground level. First-floor bedrooms in the north of Ireland were first an upper-class or at least an imported British ideal, as we have seen in earlier chapters. It was the nineteenth century before they became widespread geographically amongst the most prosperous farmers and late in that century before they became common. By that time concepts of class were becoming blurred in housing by emulation of more generalised urban attitudes spreading into rural areas. It is interesting that recent decades have seen suburban ideas of bungalows from the 1930s onwards reintroducing single-storey housing to rural areas in the 1950s, followed by a later return to two-storey houses, the most recent fad being the rapid spread of pseudo-Georgian elements, especially doors and windows, but without attention to the former fine design detail in the modern mass-produced, often plastic counterparts, again spreading from suburban living into the countryside. Perhaps the next change will be the reversion to symmetry of facade treatment, for it seems as if the sequence of vernacular borrowings from formal architecture in the nineteenth century is being repeated. What differs is the pace of change, the almost leisurely acceptance rate of innovations in the past being replaced by a seemingly frantic urge to keep up with the 'latest' ideas — but through them all so often there is a feeling of aesthetic *déjà vu*.

The house also demonstrates in a different way something of the relationship between the family and the community, and thereby speaks of the nature of the community itself.[142] Undifferentiated byre-dwellings belonged to a folk culture in which many facets of life were organised on a communal basis. In some areas farms were grouped in clusters (Figs. 237, 99) associated with infield-outfield rundale operation of farming activities, usually also related to communally organised exploitation of common pastures. Traces of this system are found in most parts of the north of Ireland.[143] Within these house clusters there was little privacy; indeed the egalitarian attitudes of householders often led to the building of houses most inconveniently sited relative to each other. Distinctions between 'outside' and 'inside' were blurred, inevitably so when cattle, which belong to 'outside', were taken into the internal family space. This system may in part have been in existence in medieval times. There has been speculation that an unfree element of land-tillers in early society lived in prototypes of these house clusters.[144] Nevertheless the whole socio-economic arrangement was sufficiently flexible to continue in operation in later periods, permitting groups of under-tenants to work co-operatively within a leasehold system imposed on native rural society from the early seventeenth century. Furthermore, as population expanded rapidly after the middle of the eighteenth century, single tenancies sometimes expanded under partible inheritance to become infield-outfield exploitation of farms on which house clusters grew, only to disintegrate in the following century as landowners rationalised the chaotic circumstances on their estates, and holdings were consolidated and the farmhouses dispersed, each to stand within the boundaries of its holding.[145]

Nevertheless, there had long been (since Early Christian times at least) an element in the settlement pattern of individual dwellings dispersed over the landscape. Known to archaeologists in a variety of forms and denominated by different terms, they had in common a dwelling defended against marauding animals, if not also marauding neighbours, by means of a surrounding embankment, wall, ditch, or water, or some combination of these. Such defence was a mediation between 'outside' and 'inside'; there was a distancing of the family from the community at large; it is believed these dwellings were the homes of a free, aristocratic class.[146]

Introduction of the lobby-entry house in the early seventeenth century had the effect of bringing this mediation between 'inside' and 'outside' into the house, in the creation of the jamb-wall lobby just within the entrance, a 'reception' area that had to be negotiated by the caller before being admitted to the family living space.

Fig. 238.   Enlarged vernacular farmhouse set back from public road at end of small laneway, Mullaghpeak Td., Co. Monaghan. UFTM L 1378.5

Fig. 239.   Formalised facade of vernacular farmhouse of hearth-lobby type, Derrycannon Td., Co. Fermanagh. UFTM L 1362.2A

Of course, the lobby-entrance house also had the effect of bringing the mediation between 'outside' and 'inside' down the social scale, for this dwelling type became a widespread form of traditional housing within its geographical distribution. It can be no coincidence, either, that it was introduced alongside concepts of leasehold tenure and consolidated farms, and that subsequently it only rarely seems to have been built within the house clusters associated with infield-outfield agricultural organisation.

Later developments within the vernacular house, of the eighteenth and especially the nineteenth centuries, traced in the previous chapter may readily be interpreted as the extension of this mediation between 'outside' and 'inside' within the dwelling — the drive towards the full, formal reception space inside the front door. This emphasis on increased privacy, separation first of the family from the community as the nature of social life and organisation changed, and then of members of the family from one another as demands for separate sleeping spaces grew, and became universal in the second half of the nineteenth century, is obvious in what happened in the later development of both vernacular house types. Extension of the jamb wall across the kitchen unit consolidated the reception function of the earlier, open lobby screened only by the jamb wall, and access to the

upper bedrooms when these were provided became centred on a stairway rising from the enlarged reception area. Similarly within the direct-entry house, the earliest stage of stairs rising from inside the front door, open to the kitchen, rapidly gave way, except in the most traditionally oriented community, to stairs rising from a separate hallway closed off from the kitchen. So, after the beginning of the seventeenth century, an historical change from emphasis on communal attitudes to increased emphasis on the individual was mirrored in the development of the house from an early, open sociability in how it was used to increased emphasis on personal privacy.

These changes in attitudes were implicit also in changes in the settlement pattern over the same period. Dispersal of the older house clusters, whenever it occurred, inevitably reduced personal contacts within the community. Then, as often happened in more prosperous farming communities, the farmhouse and yard were set back from the roadside at the end of a laneway imparting a sense of privacy often enhanced by surrounding plantations of sheltering trees (Fig. 238). This was commented upon by the Ordnance Survey memoir compilers in some of the most prosperous parishes in the southern parts of Antrim in the 1830s.[147] A typical comment is from the memoir for Camlin where, as

Fig. 240.   Rear of the same farmhouse, presenting impression of direct-entry internal layout. UFTM L 1362.1A

in the neighbouring parish of Killead, farmhouses 'are almost hidden from view in clusters of shady trees'.[148] These parishes were some of the districts most successfully colonised by British settlers in the late sixteenth and seventeenth centuries. It is no coincidence that other areas for which comparable evidence in the 1830s is available were also similarly colonised — for example: in Londonderry, Ballyscullion away from the low ground close to the River Bann,[149] and Desertoghill[150] in the east of the county; in Fermanagh, Derryvullen,[151] Enniskillen,[152] and Magheracross.[153] A century earlier, attributing the circumstances to industrious Protestants, that is to say families mainly of British settler origin, the same comment was made about the Waringstown area in north-west Down.[154]

These shifts of attitudes reflected externally in the disposition of houses on the landscape, and internally in houses in their historical development, were mainfested earliest at upper social levels, whether in earlier Irish society or amongst planted British settlers mainly of the seventeenth century and after. Thereafter they spread socially to all parts of the northern Irish community, and from more innovative prosperous districts to the most traditionally oriented, remoter areas. So in the 1830s when the county Antrim evidence for the presence of these changed attitudes amongst farmers, even 'second class farmers' in Aghagallon parish, is quite clear, in many western parts, as in Donegal and Leitrim, parts of Tyrone and west Fermanagh, the undifferentiated byre-dwelling, found often in clusters of farm buildings including from five to ten houses, was still usual.

Yet the strength of tradition was impressive. A harking back to the older attitudes of neighbourliness is evident in the ways in which houses were used in most districts, and even in the ways they were adapted. Almost everywhere until recently, and in many districts yet, when farmhouses have front and rear doors, patterns of neighbourliness are evident simply from observing who calls at the front door (outsiders) and who automatically goes to the back door (neighbours who are accepted, 'friends', meaning more distant relatives, and family). It is interesting, too, that in districts close to the distributional limits of the hearth-lobby house, many more of these houses have rear doors into their kitchens than in the heart of the distribution. Perhaps one sees here that this house distribution, at the time when it became fixed about the end of the eighteenth century or early in the nineteenth century, represented the zone of greatest interaction between the older attitudes descended from the pre-plantation culture, and the newer ones attributable to introduction by British settlement in the plantation of Ulster.

A house I visited some years ago in east Fermanagh in Derrycannon townland neatly exemplifies these differences in attitudes. It survives as a three-unit farmhouse with scollop-thatch hipped roof (Figs. 239, 240). Formally, from the front, it is a classic northern Irish lobby-entry farmhouse, its facade treatment tending towards symmetry. The implicit desire of its builders for social acceptability in terms of status is evident. Yet the front of the house looks out on a field, and although it can be seen from the road, it can be approached only by coming round from the rear. Access for all off the public road is up a very short laneway past one end of the house into the farmyard, of which the dwelling closes an end, outhouses defining two sides of the yard at right angles to the house. Perforce one is led to the back door. A sense of friendliness and openness is inescapable on entering within. Although internally the house is of lobby-entry form, because of the way it is set in relation to the road and the yard, the kitchen is *used* as a direct-entry byre-dwelling derivative house-type kitchen would be, entered from the yard by the back door at the 'low' end away from the hearth. The front door is seldom opened. Indeed, I have visited other comparably 'ambivalent' houses where the front door had not been opened for years, and in one or two instances I have seen front doors no longer capable of being opened. The story is told of one such house in south Tyrone where the family knew their clergyman so well that he had always come in like one of the family by the back door. A new clergyman arrived in the parish and one day was seen coming towards the house. In the panic to release the jammed front door, the new clergyman heard the comment urgently shouted back into the kitchen within, from behind the front door, 'Quick, get the axe, it's the new minister come to call!'

TEN

Farmhouse and Farmyard

BRIEF reference was made towards the end of the previous chapter to the traditional house as the basic element in the settlement pattern, and how changes in settlement pattern reflected fundamental shifts in social organisation and attitudes. It is not the purpose of this book to go on to consider settlement patterns in the north of Ireland. Settlement studies have proceeded for many years inspired by the pioneering researches of Estyn Evans and students he stimulated at Belfast. Yet a gap remains between the narrower study of the dwelling, and how dwellings are distributed in the landscape. Except for cottiers' cabins and labourers' cottages, which as structures were more or less sufficient unto themselves, reflecting the landless basis of their occupiers' life-styles, the farmhouse does not represent all of the farmer's building requirements. Exploiting the environmental resources at his disposal, the farmer rears animals and grows crops, and so has other space requirements to safeguard his harvests, especially from the weather. Only in the case of the combined byre and dwelling could the small farmer perhaps operate without other buildings (Fig. 237), and even many byre-dwellings had small outhouses associated with them. Farmhouses, then, existed in relationship to byres or cow-houses, stables for horses, barns, pig-sties, implement shelters and small structures to accommodate domestic fowl and even dogs. From place to place the numbers of these outhouses and their spatial relationships to the dwelling have varied, as they have through time. Potent factors in changes in functions and layout of the farmyard were gradual increase in sizes of holdings, and shifts in the greater economic structures within which farmers operated. Yet whereas there has been considerable study over the past four decades of the vernacular house, the farmers' outhouses have received relatively little attention. This chapter aims only to provide the simplest outline of the relationship of the dwelling to other farm buildings, and to describe briefly the categories of buildings involved.

Buildings specifically designed to accommodate animals and various farming activities are not recent. The early Irish laws, in setting out the rights and obligations of certain social grades, specify that the fairly prosperous farmer of the seventh or eighth century A.D. was expected to have 'seven houses' — dwelling, kiln, barn, calf-house, sheep-house, pig-sty, and at least share in a mill for grinding grain.[1] Another grade of farmer was to have 'a big house and a cow house and a pig-sty, a sheep shed and a calf shed'.[2] Obviously arrangements for housing of cattle other than byre-dwellings existed in early times.

Outhouses are noted in later sources. For example in a survey of north-east Donegal in 1611 an 'Irish barn of coples' is listed.[3] Incidental reference occurs in four of the eighteenth-century Ballyhagan inventories in county Armagh to a cow house, two barns, a stable and two 'carr houses'.[4] Barns, stables and cow houses are noted in the Manor of Castledillon in the same area slightly earlier, about 1700,[5] and elsewhere in Armagh and in Tyrone in 1703.[6] No details exist of how these buildings were constructed, what they looked like, how they were fitted out internally, or what was their spatial relationship to the farmhouses.

Nineteenth-century evidence may be greater in quantity, but often may have no greater value. Describing county Antrim in his *Ireland Exhibited to England . . .*, written in 1816, Atkinson generalised:

> The offices of a farm house consist of a stable according to the number of horses required, cow house of the same capacity, and a barn sufficient to contain a stack of grain, such as the owner thinks fit; to these may always be added, a house for one or more pigs, a shed for his calves, and in many instances, an open house to contain turf, cars, and other farming implements, to protect them when not in use from the inclemency of the weather.[7]

If evidence from contemporary county Armagh is a fair guide, we shall see that Atkinson's implication that a barn was a standard farm building was far from true, and he gives no clue as to how rare might be a building to accommodate implements and vehicles.

Generalised comments on the nature and standard of farm buildings were included in the Ordnance Survey memoirs in the 1830s, mainly for Antrim and Londonderry. Typical are the reports for Aghalee: 'office houses too are generally clean and in neat order';[8] Kilbride, where there were affluent farmers: 'There offices are in keeping with the dwelling house, as to substance of construction and extent — but they are not neatly kept', and — telling of the properties of less prosperous farmers — 'Nor is there much regularity in the arrangement of their offices or homesteads';[9] and Templepatrick, where 'Their offices are more carefully constructed . . ., and are pretty much after the Scottish plan'.[10] Improvements in and rebuilding of outhouses were going on in some places at this time. In Glynn,

> . . . barns and out offices, which are constructed on an excellent plan, and in extent in proportion to that of the farm, exhibit a compactness, regularity and substance very rarely to be met with in Ireland. All are slated, substantially built of stone, rough-cast and whitened.[11]

But then there was an improving landlord, Mr. Irving, in Glynn who in a decade had encouraged construction of eighty-five new barns, thirty-one stables and ninety-two byres, alongside ninety-five new dwellings.[12] Ballylinny, also an Antrim parish, exhibited the contrast between recently constructed farms with well planned roomy offices, and older farms with regularly constructed outhouses kept in ill repair, or with inferior-quality, dilapidated small outhouses on some smaller farms.[13] Two of the London companies tried to encourage their tenant farmers in county Londonderry to build better outbuildings in properly laid-out farmyards, by building demonstration model farms. That near Ballykelly in Tamlaght Finlagan parish, built in 1824, 'was much too large and expensive a building to suit the circumstances of the farmers of the parish' — it cost £900.[14] The Drapers' Company tried a similar scheme in the east of the county slightly earlier 'with suitable buildings in the English manner',[15] but there is no evidence it ever had significant influence amongst local farmers.

The county Armagh Gosford[16] and Drumbanagher[17] estates about 1820 provide the only detailed nineteenth-century evidence yet known to survive as to the frequency and capacity of farm outhouses on typical small northern Irish farms. In his meticulously recorded surveys William Greig recorded on a farm-by-farm basis all the byres, stables, and barns on the Gosford estate, and on the Drumbanagher estate all those buildings in the same categories as well as car-houses. He also noted the numbers of animals on each farm. Statistics given in the following paragraphs are summarised from his reports.

Byres and Cattle

TABLE 9.   BYRES ON COUNTY ARMAGH FARMS ABOUT 1820

	Houses	Byres	Cows	% Houses with Byre	Cows per Byre
Drumbanagher	162	140	275	86	1.7
Coolmalish	255	210	315	82	1.5
Baleek	346	260	524	75	2.0

The numbers of houses listed in Table 9 include the dwellings of cottiers and other landless people, so the percentages of farmhouses having byres was actually higher than the range calculated, but on these estates, particularly the Drumbanagher one, cottiers were few, so that there a figure of perhaps about 90% obtained. Obviously the great majority of farms had a byre, although it was possible for a poor farmer to get by without one, but he was taking a great risk in not having his most important animal, and perhaps his most important asset, the breeding cow, protected during hard winter weather. It is also abundantly obvious that on average the byres on the small farms of these Armagh estates held no more than a couple of cows, and not infrequently only one. From surviving small byres it is probable that a drain ran across the building inside the entrance separating a smaller end where calves might be kept, from the other end where there was only room for one or two cows. Such is the layout of the byre on the farm from Drumnahunshin townland, in the Manor of Baleek, now at the Ulster Folk and Transport Museum (Fig. 241). Map evidence suggests it may have originated after the time of Greig's survey, but its size and cobbled floor reflect what was usual at his time. On some larger farms the drain ran along the byre, like one excavated in the nineteenth-century house cluster of Murphystown in south-east Down.[18]

Byres like those listed in county Armagh by Greig were simple thatched buildings. As farming progressed in the nineteenth century, and, from earlier, on prosperous farms where the superior conditions displayed in improving landlord's demesnes were being copied, elaborate arrangements for tying cattle in place and for feeding them were installed, but a cobbled floor and a stone-lined drain remained usual in most of the north of Ireland until within the present century. Apart from the entrance, the walls were pierced by the drain and often by a mucking-out hole through which manure could be forked to the midden outside. A shuttered window opening provided ventilation — vertical slits were an improvement that came from landlords' properties and usually only appear in the walls of larger byres.

Stables and Horses

TABLE 10. STABLES ON COUNTY ARMAGH FARMS
ABOUT 1820

	Houses	Stables	Horses	% Houses with Stables	Horses per Stable
Drumbanagher	162	72	89	44	1.2
Coolmalish	255	49	129	19	2.6
Baleek	346	90	170	26	1.9

Many fewer farms on these Armagh estates had stables than had byres; there is also a significant difference between Drumbanagher, where approaching half of the houses had a stable, and the Gosford estate where the percentage was lower. It is difficult to explain this difference on the basis of the data in Greig's surveys, particularly when the ratio between horses and houses (about one horse per two dwellings) is almost constant over the two estates. The usual pattern was a single horse on those farms that had one, reflected in the ratio of horses per stable, where, however, the higher figure for Coolmalish merely reflects the keeping of a horse on some farms without benefit of a separate stable. Probably in these circumstances it was accommodated when necessary in the byre. Access to the use of a horse was vital for farm labour, drawing home turf for fuel, and transporting produce to market. The fact that a few tenants on these estates had a pair of horses emphasised how essential it was that there be co-operation among most neighbouring farms to share the use of these animals, a situation attended also with some inconvenience. Greig explained in his Gosford report, 'Those who cannot keep a horse or horses must of course wait until those who do possess them have their own lands tilled, and thereby lose the best part of the season, and the crops rendered later and more uncertain than those of their neighbours round them'.[19]

Barns

TABLE 11. BARNS ON COUNTY ARMAGH FARMS
ABOUT 1820

	Houses	Barns	% Houses with Barns
Drumbanagher	162	59	36
Coolmalish	255	108	42
Baleek	346	117	34

Only marginally more than a third of the houses on the Gosford and Drumbanagher estates had a barn attached. These figures may seem low, but are understandable in view of the common northern Irish practice of storing grain in the sheaf in stacks built in a haggard beside the farmyard, grain being threshed as required. Some small, apparently conical thatched structures on a military map of Enniskillen in 1593[20] have been interpreted as grain storage bins constructed of heavy twisted-straw ropes coiled upon each other (Fig. 60), a technique of grain storage which survived in the extreme south of Ireland until recent times.[21] No other evidence for this practice is known in the north of Ireland. By contrast, the usual northern Irish practice of having 'no farm buildings attached to the houses of the farmers for receipt of their crops'[22] is noted in the Ordnance Survey memoirs for Templecairne parish in north Fermanagh in 1834, and is echoed in Londonderry in the parish memoirs for Clondermot in the north[23] and Lissan[24] in the south of the county, and in the south-east Antrim parishes of Kilroot[25] and Templecorran.[26] Indeed, what barns there were on the Armagh estates surveyed by Greig perhaps served purposes other than grain storage, at least in part, for example housing of implements and horse-drawn vehicles; car-houses, not listed by Greig at all in his Drumbanagher survey, were associated with only about 16% of the houses on the Gosford estate.[27]

Building of some new barns in the second half of the nineteenth century was attributable to installation of horse-operated threshing machines made in northern Irish foundries like those of Scott of Belfast, Kane of Ballymena and Kennedy of Coleraine. Experimentation with threshing machines in Ireland had started about 1800 when landowners in a few places acquired machines, usually water-powered. Mr. Christy in county Down was 'the first in this kingdom' to have one built on a model he had seen in Scotland in 1796, and Mr. Ward of Bangor in the north of the same county had one as early as 1802,[28] when there was also one at Farnham in Cavan.[29] By 1810 seven landowners in county Antrim had threshers, some at least of which were water-powered, and so special mill buildings had been constructed attached to their farm steadings. At this period the machines were costly, although their price had fallen from the £100 Mr. Christy had laid out on his, to under £50 which was being paid in 1812 in Scotland for machines which could be brought over to Ireland.[30] None of the other northern Irish county surveys commissioned by the Royal Dublin Society in the early 1800s mentions threshing machines, and it is obvious from the concentration of references in the Ordnance Survey memoirs of the 1830s in mainly east Ulster parishes that the innovation was only then taking root at prosperous farmer level. Threshing machines were noted in the memoirs in Ardglass, Ballee and Kilmegan in south-east Down, in Tynan and Clonfeacle in west Armagh, and in Templemore outside Londonderry city; in most of these cases the numbers involved were very small, although in the south-west Antrim parish of Killead they were 'becoming more general'. However, the kernel of what was later to become widespread acceptance was in south-east Antrim. There were three threshing machines, one water-powered in Kilwaughter, seven in Templecorran of which six were horse-powered, and no fewer than twenty in Islandmagee, unlikely as it may seem in such a relatively isolated parish of small farms where only one was water-powered. The small thresher with circular open-air horse walk outside the barn, driven by two or three, rarely four horses, suited to the needs of the small Ulster farm where capital was limited, was at last becoming available. Adoption of the innovation was slow, however, and it is paradoxical that it was not until after 1855, when there was a general shift from tillage to pasture in northern Irish agriculture, that the widespread installation of threshing machines was seen on northern Irish farms. Late in the century even very small farmers were installing them, and the circular horse-walk at the rear of the barn became a common sight in most parts of Ulster. Records of the Kennedy foundry at Coleraine which I saw in the early 1960s[31] showed that installation of Kennedy threshers continued until 1940, when the last, powered by an oil engine, was installed in Gweedore in north-west Donegal. Their machines were first available in the Coleraine area in 1860, and by the 1880s were being installed widely in Antrim, Londonderry, Tyrone, east Donegal, mid Down, and north Armagh. Ruins of older farms all over the north of Ireland have traces of horse-walks attached to them, sometimes the threshing machines or fanners surviving in the barns, and occasionally a secondary drive was taken off for churning in a dairy placed end-to-end with the barn, often placed between it and the dwelling, sometimes the dairy being merely a rear room in the house itself (cf. Corcreeny 'B' house in Chapter 5, Fig. 74).

It is interesting that this pattern of development effectively prevented appearance in Ulster of the distinctive-looking covered horse walks of the large farms of eastern Scotland and the north-east of England. Five have been located in the north of Ireland, and seemingly only one of these predates the first edition of the six-inch Ordnance Survey maps. It was built in The Grange, the home farm of the Annesley family at Castlewellan in county Down. Three others were in Down also, at Myra Castle in Walshestown townland near Strangford in a mid-nineteenth-century context, on a more modestly sized farm in Ballywilliam townland near Donaghadee, and a later nineteenth-century example is under a metal roof supported on cast-iron pillars in Ballynaskeagh townland near Banbridge. The fifth covered horse walk was just west of county Down on the Drumbanagher estate in east Armagh.

To the extent that the evidence from the Armagh estates surveyed by William Greig is more generally representative, the small Ulster farmyard of the early nineteenth century may be characterised as having usually had a byre for cattle which may have served also for housing of calves and sometimes a horse. Significantly fewer than half of the farms had a stable, and only something more than one in three had a barn. Fewer than one in five had accommodation specifically for horse-drawn vehicles and implements. By the end of the century, outbuildings around the typical Ulster farmyard were more numerous and usually larger than they were about 1820, and the growth in specialisation of use of farmyard accommodation implicit in this change parallels the growth in specialisation of space usage inside the farm dwelling which we have observed was mainly concentrated within the same period. Towards the end of the century, too, the ubiquitous thatched roofs covering the byres, stables and barns listed by Greig were giving way to slating, tarred felt and corrugated metal sheeting.

Farmyard Layout

It is important to consider the relationships between the dwelling and the other buildings grouped in the farmyard. Preliminary studies have been published which deal with this aspect, based on analysis of farmyard layouts recorded on the first edition of the six-inch Ordnance Survey maps mainly of the 1830s (Fig. 241). An important qualification to this approach is that it considers the situation only in the 1830s. Examination of many farmyards shows that buildings were added at different times. A layout of buildings could alter fundamentally from one form to another by this process of change or

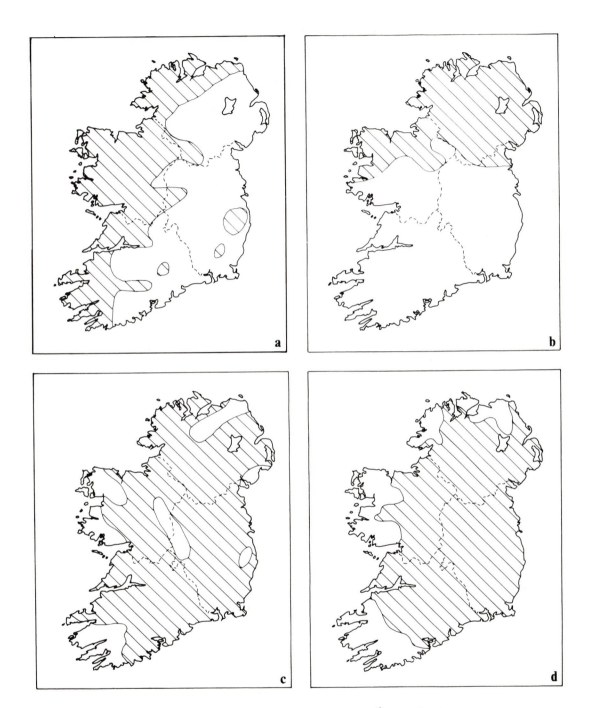

Fig. 241. Generalised distributions of farmyard types in Ireland, 1841 (after Ó Danachair).
a: buildings scattered, no formal yard;
b: outhouses extended along long axis of dwelling;
c: buildings around three sides of rectangular yard;
d: buildings along two sides of rectangular yard.

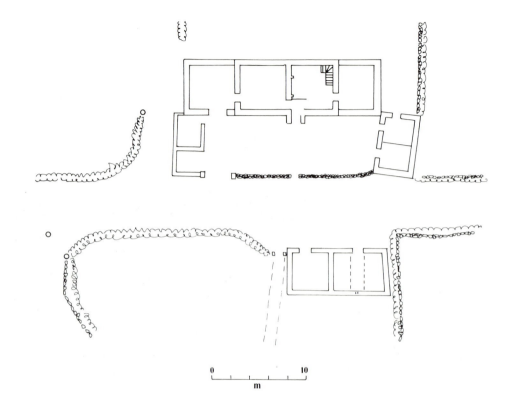

Fig. 242. Layout of farmyard at Drumnahunshin Td., Co. Armagh, recreated at UFTM (cf. Fig. 267). Above, to west side of road, dwelling with unit at left end converted to use as cartshed, and small outhouses closing the ends of the yard, pigsty and implement store at left, fowl and calf house at right. At bottom, east of road, stable left, and byre right.

enlargement. For example, the farm from Drumnahunshin townland in county Armagh (Fig. 242) removed to the Ulster Folk and Transport Museum commenced as a dwelling on one side of the road with a stable/byre building on the opposite side. Addition of small outhouses at each end of the dwelling late in the nineteenth century transformed its layout to a three-sided enclosed yard on one side of the road (Fig. 267), with the byre/stable remaining opposite. In the Ballymena area of mid Antrim some early nineteenth-century farm clusters first became single farms with some cottier houses and other former dwellings converted to outhouse use; later, all of the old dwellings became outhouses. Traces of many of these changes have now been swept away as the demands of modern farming technology necessitate removing older buildings, to replace them with large covered cattle courts, silos, barns to store baled hay and straw, and machinery sheds. Modern farm machinery is usually too wide to permit older gate widths to be maintained, and often the dwelling is rebuilt further away from the other buildings than in the past.

It must be recognised that some farmyards in the early nineteenth century did not have their outhouses related to the dwelling in any formal manner (Figs. 243, 244), idiosyncracies of individual farmers and the exigencies of site being predominant amongst the factors controlling the layout of buildings. Many others developed in this way from simple beginnings, such as having the outhouses and dwelling in an extended range. Nevertheless, certain distinctive farmyard layouts existed in the nineteenth century, but to what degree they may have been in widespread existence before 1800 is unknown. The evolution of the byre-dwelling described in Chapter 8 makes it clear that removal of cattle from the dwelling necessitated building a separate byre, and this often, indeed usually, was added at the 'low' gable of the house, under a continuation of the dwelling's thatched roof. Development of a distinctively northern Irish[32] farmyard layout starts here, and farm buildings laid out along a continuation of the long axis of the dwelling were, by the 1830s, found all over the area north from Clew Bay in county Mayo in the west to south county Louth in the east. Dwelling, byre, stable and barn, though not all were always present as we have seen (Figs. 245-248),

Fig. 243.   Early 20th-century informally arranged small farmhouse and outhouses, possibly Inishowen, Co. Donegal. UFTM WAG 3356

Fig. 244.   Informally arranged small dwelling and outhouses, Rosguill, Co. Donegal, early 20th-century. UFTM WAG 2590

Fig. 245.   Original extended farmyard, with later outhouses added opposite, early 20th-century, Trassey Valley, Mourne Mountains, Co. Down. UFTM WAG 3084

Fig. 246.   Extended farmyard, outhouses in line at each end of farmhouse, Mullan Td., Co. Londonderry. UFTM L 899.14A

Fig. 247. Earlier extended farm, later outhouses added at right angles along approach road to left, Terryglassog Td., Co. Tyrone. UFTM L 1509.8

Fig. 248. Earlier extended farmyard with later outhouses added opposite forming parallel ranges of building, Cloncore Td., Co. Armagh. UFTM L 1002.9

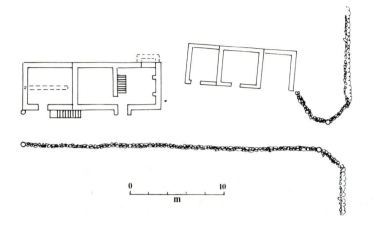

Fig. 249. Extended farmyard layout, originally in Coshkib Td., Co. Antrim, recreated at UFTM (cf. Fig. 269). Nearest public road at right are cartshed, stable and store under thatch roof; lower down yard, dwelling with byre at lower end and hay loft over.

Fig. 250. Rectangular farmyard at edge of house cluster, Ballymorran Td., Co. Down. Farmhouse and outhouses arranged around three sides of yard, gate on fourth side near corner, early 20th-century. UFTM WAG 2090

formed a continuous range. In some later examples at least two separate structures might be involved; for example, in the farmyard which originated in the 1850s in Coshkib townland north of Cushendall in the Glens of Antrim, now at the Ulster Folk and Transport Museum, the byre with a barn loft above it was attached to the 'low' end of the house, while the cart-shed, stable, and store all share a thatched roof over a separate building at the upper end of the yard, their facade set slightly behind the line of that of the dwelling (Fig. 249). Some of these extended farmsteads had become very long by the end of

the nineteenth century, as specialised spaces were added for a variety of purposes, including dairies, workshops and stores. Records of the type in the 1830s are available in the Ordnance Survey memoirs in the north-east part of the Barony of Raphoe in east Donegal,[33] in east Londonderry[34] and various parts of county Antrim.[35] The comments from east Londonderry and Carnmoney are typical. In the former district '. . . as the car house and barn are mostly under the same roof with the dwelling house there is an accumulation of filth in front', and in Carnmoney, just north of Belfast,

Fig. 251.   Farmhouse and outhouses along two sides of rectangular yard, Derryall Td., Co. Armagh (cf. Fig. 8). UFTM L 1002.15

Fig. 252.   Modernised farm with dwelling and outhouses at right angles, new outhouses at rear. Approach to yard from road at right, Ballyoglagh Td., Co. Antrim. UFTM L 1490.14

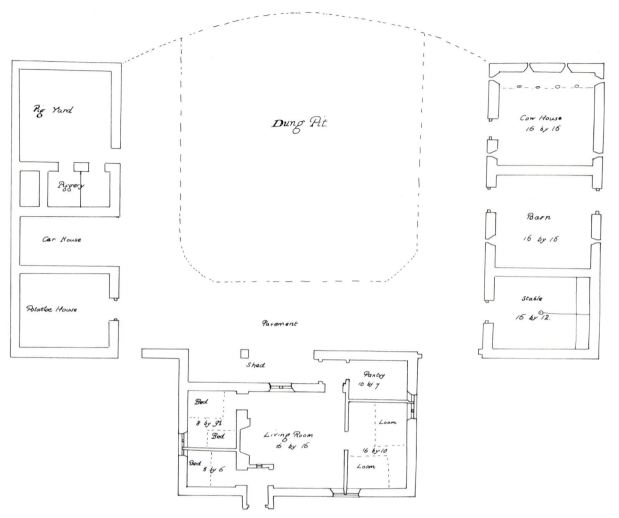

Fig. 253.   Improved farmyard layout by William Greig advocated in his reports on the Gosford and Drumbanagher estates in Co. Armagh, *c.* 1820. Redrawn from plan in PRONI T 3097.

In the construction of their offices, and in their arrangement there is a want of regularity. They generally are attached to or form a continuation of the dwelling house — along their front a narrow and ill-paved causeway extends and beyond it are usually receptacles for the manure from the stable and cow-house.

In Racavan parish in Antrim we learn that if there was no pig-sty included in the range of accommodation, 'a recess formed in the turf stack when building it' served as well. On the other hand some south-east county Down farmyards of the nineteenth century had elaborate, sometimes relatively sophisticated pig-sties; corbelled sties, comparable to those in south Wales,[36] existed there,[37] and in Grangewalls townland, which is also in Lecale barony, on a farmstead with a remarkably high standard of stonework, feeding chutes through the sty

walls allowed feed to be delivered from outside to pigs inside.

Folk belief often functions to maintain communal attitudes and traditions. From within the area where farmsteads consisting of outbuildings added onto the dwelling were usual, in the Strabane area of west Tyrone, there is an interesting account of dwelling renewal and lengthways extension of the range of building:

It was considered unlucky for a man to build a new house, and go and live in it. It was said that a man, when he built a new house, would never live to enjoy it. To get over this, when more room was needed, the new house was attached on to the old, and a door left between the old and new houses. The old portion of the house could then be used as a byre or calf-house, and when the man who built the new house died, the door would be closed up between the old and new portions of the house. This may account for the difference in height of the roofs of byre and dwelling house, as often noticed.[38]

In 1821 the respondent from the north-east part of the Barony of Raphoe to the North-West of Ireland Farming Society's questionnaire, quoted above, also noted a farmyard arrangement where the dwelling and the outbuildings were in two parallel ranges. Analysis of the Ordnance Survey six-inch maps, mainly of the 1830s, suggests that although there was a marked concentration of this farmyard layout in the extreme south-west of Ireland, it occurred elsewhere, if only sporadically in the north, especially in Armagh (Fig. 248), Monaghan, south Down and mid Tyrone. One way in which this form developed, noted in south-west Donegal, was by the building of a new dwelling in front of the old one, abandonment of the old byre-dwelling by its human occupants taking place instead of building new accommodation for the cattle, as happened so often.[39]

Other arrangements aimed towards forming a rectangular yard in front of or behind the dwelling. Where there were larger farms earlier in the nineteenth century, and a sufficient range of outhouses to complete the arrangement, outhouses were laid out in parallel ranges at each end of the dwelling, thereby forming three sides of a courtyard, the fourth often being delimited by a roadside wall. Layouts of this kind were much commoner throughout Leinster, Munster and east Connacht, where farms on average were larger than in most of Ulster; only rarely is this layout encountered in the north[40] (Fig. 250). Throughout the same distribution, a minority form of smaller farms in Leinster, Munster and east Connacht had only two sides of the yard identified by the dwelling and a range of outhouses at right angles to it. In the northern province where farms were smaller, this layout was of commoner occurrence than the three-sided one, being represented in all counties, although rare in north Londonderry and west and north Antrim[41] (Figs. 251, 252). It is likely that these two-sided and three-sided rectangular farmyard layouts represent the extent to which at vernacular level there was any significant influence exerted by those improving landlords who built formally laid-out yards on their own demesnes, in their home and model farms. Extensive accommodation provided in these for the needs of the larger-scale operations of wealthy farmers could not realistically be scaled down to the requirements of the average small farmer with his one or two milk cows, his horse which he perhaps shared with a neighbour, and his couple of sheep and a pig (Fig. 253). Enclosed rectangular, well laid-out farmyards, like those built widely in Scotland in the nineteenth century, never became a vernacular form in the north of Ireland where they remained firmly at the formal end of the architectural continuum.

ELEVEN

Conservation and Restoration

FOUR generations have passed since Maurice Collis compiled the housing statistics included in his surveys of northern Irish estates. It will be recalled from Chapter 5 that, except for the use of local slate on the north Down estate of the Londonderry family, 95% or more of rural houses in the 1840s were single-storey thatched buildings. Now, in the early 1980s, no more than a few hundred houses answering this description remain in northern Ireland. No hope remains of retaining *in situ* a regionally representative sample of these dwellings with all their variations of materials, roof cover and plan form, although in the six counties of Northern Ireland (Antrim, Armagh, Down, Fermanagh, Londonderry and Tyrone), where historic buildings legislation was implemented in 1972[1] akin to that of Britain, some may survive. However, the very existence of this legislation compounds the problem of the representativeness of the sample retained. A few thatched houses illustrating what were the majority of all rural dwellings down to the end of the nineteenth century will survive alongside a greater number of what were the minority of larger, usually later, two-storey slated vernacular farmhouses, some of which are graced with modest architectural detailing and decoration. At least the modified enlarged houses preserve something of the kernel of the vernacular tradition — internal relationships of entrances and hearths, and their external reflection in facade arrangements of piercing and chimney stacks.

In regard to traditional rural housing, the problems facing the conservation lobby and, to be fair, the sometimes reluctant owners of vernacular houses, are formidable. So far as one-storey thatched houses are concerned, most attempts to upgrade interiors to accord with modern living requirements have been disastrous. The scale of many traditional houses presents a straitjacket within which often only small dwellings can be provided, suitable for single people, childless couples and the retired. Windows of limited size, absence of amenities like bathrooms, low ceiling heights, and insurance problems posed by thatch militate against preservation.

Furthermore, the social desirability felt by many owners to add pebble-dashing, large flat-roofed porches front and rear, picture windows, and to replace thatch by coarse-textured tiling, all detract from the 'feel' of the vernacular. Examples of unsympathetic treatment of older houses are numerous, sadly sometimes in visually prominent locations where unsympathetic 'improvements' seem strikingly obtrusive. Escape from the design straitjacket of the traditional house in the north of Ireland has yet to be achieved in a satisfactory manner, and architects have not achieved in Northern Ireland a modern 'vernacular' form such as they have in some other countries. Perhaps the artist in the architect rebels against creation of a dwelling that blends with its surroundings; perhaps he and his client want a 'creation' that is immediately obvious, which is also to say obtrusive.

Study of the vernacular tradition suggests that close attention to a limited range of criteria might achieve a new vernacular style suited to rural areas. First is the problem of scale. Relationships of length to depth from front to rear have always been critical. A single-pile building, without significant gable piercing, if coupled with choice of a roof covering of subdued texture, yet managing to appear as unmechanical as older natural slating, would go far to provide a basis for an acceptable modern form. A major problem with most modern synthetic slates is their large size; smaller sizes can be achieved, as for example ones used widely in Brittany. Perhaps it needs only a demand to achieve graded sizes which would help create a distinctive and traditional character.

Attention is needed to the ratio of void to mass in wall piercing. Sufficient possibilities exist within traditional door and window design to allow adequate natural lighting of interiors. Some Northern Ireland Housing Executive projects in urban areas have recently shown that traditional solutions exist, for example in pairing conventionally sized sash windows where large windows are needed. Picture windows are seen to have been a

Fig. 254. Ballymorran Td., Co. Down. Farmhouse of 1702, from a transparency. UFTM L 1222.10

matter of fashion rather than necessity; witness the modern fad for small-paned 'Georgian' windows in suburbia, now spreading to the country.

External rendering needs careful attention. The traditional whitewashed house was enlivened by subtle variations of surface created by successive layers of lime wash applied direct to uneven stonework, or to plaster that softened but did not hide surface variations of the underlying material. The modern tendency is to apply smooth cement rendering, or self-coloured limestone chips, neither of which retains the individuality of the original wall surface. On the other hand, modern cement-based white paints are usually as acceptable as lime wash and, needing to be applied less regularly may be more economical in the long run. Nor should it be thought that white is the only acceptable colour, although bright strident colours normally should be avoided on vernacular dwellings.

In the conservation of many listed vernacular houses, all that can be hoped is to retain the traditional appearance from the front, when possible carried round to include gables. In meeting the necessary requirement for upgrading the quality of life for those who live in these houses, rear extensions will often be inevitable; but they should be completed within the parameters of vernacular building, having regard to correct balances between void and mass in piercing, and in maintaining pitched roofs

with suitable coverings, preferably of slate. Interiors are rarely of sufficient architectural quality to warrant insistence on their preservation *in toto*; if essential internal relationships of principal entrances and hearth positions can be reflected externally, modernisation should be permitted to an extent to encourage continued occupation. A minority of vernacular houses have been successfully modernised, usually with slate roofs. They have a full range of modern conveniences, damp problems have been countered, and usually they prove to be thermally efficient, having thick mass walls. But above all, there is a determination amongst their owners that traditional houses in sympathy with their surroundings shall survive. Overall architectural education of the general population throughout the north of Ireland must be extended to swell the numbers of these owners.

Thatch represents the single most difficult problem in preserving even a few of what were the commonest vernacular forms in the nineteenth century. Really competent thatchers no longer remain to carry out the full range of traditional thatching techniques, and materials are difficult to find. Straw suitable for thatching is not generally available. Modern wheat strains have been developed with short straw for combine harvesting, a process which in any case renders the straw unusable. Straw grown and handled suitably for thatching can be

Fig. 255. The same farmhouse following modernisation. UFTM L 1197.18

obtained in limited amounts but it is very expensive. Thatching skill has become equally difficult and expensive to commission. The north-eastern counties of Ireland are now served by a handful of men, only two or three of whom seem prepared to work outside their local districts. Sadly also, the duration of the roofs they re-thatch does not accord with what oral tradition suggests should be achieved. It is wrong to lay the whole blame at the thatchers' own door, by suggesting that they are not competent. At least as relevant a consideration is the fact that in the past, when thatching skills existed generally in rural districts, occasional patching was carried out as and when required. Now that this does not happen deterioration proceeds unchecked once things start to go wrong.

In these circumstances it is sensible that official concern to preserve thatched buildings is concentrated in two directions: by conserving resources to be applied on the best examples which may reasonably be expected to survive *in situ*, and in so doing by being as liberal as possible in regard to grant-aid to owners recognising that they undertake a conservation role for the community at large; and by insisting that a suitable sample of traditional buildings is preserved by public agencies. Recognising the design constraints that older buildings provide in relation

to modern living, this approach needs to be wider in its application than merely to thatched buildings. A significant number of vernacular houses, thatched and slated, have now been statutorily listed in Northern Ireland, although undermanning of the *Historic Monuments and Buildings Branch of the Department of the Environment for Northern Ireland* is delaying completion of statutory listing and preventing adequate supervision of renovation and modernisation schemes. The legislation, however, needs strengthening. It is too easy for an unsympathetic owner simply to allow a good building, even an historically important one, to moulder away through neglect.

Hopefully the existing legislation, even with its weaknesses, provides some basis for successful preservation of an adequate sample of vernacular houses. Progress of statutory listing, on the advice of the *Northern Ireland Historic Buildings Council*, and of grant-aided conservation projects may provide a climate of opinion educated to prevent some of the more unfortunate instances of unsympathetic modernisation of vernacular houses. Two cases may be quoted, in both of which alterations were implemented before statutory listing had been undertaken. An interesting and locally typical three-unit direct-entry farmhouse in Ballymorran

Fig. 256.   Coagh, Co. Tyrone. Vernacular house and shop at the end of Hanover Square. UFTM L 76.10

Fig. 257.   The same building following modernisation. UFTM L 1252.14

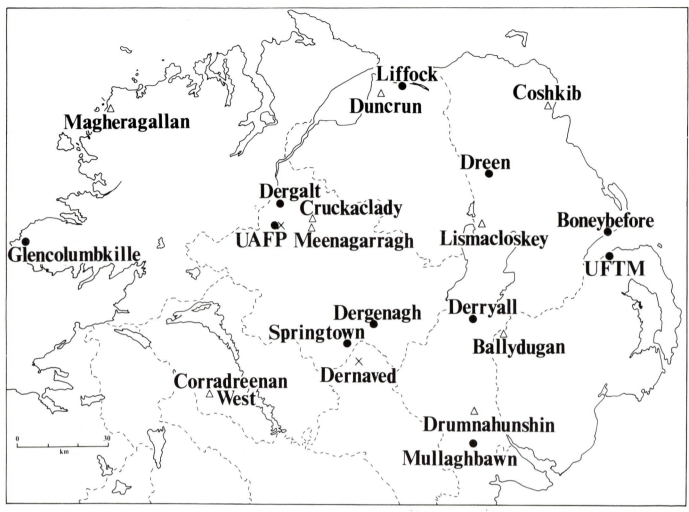

Fig. 258. Locations of preserved vernacular houses in northern Ireland, black circles. UAFP: Ulster-American Folk Park; x: original locations of exhibit houses reconstructed at UAFP. UFTM: Ulster Folk and Transport Museum; triangles: original locations of exhibit houses at UFTM.

townland near Killinchy in east Down had its thatched roof (Figs. 250, 254) replaced with modern tiles, and an inappropriately designed door and unsympathetic rendering were applied (Fig. 255), although the margined sash windows, the basic layout and date stone of 1702 were retained. More severe was the treatment of the formerly fine two-storey scollop-thatched house and shop which closed the vista at the top of Hanover Square in the east Tyrone village of Coagh (Fig. 256). The balance of mass to void in the facade piercing was fundamentally changed and a modern roof and rendering were applied. The changes in this house were visually disastrous in view of its dominant location (Fig. 257).

An important role has been played in conservation work in the north of Ireland since the late 1960s by the

Ulster Architectural Heritage Society.[2] Its listings of buildings of architectural merit have understandably concentrated on urban areas. Some vernacular houses have received the attention of the Society, and hopefully their work can be extended. An approach badly needed is provision of a complement to the district statutory lists of buildings by provision of Ulster-wide lists of thematic interest, of which examples might include houses, planned farmyards, dovecots, and other classes of buildings of vernacular interest.

A couple of decades ago official recognition was given to the ancestral houses of a number of presidents of the United States of America, partly in an attempt to stimulate American tourist interest in Northern Ireland. Ancestors of Ulysses S. Grant came from a two-unit hearth-lobby farmhouse in Dergenagh townland in east

Fig. 259. Model of the Woodrow Wilson ancestral homestead, Dergalt Td., Co. Tyrone. UFTM L 1614.3

Fig. 260. Model of the Chester Allan Arthur ancestral homestead, Dreen Td., Co. Antrim. UFTM L 1614.11

s

Fig. 261.   The Mellon family ancestral home, Castletown Td., Co. Tyrone, preserved *in situ* as part of UAFP. Photo by courtesy of UAFP.

Fig. 262.   Ancestral home of Archbishop Hughes of New York, removed from Dernaved Td., Co. Monaghan, reconstructed at UAFP. Photo by courtesy of UAFP.

Fig. 263. Former farmhouse at Boneybefore, Carrickfergus, Co. Antrim, now preserved by the district council. UFTM L 1029.12

Tyrone. It was one of the minority type, with the jamb wall at a gable and not in the centre of the house, although addition of a third brick-walled unit converted it into the usual layout early in the present century. It has recently been taken in hand by Dungannon District Council for restoration to its original layout and presentation as an historic and tourist site (Fig. 258). Commemorative plaques were mounted at Boneybefore, Carrickfergus, close to the site of the ancestral home of Andrew Jackson and on a potato store at Conagher, in north Antrim, an ancestral home of President McKinley, known from photographs taken early this century to have been of direct-entry type. Ancestors of Woodrow Wilson came from a farm in Dergalt townland near Strabane in west Tyrone, still owned by Wilsons until it was acquired by the Northern Ireland government in the 1960s. It is a direct-entry house with outshot, a second slated storey having been added over the second unit, the kitchen retaining its scollop-thatched roof (Fig. 259). What is believed to have been the home of the ancestors of Chester Allan Arthur in Dreen townland near Cullybackey in west Antrim was taken into state care about the same time and restored. The house is of direct-entry type and of two units (Fig. 260).

Initially the 'presidential' houses at Dergalt and Dreen

were taken into the administrative care of the *Northern Ireland Committee of the National Trust*. However, the Trust's interests in Northern Ireland have concentrated on coastline and on classic Georgian and earlier architecture of the Great Tradition. Apart from its earlier care for these two houses, only the fine cruck house of direct-entry type at Liffock, near Castlerock in north Londonderry, and the earliest house at The Argory in north-west Armagh, a British vernacular building of the late seventeenth century, represent the National Trust's concern for vernacular houses, although the latter is not intended for public visiting.

The National Trust was involved in the early stages of preservation of the ancestral home of the famous American banking Mellon family, at Camphill near Omagh in Tyrone. With some Mellon money in the early stages, and considerable state funding, the project grew to become the *Ulster-American Folk Park*, a largely open-air museum developed on a small site, its two parts intended to illustrate the domestic social conditions of northern Irish emigrants to America before and after their emigration. Apart from the Mellon homestead which is a two-unit direct-entry farmhouse (Fig. 261), a three-unit weaver's house typical of the district has been reproduced, and a lobby-entry farmhouse from north

Fig. 264.   Cottier's house from Duncrun Td., Co. Londonderry, reconstructed at UFTM. UFTM L 129.4

Fig. 265.   Complete and ruinous byre-dwellings, sharing a gable, from Magheragallan Td., Co. Donegal, reconstruction at UFTM. UFTM L 1190.8

Fig. 266.   Hearth and bed in outshot in kitchen of farmhouse from Cruckaclady Td., Co. Tyrone, reconstructed in UFTM. UFTM L 736.21

Monaghan has been based upon the incomplete remains of the ancestral home of the Roman Catholic Archbishop Hughes of New York removed from the original site (Fig. 262). Recent investigations have been undertaken of another Mellon homestead, again of direct-entry type with outshot.

Two small folk museums at opposite ends of Ulster may be mentioned. In *Glencolumbkille* in south-west Donegal a group of traditional byre-dwelling derivative houses was created as a 'folk village', some furnished with an intention to illustrate domestic conditions at different periods. Built of local stone with rounded roof ridges and roped thatch, the buildings are not entirely successful. Some modern materials were used, sometimes exposed to view, and the building work was completed with an attention to geometric precision not usually seen in west Donegal traditional houses. For the most part the Glencolumbkille buildings are not originals, but constructed by local people working within their own tradition, and they capture some of the authentic flavour of vernacular houses in the area. The local folklore and historical society in *Mullaghbawn*, south Armagh adopted a different approach. A tiny farm unit, with outhouse and two-unit thatched direct-entry dwelling was acquired to accommodate a collection of mainly domestic artifacts presented by local people.

Apart from the Hughes home at the Ulster-American Folk Park, the houses so far mentioned are all of direct-entry type. A notable hearth-lobby house is the concern of local people in the Clogher Valley in east Tyrone. It is on the small farm in *Springtown* townland where the nineteenth-century novelist William Carleton lived when young (Fig. 180); Carleton wrote tellingly from personal involvement of the peasant life-style of his time. The future of the Carleton house is uncertain, the last occupant having recently died. A private individual possesses a farm group of thatched outhouses and three-unit hearth-lobby house in *Derryall* townland, alongside the M1 motorway north-west of Portadown in county Armagh. For some years its thatch has been well maintained and its exterior regularly whitewashed (Fig. 251).

In west Down in the Loughbrickland-Katesbridge area there are two houses, one of hearth-lobby plan, one end of which was raised by addition of an upper room, the other a two-unit two-storey slated direct-entry farmhouse nearby in Ballynaskeagh townland; they were associated with forebears of the famous novelists, the Brontë sisters.

Fig. 267. Farmhouse and yard alongside public road in Drumnahunshin Td., Co. Armagh, reconstructed in UFTM. Copy of original photograph of *c*.1935. UFTM L 1585.8

Neither, however, is a good example of its kind, the former being in a very poor state, and their interest is solely the historical/literary one. Not so, however, the fine building at *Boneybefore*, Carrickfergus, acquired for preservation and use as a local museum by Carrickfergus District Council (Fig. 263). The three-unit direct-entry house is of one storey with a scollop thatch roof, and has outhouses at each end, mostly under thatch continuous with the dwelling. Vandals recently damaged the house severely by setting fire to its roof, but full restoration is being undertaken and it will become one of the few thatched vernacular houses surviving within easy reach of Belfast, outside the Ulster Folk and Transport Museum. The site of the ancestral home of the American president Andrew Jackson is nearby, and tourists will be attracted to visit both.

A convenient authentic overview of vernacular housing in the north of Ireland is possible at one place: the *Ulster Folk and Transport Museum* in Ballycultra townland, east of Holywood in north Down, seven miles from the centre of Belfast. The folk museum was initiated as a national institution by legislation at the end of 1958,[3] purchased its site in mid-1961, and opened to the public in July 1964 when vernacular housing was represented by a two-unit cottier's dwelling from Duncrun townland in north Londonderry (Fig. 264). It has roped marram thatch, a scarfed-cruck roof truss, bed outshot and wicker chimney canopy. It dates probably from the latter part of the eighteenth century and is one of five direct-entry houses in the museum. The typologically most archaic of these is an unpartitioned small byre-dwelling from Magheragallan townland in north-west Donegal (Figs. 265, 146), which has a wall-bed, rounded roof ridge and roped marram thatch. Scollop thatch covers two others. One is a two-unit farmhouse with an outshot in the kitchen and a byre under the other unit (Fig. 266). Removed from Cruckaclady townland in west Tyrone, it stood across the road from a single-unit house with outshot built about 1880 in Meenagarragh townland (Fig. 27). The two houses stand in a comparable physical relationship to each other again in the museum. Upward enlargement of the direct-entry type is represented by a two-unit house from Coshkib townland, north of Cushendall in the Glens of Antrim. It was built in the mid-nineteenth century as a two-unit one-storey house with roped thatch and bed outshot. About 1906 the roof was removed, the outshot closed off, and an upper floor of two bedrooms was added under a slate roof, stairs rising from inside the front door but not sheeted off from the rest of the kitchen.

Three hearth-lobby rural houses have been completed in the museum. A developed farmhouse, with an upper

Fig. 268.   Farmhouse from Corradreenan West Td., Co. Fermanagh, reconstructed in UFTM. UFTM L 444.1

floor above its kitchen and one of its other two units, has been removed from Drumnahunshin townland in south Armagh (Fig. 267). At least part of the house was originally thatched, but all was eventually covered with slate. Its kitchen layout remained in the basic form with undeveloped jamb wall, stairs having been set in the rear corner away from the fire, rising around the wall angle. The layout from which this house developed is represented by the other two houses of hearth-lobby type in the museum. One was removed from Corradreenan West townland in west Fermanagh. Unlike the Drumnahunshin farmhouse, it had a rear kitchen door (perhaps a later insertion) as well as the front entrance which gives onto the brick-built jamb wall (Fig. 232). The brick chimney breastwork was discovered during dismantling to have replaced an earlier chimney canopy, presumably of wattle-work. Brick partition walls, also nineteenth-century alterations, closed off two small bedrooms in the rear of the kitchen unit, while a stud-and-plank partition separated a small bedroom from a front parlour in the other unit. A notable feature of this house is the floor of locally fired clay tiles, dating from about 1850 or later, in the kitchen. They were a product of the Florence Court works which were close to Corradreenan West townland. The house has a scollop-thatch hipped roof (Fig. 268), the only one of this form in

the museum collection. The other hearth-lobby house has a three-unit plan but has gables supporting a purlin roof covered with scollop thatch. Unlike all the other buildings in the museum collection, it is modelled on an original that stood in Ballydugan townland in west Down, a short distance south of Lurgan. It was built in the mid-nineteenth century of stone with earth mortar in front and rear walls. Gables and internal walls separating the units were built with solid earth (mud), so it was decided that in the museum the house should be recreated, modelled on the original, using the correct materials handled in the traditional manner. It was a weaver's house with a 'shop' that originally accommodated four linen looms. A brace beam supported on the end of the jamb wall spans the kitchen but the chimney is in a constricted brick flue, so there is a large 'skeagh' or loft covering the whole of the hearth area (Fig. 130). Beam, jamb wall and loft flooring had all been replaced in modern timber, probably early in the twentieth century.

It is hoped that the collection of lobby-entry houses in the museum can be completed by inclusion of an example perhaps with a symmetrically arranged facade, where the jamb wall has been extended across the front of the kitchen unit to form a hallway from which stairs rise to an upper floor, either of lofts or of full height.

British vernacular housing in the north of Ireland is

Fig. 269.   Hill-farm from Coshkib Td., Co. Antrim, reconstructed at UFTM, with byre at near, low end of dwelling. Note traditional stone field walls. UFTM L 1587.10A

represented at the museum by one large house removed from Lismacloskey townland in west county Antrim (Figs. 213, 214). Of two storeys, it has an older portion dated dendrochronologically to about 1717, with a three-bay roof carried on two principal-rafter collar trusses with butt purlins. This timbering system contrasts with the through-purlin roofs on collar trusses of the Corradreenan, Cruckaclady, Meenagarragh houses, the scarfed-cruck truss bearing through purlins of the Duncrun house, and the purlin roof of the Ballydugan weaver's house. Its English antecedents are further demonstrated unmistakably by the presence of a brick-lined hemispherical oven to the right-hand side of the hearth (Fig. 128), under the massive stone chimney canopy which is carried on an oak bressumer of very substantial proportions. It is believed the original entrance to the house was through the kitchen hearth gable, but this door now gives ground-floor access to an addition of 1800–25, stairs to the upper floor having been inserted on the inside of the front wall, which necessitated blocking up a window.

Other vernacular houses, urban ones, are already included in the museum collection, and it is hoped that it will be possible to include a labourer's cottage from the early twentieth century, preferably one of vernacular inspiration.

Composition of the total collection of buildings at the museum is intended to be as broadly representative of northern Irish vernacular building as possible, while accepting that obvious limitations of scale are imposed by the confines and nature of the museum site. Already the reader will be aware that the typological variations in rural vernacular housing are well represented. The basis for the museum's representative development lies in the continuing programme of field and documentary research carried out, work which is justified also because the resultant archive fulfills for Northern Ireland the role played in Britain by the various Royal Commissions on Historical Monuments and National Monument Records in regard to recording of vernacular housing. A consequence of the museum's policy is that its folk park cannot be seen as an ultimate resting place for every valued vernacular building that may be in danger for whatever reason; once a particular item in the museum's 'list' of representative requirements has been filled, other similar buildings will not be reconstructed there. Selection of buildings proceeds in the hope that the final complete collection will form the suitable exhibition environment for any one particular building within it. Unlike many other open-air museums where reconstructions recreate domestic conditions at different historical periods, the entire folk park at the Ulster Folk and Transport Museum will provide a view of the vernacular part of the northern Irish built environment between about 1880 and 1910. The diachronic approach will be presented at the museum in other ways, although it is implicit in the historical development of each of the exhibit buildings up to its state about the turn of the century; and of course the houses originated at a variety of periods before then.

Viewing the collection as an entity is fundamental to an environmental approach to re-siting the various buildings in the folk park. Individually they are reconstructed on sites as close to their originals as possible, having regard to characteristics of slopes, aspect and relationships to roads and field systems (Fig. 269). Attention is also paid to spaces between the buildings, appropriate field boundary types being provided and suitable vegetation encouraged or planted. Nevertheless, at its best, the folk park will be a compromise, limited as it is to some sixty-five acres. Yet it will be an acceptable compromise insofar as its rural and urban sections together provide the necessary variety of settings to permit the whole collection to be as representative as possible.

In choosing and acquiring buildings for removal to the museum, an attempt is made always to work on structures already derelict, even partly ruinous, and certainly whose future is seriously endangered. Most have been buildings which would not have been the subject of *in situ* preservation projects. However, the museum has been able to accommodate an already statutorily listed building which finally could not be retained on its original site, and one or two such cases may occur in the future. Of its vernacular houses, only the Lismacloskey one conceivably would have been considered worthy of listing in the state in which it was found on the original site; it was acquired and moved to the museum site before statutory listing commenced, it was already uninhabited and being used to rear turkeys, and its fabric was deteriorating rapidly.

As a coherent collection, the Ulster Folk and Transport Museum allows viewing of any one of its vernacular houses in an architectural environment appropriate to a time when such houses were more nearly the norm. Accordingly the museum provides the necessary complement to viewing any vernacular house conserved *in situ* throughout the north of Ireland, where it now inevitably exists within an architectural environment, even a landscape, in which it becomes increasingly anachronistic. In this light the folk park at the museum fulfils a significant role in the range of architectural conservation and preservation agencies and legislation in the north of Ireland.[4]

Glossary

ABBREVIATIONS

Adams (a) 'Glossary of Household Terms' compiled by G.B. Adams, appended to Gailey, Alan 'Kitchen Furniture', *Ulster Folklife*, 12 (1966), 31–34.

Adams (b) 'A Note on the Term Thawluck', by G.B. Adams, appended to Aalen, F.H.A., 'Furnishings of Traditional Houses in the Wicklow Hills', *Ulster Folklife*, 13 (1967), 68.

Bliss Bliss, A.J., 'Thallage, Thawlogue and Thawluck', *Ulster Folklife*, 14 (1968), 28–33.

Counties Ant: Antrim; Arm: Armagh; Don: Donegal; Dn: Down; Ferm: Fermanagh; Ldy; Londonderry; Lo: Louth; Mon: Monaghan; Tyr: Tyrone.

DOST *Dictionary of the Older Scottish Tongue* (London, 1937 — in progress), eds. W.A. Craigie and A.J. Aitken.

EDD *The English Dialect Dictionary* (Oxford, reprint 1961), ed. J. Wright.

Dineen *An Irish-English Dictionary* (Dublin, 1927, reprinted 1965), by P.S. Dineen

Evans Evans, E. Estyn, *Irish Folk Ways* (London, 1957).

Fenton and Walker Fenton, Alexander and Walker, Bruce, *The Rural Architecture of Scotland* (Edinburgh, 1981).

Lucas (a) Lucas, A.T., 'Contributions to the History of the Irish House: A Possible Ancestry of the Bed Outshot', *Folk Life*, 8 (1970), 81–98.

Lucas (b) Lucas, A.T., 'Contributions to the History of the Irish House: Smokehole and Chimney', in *Gold Under the Furze* (Dublin, 1982), eds. Alan Gailey and Dáithí Ó hÓgáin.

Patterson Patterson, William Hugh, *A Glossary of Words in use in the Counties of Antrim and Down* (London, 1880).

Robinson Robinson, Philip, 'Vernacular Housing in Ulster in the Seventeenth Century', *Ulster Folklife*, 25 (1979), 1–28

SOED *The Shorter Oxford English Dictionary* (Oxford, 3rd edn. rev. with addns., 1959), revised and ed. C.T. Onions.

SND *The Scottish National Dictionary* (Edinburgh, n.d., but 1934–1976), eds. W. Grant and D.D. Murison.

Traynor Traynor, Michael, *The English Dialect of Donegal* (Dublin, 1953).

UFTM 611..., 641... Ulster Folk and Transport Museum questionnaires, 1961, no. 1, reply no. . . ., 1964, no. 1, reply no. . . . .

Wakelin Wakelin, Martyn F., 'Welsh Inlfuence in the West of England: Dialectal TALLET', *Folk Life*, 8 (1970), 72–80.

BALK. Also in a variety of spellings reflecting dialect variations in pronunciation.

1. BAAK, collar truss, Maghera, Ldy, UFTM 611 unnumbered; collar-beam, Dromore/Irvinestown, Tyr/Ferm, UFTM 611. BACK, 'The main roof was a back [? = truss] and wattles', Leckpatrick, Tyr, UFTM 611392. BAKS, rafters, Termoneeny, Ldy, UFTM 611349. BAWKS, referring either to timbers overlying purlins, or to collar beams, Kilskeery, Tyr, UFTM 611231.

2. BAK, big beam over the fire, Castledawson, Ldy, UFTM 611311. BAULK, clay-plastered chimney was 'supported on a plank of wood strapped across the kitchen', Knocknamuckley, Arm, UFTM 611022. BOCK, a sallyrod chimney rested on the bock, Cleenish, Ferm, UFTM 611287.

3. BACK, 'a protected canopy made of rods sloped from the roof down', Drumragh, Tyr, UFTM 611347. BOCK, a chimney canopy or brace, Tydavnet, Mon, UFTM 611287.

Meaning 1 above occurs widely in Britain (EDD), and Traynor for Don quotes this meaning, equating balk with either a 'couple' (q.v.) or a 'collar beam' (q.v.). It seems probable that the usage developed by extension of meaning in the sequence 1 to 3 set out here.

BAY. Shifts in meaning since the seventeenth century as applied to buildings in northern Ireland are discussed in Chapter 3; earlier usage refers to the spacing between roof trusses, later to the spacing between partition walls between rooms or units. Formal architectural usage often relates to piercing spacings on facades of buildings. Evolution from trusses to load-bearing walls supports the idea that application of the word to truss spacings is the earlier meaning; however, this is the opposite to what SOED outlines, which documents our later usage as early as the late eighteenth century, and the application to roof timbering spacings no earlier than 1823.

BENT. A name given to grass of a reedy habit; also to various grass-like rushes, sedges, etc. (SOED). In the north of Ireland the meaning is commonly restricted to the grass growing on sand or sandhills, otherwise known as marram (*Psamma arenaria*).

BLADE. Standard vernacular architectural term for one of the side members of a roof truss; usually needs qualification, as in 'cruck blade', 'collar-truss blade', etc. A blade may consist of a continuous timber, or of pieces of timber securely jointed together so that they serve as a continuous timber.

BOOLEY. Anglicisation of Irish *BUAILE* (Dineen: a second, temporary or disused milking place; used often in place names). Refers particularly to seasonal pastures and their associated temporary dwellings, often located in upland, coastal or insular places. Exploitation of such seasonal pastures referred to as 'booleying', and was often an integral part of 'rundale' (q.v.) organisation. In place names occurs particularly in the form -BOLEY.

BRACE. Responses to UFTM 611 provide two meanings:

1. More restricted application is to the bressumer (q.v.), the

256

horizontal cross timber parallel to the hearth wall which supports the outer face of the chimney breast. Attested for locations across south Ulster, usually in the form of a timber spanning the kitchen across the hearth area from front to rear of the house, in hearth-lobby type houses resting on, and sometimes terminating on, the end of the jamb wall (q.v.).
2. Wider usage relates the word to the chimney canopy supported on the bressumer, usually a wattled canopy, but occasionally a stone one (e.g. Seagoe, Arm, UFTM 611399; Taughboyne, Don, UFTM 611280). Many references in UFTM 611 except for Ant. This meaning cited by Patterson.

Similar usages quoted in SND for Scotland, and EDD suggests a Middle English derivation from Old French with the sense of two arms, or the span of two arms, which suggests that meaning 1 above may be earlier than 2, a view supported by Traynor.

Wider application of brace to the canopy perhaps arose from dialect confusion with 'breast', a standard word for the chimney canopy, or more especially for what superseded it, the stonework surrounding a chimney flue only partially contained within the hearth wall thickness.

BRESSUMER [= Breast + Summer]. A summer or beam extending horizontally over a large opening, and sustaining the whole superstructure of a wall, etc. SOED. As used in this book, and commonly in vernacular architectural writings, the word refers particularly to the beam spanning a hearth and supporting a chimney canopy or breast. See BRACE.

BYRE-DWELLING. Combined, unpartitioned quarters for people and cattle, especially milk cattle. An academic term in Irish vernacular architecture literature for houses of a type related to 'longhouses' in England and Wales, and to certain kinds of 'blackhouses' in Highland and insular Scotland.

CABIN, CABBIN. A booth, hut, (soldier's) tent or other temporary shelter (until 1649, now obsolete); a permanent mud of turf-built hovel or the like (Middle English), rhetorically 'a poor dwelling' (1598) — SOED. See Chapter 9 for full discussion of the northern Irish connotations and relationships in meaning with CREAT (q.v.) and COTTAGE (q.v.).

CAILLEACH. Irish, a veiled woman, a nun, a woman celibate; an old woman, a hag — Dineen. Applied in other connotations to the last or oldest of something, e.g. the last sheaf of harvest cut ceremonially. In northern and western Irish housing the word occasionally refers to the bed outshot (q.v.); perhaps this usage relates to the connotation of being veiled, with reference to the interior screening of the bed in the outshot from the remainder of the kitchen space.

COLLAR (BEAM). The cross member of an A-shaped roof truss.

COTTAGE. A small or humble dwelling-house — SOED. See Chapter 9.

COTTIER, COTTAR, COTTER. SOED suggests a different derivation from that of cottager (one who lives in a cottage) — a peasant who occupies a cottage belonging to a farm as a sort of out-servant (1552). However, this implies a tenurial status associated with the cottage, a connotation absent from SOED's definition, but according with Irish usage. The Irish form with -i-SOED dates from 1791. See Chapter 9.

COUPLE. A pair of blades tied by collar(s) and/or tie beam to form a roof truss; a roof truss, sometimes applies to a single blade (q.v.). Widespread colloquial use in the north of Ireland. SOED notes this meaning prior to 1611, and quotes the meaning principal rafter, i.e. a truss blade, as Middle English. However, Irish usage normally restricts COUPLE to blades in double-skin roof systems — see discussion under RAFTER in this glossary.

EDD cites references for Scotland, northern and south-western England. COUPLINGS, meaning couples, truss blades, attested for Banagher, Ldy, UFTM 611256.

CREAT, CREAGHT, CRATE, CREET, CRETE. Irish *caoraidheacht* (a foray or plundering of cattle, a foray party; cattle and their caretaker — Dineen) was variously anglicised in the seventeenth century and earlier. At that time the principal motivation for movement of people and cattle so denominated was economic, although some contexts make it clear that movements took place on account of war or civil disturbance. Irish *creata* (a frame or frame-work, as of a roof; the ribs of a house-roof — and comparable and related meanings — Dineen) was also anglicised with the same spellings, in some cases to apply to the temporary dwellings of people migrating with their cattle, in other contexts to describe wattled structures in any circumstances. Following Robinson, I reserve CREAT for the structures, and CREAGHT, CREAGHTING, for the people and the activity.

CRUCK. Functionally defined, a cruck blade, whether continuous or composed of wall and roof sections securely jointed together, provides fundamental support for the roof of a building largely independently of the side walls, and may stretch from the ground, or from a position significantly below the wall-heads, to the apex of the roof. Crucks, or cruck blades in pairs, form cruck trusses, which may be referred to as of tie-beam (q.v.) type, because a tie-beam joins the cruck blades at about wall-head height, or 'open' because there is no tie-beam, the truss being tied only by a collar (q.v.) or collars, and sometimes also by a yoke (q.v.). Cruck trusses, together with end crucks, can constitute an entire timber framework which will provide independent support for a roof. There are variations (perhaps historically later derived forms) in which the walls play a partial load-bearing role, e.g. in cases where crucks spring from a level within the walls above ground level. Observed examples range along a continuum of types at one end of which the crucks spring from ground level, and at the other end they become principal rafters (q.v.) or collar-truss blades springing from the wall-heads.

CÚILTEACH, and various anglicisations, e.g. COOLTYE. The usual Irish word for the bed outshot (q.v.), although this meaning is not provided by Dineen. Literally, back house. A full discussion of the various colloquial and literary connotations is found in Lucas (a).

DAIS. SOED provides the meaning, a seat, bench, in northern dialects deriving from Middle English, as well as the more widely known application, a raised platform in a hall for the high table or for seats of honour. EED (under DEAS) quotes usages with the general meaning of seat, from Scotland and northern England, and for Ireland (following Patterson) only the quotation cited in Chapter 9, a log used as a seat, and placed against the gable of a cottage at the back of the fire, that is, where a 'round about' fire was used.

DIRECT-ENTRY. Describes a kitchen layout where entry into the house from out-of-doors is straight into the living space at the opposite end of the room from the hearth. There may be a single door in the front wall, or there may also be an opposite door in the rear wall. In house classification in this book, developed forms where an entry lobby has been enclosed inside the entrance within the kitchen, or a passage inside the front door, or between front and rear doors provides for stairs rising to an upper floor or lofts or attics, are included in the family of plan types under this term.

DORMER. A projecting vertical window in the sloping roof of a house, having a roof of its own. Derives from the fact that it usually lights sleeping accommodation. Applied also in Ireland to a window in a gablet projecting above eaves level in the same plane as the house wall.

FARRA, FARRAY, FAROW, *FARADH.* Irish, a hen roost, a loft of any kind, a roofing — Dineen. Informant from Maghery, Arm, UFTM 611077 (in the hearth-lobby house type area) provides, FARRA, FARRAY, a loft over the hearth, between chimney canopy and front of house, over entrance lobby. Farra = hen roost or loft (obviously quoting Dineen) — it was customary in some houses to keep a few hens in a roost behind the door. Only very old people used the word. From Cleenish, Ferm, UFTM 611092 and Donagh, Mon, UFTM 611376, the meaning, lofts to either side of chimney canopy or brace; although both locations are within the hearth-lobby house type area, these definitions do not specify that the lofts concerned are in such houses, but this is probable.

FLAKE. SOED provides, a frame or rack for storing provisions, from Middle English; other connotations cited suggest it may be of wattle-work. EDD provides mainly northern English evidence for, a frame or rack suspended from the ceiling, on which oat-cake, bacon, etc., is laid to dry; and quotes south-west Scottish material suggesting such a flake was over the hearth area, cited also in SND. Patterson, for Dn and Ant defines flake, a hurdle on which flax was dried over the fire. Informant for Cleenish, Ferm, UFTM 611092, equates flake with brace, a sally-rod chimney canopy; perhaps an extension from the south-west Scottish meaning, in support of which Evans states that in Ulster a wattled shelf or loft resting on the brace-tree (bressumer) goes under various names, as skeagh, hurdle or flake.

FOREST CHIMNEY. Quoted by Lucas (b) from late medieval urban contexts in Leinster, describing wattled or timber chimney canopies. See Chapter 9.

FORLÉS. Lucas (b) has discussed this word exhaustively, and plausibly argues that it means, smoke-hole, when it occurs in early literary contexts, not, skylight, as formerly translated by literary scholars. See Chapter 7.

GABLE. The vertical triangular piece of wall at the end of a ridged roof, from the level of the eaves to the apex. The triangular-topped end wall of a building — SOED. Middle English adoption of Old French *gable, jable,* probably from Old Norse *gafl,* of the same meaning. Common dialectal rendering in northern Ireland is 'gavel', perhaps closer to the origins of the word than the modern standard form.

GALLETING. Insertion of pieces of stone of contrasting colour into mortar bonding masonry, mainly for decorative effect.

GROUP, GRIP, GRIPE. The stone-lined drain in a byre which drains liquid manure, usually through an opening in the bottom of a wall to the exterior. SOED quotes the derivation from Middle and Old English with the meaning, a trench, drain; gutter in a cowhouse (1825). EDD and SND provide usages widely for Scotland and northern England.

HAGGARD Bed. An informant for Loughguile, Ant, UFTM 611249 states, an old man used to call the outshot bed the haggard bed.

HALF-LOFT. A loft extending over a portion of the kitchen space at wall-head level in a single-storey vernacular house, normally at the end opposite the hearth and open to the fire, its outer edge often carried on a heavy beam spanning the kitchen from front wall to rear wall.

HALLAN, HOLLAN. UFTM 611 informants for Islandmagee, Connor (Ant), Warrenpoint, Garvaghy, Clonduff, Ballyculter, Dromara, Aghaderg and Banbridge (Dn) report the word, in a variety of spellings, applied to the jamb wall. Interestingly, some of these locations are at or just beyond the distributional limit mapped in this book for the hearth-lobby house type with jamb wall. Patterson also provides HADDIN, DOST notes HALLAND in late northern Middle English. EDD and SND provide mainly northern English and southern Scottish evidence for application to a screen or wall, often associated with the hearth, and some references are specifically to the form of screen wall between hearth and entrance normal in northern Ireland. Fenton and Walker cite references elsewhere in Scotland to other applications, e.g. in Lanarkshire to a chimney.

HEARTH-LOBBY. Describes a kitchen layout where entry is directly into the living space, adjacent to the hearth. A screen wall, usually provided with a small opening or window, separates entrance and hearth, and therefore forms a reception area or lobby immediately inside the entrance. The term can also be applied to various layouts developed from that outlined here, e.g. where a door closes between the end of the jamb wall and the inside of the front wall of the house, or where the jamb wall is continued across the whole of the front of the kitchen unit to form a passage-like reception hall.

HIP. A projecting inclined edge on a roof, extending from the ridge or apex to the eaves, and having a roof slope to each side — SOED. Therefore, in Irish vernacular buildings a hip or hipped roof is one with four sloping surfaces. On a HALF-HIP roof the inclined edges extending down from the ends of the ridge do not reach eaves level.

JAMB WALL. The screen wall between entrance and hearth in a lobby-entry kitchen layout. Interestingly, Patterson does not record the word although the jamb wall was common throughout much of the area to which his glossary refers, yet Traynor quotes the term with this meaning, although the lobby-entry house has not been recorded in the field in Don in the present study. The usage seems confined to Ireland, and fairly obviously is compounded from jamb, the side post or cheek of a fireplace — SOED, EDD.

KEEPER. Bent wooden thatching pin or scollop holding down a stretcher (q.v.) on the surface of a thatch roof by being driven over the latter and obliquely into the thatch material, Garrison, Ferm, UFTM 611215.

LOGIE HOLE. Ballinascreen, Ldy informant, UFTM 611382, cites this term for the window in a jamb wall. Meanings provided by EDD and SND for northern Ireland, Scotland and Cumberland suggest a small aperture or hole, e.g. in south Don, the eye of a lime kiln. Meanings are all associated with a kiln, hearth or fireside.

LONGHOUSE. See BYRE-DWELLING.

OSIER. A species of willow (*Salix viminalis*) — SOED. In Ireland more widely applied to a number of *Salix* species, all producing pliable rods or wattles (q.v.) suitable for basket making and for use as thatching scollops (q.v.).

OUTSHOT. The projection outside the rectangular plan of a northern or western Irish traditional house, located near the hearth in a corner (usually the rear corner) of the kitchen, accommodating a bed so that it obtrudes only minimally upon the living space. Commonly the bed in the outshot is screened from the remainder of the kitchen, e.g. by means of curtains or wooden doors. See also *Cailleach, Cúilteach.*

OUTSHUT. A space or room added at the rear (usually) of a house roofed by continuation of the slope of the main roof. It may extend along part or all of the length of the house, and its proportions, therefore, are greater than those of an OUTSHOT, which merely extends the kitchen space sufficiently to accommodate a single item of furniture.

PURLIN. A horizontal, longitudinal timber providing support for common rafters of a roof. It may be supported by a truss or trusses, or by transverse walls, including gables. Specifically qualified as ridge or side purlins according to position in the roof structure (collar purlins are yet unrecorded in northern Irish vernacular buildings), and as through or butt purlins according to relationship to supporting trusses. See Chapters 5 and 8. Widely known in Ulster in the dialect form PURLOIN.

QUOIN. One of the interlocking stones or bricks serving to form the corner of a building; a corner-stone.

RAFTER. One of the timbers which give slope and form to a roof, and bear the outer covering. PRINCIPAL RAFTERS are truss blades in butt-purlin roof systems where the backs of the principal and common rafters lie in a single plane — single-skin roofs. COMMON RAFTERS occur in single-skin roofs as above, and also in double-skin roofs overlying through purlins; common rafters always carry the roof covering, principal rafters only do so in single-skin roofs.

RANTLE-TREE. The beam across a chimney on which the crook is hung. Trainor suggests the term is of Scandinavian origin. Widely known also in Scotland and northern England — SND, EDD.

RENDER. To cover walling material with a coating, e.g. of plaster. Thus, RENDERING, plaster, e.g. of lime and sand, or earth, etc.

RIBS, RIBBERIES. Roof rafters, Banagher, Ldy, UFTM 611256. RIGGING-RIB, ridge purlin, Kilskeery, Tyr, UFTM 611231. These meanings are also in SOED, EDD. SND has only the application to purlins.

ROOM. An interior portion of a building divided off by walls or partitions, especially a chamber or apartment in a dwelling — SOED. In this book, when all of the walls surrounding such an apartment support the roof and share in front and rear exterior walls, unit or structural unit, is used. Colloquially, in a special sense, a room may be a formal parlour; SND, EDD quote this specialised meaning also for Scotland and northern England.

RUNDALE. A form of joint, co-operative or common occupancy or tenancy of land, each individual having rights to shares in each quality of land for cultivation, holdings therefore often being in scattered strips intermixed with those of neighbours. Common rights of rough grazing, turbary, and in coastal areas of seaweed collection, also featured regularly. Operation of cultivable land was often divided between infield, permanently worked, receiving all available animal manure, and outfield where lea land was broken in on lengthy or irregular rotations, unfertilised, and crops were taken for a few years until diminishing returns rendered continued tillage useless. Periodic reallocation of infield holdings sometimes was practised.

SADDLE. See under YOKE.

SCARFED JOINT. A joint whereby two timbers are connected longitudinally into a continuous piece, by having their ends in contact halved, notched or cut away to fit into each other with mutual overlapping. Such joints are often secured by pegging through the overlapping portions.

SCOBE, SCOLLOP. Rod of hazel, osier, briar, or other pliable wood, sharpened at both ends, for pinning down thatch material to the scraw in thatching a roof. SCOBE is known with this meaning also in Scotland, especially the south-west — SND. EDD quotes SCOLLOP for Pembrokeshire with the same meaning. Probably both words are from Gaelic *scolb*, a splinter of wood or bone, a split or thin stick, a wattle (e.g. Dineen). Scottish usage may be a direct translation between Gaelic and Scots, and not a borrowing from Ireland as the Pembrokeshire usage probably is.

SCRAW. From Irish *scraith*, a green sod, scraw, sward, etc. — Dineen. The turf underthatch on a roof. Occurs with this meaning also in south-west Scotland and the Isle of Man — EDD.

SHED, SHOP. The apartment or unit in a vernacular house, or attached to such, accommodating handlooms, in Ulster particularly for the weaving of linen.

SKEAGH, SKAY, SCEIH. Four informants from Arm (all from within the lobby-entry house type distribution) define the word as a loft of some kind. In north Arm UFTM 611109, and Ballymyre, Arm, UFTM 611176, lofting over the lobby between the jamb wall and the entrance; Derrynoose, Arm, UFTM 611358, (?) any half-loft; Maghery, Arm, UFTM 611077, loft over hearth area between chimney canopy and rear wall. Apart from Ballymyre, these locations are all just south of Lough Neagh. An informant for Moy, Tyr, UFTM 611394, does not clearly distinguish if the word refers to lofting or to the chimney canopy. From Irish *sciath*, shield, wing, wickerwork partition — Dineen. See Adams (a).

SMOKE WALK. The black track formed by deposits of soot and tar from smoke, especially peat smoke, as it makes its way up a wall face from a hearth to a chimney above, Cushendall area, Ant, UFTM 611372.

SPALDRICK. A thatcher's small rake for combing straws, Cullybackey, Ant, UFTM 611271. Perhaps from SPALD, to split, lay open, or to stretch, spread, lay out — EDD + RAKE.

SPURTLE, SPURTICLE. A thatcher's narrow, two-pronged fork with long handle, for pushing straw into the roof in thatching, Cullybackey, Ant, UFTM 611271. EDD quotes this meaning also from Cumberland, but other meanings, usually referring to long thin implements, e.g. for stirring, are more widespread in northern England and in Scotland.

SPY (WINDOW, HOLE). The aperture in a jamb wall between hearth and dwelling entrance. See LOGIE HOLE. EDD quotes this usage for Wexford where lobby-entry houses with jamb walls were common, and following Patterson, also for northern Ireland.

STAPPLE, STOPPLE. A handful or bundle of straw, usually folded over or tied at one end, used in thatching. EDD quotes the usage in west lowland and south-west Scotland, northern Ireland and north-west England. Patterson quotes the word for a knot of hair in a hair-brush. In the sense of a 'stopper', SOED cites the word for Middle English; its application to a bundle of straw thrust into a hole in a roof by means of a spurtle as a means of patching is therefore readily understandable.

STRETCHER. A scollop laid on the surface of a roof, held in place by keepers (q.v.), Garrison, Ferm, UFTM 611215.

THALLAGE. The word has been recorded a number of times from informants in south Arm (Adams (a)), neighbouring parts of south Mon (UFTM 641042b, Bliss) and in north Lo (Bliss), and refers to a 'half-loft', or in most cases more specifically to lofting to one or other side of the chimney canopy. By a separate linguistic derivation the ultimate source of this word also produced the Leinster forms THAWLOGUE and THAWLUCK, with comparable meanings (Adams (b), Bliss). Similarly related variants of TALLET are found in the west of England (Wakelin).

The ultimate etymon is Latin *tabulatum*, but it entered our area through the medium of Welsh *taflod* via a putative dialectal pronunciation *talod*. Studies of the word by Adams and Bliss agree on this sequence; they disagree on the probable dating of the borrowing into south Ulster speech, Adams suggesting this was in the thirteenth or fourteenth century, Bliss preferring a significantly later dating.

It is important to consider the dominant meaning of the word, lofting associated with (1) covering a hearth area, and (2) a chimney canopy (indeed, surely the former presupposes the latter, in view of the smokiness of a lofted area without a chimney?). Chapter 6 in this book shows that chimney canopies were only being introduced in the late sixteenth century, at the earliest. If the word and that to which it applied were introduced together, which seems likely in this case since the meaning is so specifically related to the presence of a chimney canopy both in the case of the recorded meanings and on account of sheer practicality, then the word must have been borrowed into south Ulster speech also no earlier than the late sixteenth century, a conclusion seemingly favouring Bliss's opinion.

Since the more recent source of the word was Welsh, it may have lain in the northern end of the Welsh borderland. Many British settlers to northern parts of Ireland are known to have migrated through the port of Chester, and some indeed came from its hinterland.

TIE (BEAM). A timber connecting truss blades, placed lower than a collar and usually at wall-head level. In a tie-beam truss it is jointed to the bottom ends of the truss blades resting on the wall-heads, but the blades of a cruck truss extend below a tie beam if one is present.

TOWNLAND. The smallest administrative territorial unit in Ireland, averaging about half a square mile in extent. Townland limits are intimately known throughout rural Ireland and provide the most readily used, detailed referencing system for locating houses (indeed, being still of greater utility than modern postal addresses!). Townland names have been cited wherever possible in this book.

TRINKET. From a south Arm informant quoted in Chapter 8; a name for the drain in a byre-dwelling. The word was widely used in northern Ireland, in the sense of a small, especially artificial water course, or drain. Cited in EDD, Patterson and Traynor for Ulster, and by Traynor for Dublin. In form TRINK, EDD and SND cite references for Ulster, and for Scotland south from Shetland to Fife in the east, with comparable meanings.

TRUSS. A frame, usually of timbers jointed firmly together, either resting on wall-heads or springing from some level between them and the ground, or from the ground itself, and serving with other trusses and/or transverse walls (including gables) to support other roof timbers, e.g. purlins and common rafters, and the roof covering.

UNIT, STRUCTURAL UNIT. A portion or apartment of a house, extending between and participating in the front and rear walls, surrounded by walls all of which are load-bearing and support the roof.

VERNACULAR. From Latin *vernaculus*, domestic, indigenous. Usage has been mainly linguistic, but since at least 1857 the word has been adjectivally used to denominate buildings — SOED. Definition of the word as used in this book is in Chapter 1.

WALL PLATE. A continuous timber extending along a wall-head, especially in timber-framed structures, from which rafters spring towards the apex of the roof.

WATTLE. Rods or stakes, interlaced with twigs or branches of trees, used to make fences, walls, and roofs. Also, rods and branches of trees collected for this purpose — SOED. The first meaning in SOED is more usually provided in WATTLE-WORK in Ireland.

YOKE. A short timber upon the upper edge of which a ridge purlin rests just below the apex of, and jointed to the faces of one side of the blades of, a roof truss. It contrasts with a saddle in that the latter is fixed across the tops or ends of the truss blades and supports the ridge purlin on its back. The directions of the pegs securing the respective joints identify clearly a yoke from a saddle. The pegs in yoke joints are driven horizontally through the yoke and truss blades; in saddle joints they are driven downwards, often vertically. Very few instances of saddles have been encountered in northern Irish roof trusses.

Notes and References

ABBREVIATIONS USED IN REFERENCES

A	*Antiquity*
B	*Béaloideas*
Devon Commission	*Report from and Evidence taken before H. M. Commissioners of Inquiry into the Law and Practice in respect of the Occupation of Land in Ireland* (1845)
FL	*Folk Life*
IFC MS	Irish Folklore Collections (formerly, Irish Folklore Commission), now, Department of Irish Folklore, University College, Dublin, manuscript
JCHAS	*Journal of the Cork Historical and Archaeological Society*
JRSAI	*Journal of the Royal Society of Antiquaries of Ireland*
MA	*Medieval Archaeology*
O S Mem	Ordnance Survey Memoir
Poor Inquiry (Ireland)	*First Report of the Commissioners of Inquiry into the Conditions of the Poorer Classes in Ireland* (1836)
PRIA	*Proceedings of the Royal Irish Academy*
PRONI	Public Record Office for Northern Ireland
TCD	Trinity College, Dublin
UF	*Ulster Folklife*
UFTM	Ulster Folk and Transport Museum; if followed by a six-digit number, this identifies a response to a questionnaire issued in the year denoted by the first two digits.
UFTMYB	*Ulster Folk and Transport Museum Year Book*
UJA	*Ulster Journal of Archaeology*
UM	Ulster Museum, Botanic Gardens, Belfast

Abbreviated back referencing, e.g. using op. cit., has been carried out only to works earlier cited within discrete chapters, and not across chapters. Within abbreviated back references, multiple publications by a single writer are suitably identified, usually by inclusion of the year of publication in the abbreviated reference.

Preface
1. Smith, Peter, 'The Architectural Personality of the British Isles', *Archaeologia Cambrensis*, 129 (1980), 1-36.
2. Gaillard-Bans, Patricia, *Aspects de l'architecture rurale en Europe occidentale* (UNESCO, n.d., but 1979).
3. Fenton, Alexander and Walker, Bruce, *The Rural Architecture of Scotland* (John Donald Publishers Ltd., Edinburgh, 1981).
4. Meirion-Jones, Gwyn I., *The Vernacular Architecture of Brittany* (John Donald Publishers Ltd., Edinburgh, 1982).
5. Ó Danachair, Caoimhín, *A Bibliography of Irish Ethnology and Folk Tradition* (Mercier Press, Dublin and Cork, 1978); Danaher, Kevin and Lysaght, Patricia, 'Supplement to A Bibliography of Irish Ethnology and Folklore', *Béaloideas*, 48-49 (1980-81), 206-227.

Chapter 1
1. Howard Wight Marshall uses this idea also, in Chapter 2, 'The Notion of Folk Architecture', in his *Folk Architecture of Little Dixie* (Columbia, 1981), 17-29.
2. Ibid., 19; Redfield, Robert, *Peasant Society and Culture* (Chicago, 1956), 70. In dealing with architecture, see Rapoport, Amos, *House Form and Culture* (Englewood Cliffs, 1969), 1-8; and Oliver, Paul, 'Primitive Dwelling and Vernacular Architecture', in idem (ed.), *Shelter and Society* (London, 1969), 7-12.
3. Redfield, Robert, op.cit., Chapter 3, 'The Social Organisation of Tradition', 70.
4. Craig, Maurice, *Classic Irish Houses of the Middle Size* (London, 1976), 17. The earliest dated northern Irish instance of the practice of carrying an internal wall up to roof-ridge height to carry the roof is in the National Trust's Ardress House in north county Armagh. The house originated as a relatively modest three-unit dwelling, probably harking back to English vernacular exemplars, in 1667. One of the two internal partition walls rising to the roof ridge is in brickwork of apparently contemporary character, and its relationship with the butt-purlin roof timbering system makes it clear that the wall treated thus is an original feature, taking the place that would otherwise be occupied by a principal-rafter truss. Much of the other internal partition wall is in a later brick size, but again, its relationship with the roof timbering suggests it more probably replaces an earlier brick wall than a roof truss.

5. Ó Danachair, Caoimhín, 'Hearth and Chimney in the Irish House', *B*, 16 (1946), Figs. 5 and 6 illustrate hearth walls of mass construction that do not support a roof structure; Aalen, F.H.A., 'The Evolution of the Traditional House in Western Ireland', *JRSAI*, 96 (1966), 50, also refers to such walls.

6. Browne, C.R. and Haddon, A.C., 'On the Ethnography of the Aran Islands, Co. Galway', *PRIA*, 3rd ser., 2 (1891-3), 768-834; Browne, C.R., 'The Ethnography of Inishbofin and Inishark, Co. Galway', ibid., 3 (1893-6), 587-649; idem, 'The Ethnography of Ballycroy, in the County of Mayo', ibid., 4 (1896-8), 74-111; idem, 'Ethnography of Clare Island and Inishturk, in the County of Mayo', ibid., 5 (1898-1900), 40-72; idem, 'Ethnography of Garumna and Lettermullen, in the County of Galway',' ibid., 5 (1898-1900), 223-268; idem, 'The Ethnography of Carna and Mweenish in the Parish of Moyruss, Connemara', ibid., 6 (1900-2), 503-534.

7. Mülhausen, Ludwig, 'Contributions to the study of the tangible material culture of the Gaeltacht', *JCHAS*, 38 (1933), 67-71 and ibid., 39 (1934), 41-51; idem, 'Haus und Hausbau in Teilinn (co. Donegal)', *Zeitschrift für keltische Philologie*, 22 (1941), 33-360.

8. Campbell, Å, 'Irish Fields and Houses', *B*, 5 (1935), 57-64; idem, 'Notes on the Irish House', *Folk Liv*, 1 (1937), 207-234 and ibid., 2 (1938), 173-96.

9. Ó Danachair, Caoimhín, 'Old House Types in Oighreacht ui Chonchubhair', *JRSAI*, 75 (1945), 204-212.

10. He discussed the postal enquiry system in Ó Danachair, Caoimhín, 'The questionnaire system', *B*, 15 (1945), 203-217.

11. Evans, E. Estyn, 'Donegal Survivals', *A*, 13 (1939), 207-222; idem, 'Some Survivals of the Irish Openfield System', *Geography*, 24 (1939), 24-36.

12. Idem, *Irish Heritage* (Dundalk, 1942).

13. Harrison, John, 'A Note on Two Houses in North County Dublin', *Sinsear*, 3 (1981), 108-111.

14. Aalen, F.H.A., op. cit. ref. 5 above; idem, 'Furnishings of Traditional Houses in the Wicklow Hills', *UF*, 13 (1967), 61-68; idem, 'The House Types of Gola Island, co. Donegal', *FL*, 8 (1970), 32-44.

15. McCourt, Desmond, 'The outshot house type and its distribution in county Londonderry', *UF*, 2 (1956), 27-34.

16. Idem, 'Cruck Trusses in north-west Ireland', *Gwerin*, 3 (1961), 165-185; idem, 'Roof-timbering techniques in Ulster: a classification', *FL*, 10 (1972), 118-130.

17. Buchanan, R.H., 'Thatch and Thatching in North-East Ireland', *Gwerin*, 1 (1957), 123-142.

18. Gailey, Alan, 'The Thatched Houses of Ulster', *UF*, 7 (1961), 9-18.

19. Robinson, Philip, 'Vernacular Housing in Ulster in the Seventeenth Century', *UF*, 25 (1979), 1-28; idem, 'Urban Vernacular Housing in Newtownards, County Down', *FL*, 17 (1979), 20-38.

20. E.g. Evans, E. Estyn, 'Gleanings from County Cavan', *UF*, 26 (1980), 1-7; idem, 'Traditional Houses of Rathlin Island', ibid., 19 (1973), 13-19.

21. Idem, *Irish Folk Ways* (London, 1957); Evans used the original basis of classification also in his *The Personality of Ireland* (Cambridge, 1973).

22. Innocent, C.F., *The Development of English Building Construction* (Cambridge, 1916).

23. Addy, S.O., *The Evolution of the English House* (London, 1898).

24. Fox, Sir Cyril and Raglan, Lord, *Monmouthshire Houses*, I (Cardiff, 1951), II (Cardiff, 1953), III (Cardiff, 1954). A basis for Welsh house studies was laid in Peate, Iorwerth C., *The Welsh House* (Liverpool, 1946).

25. Smith, Peter, *Houses of the Welsh Countryside* (London, 1975); Mercer, Eric, *English Vernacular Houses* (London, 1975).

26. Cordingley, R.A., 'British Historical Roof-types and their members: a classification', *Transactions of the Ancient Monuments Society*, new ser., 9 (1961), 73-118; Brunskill, R.W., 'A Systematic Procedure for recording English vernacular architecture', ibid., 13 (1965-6), 43-126; idem, *Illustrated Handbook of Vernacular Architecture* (London, 1970).

27. This point was probably not apparent to J.T. Smith when in 1963 he commented, 'In Ireland . . . the distributional study of house types has proceeded further than in England, . . .', in 'The Long-house in Monmouthshire: a Re-appraisal', in Foster, I. Ll. and Alcock, L. (eds.), *Culture and Environment* (London, 1963), 411-412.

28. *Ulster Folk Museum Act (Northern Ireland)*, 1958, section 2.

29. *An Archaeological Survey of County Down* (HMSO, Belfast, 1966).

30. Barley, M.W., *The English Farmhouse and Cottage* (London, 1961).

31. E.g. Adams, G.B., 'Glossary of Household Terms', appended to Gailey, Alan, 'Kitchen Furniture', *UF*, 12 (1966), 31-34.

32. Glassie, Henry, *Passing the Time* (Dublin, 1982), 379.

33. For the Welch collection, see Evans, E. Estyn and Turner, Brian, *Ireland's Eye* (Belfast, 1977).

34. 'Illustrations of the Irish Linen Industry in 1783 by William Hincks', *UF*, 23 (1977), 1-32.

35. *Poor Inquiry (Ireland), Appendix E* (London, 1836).

36. Original MSS of the Ordnance Survey memoirs are in the Library, Royal Irish Academy, Dublin. Microfilm copies may be consulted at the National Library, Dublin; Public Record Office for Northern Ireland, Belfast; the Library, The Queen's University, Belfast; and at the Ulster Folk and Transport Museum, Holywood, Co. Down. Some fragments of memoirs not included in the microfilms or at the Royal Irish Academy are housed at the Ordnance Survey of Ireland, Phoenix Park, Dublin.

37. Mason, W. Shaw, *A Statistical Account or Parochial Survey of Ireland*, I (Dublin, 1814), II (Dublin, 1816), III (Dublin, 1819).

38. A useful summary of the background to these county surveys is McClelland, Aiken, 'The Irish County Statistical Surveys', *UFTMYB*, 1967-8, 17-18.

39. Robinson, Philip, used this material to good effect in 'Vernacular Housing in Ulster in the Seventeenth Century', loc. cit. ref. 19.

40. A Breife Survey of the severall leases . . . within the Manor of Brownlowes Derry . . . 1667 . . ., PRONI, T 970/1.

41. Gailey, Alan, 'The Ballyhagan Inventories, 1716-1740', *FL*, 15 (1977), 36-64.

42. PRONI, Mic 80/3.
43. Greig, William, *General Report of the Gosford Estates in County Armagh 1821*, eds. F.M.L. Thompson and D. Tierney (Belfast, 1976).
44. General Report on the Estate of Drumbanagher . . . by William Greig . . . 1820, PRONI, T 3097; original MS in the possession of Mrs. Don Best, Drumbanagher, Co. Armagh, to whom the author is indebted for initial access to the document.
45. Statistical Survey of the Estate of the Most Noble the Marquis of Londonderry situate in the County of Down 1848, by Maurice Collis, PRONI, T 1536/4; surveys also by Maurice Collis of the Trinity College Estates, dated 1845 but enumerated in 1843, TCD, Mun. V, 79/1, 3-7.
46. Glassie puts it well: 'Houses are constantly rebuilt. Scholars accustomed to traditions in which rebuilding is rare or neatly periodic become frustrated by the impossibility of assigning dates to Irish houses. New houses contain early stone corners; homes expand and shrink and shift over old sites, continually absorbing diverse materials into their walls. The roof is frequently repaired and re-thatched, and inside it is the same.' Glassie, Henry, op. cit., 390.
47. Baillie, M.G.L., 'Dendrochronology as a Tool for the Dating of Vernacular Buildings in the North of Ireland', *VA*, 7 (1976), 3-10. See also idem, *Tree-Ring Dating and Archaeology* (London, 1982), Chapters 5 to 8.

Chapter 2
1. Herity, Michael and Eogan, George, *Ireland in Prehistory* (London, 1977), 44-50; see also O'Riordan, S.P., 'Lough Gur Excavations: Neolithic and Bronze Age Houses on Knockadoon', *PRIA*, 56 C (1954), 297-459.
2. Ó Nualláin, Seán, 'A Neolithic House at Ballyglass near Ballycastle, Co. Mayo', *JRSAI*, 102 (1972), 49-57; ApSimon, A. M., 'An Early Neolithic House in Co. Tyrone', *JRSAI*, 99 (1969), 165-168.
3. Herity, M. and Eogan, G., op. cit., 70, 99, 103-106.
4. Ibid., 125, 129, 142, 170-1, 189.
5. Ó Riordáin, S.P., 'Excavations at Cush', *PRIA*, 45 C (1940), 83-181.
6. Lynn, C.J., 'Early Christian Period Domestic Structures: A Change from Round to Rectangular Plans?', *Irish Archaeological Research Forum*, 5 (1978), 36, 37.
7. Ibid., 38. In the 'Martyrology of Donegal', we learn that Mochaoi, abbot of Nendrum in east county Down, 'went with seven young men to cut wattles to make a church'; Mochaoi is said to have been alive in 496: quoted in Mitchell, A., 'Wattled Houses in Scotland', *A*, 13 (1939), 343-4.
8. Lynn, C.J., op. cit., for lists of investigated sites, 31-6.
9. Murray, Hilary, 'Documentary evidence for domestic buildings in Ireland c. 400-1200 in the light of archaeology', *MA*, 23 (1979), 81-2.
10. Ibid., 82-3; for *Críth Gablach*, see Binchy, D.A. (ed.), *Críth Gablach* (Dublin, 1970).
11. Murray, H., op. cit., 82.
12. Quoted in Radford, C.A., 'The Earliest Irish Churches', *UJA*, 3rd ser., 40 (1977), 1-11.
13. Murray, H., op. cit., 93.
14. Ibid., 85-87; see also Lucas, A.T., 'Wattle and Straw Mat Doors in Ireland', *Studia Ethnographica Upsaliensia*, 11 (1957), 32-4.
15. Lucas, A.T., 'Contributions to the Study of the Irish House: a possible ancestry of the bed outshot', *FL*, 8 (1970), 81-98.
16. Binchy, D.A. (ed.), op. cit., 4, lines 99-100.
17. *The Ancient Laws of Ireland*, IV (Dublin, 1879), 313.
18. Murray, H., op. cit., 91-2.
19. For some discussion of the settlement background to this apparent problem, see Proudfoot, V.B., 'Clachans in Ireland', *Gwerin*, 2 (1959), 110-122; idem, 'The People of the Forths', *UF*, 1 (1955), 25-6.
20. Murray, H., op. cit., 93-4.
21. The situation remains essentially as described in Glasscock, R.E., 'The Study of Deserted Medieval Settlements in Ireland (to 1968)', in Beresford, Maurice and Hurst, John (eds.), *Deserted Medieval Villages* (London, 1971). 289-291.
22. Ó Riordáin, S.P. and Hunt, John, 'Medieval Dwellings at Caherguillamore, Co. Limerick', *JRSAI*, 72 (1942), 37-63. Publication of the Tildarg excavation is eagerly awaited. I am indebted to the excavator, Mr. N. F. Brannon, for preliminary information.
23. Davison, B.K., 'Excavations at Ballynarry, Co. Down', *UJA*, 3rd ser., 24-25 (1961-62), 37-9.
24. Waterman, D.W., 'Excavations at Ballyfounder rath, Co. Down', *UJA*, 3rd ser., 21 (1958), 31-61.
25. Idem, 'A pair of raths at Glenkeen, Co. Derry', *UJA*, 3rd ser., 30 (1967), 49-52.
26. Rynne, E., 'Some destroyed sites at Shannon airport, Co. Clare', *PRIA*, 63 C (1962-64), 245-277.
27. Leask, H.G. and Macalister, R.A.S., 'Liathmore-Mochoemóg (Leigh), County Tipperary', *PRIA*, 51 C (1946), 1-14.
28. Robinson, Philip. 'Vernacular Housing in Ulster in the Seventeenth Century', *UF*, 25 (1979), 1-13.
29. Quoted in Prendergast, J.P., 'The Ulster creaghts', *Proceedings and Transactions of the Kilkenny and South-East of Ireland Archaeological Society*, 3 (1854-55), 422.
30. *Calendar of State Papers, Ireland, 1608-1610* (London, 1875), 65.
31. *Memoirs of Edward Ludlow*, I (Edinburgh, 1751), 365.
32. *Calendar of State Papers relating to English Affairs (Rome), 1572-1578* (London, 1923), 62.
33. Ó Danachair, Caoimhín, 'Representations of Houses on some Irish Maps of 1600', in Jenkins, J.G. (ed.), *Studies in Folk Life* (London, 1969), 93-4.
34. Robinson, P., op. cit., 3.
35. Hayes-McCoy, G.A. (ed.), *Ulster and Other Irish Maps c. 1600* (Dublin, 1964), 6 pl. III.
36. Quoted in Camblin, G., *The Town in Ulster* (Belfast, 1951), 15. With reference to the north-east of Ireland, a Gaelic satire of c. 1595 tells of: '. . . the hungry kerne, That did not build a crib-house of rods on a mountain.' Quoted in *UJA*, 2nd ser., 14 (1908), 43.
37. Hill, G. (ed.), *The Montgomery Manuscripts, 1603-1706* (Belfast, 1869), 59.
38. Robinson, P., op. cit., 6.
39. Ibid., 7-13.
40. Quoted in Treadwell, V., 'The Plantation of Donegal — A Survey', *Donegal Annual*, 3 (1954), 7, 42.

T

41. Ibid., 41.
42. *Hastings Manuscripts*, IV (London, 1947), 163.
43. Ibid., 168.
44. Ibid.
45. Ibid., 173.
46. Ibid., 164.
47. Whyte, Ian D., 'Rural Housing in Lowland Scotland in the Seventeenth Century: The Evidence of Estate Papers', *Scottish Studies*, 19 (1975), 62-5.
48. Robinson, P., op. cit., 9.
49. Hayes-McCoy, G.A. (ed.), op. cit. ref. 35 above; these maps are discussed in Ó Danachair, C., op. cit. ref. 33 above, 92-103, and in Robinson, P., op. cit. ref. 26 above, 10-12.
50. Robinson, P., op. cit., 11.
51. Chart, D.A. (ed.), *Londonderry and the London Companies, 1609-1629: The Phillips Manuscripts* (Belfast, 1928); these maps are discussed in Robinson, P., op. cit., 12.

Chapter 3
1. Aalen, F.H.A., 'The House Types of Gola Island, county Donegal', *FL*, 8 (1970), 34.
2. O S Mem, Box 40, I, 5 (1835-6), 59.
3. Robinson, Philip, 'Vernacular Housing in Ulster in the Seventeenth Century', *UF*, 25 (1979), 17, 19.
4. *Memoirs of Edward Ludlow*, I (Edinburgh, 1751), 356.
5. PRONI, T 2985, 54-56; see Buchanan, Gwen, 'Talk of the Ten Towns by Francis Chambers', *UF*, 20 (1974), 61-4.
6. Hill, Lord George, *Facts from Gweedore*, 5th edn. (London, 1887, first published 1845; reprinted Belfast 1971), 40-1. Henry Morris provided a graphic account of communal housebuilding following a wedding in the Dungloe area of west Donegal, to the south of Gweedore, in 1909, in 'Reliques of the Brehon Laws and other Ancient Usages in Ulster', *B*, 9 (1939), 292-3.
7. O'Dowd, Anne, *Meitheal* (Dublin, 1981), 147, 51.
8. Synge, John M., *The Aran Islands* (London, 1912), 156. The community of architectural experience in rural districts in recent times is neatly illustrated in Glassie's observation about the design of a house in west Fermanagh: '. . . he went to his neighbour, the mason, and described the house in his mind, designed "on the track" of one in which he had lived in Drumbargy. The mason's wife sketched the plans. The mason suggested an additional door to ease internal flow, Paddy agreed, and the house was built down the hill in Rossdoney. They staked it out together, and Mr. Moore laid it up, while Mr. McBrien brought in the material, mixing the mortar, cutting the timber himself from land near the Arney . . . he sits in an object formed within his own control.' Glassie, Henry, *Passing the Time* (Dublin, 1982), 578-9.
9. UFTM 611032. Glassie reports the belief in mid-west Fermanagh that one should not build to the east or south of an existing house, and rationalises this with the comment that, obviously, such new construction would perhaps keep natural warmth and light from the sun out of the old kitchen: Glassie, Henry, op. cit., 344.
10. Ó Súilleabháin, Seán, 'Foundation Sacrifices', *JRSAI*, 75 (1945), 45-52.
11. Gailey, Alan, 'Horse Skulls under a County Down Farmhouse Floor', *UFTMYB*, 1968-69, 18-20.
12. UFTM 611307.
13. Gailey, Alan, 'The Thatched Houses of Ulster', *UF*, 7 (1961), 16-17.
14. O S Mem, Box 11, IV, 4 (1840), B, 59-61.
15. Young, Arthur, *A Tour in Ireland . . . in the Years 1776-1779)*, I (Dublin, 1780), 186, 206, 214.
16. PRONI, D 1939/22/3/9.
17. M'Parlan, James, *Statistical Account of the County of Donegal* (Dublin, 1802), 65.
18. Idem, *Statistical Survey of the County of Leitrim* (Dublin, 1802), 63; idem, *Statistical Survey of the County of Sligo* (Dublin, 1802), 70.
19. Coote, Sir Charles, *Statistical Survey of the County of Cavan* (Dublin, 1802), 86.
20. Idem, *Statistical Survey of the County of Armagh* (Dublin, 1804), 251.
21. M'Evoy, John, *Statistical Survey of the County of Tyrone* (Dublin, 1802), 148.
22. Sampson, G. Vaughan, *Statistical Survey of the County of Londonderry* (Dublin, 1802), 301; Sampson republished his costings in his *A Memoir, explanatory of the Chart and Survey of the County of Londonderry, Ireland* (London, 1814), 277.
23. *Devon Comm., Evidence*, I (Dublin, 1845), witness 127, questions 14-17.
24. Binns, Jonathan, *The Miseries and Beauties of Ireland*, I (London, 1837), 111-3.
25. O S Mem, Box 49 (IV), II, 1 (1835), 10.
26. Binns, J., op. cit. I, 50-2, 215-6.
27. *Poor Inquiry (Ireland), Appendix E, Suppt.* (London, 1836), 48, 64, 66, 66-7, 65.
28. PRONI, D 627/243.
29. PRONI, D 1939/15/10/8, 21.
30. Murray, Hilary, 'Documentary Evidence for domestic buildings in Ireland *c.* 400-1200 in the light of archaeology', *MA*, 23 (1979), 83.
31. Richmond, I.A., 'The Irish Analogues for the Romano-British Barn Dwelling', *Journal of Roman Studies*, 23 (1932), 101-2.
32. Robinson, P., op. cit., 15.
33. PRONI, D 1932/8/15.
34. PRONI, T 970/1, f. 67.
35. PRONI, Mic 80/3, ff. 11-3, 63-4, 29-31.
36. PRONI, D 859/6.
37. PRONI, T 877/127; D 1741/12; D 2394/1; D 1932/8/101.
38. O S Mem, Box 39, I, 2 (1835), 37.
39. Mason, W. Shaw, *Statistical Account or Parochial Survey of Ireland*, I (Dublin, 1814), 311-2.
40. *Poor Inquiry (Ireland), Appendix E, Suppt.*, 355.
41. Binns, J., op. cit. I, 291-2.
42. Gailey, Alan, 'The Housing of the Rural Poor in Nineteenth-Century Ulster', *UF*, 22 (1976), 34-58.
43. This limitation was cited by Evans for houses he studied in the 1930s in north-west Donegal: Evans, E. Estyn, 'Donegal Survivals', *A*, 13 (1939), 212.
44. PRONI, D 2223/2/18.
45. PRONI, D 266/219.
46. O S Mem, Box 18, XVI, 2 (1835), 14.

47. *Poor Inquiry (Ireland), Appendix E, Suppt.*, for Armagh, 63, 281; for Monaghan 66-7 and Binns, J., op. cit. I, 215-6.
48. The use of 'bay' referring only to the arrangement of facade piercing will be found in many of the district lists of buildings published by the Ulster Architectural Heritage Society.
49. Wakefield, Edward, *An Account of Ireland, Statistical and Political,* II (London, 1812), 728-9.
50. Ibid., 685-8.
51. Connell, K.H., *The Population of Ireland, 1750-1845* (Oxford, 1950), 12.
52. PRONI, T 970/1.
53. Dubourdieu, Rev. John, *Statistical Survey of the County of Down* (Dublin, 1802), 33.
54. Wakefield, E., op. cit. II, 688.
55. Hill, Lord G., op. cit., 16.
56. Detailed discussion of the census data on one-room houses is available in Gailey, A., op. cit. (1976), 36-8.
57. PRONI, Mic 80/3, ff. 26-8, 21-5, 40-1.
58. PRONI, T 848/1, 36, 29, 49.
59. Atkinson, A., *Ireland Exhibited to England . . .* (London, 1823), 284-5 (known to have been written in 1816).
60. Figures derived from PRONI, T 1536/4, and TCD, Mun. V, 79/1, 3-7.

Chapter 4
1. Quoted in Robinson, Philip, ' "English" Houses Built at Moneymore, county Londonderry, c. 1615', *Post-Medieval Archaeology, 17 (1983),* forthcoming.
2. PRONI, Mic 80/3, ff, 29-31, 40-1.
3. 4 Anne, Cap. 9, Section IX.
4. IFC MS 1076, 1372.
5. Evans, E. Estyn, 'Gleanings from County Cavan', *UF,* 26 (1980), 6.
6. IFC MS 1077, 232.
7. See the maps reproduced in Chart, D.A. (ed.), *Londonderry and the London Companies, 1609-1629: The Phillips Manuscripts* (Belfast, 1928).
8. Moody, T.W., *The Londonderry Plantation, 1609-1641* (Belfast, 1939), 308. These houses are fully discussed in Robinson, Philip, 'Vernacular Housing in Ulster in the Seventeenth Century', *UF,* 25 (1979), 13-24; see also Blades, Brooke S., ' "In the Manner of England": Tenant Housing in the Londonderry Plantation', *UF,* 27 (1981), 39-56.
9. PRONI, D 1932/8/15.
10. PRONI, D 652/1.
11. Young, R.M., 'An Account of the Barony of O'Neiland, Co. Armagh, in 1682', *UJA,* 2nd ser., 4 (1898), 241.
12. O S Mem, Ballyscullion parish, in PRONI, Mic 6/210.2.
13. O S Mem, Box 10, IV, 3 (1837), 36.
14. O S Mem, Box 43, I, 3 (1836), 14.
15. IFC MS 1076, 142, quoted in Ó Danachair, Caoimhín, 'Materials and Methods in Irish Traditional Building', *JRSAI,* 87 (1957), 73.
16. Ó Danachair, C., op. cit., 62.
17. PRONI, T 3381/10/2.
18. PRONI, Mic 80/3.
19. Evans, E. Estyn, 'Sod and Turf Houses in Ireland', in Jenkins, J.G. (ed.), *Studies in Folk Life* (London, 1969), 80-90.
20. Thompson, George, McCourt, Desmond and Gailey, Alan, 'The First Ulster Folk Museum Exhibit: The Magilligan Cottier House', *UF,* 10 (1964), 25, 27.
21. Evans, E.E., op. cit. (1980), 6. It has been recorded in recent times in west Fermanagh that upland sod, 'sod with a kind of a grip in it that wouldn't moulder away', was cut with spades, laid in courses like bricks, clay being used as mortar, for building both dwellings and outhouses: IFC MS 1076, 134, reported in Glassie, Henry, *Passing the Time* (Dublin, 1982), 439.
22. Evans, E.E., op. cit. (1969), 83-5.
23. Robinson, P., op. cit. (1979), 21.
24. Figures derived from PRONI, T 1536/4, and TCD, Mun. V, 79/1, 3-7.
25. PRONI, T 1536/4.
26. The Rev. Mr. Henery's Account of the County of Fermanagh written Ao. 1739, Henry's Topographical Descriptions, Cathedral Library, Armagh, MS g.I.14.
27. Young, Arthur, *A Tour in Ireland . . . in the Years 1776-1779,* I (Dublin, 1780), 239.
28. O S Mem, Box 26, VII, 1 (1834), Clones parish, counties Monaghan/Fermanagh.
29. UFTM 611060.
30. Bigger, F.J., 'Some Notes on the Churches of Saint Tassach of Raholp and Saint Nicholas of Ardtole and their surroundings, in the Barony of Lecale in Down', *JRSAI,* 46 (1916), 123.
31. Barrow, John, *A Tour Round Ireland . . . in the Autumn of 1835* (London, 1836), 116.
32. Pilson, Aynsworth, 'Reminiscences of the Latter Part of the Eighteenth Century', *Downpatrick Recorder,* 8 Sept. 1855; idem, 'Reminiscences of the Middle and Latter End of the 18th Century', ibid., 31 Dec. 1859.
33. PRONI, T 970/1.
34. M'Evoy, John, *Statistical Survey of the County of Tyrone* (Dublin, 1802), 95.
35. This suggestion, made by a number of writers, is best supported by the recently published, earliest known clear reference to earth walling in Ireland, from an Anglo-Norman context in the manor of Insula, county Kerry, dated 1298: extent of the Irish lands of Thomas Fitz Maurice, 'one hall of forks constructed with earth walls and straw thatch . . .', Public Record Office, London, E101/233(6), quoted in Alcock, N.W. and Hall, Sir R. de Z., 'Documentary evidence for crucks', in Alcock, N.W., *Cruck Construction. An Introduction and Catalogue* (London, 1981). 33.
36. Robinson, P., op. cit. (1979), 13, 21.
37. PRONI, Mic 80/3, ff. 5-8, 8-10, 11-3, 44-5, 54-6, 65-6.
38. PRONI, T 848/1, 43, 45.
39. PRONI, Mic 80/3, ff. 63-4.
40. Young, A. op. cit. I, 184.
41. Wakefield, Edward, *An Account of Ireland, Statistical and Political,* II (London, 1812), 794.
42. O S Mem, Box 23, XXXVII, 1 (1834), 11.
43. Sampson, G. Vaughan, *Statistical Survey of the County of Londonderry* (Dublin, 1802), 298.
44. Benn, George, *History of the Town of Belfast* (Belfast, 1823), 161; this was earlier reported by Dubourdieu, Rev. John, *Statistical Survey of the County of Antrim* (Dublin, 1812), 145.

45. 'Y', 'On the Improvement of the Habitations of the Poor in Ireland', *Dublin Penny Journal*, 1, No. 40, 30 March, 1833, 316-7.
46. PRONI, T 1888/1.
47. Binns, Jonathan, *The Miseries and Beauties of Ireland*, I (London, 1837), 157.
48. M'Evoy, J., op. cit., 95.
49. Ibid., 96.
50. O S Mem, Box 49, (IV), II, 1 (1835), 10.
51. Ó Danachair, C., op. cit., 68.
52. Robinson, P., op. cit. (1979), 21; Meek, H. and Jope, E.M., 'The Use of Brick in the North of Ireland, 1580-1640', appendix to idem, 'The Castle of Newtownstewart, Co. Tyrone', *UJA*, 3rd ser., 21 (1958), 113-4.
53. B(igger), F.J., 'Sir Moyses Hill at Malone in 1635', *UJA*, 2nd ser., 8 (1902), 49.
54. *Belfast News-Letter*, advertisement, 5 March 1754.
55. PRONI, T 2541/IA1/6c.
56. McCourt, Desmond, 'Some Cruck-framed Buildings in Donegal and Derry', *UF*, 11 (1965), 42-3.
57. PRONI, Mic 80/3, ff. 21-5, 61-2.
58. PRONI, T 848/1, 36, 49.
59. PRONI, T 877/122; D 1939/22/3/9; D 1932/8/101.
60. Coote, Sir Charles, *Statistical Survey of the County of Monaghan* (Dublin, 1801), 99.
61. Sampson, G.V., op.cit., 298.
62. Dubourdieu, J., op. cit., 146.
63. O S Mem, Box 27, I, 1 (1834); Box 27, IV, 1 (1835). Glassie, Henry, op. cit., 552-571, provides an excellent account of the end of the brick-making activity in this area.
64. PRONI, T 970/1, passim.
65. Ó Danachair, C., op. cit., 66, 67.
66. O S Mem, Box 27, I, 1 (1834).
67. O S Mem, Box 11, II, 2 (n.d.).
68. O S Mem, Box 7, 5, Vol. III (1839), 47.
69. O S Mem, Box 37, II, 3.
70. *Poor Inquiry (Ireland), Appendix E, Suppt.*, 294.
71. O S Mem, Box 49, IV, II, 1 (1835), 10.
72. PRONI, D 2223/2/18.
73. Mason, W. Shaw, *Statistical Account or Parochial Survey of Ireland*, II (Dublin, 1816), 233; Atkinson, A., *Ireland Exhibited to England . . .* (London, 1823), 284-5.
74. O S Mem, Box 3, V, 4 (1839), 26.
75. O S Mem, Box 18, VII, 2 (1835), 9.
76. O S Mem, Box 37, III, 5 (1837), 18.
77. Robinson, P., op. cit. (1979), 12.
78. See the maps of the Phillips MSS, reproduced in Chart, D.A. (ed.), op. cit; see also Robinson, P., op. cit. (1979), 17.
79. PRONI, T 970/1, 87.
80. Johnston, John Moore, 'A Description of the Parish of Magheradroll in the County of Down', *Heterogenea* (Downpatrick, 1803), 20; this was first published in *Hibernian Magazine*, Sept. 1797, but was written in 1791.
81. Coote, Sir Charles, *Statistical Survey of the County of Armagh* (Dublin, 1804), 134.
82. Johnston, John Moore, 'A Description of the half barony of Masseereene . . .', *Heterogenea* (Downpatrick, 1803), 127, referring to houses on the Hertford estate.

83. Dubourdieu, J., op. cit., 145.
84. Sampson, G.V., op. cit., 300.
85. Johnston, John Moore, 'To the Patriotic Committee conducting the farming or agricultural Society of Down', *Heterogenea* (Downpatrick, 1803), 89-90.
86. Mason, W.S., op. cit. I (Dublin, 1814), 611.
87. O S Mem, Box 4, IV, 4 (1838); Box 4, IV, 2 (1837), 20.
88. O S Mem, Box 11, IV, 1 (1840), 13; Box 11, IV, 4 (1840), 60.
89. O S Mem, Box 42, I, 2 (1837), 28: Kilcronaghan; Box 43, I, 3 (1836): Lissan.
90. O S Mem, Box 1, III, 2 (1837), 36: Aghalee; Box 1, II, 2 (1835), 34: Aghagallon.
91. O S Mem, Box 2, V, 2 (1840), 9: Inver; Box 16, IV, 2 (1840), 51.
92. O S Mem, Box 21, IX, 1 (1821), 42.
93. O S Mem, Box 51, X, 5 (1825).
94. O S Mem, Box 21, III, 1 (1821), 9: Clonleigh; Box 21, VII, 1 (1834), 4: Desertagney.
95. Hill, Lord George, *Facts from Gweedore*, 5th edn. (London, 1887; Belfast, 1971), 43, 45.
96. UFTM, Colhoun photograph collection.
97. Evans, E. Estyn, 'Traditional Houses of Rathlin Island', *UF*, 19 (1973), 14.
98. O S Mem, Box 12, III, 2 (1838), 50.
99. O S Mem, Box 37, I, 3 (1836).
100. O S Mem, Box 14, VIII, 1 (1838), 19.
101. O S Mem, Box 51, V, 1 (1835).
102. O S Mem, Box 3, V, 4 (1839), 27-8.
103. PRONI, D 3464/1.
104. Glassie, H., op. cit., 390.

Chapter 5
1. PRONI, D 859/6.
2. PRONI, D 2223/2/18.
3. Registry of Deeds, Dublin: lease of 1712, Lavehill (now Longfield) townland, Laragh Parish, county Cavan.
4. M'Evoy, John, *Statistical Survey of the County of Tyrone* (Dublin, 1802), 96.
5. PRONI, T 2125/3/1.
6. UFTM WAG 2520.
7. McCracken, Eileen, *The Irish Woods since Tudor Times* (Newton Abbot, 1971).
8. Gailey, Alan, 'A House from Gloverstown, Lismacloskey, County Antrim', *UF*, 20 (1974), 34-7.
9. *Ordnance Survey Memoir, Antrim* (Belfast, 1969), 14.
10. PRONI, D 859/6.
11. PRONI, D 75. Traditionally oak was insisted upon for jointed crucks in earth-wall houses in west Fermanagh because it was regarded as especially resistant to damp and therefore to rotting: Glassie, Henry, *Passing the Time* (Dublin, 1982), 527.
12. *Ancient Laws of Ireland*, I (Dublin, 1865), 130-3.
13. Moryson, Fynes, *An Itinerary*, IV (Glasgow, 1908), 196.
14. Petty, Sir William, *Political Anatomy of Ireland* (London, 1691), 82.
15. Mason, W. Shaw, *Statistical Account or Parochial Survey of Ireland*, II (Dublin, 1816), 82: Ballymoyer (sic) parish, county Armagh.
16. O S Mem, Box 22, VII, Lough Swilly No. 5 Papers.
17. 'Belfastiensis' (Ward, I.W.), 'Shipwreck at Tyrella, County Down', *UJA*, 2nd ser., 11 (1905), 139.

18. M'Evoy, J., op. cit., 147-8.
19. Coote, Sir Charles, *Statistical Survey of the County of Armagh* (Dublin, 1804), 134.
20. Mason, W.S., op. cit. I (Dublin, 1814), 289.
21. Idem, op. cit. II (Dublin, 1816), 247.
22. Donaldson, John, *A Historical and Statistical Account of the Barony of Upper Fews in the County of Armagh* (1838; republished Dundalk, 1923), 49 (written 1818).
23. O S Mem, Box 27, III, 1 (1835).
24. O S Mem, Box 49, XIX, 1 (1838), 5.
25. O S Mem, Box 21, iI, 1 (1835), 47; Box 21, X, 1 (1836), 19; Box 22, II, 1 (1834); Box 22, X, 1 (1834), 57.
26. Evidence from IFC MSS, quoted in A.T. Lucas's excellent study, 'Bog Wood. A Study in Rural Economy', *B, 23* (1954), 84.
27. Pilson, Aynsworth, 'Reminiscences of the Last Century', *Downpatrick Recorder*, 16 Dec. 1854.
28. *Ordnance Survey Memoir, County Londonderry. Vol. I. Templemore Parish* (Dublin, 1837), 200.
29. O S Mem, Box 4, II, 5 (1840); Box 7, 5, Vol. III (1839), 242-3; Box 14, III, 3 (1835).
30. O S Mem, Box 23, XXVIII, 1 (1836), 34.
31. O S Mem, Box 25, XII, 1 (1836), 15-6.
32. O S Mem, Box 25, I, 1 (183?), 46-7; Box 25, I, 3 (183?), 3.
33. O S Mem, Box 25, VII, 2 (1837), 17.
34. O S Mem, Box 45, I, 4 (1836).
35. O S Mem, Box 44, I, 5 (1836); Box 40, I, 5 (1835-36), 59; Box 30, II, 1 (1835), App. 3.
36. O S Mem, Box 38, I, 15 (183?).
37. O S Mem, Box 27, VI, 1 (1834).
38. Evans, E. Estyn, 'Traditional Houses of Rathlin Island', *UF, 19* (1973), 16.
39. Gailey, Alan, 'Traditional Houses at Riasc, near Ballyferriter', *Journal of the Kerry Archaeological and Historical Society*, 14 (1981), 94-111.
40. These references are quoted in Ó Danachair Caoimhín, 'Materials and Methods in Irish Traditional Building', *JRSAI*, 87 (1957), 63, 72-3.
41. Dutton, Hely, *Statistical Survey of the County of Galway* (Dublin, 1824), 343.
42. IFC MS 1076, 83a.
43. Alcock, N.W. and Hall, Sir R. de Z., 'Documentary evidence for crucks', in Alcock, N.W., *Cruck Construction. An introduction and catalogue* (London, 1981), 33.
44. Ibid., 32.
45. Quoted from Drapers' Company records in Robinson, Philip, ' "English" Houses Built at Moneymore, county Londonderry, c. 1615', *Post-Medieval Archaeology*, 17 *(1983)*, forthcoming.
46. Gailey, Alan, 'Further Cruck Trusses in East Ulster', *UF, 18* (1972), 88-9.
47. Atkinson, Edward Dupré, *An Ulster Parish* (Dublin, 1898), 23.
48. Pender, Séamus (ed.), *A Census of Ireland circa 1659* (Dublin, 1939), 79.
49. Gailey, Alan, op. cit. (1972), 84-7: Magherana 'B'.
50. Cooper, S.J.W., 'House with Cruck Truss at Magherana, near Waringstown', *UF, 14* (1968), 60-2.
51. Details of all of these trusses will be found in: Evans, E.E., op. cit. (1973), 16; McCourt, Desmond, 'The Cruck Truss in Ireland and its West European

Connections', *Folkliv, 28/29* (1964/65), 28-9; idem, 'Some Cruck-framed Buildings in Donegal and Derry', *UF, 11* (1965), 39-50; idem, 'Cruck Trusses in North-West Ireland', *Gwerin, 3* (1961), 179.
52. Stokes, G.T. (ed.), *Pococke's Tour in Ireland in 1752* (Dublin, 1891), 55.
53. For the Donegal and Tyrone cruck corbels, McCourt, D., op. cit. (1964/65), 67, 75; for the Fermanagh cruck corbel, Glassie, H., op. cit., 415, 519; for the cruck house noticed near Newtownstewart, ibid., 770.
54. Evans, E. Estyn, 'Some Cruck Roof-trusses in Ulster', *UF, 12* (1966), 35-7.
55. See entries in Gailey, A. and McCourt, D., 'Crucks in Ireland', in Alcock, N.W., op. cit., 91, under Ballinderry 'A', Ballylinny, Allistragh, Ballymoney (Down), Clare 'B', ? Waringstown 'C', ? Corry, Drumcullion, Kingarrow South, Knockarevan, Rossavally, Ballymultimber, Duncrun 'B', Glengomna and Drumgaghan. Glassie, H., op. cit., 347, 415, gives details of an abandoned turf house/hayshed he recorded in Derryhowlaght townland, west Fermanagh, with apparently six trusses of this type.
56. Sampson, G. Vaughan, *Statistical Survey of the County of Londonderry* (Dublin, 1802), 300.
57. O S Mem, Box 16, IV; *Ordnance Survey Memoir, Templecorran Parish, 1839* (Belfast, 1971), 12.
58. Gailey, A. and McCourt, D., op. cit., 90-2.
59. O S Mem, Box 9, I, 1 (1837), 12.
60. IFC MS 1077, 232.
61. See entries in Gailey, A. and McCourt, D., op. cit., 91, under Drumderg, Kinbally, Derrybrughas, Clare 'A', Corcreeny 'A', Blunnick, ? Derryaghna, Sessiagh East, Articlave Lower, Ballyhenry, Ballywoollen, Clooney, Duncrun 'A', Gortmore, Rathfad and Shanvey.
62. McCourt, D., op. cit. (1961), 177: Ballyhenry; idem, op. cit. (1965), 40: Articlave; idem, op. cit. (1961), 179: Shanvey.
63. This dating is based on Gailey, Alan, 'Two Cruck Truss Houses near Lurgan', *UF, 8* (1962), 63; and on Baillie, M.G.L., 'Dendrochronology as a Tool for the Dating of Vernacular Buildings in the North of Ireland', *VA, 7* (1976), 7.
64. Robinson, Philip, 'Further cruck houses in south Antrim: problems of historico-cultural interpretation', *JRSAI*, 112 (1982), 101-111.
65. Gailey, A. and McCourt, D., op. cit., 92: Ballynabraggett.
66. I am indebted to Dr. M.G.L. Baillie, of the Palaeoecology Laboratory, Queen's University, Belfast, for this as yet unpublished dating.
67. Baillie, M.G.L., op. cit., 7.
68. McCourt, Desmond and Evans, David, 'A Seventeenth-Century Farmhouse at Liffock, County Londonderry', *UJA*, 3rd ser., 35 (1972), 48-56; Baillie, M.G.L., op. cit., 7. McCourt originally classified the Liffock trusses as open, i.e. without tie-beams, because unequivocal evidence for their existence was not available to him when he was writing; nevertheless, he suggested the possible presence of tie-beams which were revealed in the course of restoration work carried out after acquisition of the house by the National Trust. As yet tie-beams have been confirmed in the cases of only two trusses, but it seems likely from the general consistency of the carpentry in this house that all of the trusses had tie-beams.

69. Gailey, A., op. cit. (1972), 84-7.
70. McCourt, Desmond and Evans, E. Estyn, 'A Late 17th-Century Farmhouse at Shantallow, near Londonderry', *UF,* 14 (1968), 17-9, and 17 (1971), 37-41.
71. Gailey, Alan, 'Notes on Three Cruck-Truss Houses', *UF,* 10 (1964), 91-4.
72. McCourt, Desmond, 'Weavers' Houses around Southwest Lough Neagh', *UF,* 8 (1962), 43-56; the various arguments for the derivation of the purlin roof are set out in idem, 'Roof Timbering Techniques in Ulster: A Classification', *FL,* 10 (1972), 128-130. Data on Icelandic purlin roof forms which have a 'long and unbroken tradition' are in Ágústsson, Hörthur, 'Kyrkjehus i ei Norron Homilie', *By og Bygd,* 25 (1974-75), 1-38.
73. McCourt, Desmond, op. cit. (1972, 'Roof Timbering Techniques in Ulster'), 129.
74. Evans, E. Estyn, *Irish Heritage* (Dundalk, 1942), 63.
75. Glassie, H., op. cit., 414, 770.
76. Evans, E. Estyn, 'The Ulster Farmhouse', *UF,* 1 (1955), 28-9.
77. Seen by Professor Evans, reported by Buchanan, R.H., 'Thatch and Thatching in North-East Ireland', *Gwerin,* 1 (1957), 126.
78. O S Mem, Ballyrashane parish, Queen's University Library, Mic 6/209.
79. (Smith, C. and Harris, W.), *The Antient and Present State of the County of Down* (Dublin, 1744), 24.
80. Quoted in Hall, Mr. and Mrs. S.C., *Ireland, its Scenery, Character, etc.,* III (London, *c.* 1847), 54.
81. Stokes, G.T. (ed.), op. cit., 18-9.
82. Pilson, Aynsworth, 'Downpatrick in 1708', *Downpatrick Recorder,* 24 May 1856.
83. Idem, 'Reminiscences of the last Century', *Downpatrick Recorder,* 16 Dec. 1854; idem, 'Reminiscences of the middle and latter end of the 18th Century', *Downpatrick Recorder,* 17 Dec. 1859.
84. Percentages calculated from figures quoted in the relevant parish accounts in O S Mem.
85. PRONI, T 1536/4.
86. Table 6 is derived from data in PRONI, T 1536/4, and TCD, Mun. V, 79/1, 3-7.
87. O'Dowd, Anne, *Meitheal* (Dublin, 1981), 78, 147.
88. Ó Danachair, Caoimhín, 'The Questionnaire System', *B,* 15 (1945), 203-17.
89. Buchanan, R.H., op. cit., 123-42.
90. *Poor Inquiry (Ireland), Appendix E, Suppt.,* 64; see also Binns, Jonathan, *The Miseries and Beauties of Ireland,* I (London, 1837), 112.
91. Glassie, H., op. cit., 416-21.
92. M'Evoy, J., op. cit., 147.
93. UFTM 611077.
94. UFTM 611366.
95. UFTM 611360.
96. UFTM 611036.
97. Stokes, G.T. (ed.), op. cit., 62.
98. Thompson, George, McCourt, Desmond and Gailey, Alan, 'The First Ulster Folk Museum Exhibit: The Magilligan Cottier House', *UF,* 10 (1964), 27.
99. Evans, E.E., op. cit. (1973), 18.
100. Idem, 'Gleanings from County Cavan', *UF,* 26 (1980), 6.
101. UFTM 611271.
102. UFTM 611215.
103. UM, R.J. Welch photograph RW 471.
104. UM, R.J. Welch photograph RW 993; also RW 984 shows roped thatch on houses at the Giants Causeway. Roped thatch at Portstewart is shown in photographs of about 1870 and 1900, included in McDonald, Tom and Anderson, Robert (eds.), *Memories in Focus* (Coleraine, 1981), Plates 59 and 69.
105. Original in possession of Mr. McPolin, Portaferry; copy in UFTM archives 35/8.
106. UM, R.J. Welch photographs, RW 319, RW 761.
107. UFTM, WAG 1196, 1708, 1796, 1799, 3383.
108. Evans, E. Estyn, *Mourne Country* (Dundalk, 1951), 185.
109. Buchanan, R.H., 'Stapple Thatch', *UF,* 3 (1957), 20-1.
110. Stokes, G.T. (ed.), op. cit., 62.
111. Evans, E. Estyn, 'Donegal Survivals', *A,* 13 (1939), 221.
112. Lucas, A.T., op. cit., 105.
113. Evans, E.E., op. cit. (1939).
114. Idem, op. cit. (1973), 15.
115. McDonald, T. and Anderson, R. (eds.), op. cit., Plates 73 and 42.
116. UFTM WAG 1646: Glendun; WAG 1943: Glenshesk.
117. Ó Danachair, C., op. cit. (1945), 210, 213.
118. Buchanan, R.H., op. cit. (*Gwerin,* 1957), 135; idem, op. cit. (*UF,* 1957), 19-28.
119. UFTM archives, Cassidy transcripts, 269.
120. Evans, E.E., op. cit. (1980), 6.
121. Boate, Gerard, *Ireland's Naturall History* (London, 1652; first written in Latin, 1641), in *A Collection of Tracts and Treatises . . .* (Dublin, 1860), 122.
122. All of this material, and more, is fully documented in Robinson, Philip, 'Vernacular Housing in Ulster in the Seventeenth Century', *UF,* 25 (1979), 22-3.
123. PRONI, T 970/1.
124. O S Mem, Box 23, XXVI, 2 (1834); Atkinson dates the house one year later, and also states that the shingles were removed in 1834: Atkinson, E.D., op. cit., 87, 88.
125. Communicated by Samuel Molyneux, in Part II, *A Collection of Such Papers as were communicated to the Royal Society, Referring to some Curiosities in Ireland,* 124-5, in *A Natural History of Ireland in Three Parts, By Several Hands* (Dublin, 1726).
126. PRONI, T 848/1, 39.
127. O S Mem, Box 1, II, 2 (1835), 29.
128. Robinson, P., op. cit. (1979), 22.
129. Boate, G., op. cit., 122.
130. *Belfast News-Letter,* 12 Dec. 1738.
131. Portlock, J.E., *Report on the Geology of the County of Londonderry, and of parts of Tyrone and Fermanagh* (Dublin, 1843), 680.
132. Robinson, P., op. cit. (1979), 22-3.
133. B(igger), F.J., 'Sir Moyses Hill at Malone in 1635', *UJA,* 2nd ser., 8 (1902), 49.
134. Montgomery, William, 'Description of the Ardes Barony . . . 1683', in Young, R.A., *Historical Notices of Old Belfast and its vicinity* (Belfast, 1896), 140; cf. also Quinn, D.B., 'William Montgomery and the description of the Ards, 1683', *Irish Booklore,* 2 (1972), 37.
135. Ibid.
136. PRONI, D 765/19.

137. Johnston, John Moore, 'A Description of the Parish of Magheradroll in the County of Down', *Heterogenea* (Downpatrick, 1803), 20-1.
138. Idem, 'To the Patriotic Committee conducting the farming or agricultural Society of the County of Down', *Heterogenea* (Downpatrick, 1803), 90.
139. Hoare, Sir Richard Colt, *Journal of a Tour in Ireland AD 1806* (London, 1807), 219.
140. Dubourdieu, Rev. John, *Statistical Survey of the County of Down* (Dublin, 1802), 34-5.
141. M'Evoy, J., op. cit., 96-7.
142. Atkinson, A., *Ireland Exhibited to England . . .* (London, 1823), 284.
143. Mason, W.S., op. cit. II, 20.
144. Ibid., 233.
145. PRONI, T 3097.
146. Greig, William, *General Report on the Gosford Estates in County Armagh* (Belfast, 1976), 53.
147. PRONI, D 3113/8/2.
148. *Devon Commission*, Evidence Pt. I, witness 21.
149. *Devon Commission*, Evidence Pt. II, witness 333.
150. PRONI, D 1118/1/1/1.
151. PRONI, D 1214/2/21, letter dated 26 Nov. 1879.
152. O S Mem, Box 38, I, 15 (1830); cf. O S Mem, Box 22, VI, 1 (1836).
153. PRONI, D 1767/2.

Chapter 6
1. Robinson, Philip, 'Vernacular Housing in Ulster in the Seventeenth Century', *UF*, 25 (1979), 13-24.
2. *Hastings Manuscripts*, IV (London, 1947), 173.
3. PRONI, T 970/1.
4. PRONI, D 1453/1.
5. PRONI, Mic 80/3, 16, 21-5.
6. Lucas, A.T., 'Contributions to the History of the Irish House: Smokehole and Chimney', in Gailey, Alan and Ó hÓgáin, Dáithí (eds.), *Gold Under the Furze* (Dublin, 1982), 50-65.
7. Morris, Henry, 'Reliques of the Brehon Laws and other Ancient Usages in Ulster', *B*, 9 (1939), 293.
8. 'The Rosses, County Donegal, in 1753-1754', *UF*, 19 (1973), 21.
9. Evans, E. Estyn, 'Donegal Survivals', *A*, 13 (1939), 219.
10. Glassie, Henry, *Passing the Time* (Dublin, 1982), 327, 455-6.
11. Ó Danachair, Caoimhín, 'Hearth and Chimney in the Irish House', *B*, 16 (1946), 97.
12. (Smith, C. and Harris, W.), *The Antient and Present State of the County of Down* (Dublin, 1744), 15-6.
13. Sampson, G. Vaughan, *Statistical Survey of the County of Londonderry* (Dublin, 1802), 298-9, referring to the district lying east of the River Bann.
14. UFTM 611297.
15. Millen, William, in 'Antiquarian Notes and Queries', *UJA*, 1st ser., 5 (1857), 160.
16. Brannon, N.F., 'Three Bed-outshot Houses in Castletown Townland, County Tyrone', *UF*, 29 (1983), 29-32.
17. UFTM 611302.
18. UFTM 611372.
19. Hill, Lord George, *Facts from Gweedore*, 5th edn. (London, 1887; Belfast, 1971), 25.

20. Foster, T.C., *Letters on the Condition of the People of Ireland* (London, 1846), 111.
21. Mason, W. Shaw, *Statistical Account or Parochial Survey of Ireland*, II (Dublin, 1816), 156.
22. Binns, Jonathan, *The Miseries and Beauties of Ireland*, I (London, 1837), 254.
23. O S Mem, Box 27, X, 1 (183?).
24. *Poor Inquiry (Ireland)*, Appendix E, Suppt., 48.
25. Binns, J., op. cit. I, 86-7.
26. Marshall, J.D., 'Notes on the Statistics and Natural History of Rathlin Island', *Transactions of the Royal Irish Academy*, 17, pt. 3 (1832-37), 54.
27. PRONI, T 1536/4.
28. Ibid.
29. Barrow, John, *A Tour Round Ireland . . . in the Autumn of 1835* (London, 1836), 116.
30. O S Mem, Box 18, XXIII, 2 (1835), 8.
31. O S Mem, Box 27, I, 1 (1834).
32. *Poor Inquiry (Ireland)*, Appendix E, Suppt., 48.
33. *Reports of Deputations who in Pursuance of Resolutions of the Court of Assistants of the Drapers' Company . . ., visited the Estates of the Company in the County of Londonderry* (London, 1829), 15.
34. Binns, J., op. cit. I, 215-6.
35. O S Mem, Box 34, I, 4 (183?), and Box 34, I, 24 (1836).
36. O S Mem, Box 15, VI, 1 (1840), 57.
37. O S Mem, Box 15, IV, 1 (1835), 16-7.
38. O S Mem, Box 16, IV, 2 (1840), 52.
39. Gailey, Alan, 'Kitchen Furniture', *UF*, 12 (1966), 26.
40. Evans, E. Estyn, 'The Ulster Farmhouse', *UF*, 1 (1955), 31; idem, *Irish Folk Ways* (London, 1957), Fig. 18, county Armagh, and Fig. 21, county Cavan.
41. McCourt, Desmond, 'The Outshot House-Type and its Distribution in County Londonderry', *UF*, 2 (1956), 28-30, Plate I.
42. Lucas, A.T., op. cit., 50-65.
43. Evans, E. Estyn, 'Gleanings from County Cavan', *UF*, 26 (1980), 5.
44. Full details of this house are in Gailey, Alan, 'Vernacular Dwellings of Clogher Diocese', *Clogher Record*, 9, No. 2 (1977), 192-4.
45. Millen, W., op. cit., 160.
46. O S Mem, Box 32, I, 1 (1821), 22.
47. O S Mem, Box 27, I, 1 (1834).
48. *Poor Inquiry (Ireland)*, Appendix E, Suppt., 66-7, 48, 65.
49. Ibid., 319.
50. See hearth-tax figures for 1791 quoted in Wakefield, Edward, *An Account of Ireland, Statistical and Political*, II (London, 1812), 688.
51. O S Mem, Box 47, I, 2 (1835?), 10-1; also Box 47, I, 5 (1835), 21-2.
52. O S Mem, Box 29, I, 3 (183?), 37.
53. Binns, J., op. cit. I, 112.

Chapter 7
1. O S Mem, Box 12, III, 2 (1838), 47.
2. O S Mem, Box 11, II, 2 (n.d.).
3. O S Mem, Box 23, XXVI, 2 (1834).

4. Foster, T.C., *Letters on the Condition of the People of Ireland* (London, 1846), 106, Glenties area; and 111, Aranmore Island.
5. O S Mem, Box 27, X, 1 (183?).
6. O S Mem, Box 15, VI, 1 (1840), 59: Raloo parish, county Antrim; Binns, Jonathan, *The Miseries and Beauties of Ireland*, I (London, 1837), 50-2: Upper Iveagh Barony, county Down. For west Fermanagh, see Glassie, Henry, *Passing the Time* (Dublin, 1982), 527.
7. Binns, J., op. cit. I, 111-3; *Poor Inquiry (Ireland), Appendix E, Suppt.*, 65.
8. Binns, J., op. cit. I, 215-6; *Poor Inquiry (Ireland), Appendix E, Suppt.*, 66-7.
9. O S Mem, Box 32, I, 1 (1821).
10. *Poor Inquiry (Ireland), Appendix E, Suppt.*, 63; Binns, J., op. cit. I, 186.
11. Thompson, George, McCourt, Desmond and Gailey, Alan, 'The First Ulster Folk Museum Exhibit: The Magilligan Cottier House', *UF*, 10 (1964), 28.
12. O S Mem, Box 11, VI, 3 (1839), 46.
13. Evans, E. Estyn, 'Traditional Houses of Rathlin Island', *UF*, 19 (1973), 18.
14. Ayres, James, *The Shell Book of the Home in Britain* (London, 1981), 112-3.
15. Ibid., 110-1; Peate, Iorwerth C., *The Welsh House* (Liverpool, 1940), 174.
16. Lucas, A.T., 'Decorative Cobbling: Examples from counties Limerick, Wexford and Cork', *JRSAI*, 106 (1976), 31-72.
17. Brannon, N.F., 'Three Bed-outshot Houses in Castletown Townland, County Tyrone', *UF*, 29 (1983), 29-32.
18. O S Mem, Box 51, X, 5 (1825).
19. O S Mem, Box 37, I, 3 (1836?).
20. PRONI, T 2826/4.
21. Mason, W. Shaw, *Statistical Account or Parochial Survey of Ireland*, III (Dublin, 1819), 13.
22. O S Mem, Box 31, II, 22 (1835), 4.
23. UM, R.J. Welch photograph, RW 400.
24. Atkinson, A, *Ireland Exhibited to England . . .* (London, 1823), 284-5.
25. Mason, W.S., op. cit. II (Dublin, 1816), 233.
26. PRONI, T 1536/4.
27. Gailey, Alan, 'A House from Gloverstown, Lismacloskey, County Antrim', *UF*, 20 (1974), 24-41.
28. Idem, 'House with Built-in Oven, Carrickreagh, County Fermanagh', appended to idem, op. cit. (1974), 45-8.
29. McCourt, Desmond and Evans, David, 'A Seventeenth-Century Farmhouse at Liffock, County Londonderry', *UJA*, 3rd ser., 35 (1972), 48-56.
30. Gailey, Alan, 'Further Cruck Trusses in East Ulster', *UF*, 18 (1972), 84-7.
31. Robinson, Philip, 'Vernacular Housing in Ulster in the Seventeenth Century', *UF*, 25 (1979), 17; Blades, Brooke S., ' "In the Manner of England": Tenant Housing in the Londonderry Plantation', *UF*, 27 (1981), 50-3.
32. PRONI, T 848/1.
33. Gailey, Alan, 'The Ballyhagan Inventories, 1716-1740', *FL*, 15 (1977), 42-6.
34. O S Mem, Box 4, V, 1 (1838); Box 7, 5, Vol. III (1839), 46; Box 11, VI, 1 (1840), 80-1.
35. O S Mem, Box 37, I, 3 (1836); Box 37, III, 2 (1837); Box 34, I, 4 (183?).
36. O S Mem, Box 51, VIII, 2 (1834).
37. *Devon Commission*, Evidence Pt. I, witness 278, question 26.
38. Gailey, Alan, 'Some developments and adaptations of traditional house types', in Ó Danachair, Caoimhín (ed.), *Folk and Farm* (Dublin, 1976), 64-5.
39. *Archaeological Survey of County Down* (Belfast, 1966), 354, Berwick Hall, Aughnadrumman townland.
40. Donaldson, John, *A Historical and Statistical Account of the Barony of Upper Fews in the County of Armagh* (1838; republished Dundalk, 1923), 17.
41. Reid, Thomas, *Sketches of Ireland* (London, 1827), 201.
42. O S Mem, Box 27, I, 1 (1834).
43. O S Mem, Box 26, IX, 2 (1834).
44. O S Mem, Box 27, XI, 1 (1834).
45. Lucas, A.T., 'Wattle and Straw Mat Doors in Ireland', *Studia Ethnographica Upsaliensia*, 11 (1956), 16-35.
46. Quoted in Crawford, W.H. and Trainor, Brian (eds.), *Aspects of Irish Social History* (Belfast, 1969), 90.
47. Mason, W.S., op. cit. II, 233; see also Atkinson, A., op. cit., 284-5.
48. Table 7 is based on data in PRONI, T 1536/4, and TCD, Mun. V, 79/1, 3-7.
49. Maurice Collis testified to these and other matters relevant to housing on the Trinity College estates, before the Devon Commission, obviously quoting data from his surveys: *Devon Commission*, Evidence, Pt. I, witness 39.
50. Gailey, A., op. cit. (1974), 27-9.
51. Wakefield, Edward, *An Account of Ireland, Statistical and Political*, II (London, 1812), 729.
52. Ibid., 688.
53. Ibid., I (London, 1812), 598.
54. *Reports of Deputations who in Pursuance of Resolutions of the Court of Assistants of the Drapers' Company . . . visited the Estates of the Company in the County of Londonderry* (London, 1829), First Report, 1817, 11.

Chapter 8
1. Danaher, Kevin, 'Old House Types in Oighreacht Ui Chonchubhair', *JRSAI*, 68 (1938), 227-8; McCourt, Desmond, 'The outshot house type and its distribution in county Londonderry', *UF*, 2 (1956), 28.
2. Harrison, John, 'A Note on Two Houses in North County Dublin', *Sinsear*, 3 (1981), 109-110.
3. Campbell, Åke, 'Notes on the Irish House', *Folk-Liv*, 1 (1937), 207-234; 2 (1938), 173-196.
4. A recent study based on this distinction is Ó Danachair, Caoimhín, 'Traditional Forms of the Dwelling House in Ireland', *JRSAI*, 102 (1972), 77-96.
5. McCourt, Desmond, 'Innovation Diffusion in Ireland: An Historical Case Study', *PRIA*, 73 CI (1973), 2-6; Gailey, Alan, 'Vernacular Dwellings in Ireland', *Revue Roumaine d'Histoire de l'Art*, 13 (1976), 150, 152.
6. McCourt, Desmond and Evans, E. Estyn, 'A Late Seventeenth-Century Farmhouse at Shantallow, near Londonderry', *UF*, 14 (1968), 14-23; 17 (1971), 37-41.
7. Summary reference to these houses will be found in Smith, Peter, 'The Architectural Personality of the British Isles', *Archaeologia Cambrensis*, 129 (1980), 12-3, 32.

8. Ibid.

9. UFTM, WAG 2814.

10. M'Parlan, James, *Statistical Survey of the County of Donegal* (Dublin, 1802), 65.

11. Mason, W. Shaw, *A Statistical and Parochial Survey of Ireland,* II (Dublin, 1816), 156.

12. Hill, Lord George, *Facts from Gweedore,* 5th edn. (London, 1887, reprinted Belfast, 1971), 27.

13. O S Mem, Box 28, II, 1 (1837), 29: Union of Manorhamilton.

14. Evans, E. Estyn, 'Donegal Survivals', *A,* 13 (1939), 209.

15. Ibid., 216. In his analysis of the houses of the Ballymenone district of west Fermanagh, Glassie distinguishes the version with opposed doors (his 'northwestern' type) as a separate house type from that with a single entrance (his 'local' type). The evidence all over Ireland for the geographical co-existence of the two, and in many areas for the conversion of the former into the latter by the simple expedient of blocking up one door once cattle were removed from the building to a separate byre, surely argues that the two are variants of a single house form: Glassie, Henry, *Passing the Time* (Dublin, 1982), 589-599, 785-6.

16. Stokes, G.T. (ed.), *Pococke's Tour in Ireland in 1752* (Dublin, 1891), 63.

17. The evidence is quoted in Ó Danachair, Caoimhín, 'The Combined Byre-and-Dwelling in Ireland', *FL,* 2 (1964), 65.

18. Aalen, F.H.A., 'The House Types of Gola Island, Co. Donegal', *FL,* 8 (1970), 37.

19. Detailed publication of the Donegal evidence, including the houses mentioned in the previous paragraph, is in McCourt, Desmond, 'The House with Bedroom over Byre', *UF,* 15/16 (1970), 7-14.

20. Ó Danachair, Caoimhín, op. cit. (1964), 72-3. For county Leitrim, see M'Parlan, James, op. cit., 43-4.

21. Micks, William L., *An Account of the Constitution, Administration and Dissolution of the Congested Districts Board for Ireland from 1891 to 1923* (Dublin, 1925), 253.

22. Wakefield, Edward, *An Account of Ireland, Statistical and Political,* II (London, 1812), 742-3.

23. O S Mem, Box 52, XVIII, 1 (1834).

24. O S Mem, Box 49 (IV), IX, 1 (183?), 14.

25. *Poor Inquiry (Ireland), Appendix E, Suppt.,* 391.

26. *Reports of Deputations who in Pursuance of Resolutions of the Court of Assistants of the Drapers' Company . . . visited the Estates of the Company in the County of Londonderry* (London, 1829), 15.

27. Ó Danachair, Caoimhín, op. cit. (1972), 86; idem, 'Irish Vernacular Architecture in relation to the Irish Sea', in *The Irish Sea Province in Archaeology and History* (Cardiff, 1970), 102-3.

28. Details of these houses are available in McCourt, D., op. cit. (1973), 1-8, 14-6.

29. Ibid., 18.

30. McCourt, D., op. cit. (1956), Plate IV.

31. Gamble, John, *Views of Society and Manners in the North of Ireland . . . in the Year 1818* (London, 1819), 147.

32. Ó Danachair, Caoimhín, 'The bed-outshot in Ireland', *Folk-Liv,* 19-20 (1955-56), 29; Lucas, A.T. quotes sources for 1802 and the 1830s in 'Contributions to the History of the Irish House: A Possible Ancestry of the bed outshot', *FL,* 8 (1970), 81.

33. O S Mem, Box 15, IV, 1 (1835), 16-8.

34. O S Mem, Box 48, I, 2 (1821).

35. O S Mem, Box 42, V, 2 (1836), 31.

36. Ó Mórdha, Séamus, 'Miscellanea. An Old Type of Country House', *Clogher Record,* 2, No. 2 (1958), 265-6, quoting a story by Peter Maginnis of Derrygonnelly published in the *Lisbellaw Gazette,* 24 Dec. 1879.

37. Micks, W.L., op. cit., 253.

38. Details of these recent finds are in Gailey, Alan, 'Three Houses with Outshot in North Louth and South Armagh', *Journal of the County Louth Archaeological and Historical Society,* 20, No. 1 (1981), 3-9.

39. Gaillard-Bans, Patricia, *Aspects de l'Architecture rurale en Europe occidentale* (UNESCO, n.d., but 1979), Chapitre II.

40. Lucas, A.T., op. cit., 81-98.

41. Ibid., 97-8.

42. The most recent summary of the European evidence on the outshot is in Meirion-Jones, Gwyn I., 'The Bed Outshot in Brittany', *UF,* 25 (1979), 29-33.

43. Aalen, F.H.A., 'The Evolution of the Traditional House in Western Ireland', *JRSAI,* 90 (1966), 47-58, argues along these lines, but in stressing the importance of the roof form in persisting in maintaining the central hearth/gable hearth classificatory distinction, he has missed the fundamental importance of the entrance/hearth relationship.

44. Bigger, Francis Joseph, 'Thomas Beggs, an Antrim Poet, and the Four Towns Book Club', *UJA,* 2nd ser., 8 (1902), 124.

45. PRONI, T 2125/3/1.

46. Gailey, Alan, 'The Ballyhagan Inventories, 1716-1740', *FL,* 15 (1977), 36-64, provides an analysis of these houses insofar as they can be interpreted from the inventories.

47. PRONI, T 3097: General Report on the Estate of Drumbanagher . . . by William Greig . . . 1818.

48. Greig, William, *General Report on the Gosford Estates in County Armagh 1821* (Belfast, 1976), 230; the original is PRONI, D 1606.

49. Chart, D.A. (ed.), *Londonderry and the London Companies, 1609-1629* (Belfast, 1928), illustrations passim; Blades, Brooke S., ' "In the Manner of England": Tenant Housing in the Londonderry Plantation', *UF,* 27 (1981), 39-56.

50. Tighe, William, *Statistical Observations relative to the County of Kilkenny made in the Years 1800 and 1801* (Dublin, 1802), 414.

51. Gailey, Alan, 'Further Cruck Trusses in East Ulster', *UF,* 18 (1972), 84-7.

52. Idem, 'House with Built-in Oven, Carrickreagh, County Fermanagh', appended to 'A House from Gloverstown, Lismacloskey, County Antrim', *UF,* 20 (1974), 45-8.

53. See ref. 49 above.

54. Glassie describes a number of houses of this developed form in the Ballymenone district of west Fermanagh, the earliest of which was built only as recently as 1900.

He does not clearly derive this form from the earlier hearth-lobby (his 'southeastern') layout: Glassie, H., op. cit., 344, 398, 409-11, 589, 605, 763. However, I have never encountered this particular developed configuration outside the distributional limits of the hearth-lobby type, and many examples of the developed form referred to by Glassie within the area he studied as a 'new' type are actually not exactly symmetrical in their facade arrangement, their front doors being slightly off-centred towards the kitchen hearth wall; in many cases the developed or extended former jamb wall between the front 'hall' and the kitchen retains the jamb-wall spy window: cf. Glassie, H., op. cit., 398.

55. Aalen, F.H.A., op. cit. (1966), 58; Glassie, H., op. cit., 766.
56. Ó Danachair, C., op. cit. (1970), 105.
57. Campbell, A., op. cit. (1937), 221.
58. Evans, E. Estyn, *The Personality of Ireland* (Cambridge, 1973), 63; in 1955 he saw the Ulster distribution of the jamb wall as 'strikingly similar' to that of English as opposed to Scots settlement: idem, 'The Ulster Farmhosue', *UF*, 1 (1955), 28. Glassie, H., op. cit., 766.
59. McCourt, Desmond, op. cit. (1973), 1-19; in fact he first published his ideas in German, 'Hausformen in einem kulturellen Kontaktgebiet Nordirlands', *Deutsches Jahrbuch für Volkskunde*, 14 (1968), 247-60.
60. Gailey, Alan, 'The Thatched Houses of Ulster. The First Ulster Folk Museum Questionnaire', *UF*, 7 (1961), 9-18.
61. Trimble, W. Copeland, *The History of Enniskillen*, III (Enniskillen, 1921), 783.
62. *An Archaeological Survey of County Down* (Belfast, 1966), 390.
63. Atkinson, A., *Ireland Exhibited to England . . .*, II (London, 1823), 284-5, writen 1816.
64. McCourt, D., op. cit. (1973), 7.
65. Gailey, A., op. cit. (1981).
66. McCourt, D., op. cit. (1973), 4-7.
67. Evans, E. Estyn, 'Gleanings from County Cavan', *UF*, 26 (1980), 5.
68. Idem, op. cit. (1955), 28.
69. See, for example, the region defined for the Mid-Ulster dialect by Adams, G.B., 'Introduction. Ulster Dialects', in idem (ed.), *Ulster Dialects* (Holywood, 1964), xiv, 1-4. A more complex cultural-historical analysis relevant here is Robinson, Philip, 'Plantation and Colonisation: The Historical Background', in Boal, F.W. and Douglas, J.N.H. (eds.), *Integration and Division* (London, 1982), 19-47.
70. Robinson, Philip, 'Vernacular Housing in Ulster in the Seventeenth Century', *UF*, 25 (1979), 13-24; Blades, B.S., op. cit., 39-56.
71. Robinson, Philip, ' "English" Houses Built at Moneymore, County Londonderry, c. 1615', *Post-Medieval Archaeology*, forthcoming; Drapers' Company records, Ma. Dr., b1858. In late summer 1982, N.F. Brannon of the Northern Ireland Archaeological Survey excavated a directly comparable house of c. 1620 which had been added to an earlier tower house at Dungiven Priory, county Londonderry. So, what appeared on Raven's contemporary drawing to be a much larger, more complex house, turns out to be a fairly modest English vernacular house added to earlier buildings, with the further addition of a rear wing.
72. *Royal Commission on Ancient Monuments of Scotland, Roxburghshire*, I (Edinburgh, 1956), Figs. 74 and 76.
73. Fenton, Alexander and Walker, Bruce, *The Rural Architecture of Scotland* (Edinburgh, 1981), 147.
74. Ó Danachair, C., op. cit. (1972), 86.
75. Ó Ríordáin, Seán P. and Ó Danachair, Caoimhín., 'Lough Gur Excavations Site J, Knockadoon', *JRSAI*, 77 (1947), 39-52.
76. Macalister, R.A.S., 'The History and Antiquities of Inis Cealtra', *PRIA*, 33 C6 (1916), 110, 140-1.
77. The earliest examples of English lobby-entry houses are in the south-east where, for example, some Wealden houses had their cross-passages blocked by insertion of a stone chimney stack, producing the lobby-entry (or baffle-entry) configuration in the sixteenth century: Mercer, Eric, *English Vernacular Houses* (London, 1975), 61-6; see also Brunskill, R.W., *Traditional Buildings of Britain* (London, 1981), 53-4. Other trains of development leading to the lobby-entry form occurred, and most houses with this plan in England and Wales are dated from the early seventeenth century onwards: Mercer, E., op. cit., 63-6; Brunskill, R.W., *Houses* (London, 1982), 70-2; Smith, Peter, *Houses of the Welsh Countryside* (London, 1975), 161-3; idem, op. cit. (1980), passim.
78. Adams, G.B., 'Glossary of Household Terms', *UF*, 12 (1966), 32-4.
79. Information from Dr. P. Robinson, Dec. 1976.
80. *An Archaeological Survey of County Down* (Belfast, 1966), 354.
81. Trimble, W.C., op. cit. III, 758-61.
82. Ibid., 769.
83. I am indebted to the present owner, Mr. Robert McKinstry, for showing me over his house, providing plans, and discussing its development with me.
84. Jope, E.M., 'Moyry, Charlemont, Castleraw and Richhill: Fortification to Architecture in the North of Ireland 1570-1700', *UJA*, 3rd ser., 23 (1960), 111.
85. Ibid., 110; *An Archaeological Survey of County Down* (Belfast, 1966), 256-7.
86. Jope, E.M., op. cit., 110.
87. Mercer, E., op. cit., 55-9; Smith, Peter. op. cit. (1975), 159-161; Brunskill, R.W., op. cit. (1982), 68-70; idem, op. cit. (1981), 48-51.
88. Walker, Bruce, 'Notes on Cottages with Cross Passages in Inver, Tain, Ross-shire', *Scottish Vernacular Buildings Working Group Newsletter*, 4 (1978), 28-30.
89. McCourt, D. and Evans, E.E., op. cit. (1968 and 1971).
90. Smith, P., op. cit. (1975), 159-161; Brunskill, R.W., op. cit. (1982), 80.
91. Gailey, A., op. cit. (1974), 24-41.
92. Robinson, P.S. and Brannon, N.F., 'A Seventeenth-Century House in New Row, Coleraine', *UJA*, 3rd ser., 44-45 (1981-2), 173-178. Dr. Robinson has recently been re-examining a number of larger Ulster houses of the seventeenth century (summer 1982). They are not vernacular houses in the Irish sense, although some, or even all of them, owe much to English vernacular architectural exemplars. The buildings involved are Waringstown House (1666) in

north-west Down, Ardress House (*c.* 1660) in north Armagh, and Springhill (*c.* 1695) near Moneymore in south Londonderry; Ardress and Springhill are National Trust properties. Roofs of all three houses have oak principal-rafter systems with butt purlins on the sides of the roofs, but no ridge purlins, and with wind-braces in all three. Outhouses at Springhill and Waringstown House also have similar seventeenth-century roofs. I am indebted to Dr. Robinson for this information.

93. Gailey, Alan, 'House with Built-in Oven, Carrickreagh, County Fermanagh', loc. cit.

94. Idem, 'A House from Gloverstown . . .', loc. cit., 39, ref. 24 provides details of Newlands cottage.

95. McCourt, Desmond and Evans, David, 'A Seventeenth-Century Farmhouse at Liffock, County Londonderry', *UJA*, 3rd ser., 35 (1972), 48-56.

96. PRONI, T 2985; see Buchanan, Gwen, 'Talk of the Ten Towns by Francis Chambers', *UF*, 27 (1981), 64.

97. Lacy, Brian, 'Two Seventeenth-Century Houses at Linenhall Street, Londonderry', *UF*, 27 (1981), 57-62.

98. *Calendar Carew Manuscripts, 1603-1624* (London, 1873), 94, 222.

99. PRONI, D 1453/1.

100. PRONI, D 848/1, 49, 29.

101. UFTM, WAG 3297.

102. Ua Danachair, Caoimhin, 'The Traditional Houses of County Limerick', *North Munster Antiquarian Journal*, 5 (1946-1949), 28-30.

103. Brunskill, R.W., 'Distributions of Building Materials and Some Plan Types in the Domestic Vernacular Architecture of England and Wales', *Transactions of the Ancient Monuments Society*, new ser., 23 (1978), 49-50, 64; Smith, P., op. cit. (1980), 33.

104. Smith, P., op. cit. (1980), 31.

105. Ó Danachair, C., op. cit. (1970), 102-3.

106. Fenton, Alexander, *The Hearth in Scotland* (Dundee, 1981), 6 et seq; idem, *The Island Blackhouse* (Edinburgh, 1978).

107. Walton, James, 'The built-in bed tradition in north Yorkshire', *Gwerin*, 3 (1960-1962), 114-125; see also Meirion-Jones, G.I., op. cit., 32-3.

108. Gailey, Alan, 'Traditional Houses at Riasc, near Ballyferriter', *Journal of the Kerry Archaeological and Historical Society*, 14 (1981), 94-111.

109. Dutton, Hely, *Statistical Survey of the County of Galway* (Dublin, 1824), 343.

110. IFC MSS 1076, 832; 1077, 236: quoted in Ó Danachair, Caoimhín, 'Materials and Methods in Irish Traditional Building', *JRSAI*, 87 (1957), 73.

111. Alcock, N.W., 'The origin and spread of cruck construction in Britain', in idem, *Cruck Construction. An introduction and catalogue* (London, 1981), 59.

112. Smith, J.T., 'The problems of cruck construction and the evidence of distribution maps', in Alcock, N.W., op. cit., 8-16.

113. Alcock, N.W., op. cit., 59.

Chapter 9

1. Campbell, Åke, 'Notes on the Irish House', *Folk-Liv*, 1 (1937), 207-234 introduced this theme, which was taken up particularly by Evans, E. Estyn in 'The Ulster Farmhouse', *UF*, 1 (1955), 27-31, and in other publications.

The most extensive excursion into this field has been by Henry Glassie in his *Passing the Time* (Dublin 1982), especially Chapters 13 and 24. His study of the housing of a small west Fermanagh community is based mainly on material gathered from the people living in the forty-two occupied houses of the Ballymenone district, and observation of the buildings and of a further eleven unoccupied houses. He has gone further than any other writer to examine how houses are used internally and what kinds of functions they perform for the family and the community. He sees the need for this 'emic' approach to be set alongside an 'etic' consideration of his district's housing, that is, a more broadly based formal consideration of its vernacular architecture. Many of Glassie's conclusions and interpretations are certainly valid for the district he studied; further locally based emic studies are needed to determine their more general applicability. For example, it is clear that Ballymenone was late to formalise the facades of its houses, to insert longitudinal formal 'halls' in front of kitchens and to lose its thatch roofs. His emic approach does not lead to recognition of the longitudinal closed-off hall in the houses he studied as a development from the earlier lobby-entry configuration with jamb wall, which the present etic approach has shown developed elsewhere earlier than in Ballymenone but, more importantly, which shows that it occurred only in areas where the jamb wall was known. Thus I would suggest that when Glassie says that of the fifty-three houses he studied, only one was of the 'southeastern' (i.e. hearth-lobby or lobby-entry) form, it is necessary to add also that most if not all of the houses of his 'new' type also belong to the hearth-lobby *family* of plan forms.

Such criticism apart, Glassie's book is a turning point in Irish vernacular architecture studies, clearly signposting one direction in which future research endeavour should be followed at local level. Many of his conclusions are echoed in my own work in this book, although interesting differences are evident in historical timing of architectural changes.

2. Robinson, Philip, 'Vernacular Housing in Ulster in the Seventeenth Century', *UF*, 25 (1979), 1-7.

3. PRONI, T 848/1, f. 32.

4. Moryson, Fynes, 'A description of Ireland, 1600-3', in Morley, H. (ed.), *Ireland under Elizabeth and James the First* (London, 1890), 430.

5. Hayes-McCoy, G.A. (ed.), *Ulster and other Irish Maps c. 1600* (Dublin, 1964), 6.

6. Quoted in Camblin, G., *The Town in Ulster* (Belfast, 1951), 15.

7. Quoted in Lucas, A.T., 'Wattle and Straw Mat Doors in Ireland', *Studia Ethnographica Upsaliensia*, 11 (1956), 30.

8. *Calendar Carew Manuscripts, 1603-24* (London, 1873), 77.

9. Harris, W., *Hibernica, or some ancient pieces relating to Ireland* (Dublin, 1770), 194.

10. *Hastings Manuscripts*, IV (London, 1947), 159-182.

11. *Calendar Carew Manuscripts, 1603-24* (London, 1873), 228; Harris, W., op. cit., 209.

12. Glancy, M., 'The Incidence of the Plantation on the City of Armagh', *Seanchas Ardmhacha*, 1 (1954-55), 115-60.

13. PRONI, T 970/1, ff. 72, 73: Brownlow Lease Book.
14. PRONI, Mic 80/3, ff. 29-31.
15. Ibid.
16. Ibid., ff. 14-5, 51-3.
17. Ibid., ff. 61-2.
18. Robinson, P., op. cit., passim.
19. Armagh, Cathedral Library, MS.g.I.14, Rev. Mr. Henerey's Account of the County of Fermanagh written Ao. 1739.
20. Stokes, G.T. (ed.), *Pococke's Tour in Ireland in 1752* (Dublin, 1891), 63.
21. PRONI, T 2368; quoted in Crawford, W.H. and Trainor, Brian (eds.), *Aspects of Irish Social History 1750-1800* (Belfast, 1969), 90.
22. Downham, G., 'The Estate of the Diocese of Derry', *UJA*, 2nd ser., 1 (1895), 174.
23. Young, Arthur, *A Tour in Ireland*, I (Dublin, 1780), 239, 293.
24. Mason, W. Shaw, *A Statistical Account, or Parochial Survey of Ireland*, II (Dublin, 1816), 524.
25. Johnson, James, *A Tour in Ireland* (London, 1844), 327.
26. Hill, G. (ed.), *The Montgomery Manuscripts, 1603-1706* (Belfast, 1869), 59.
27. M'Skimmin, S., *The History and Antiquities of the County of the Town of Carrickfergus* (Belfast, 1939), 141.
28. Quoted in Robinson, P., op. cit., 2, 4.
29. PRONI, Mic 80/3, ff. 29-31.
30. Boate, Gerard, *Ireland's Naturall History* (London, 1652), in *A Collection of Tracts and Treatises . . .* I (Dublin, 1860), 120.
31. PRONI, T 3097, App. No. 4, ff. 99-104.
32. PRONI, D 603; Greig, William, *General Report on the Gosford Estates in County Armagh in 1821* (Belfast, 1976), 230.
33. Robinson, P., op. cit., 1-28.
34. Petty, Sir William, 'The Political Anatomy of Ireland, 1672', in *A Collection of Tracts and Treatises . . .* (Dublin, 1860), 77.
35. (Smith, C. and Harris, W.), *Antient and Present State of the County of Down* (Dublin, 1744), 105.
36. Johnson, J., op. cit., 327.
37. O S Mem, Box 27, I, 1 (1834).
38. O S Mem, Box 16, VI, 1 (1838), 57-8.
39. O S Mem, Box 27, IV, 1 (1835).
40. O S Mem, Box 24, XI, 1 (1833), 6.
41. O S Mem, Box 27, V, 2 (1835).
42. O S Mem, Box 51, II, 1 (1835).
43. O S Mem, Box 49, XVIII, 1 (1835), 19.
44. O S Mem, Box 33, I, 7 (183?), 2, 5.
45. O S Mem, Box 4, IV, 2 (1837), 20; Box 4, IV, 4 (1834).
46. Hill, Lord George, *Facts from Gweedore*, 5th edn. (London, 1887; republished Belfast 1971), Appendix I, 51-2.
47. O S Mem, Box 27, VII, 1 (1834).
48. Evans, E. Estyn, 'Introduction', in Hill, G., op. cit., xvii.
49. O S Mem, Box 11, IV, 1 (1840), 1.
50. O S Mem, Box 11, IV, 4 (1840), 59-60, 62.
51. O S Mem, Box 30, III, 1 (c. 1837).
52. O S Mem, Box 43, I, 3 (1836).
53. O S Mem, Box 37, I, 3 (1836?).
54. O S Mem, Box 48, I, 2 (1821).
55. All of these 1848 data for the Londonderry family's north Down estate are calculated from the material in PRONI, T 1536/4.
56. O S Mem, Box 51, X, 5 (1825).
57. O S Mem, Box 43, I, 3 (1836).
58. O S Mem, Box 10, II, 1 (1835); Box 16, VI, 1 (1838), 57.
59. O S Mem, Box 52, XXIV, 1 (183?).
60. O S Mem, Box 30, III, 1 (c. 1837); Box 32, I, 15 (1834?), 15-6; Box 33, I, 7 (183?), 2, 5; Box 36, I, 2 (183?); Box 44, I, 4 (1836).
61. (Smith, C. and Harris, W.), op. cit., 105.
62. Robinson, Philip, 'Plantation and Colonisation: The Historical Background', in Boal, F.W. and Douglas, J.N.H. (eds.), *Integration and Division* (London, 1982), 38-45. Nevertheless, as Glassie has shown in west Fermanagh, sectarian differences there are not, and elsewhere probably were not, evident in the occupancy of different house types: Glassie, H., op. cit., 331.
63. PRONI, D 1939/15/10/18, specification; /21, agreement to build.
64. PRONI, D 1513/1/8.
65. PRONI, D 743.
66. PRONI, D 1556/11/6.
67. 19 & 20 Vic., c. 65.
68. 23 & 24 Vic., c. 19.
69. 33 & 34 Vic., c. 46.
70. 35 & 36 Vic., c. 32.
71. 44 & 45 Vic., c. 43.
72. 45 & 46 Vic., c. 60.
73. 46 & 47 Vic., c. 60.
74. (Labourers Department, Local Government Board), 'Model Labourers' Cottages', in M(acartney)-F(ilgate), W.T. (ed.), *Irish Rural Life and Industry* (Dublin, 1907), 281-94.
75. Bigger, Francis Joseph, *Labourers' Cottages for Ireland* (Dublin, 1907); this was a pamphlet published by Independent Newspapers, Ltd. upon their invitation to Bigger, following a letter of his in the *Irish Independent*, 2 March 1907, in which he had published his criticism.
76. Brown, Robert, 'The Housing of the Irish Artizan', in M(acartney)-F(ilgate), W.T. (ed.), op. cit., 300.
77. Bigger, F.J., op. cit., 5.
78. Curwen, J.C., *Observations on the State of Ireland . . .*, I (London, 1818), 112, referring, apparently, to the north-east of Ireland.
79. Johnson, J., op. cit., 327.
80. O S Mem, Box 47, I, 2 (1835), 10-1.
81. O S Mem, Box 47, I, 2 (1835), 10-1; Box 32, I, 15 (1834), 13-4; Box 41, I, 7 (183?), 4-5.
82. O S Mem, Box 47, I, 7 (183?), 4-5; Box 47, I, 2 (1835), 10-1.
83. Pilson, Aynsworth, 'Reminiscences of the Last Century', *Downpatrick Recorder*, 23 Dec. 1854.
84. Johnston, John Moore, 'A Description of the Parish of Magheradroll in the County of Down', *Heterogenea* (Downpatrick, 1803), 20-1.
85. UFTM 611311.
86. UFTM 611143.
87. UFTM 611004, 611215.

88. O S Mem, Box 22, VI, 2 (1825), Raymoghey parish.
89. Binns, Jonathan, *The Miseries and Beauties of Ireland,* I (London, 1837), 338-9.
90. McCourt, Desmond and Evans, E. Estyn, 'A Late Seventeenth-Century Farmhouse at Shantallow, near Londonderry', *UF,* 14 (1968), 20-1.
91. Kirkham, G., 'Economic Diversification in a Marginal Economy', in Roebuck, Peter (ed.), *Plantation to Partition* (Belfast, 1981), 78, quoting *Poor Inquiry (Ireland), Appendix D,* returns for the parish of Magilligan (1836).
92. Ayres, James, *The Shell Book of the Home in Britain* (London, 1981), 118, quoting Carew, Richard, *The Survey of Cornwall* (London, 1602; 1769 edn.), 18-9.
93. McCourt, Desmond and Evans, E. Estyn, 'A Late Seventeenth-Century Farmhouse at Shantallow, near Londonderry — Part II', *UF,* 17 (1971), 41.
94. Idem and idem, op. cit. (1968), 20.
95. *Poor Inquiry (Ireland), Appendix E, Suppt.,* 63: evidence for barony of Lower Fews.
96. O S Mem, Box 10, IV, 4 (1836).
97. O S Mem, Box 32, I, 1 (1821), 22.
98. O S Mem, Box 45, II, 9 (1835), 7.
99. O S Mem, Box 22, IX, 1 (1835).
100. O S Mem, Box 51, X, 5 (1825).
101. Coote, Sir Charles, *Statistical Survey of the County of Cavan* (Dublin, 1802), 129-130.
102. See Danaher, Kevin, *The Year in Ireland* (Cork, 1972) for much of the detail on these matters.
103. *Ordnance Survey Memoir of Templecorran Parish 1839* (Belfast, 1971), 39.
104. The following paragraphs summarise parts of a fuller description of the furnishing of traditional kitchens, in Gailey, Alan, 'Kitchen Furniture', *UF,* 12 (1966), 18-34. For comparative material for west Fermanagh, see Glassie, H., op. cit., 396-7.
105. O S Mem, Box 34, I, 10 (183?), 1-4.
106. O S Mem, Box 51, X, 5 (1825).
107. O S Mem, Box 30, II, 1 (1835), 40; Box 43, II, 2 (183?).
108. Although Greer in Altnavannog was a member of the Ballyhagan community in mid county Armagh, Altnavannog is in east county Tyrone some miles to the west. The analysis of the Ballyhagan housing is in Gailey, Alan, 'The Ballyhagan Inventories, 1716-1740', *FL,* 15 (1977), 42-6.
109. O S Mem, Box 12, III, 2 (1838), 47.
110. O S Mem, Box 4, V, 1 (1838), 13.
111. O S Mem, Box 15, IV, 1 (1835), 16-8.
112. O S Mem, Box 29, I, 3 (1836?), 37.
113. O S Mem, Box 37, II, 2 (183?).
114. Gailey, A., op. cit. (1977), 42-6.
115. Idem, op. cit. (1966), 21-2.
116. McCourt, Desmond, 'Innovation Diffusion in Ireland: an historical case study', PRIA, 73 C1 (1973), 5; I do not agree with Dr. McCourt that these screen walls should be referred to as, or compared with, jamb walls. The Duncrun example is now reconstructed at the Ulster Folk and Transport Museum.
117. See, in particular, the analysis in Blades, Brooke S., ' "In the Manner of England": Tenant Housing in the Londonderry Plantation', *UF,* 27 (1981), 42-52.
118. Greig, W., op. cit., 25.
119. Ibid., 38.
120. PRONI, T 3097.
121. Campbell, Patrick, 'Growing up in Donegal', *B,* 42-44 (1974-76), 81.
122. Ibid., 81-4.
123. Bell, Jonathan, 'Hiring Fairs in Ulster', *UF,* 25 (1979), 71-2.
124. O S Mem, Box 37, I, 3 (1836?).
125. O S Mem, Box 4, V, 1 (1838), 13.
126. O S Mem, Box 7, 5, Vol. III (1839), 46.
127. O S Mem, Box 11, VI, 1 (1840), 80-1.
128. O S Mem, Box 15, VI, 1 (1840), 57.
129. O S Mem, Box 13, I, 2 (1839), 34.
130. *Ordnance Survey Memoir of Templecorran Parish 1839* (Belfast, 1971), 39.
131. O S Mem, Box 11, VI, 3 (1839), 47.
132. Bell, J., op. cit., 71.
133. Magill, Patrick, *Children of the Dead End* (London, 1914), 35.
134. Bell, J., op. cit., 71.
135. UFTM 611294.
136. Cullen, L.M., 'Wealth, Wills and Inheritance', unpublished paper presented to the IIIe Colloque Franco-Irlandais, Paris, 24-26 March 1982.
137. PRONI, D 1096/16/7.
138. UFTM archives, as yet uncatalogued.
139. Quoted in Gailey, A., op. cit. (1977), 46.
140. O S Mem, Box 15, IV, 1 (1835), 16-8.
141. O S Mem, Box 45, I, 4 (1836).
142. Rapoport, Amos, *House Form and Culture* (Englewood Cliffs, 1969), Chapter 3. Glassie, Henry, *Folk Housing in Middle Virginia* (Knoxville, 1975), also discusses the symbolic value of traditional housing in a local American study.
143. See McCourt, Desmond, 'The Decline of Rundale, 1750-1850', in Roebuck, Peter (ed.), *Plantation to Partition* (Belfast, 1981), 119-39; idem, 'The Dynamic Quality of Irish Rural Settlement', in Buchanan, R.H., Jones, Emrys, and McCourt, Desmond (eds.), *Man and his Habitat* (London, 1971), 126-164.
144. Proudfoot, V.B., 'Clachans in Ireland', *Gwerin,* 2 (1959), 112.
145. See Evans, E. Estyn, 'Introduction', in Hill, G., op. cit., where this process is illustrated on Hill's estates in north-west Donegal.
146. Proudfoot, V.B., op. cit., 111-2.
147. O S Mems for the following parishes: Aghagallon, Aghalee, Antrim, Ballylinny, Ballymartin, Ballynure, Ballywalter, Camlin, Carmavy, Mallusk, Muckamore, Grange of Nilteen, Raloo and Templepatrick.
148. O S Mem, Box 6, I, 2 (1837?).
149. O S Mem, Box 30, V, 2 (1836).
150. O S Mem, Box 37, III, 2 (183?).
151. O S Mem, Box 26, IX, 2 (1834).
152. O S Mem, Box 27, I, 1 (1834).
153. O S Mem, Box 27, VI, 1 (1834).
154. (Smith, C. and Harris, W.), op. cit. 125.

Chapter 10
1. *Ancient Laws of Ireland,* IV (Dublin, 1879), 309.
2. Ibid., V (Dublin, 1901), 515.

3. Robinson, Philip, 'Vernacular Housing in Ulster in the Seventeenth Century', *UF*, 25 (1979), 8.
4. Gailey, Alan, 'The Ballyhagan Inventories, 1716-1740', *FL*, 15 (1977), 57.
5. PRONI, Mic 80/3, ff. 5-8, 8-10, 11-3, 21-5, 54-6, 63-4.
6. PRONI, T 848/1, 29, 36, 43, 45, 49.
7. Atkinson, A., *Ireland Exhibited to England . . .* (London, 1823), 284-5, written 1816.
8. O S Mem, Box 1, II, 2 (1837), 36.
9. O S Mem, Box 12, I, 5 (1839), 27-8.
10. O S Mem, Box 16, VI, 1 (1838), 58.
11. O S Mem, Box 11, IV, 4 (1840), 60.
12. O S Mem, Box 11, IV, 1 (1840), 25.
13. O S Mem, Box 3, V, 4 (1839), 26-8.
14. O S Mem, Box 47, I, 1 (1835).
15. O S Mem, Box 48, I, 2 (1821).
16. Greig, William, *General Report on the Gosford Estates in County Armagh, 1821* (Belfast, 1976).
17. PRONI, T 3097.
18. Buchanan, R.H., Johnson, J.H. and Proudfoot, Bruce, 'Excavations at Murphystown, Co. Down', *UJA*, 3rd ser., 22 (1959), 130-3, Plate Xb.
19. Greig, W., op. cit., 154.
20. The original map is British Museum: Augustus I (ii), 39. See Belmore, The Right Hon. the Earl of, 'Ancient Maps of Enniskillen and its Environs', *UJA*, 2nd ser., 2 (1896), 218-43, where there is a copy reproduced.
21. Lucas, A.T., 'An Fhóir: A Straw-Rope Granary', *Gwerin*, 1 (1956), 18-9.
22. O S Mem, Box 27, IX, 1 (1834).
23. O S Mem, Box 34, I, 10 (183?), 1-4.
24. O S Mem, Box 43, I, 3 (1836).
25. O S Mem, Box 13, I, 2 (1839), 35.
26. *Ordnance Survey Memoir of Templecorran Parish 1839* (Belfast, 1971), 38-9.
27. Quoted by D. Tierney in 'The Tabular Reports', in Greig, W., op. cit., 54.
28. Dubourdieu, Rev. John, *Statistical Survey of the County of Down* (Dublin, 1802), 52-3.
29. Coote, Sir Charles, *Statistical Survey of the County of Cavan* (Dublin, 1802), 63.
30. Dubourdieu, Rev. John, *Statistical Survey of the County of Antrim* (Dublin, 1812), 155.
31. Sadly, this unique record was lost following the death of Mr. Kennedy in the mid-1960s.
32. Ó Danachair, Caoimhín, 'Farmyard Types and their Distribution in Ireland', *UF*, 27 (1981), 65-6; idem, 'Irish Farmyard Types', *Studia Ethnographica Upsaliensia*, 11 (1956), 6-15 was this author's first examination of this topic; since the early study did not include the distributional information derived from the Ordnance Survey maps of the 1830s, which is a central part of his 1981 paper, the 1956 paper is not quoted further here.
    In his study of the Ballymenone district of west Fermanagh, Henry Glassie sees a sequence in farmyard layout developing from houses with byres attached, through detached byres set in line along the long axis of the dwelling, to houses with byres in a parallel range behind; he sees this development as gradually 'separating living from making a living'. As a diachronic statement it underlines the synchronous nature of the farmyard-form analysis already published by Ó Danachair, for Glassie's sequence progresses from one of Ó Danachair's types into another: Glassie, Henry, *Passing the Time* (Dublin, 1982), 382. Indeed, Glassie illustrates from his small district a farmyard layout that fits into none of the categories discussed by Ó Danachair: Glassie, H., op. cit., 350. As already noted in this chapter, exigencies of site and personal assessments of convenience were potent factors. Glassie generalises for the Ballymenone district: 'Across the street, around the harggard, or dropped separately along the house's axis, other buildings stand, "outhouses" or "outoffices": the dairy, the hayshed and turfshed (often built combined), the cartshed and small houses for calves, fowl, and the broken disused, future-useful odds and ends . . . "ould trumfery". These buildings, the major ones usually strung in rows to face the south or east, parallel or perpendicular to the house, comprise the "home place" ': ibid., 344. However, this statement relates to a small part of west Fermanagh only, at present, and is based on study of farmyard layouts observed during field investigations carried out in the 1970s.
33. O S Mem, Box 22, 8 (1821), parishes of Allsaints, Taughboyne, Killea, Clonleigh and Raymoghey.
34. O S Mem, Box 48, I, 2 (1821), parishes of Ballinascreen, Kilcronaghan and Desertmartin.
35. O S Mem, Box 15, IV, 1 (1835), 16-8, Racavan; Box 6, IV, 1 (1839), Carnmoney; Box 13, I, 2 (1839), 35, Kilroot; Box 15, VI, 1 (1840), 57 and VI, 2 (1840), 16-7, Raloo; *Ordnance Survey Memoir of Templecorran Parish 1838* (Belfast, 1971), 38-9.
36. Wiliam, Eurwyn, 'Circular Corbelled Pigsties in Wales', *Scottish Vernacular Buildings Working Group Newsletter*, 6 (1980), 1-5.
37. Buchanan, R.H., 'Corbelled Structures in Lecale, County Down', *UJA*, 3rd ser., 19 (1956), 92-112.
38. UFTM 611226.
39. Ó Danachair, C., op. cit. (1981), 72-4.
40. Ibid., 68-72.
41. Ibid., 70-2.

Chapter 11

1. Historic Buildings legislation came into being under the Planning (Northern Ireland), Order 1972, which provided for a Historic Buildings Council for Northern Ireland which advises the Department of the Environment (Northern Ireland) under Article 31(3) on the listing of buildings of special architectural or historic interest; under Article 37(3) on the designation of Conservation Areas of special architectural or historic interest, the character or appearance of which it is desirable to preserve or enhance; under Article 83(3) on the making of grants or loans for the preservation of a listed building; and on the provision of financial assistance for works in Conservation Areas. The provisions of the legislation are administered through the Planning Service and the Historic Buildings Branch of the Department of the Environment (Northern Ireland).

2. The Ulster Architectural Heritage Society came into being during 1967 and has functioned principally in two ways. It has been vigilant as a pressure group concerned for architectural conservation, and it has an honourable record in publication of district lists of buildings of merit, and of thematic monographs. Of recent years it has developed its interests in architectural education and appreciation, for example, in forging links with schools, sponsoring competitions, and for many years it has conducted architectural excursions for its members.

3. The museum was established under the Ulster Folk Museum Act (Northern Ireland), 1958. Its Board of Trustees first met at the end of 1958, the museum site was purchased in 1961, and it was formally opened on 2 July 1964. The name was changed to the Ulster Folk and Transport Museum under the provisions of the Museums (Northern Ireland) Order 1973, recognition thereby being accorded to the terms of the Ulster Folk Museum (Amendment) Act (Northern Ireland) 1967 which provided for an agreement whereby the museum became responsible for the transport museum formerly operated by Belfast Corporation.

4. Gailey, Alan, 'The Ulster Folk and Transport Museum and Building Conservation in Northern Ireland', *UFTMYB*, 1976-77, 13-14.

INDEX

Notes:

1. Illustrations are indexed by the number of the page where they occur.
2. Most place names are rendered in modern spellings; main exceptions are quoted from the early 18th-century surveys of the Manor of Castledillon, and of the Archbishopric of Armagh, and from some other documentary sources.
3. Place names in Ulster (nine counties) are indexed individually, without further inclusion under county names.
   Abbreviations: Ant.: Antrim, Arm.: Armagh, Cav.: Cavan, Don.: Donegal, Dn.: Down, Fer.: Fermanagh, Ldy.: Londonderry, Mon.: Monaghan, Tyr.: Tyrone.
4. References to other Irish counties, and to places within them, are indexed under the county names.

DATE DUE

RESERVE

S-8-97

JUN 2 8 1999

JUL 1 1 2000

Jul 26

AUG 1 7 2000